For Roy Hays
With all good wishes
George E. Mowry

THE ERA
OF THEODORE ROOSEVELT

The

New American Nation Series

EDITED BY

HENRY STEELE COMMAGER

AND

RICHARD B. MORRIS

THE ERA OF THEODORE ROOSEVELT

1900 ★ 1912

By GEORGE E. MOWRY, 1909-

ILLUSTRATED

NEW YORK

HARPER & BROTHERS • PUBLISHERS

Library of Congress catalog card number: 58–8835

For John D. Hicks

Contents

Illustrations

Editors' Introduction

WITH the accession to the Presidency of the man Mark Hanna called "that damn cowboy," the comfortable world of William McKinley evaporated as a morning mist. What hastened its evaporation was the realization that it had been comfortable only for the fortunate and the privileged, and that all through the decade of the nineties these constituted an ever-shrinking segment of the population. It had not been comfortable at all for farmers trying to live on five-cent cotton and fifty-cent wheat; for workingmen sweating twelve hours a day in factory, mill, or mine; for immigrants crowded into the noisome slums of great cities. Theodore Roosevelt was born to wealth and to patrician position, raised in luxury, educated privately and at Harvard, and destined for privilege, but he sensed the disparity between the lot of the fortunate and the unfortunate—between the American dream and the American reality—as the more plebeian McKinleys and Clevelands and Mark Hannas did not, and he was the first President since poor Andrew Johnson who did sense it. That was his significance; and because he was able and eager to do something to remedy the disparity, history has given his name to an era.

When Roosevelt took the oath of office, he promised to "continue absolutely unbroken" the policies of his predecessor. In a narrow sense he was true to this promise, for there was no overt repudiation of McKinleyism. But in historical perspective Roosevelt was not so much a successor as an innovator. We can see now that he ushered in a revolution—a revolution as significant in its way as the industrial revolution of almost a century earlier. It was a fourfold revolution: in the relation of government to the economy; in the relations of the different elements of the economy—capital, labor, and agriculture—to each other; in the relation of the United States to the rest of the world; and in the social and economic thought about these and related matters. This revolution has gone on, not without challenge but without serious interruption, to our own time, and in a very real sense we can say that the modern age began when Theodore Roosevelt took over the Presidency on September 14, 1901.

There had been antecedents, to be sure; the real watershed of our history can be located in the decade of the nineties. Liberals had called for government regulation of the economy for fully a generation, and the legal foundations for such regulation had been laid in the great case of *Munn v. Illinois.* Economic dissenters like Henry George and Henry Demarest Lloyd had blazed the way for new relationships among those interests we so defiantly refuse to call classes. Tender-minded reformers like Jacob Riis and Jane Addams had inaugurated a humanitarian crusade on behalf of the poor and the exploited. The origins of world power go back to the generation of Seward, and certainly to the doctrines of Captain Mahan and the expansionism of the nineties. And that intellectual revolution which Professor Mowry has delineated with such skill began with the impact on the American mind of Darwin and Spencer.

But if it cannot be said that Theodore Roosevelt created a new era in American history, it can be said that he inaugurated one. If he did not provide it with ideas, he did imprint upon it the stamp of his own character. He was in a sense an orthodox heretic, a respectable agitator, an intellectual Philistine, a conservative revolutionist, and his sponsorship was a guarantee that the revolution would be conducted under the most high-minded auspices, in the most orderly fashion, and to the most respectable ends. What this meant was that the United States would escape those convulsions which attended the social revolutions in so many other countries, and that this revolution—like earlier American revolutions—would be essentially conservative in character.

Professor Mowry has caught with sharp insight and deep understanding the complexity lurking within the apparent simplicity of the progressive movement, and of the man who came to personify it. He has given us first a series of searching analyses of the intellectual currents that swept across America at the turn of the century, the social and economic problems that clamored for solution, and the progressive

temper that turned so buoyantly to the task. Then, with the stage carefully set, he puts Roosevelt in the center and assigns him the leading
role—but he does not for a moment permit him to steal the show.
Unlike so many historians Professor Mowry is not thrown off his stride
by the ebullient and domineering Roosevelt. He subscribes neither to
the excessive adulation of an earlier period, nor to the fashionable
depreciation of more recent years, but accepts Roosevelt for what he
was: a wonderfully successful interpreter of popular sensibilities and
aspirations; a showman with something to show; a hard-headed vision-
ary who accepted a fiduciary relationship to future generations; a
practical politician who could master politics and parties; a vital force
who restored Washington as the center of American affairs, and the
White House as the center of Washington, and who revived faith not
only in the executive but in the political process itself.

And, *mirabile dictu*, Professor Mowry has managed to be equally
judicious with President Taft—a judge who was not himself judicious
and who has inspired very little judiciousness in others. Mr. Mowry
holds nicely the balance between critics and apologists, but leaves us
in no doubt of his own verdict: that Taft, for all his good qualities and
good intentions, was out of touch with the great movements of his own
day and that for the good of his country he had to be repudiated.

Although in an earlier book in this series Professor Dulles has drawn,
in broad strokes, the contours of foreign relations during these years,
Mr. Mowry has not excluded or neglected them here. For in a sense
the self-conscious emergence of the United States as a world power
during these years was a function and product of domestic developments, particularly economic developments. And clearly, too, the new
vigor and scope in the conduct of foreign relations was a part of the
new vigor and scope in the conduct of the executive power by Roosevelt. Clearly we cannot present the Roosevelt era and ignore Panama
or Venezuela or Algeciras or Portsmouth. Mr. Mowry has fitted all of
these episodes discretely into the larger picture so as to give us a full
sense of the new energies and forces which were released during the
era of Roosevelt.

This volume is one of The New American Nation Series, a comprehensive, co-operative survey of the history of the area now embraced in
the United States from the days of discovery to the second half of the
twentieth century. Since the publication by the House of Harper of the
American Nation series, over half a century ago, the scope of history

has been immensely broadened, new approaches explored and developed. The time has come for a judicious reappraisal of the new history, a cautious application of the new techniques of investigation and presentation, and a large-scale effort to achieve a synthesis of new findings with the familiar facts, and to present the whole in attractive literary form.

To this task The New American Nation Series is dedicated. Each volume is part of a carefully planned whole, and fitted as well as is possible to the other volumes in the series; at the same time each volume is designed to be complete in itself. From time to time the same series of events will be presented from different points of view: thus the volumes on foreign affairs, constitutional history, and intellectual history will in some ways retrace ground covered in this volume. That all this may result in some overlapping is inevitable, but it has seemed to the editors that repetition is less regrettable than omission, and that something is to be gained by looking at the same period and the same material from different and independent points of view.

HENRY STEELE COMMAGER
RICHARD BRANDON MORRIS

Preface

THE first dozen years of the twentieth century were important ones for the development of modern American society. They marked the birth and growth of the so-called progressive movement, a social quest which, in its broadest aspects, attempted to find solutions for the amazing number of domestic and foreign problems spawned by the great industrial, urban, and population changes of the late nineteenth century. Workable answers to such problems had largely eluded the nineteenth century despite the persistent efforts of sundry rural political movements. Perhaps that was the main difficulty with most of the nineteenth-century answers. They were essentially rural answers to urban problems, and thus they missed their mark by a little wider margin than is customary in modern man's seemingly endless attempt to push rapidly into the unknown territory of the future without either adequate equipment or directions for the journey. Road maps of varying quality are made by historians after they are no longer of immediate use.

Possibly because the progressive movement was dotted with interesting personalities, or simply because it achieved some measure of success in finding partial legislative solutions to the period's major complexities, it has attracted more than its share of historians. A glance at the footnotes and more especially at the bibliography will indicate that this book could not have been written without the aid of their works. No one is more sensitive to the need of collaborative scholarship, perhaps, than the historian of recent societies. Faced by the torrents of print turned out by modern presses and the rivers of words carried into the pit of public discussion by modern communication facilities, the individual scholar, were he to rely entirely upon himself for verification, would be almost drowned. This book, like most such in recent history, is a synthesis of the work and views of many people, as well as twenty years of my own research in the period.

In addition to tracing the history of the nation, it contains the best answers I can give to the many still unanswered vexing questions about the origins and the nature of the progressive movement. It attempts another re-evaluation of that many-sided character, Theodore Roosevelt, whose personality and deeds dominated the American scene until 1912. And it continues the story of the evolution of the reform movement through the Taft administration until its Republican phase ended in the bitterly contested tri-cornered struggle between Roosevelt, Taft, and LaFollette in the elections of 1912.

In the making of this book there were many hands. My thanks are especially due to the University of California, which supplied the sabbatical leave during which much of it was written, and to the Research Committee of the University Senate for the funds which subsidized work in the eastern United States and provided a research assistant, Joseph Brent, who saved me a good many weary steps up and down the levels of library stacks. Over the course of years a host of gracious and helpful librarians in depositories scattered from California to New England have been of inestimable service. Especially was this true of Katherine E. Brand of the Recent Manuscripts Section of the Library of Congress. My thanks are also due to the editors of this series, Henry Steele Commager and Richard B. Morris, whose comments and helpful suggestions aided greatly, and lastly, to my wife, LaVerne Mowry, who read and edited the entire manuscript.

GEORGE E. MOWRY

Los Angeles, California
April 1, 1958

THE ERA
OF THEODORE ROOSEVELT

CHAPTER 1

Material America

MATERIAL conditions as measured by production indices, consumption figures, and statistics on income are rather unsatisfactory data with which to start a study of a society. Contrasted with the creations of the mind and spirit, they are stubbornly cold, narrowly clinical, and more limited in their usefulness than is generally appreciated. Like the foundations of a building, they have a utilitarian ugliness about them, a rigidity that gives no hint of the airy and elegant structure that may appear aboveground. But they are at least necessary to an understanding of what rises above. Material facts have an injunctive force, perhaps, which helps dictate both a civilization's general order as well as the upper limits to which it may attain.

If material facts about their country have always held an attraction for Americans, they have also been of intense interest to visiting foreigners. Alexis de Tocqueville, St. Jean de Crèvecoeur, and James Bryce, to name but a few, were all intrigued by material conditions in America. So was a friendly visiting Englishman in 1900, Frederic Harrison. By virtue of its intelligent, industrious citizens and its magnificent natural resources, the United States, he observed, would soon lead the world in material progress. Harrison had a great many other compliments for the United States, including the comment that in values the average American was closer to the English than the latter were to the people living north of the Tweed River in his homeland. But if Harrison was full of praise for most aspects of American life, he was also somewhat disconcerted by its other phases. "Life in the States," he commented, "is one perpetual whirl of telephones, telegrams, phonographs, electric bells, motors, lifts, and automatic instruments." Obviously, American life was too fast, its sound level too high, its change too rapid for this quiet British visitor.[1]

Change was not confined to technology in 1900; it touched almost every facet of American society. For the most part Americans were quite aware, possibly overaware, of the alterations being made. The word "new" occurred with astonishing frequency to describe all manner of changes quite divorced from electronic gadgets. The "new theology," the "new morality," the "new woman," the "new immigration," the "new city," and the "new South" were phrases both current and familiar to the well-informed of the day. As the years progressed, few political programs and tracts dared not include in their descriptive title an allusion to their uniqueness and their novelty, the "New Nationalism," the "New Freedom," and New Jersey's "New Idea" being paralleled in more literary channels by such titles as the *New Republic* and the *New Democracy*.

This emphasis upon change in part reflected the real alterations taking place at an amazing rate in society; in part it probably reflected a deep desire to forget the troublesome decade of the nineties. The great depression of 1893 had sharply curtailed the progress of industry. It had also witnessed thousands of business bankruptcies and millions of hungry and angry unemployed men walking the city streets. The depression had added to the troubles of an already long-distressed agriculture, a condition which led to the bitter election campaign of 1896 between the rural have-nots and the urban haves. The bloody strikes of the nineties, the march of desperate men to Washington, the rise of socialism, and the farmer's startling political protest in 1896 were all episodes which most Americans wished to forget at the beginning of the new century. For, following the Bryan campaign and the Spanish-American War, a sharp change had taken place in the economic climate. As industrial production increased steadily from 1898 on, farm prices rose and unemployment sank to more normal levels. A relative sense of well-being possessed the nation and the average man assumed a feeling of optimism about the future that he had not had since the eighties.

In September, 1901, a popular magazine carried a study of what it called the average American adult male. He was British by ancestry,

[1] Frederic Harrison, "Impressions of America," *Current Literature,* XXXI (1901), 135.

but had some German blood. He was five feet eight inches tall, married, and had three living children and one who had died in infancy. He was a Protestant in religion and a Republican in politics, who subscribed to one daily and one weekly newspaper. He consumed twenty pounds of tobacco a year, seven and a half gallons of hard spirits, and seventy-five gallons of beer. He lived in a two-story, seven-room house; and if he was a farmer, he had a cash return of $540 a year; if a city man, a yearly income of $750. His estate was estimated at about $5,000, of which $750 was in a bank account or in securities. The article concluded with a note of thanks for the well-being of the American people. Some years later another such self-congratulatory study pointed out that in average per capita income the United States led the world with a figure of $227 as against Great Britain's $181 and France's $161. Moreover, taxes took only 3 per cent of the average income in the United States as compared with 9 per cent in England and 12 per cent in France.[2]

While such figures are useful for the purpose of gross comparisons, they are extremely deceptive if applied to particular classes. After years of hardship, the farmer was to do moderately well in the new century. With the return of world prosperity the prices of farm products increased by nearly 50 per cent between 1900 and 1910. In the same period the average value of farm land per acre increased slightly and the average value per farm unit went up from $5,471 to $6,444. As a degree of farm prosperity returned, the foreclosure rate dropped from its peak in the nineties, new machinery was purchased, and new land was rapidly put into cultivation.[3] The American worker also profited by the return of prosperity. Especially after the industrial boom triggered by the Spanish-American War, unemployment levels dropped and, although no trustworthy figures exist, the degree of job opportunity and job security in the first decade of the century appeared to be rather high. Otherwise the relative fortune of the industrial worker was not commensurate with that of the farmer. According to one authority the average real earnings of all urban workers in that period dropped from those of the previous decade. In only three years, from 1900 to 1912, apparently, was the average real

[2] "The Average American," *Current Literature*, XXXI (1901), 421; *Literary Digest*, XXXVI (1908), 896.
[3] United States Department of Agriculture, *Yearbook, 1911* (Washington, 1912), p. 695.

wage above the 1890–99 average. During the other nine years it was lower. While the urban working class as a whole was much better off than it had been in the nineties, since more of the group held steadier positions, the individual worker seemed to command no greater amounts of goods and services other than those provided by public bodies.[4]

Measured against the gains of agriculture and labor, the rate of growth of and the returns from American industry and finance were impressive. Total physical production increased in the decade somewhere between 75 to 90 per cent, and the total national wealth approximately doubled. The nation's relative position in the world economy was also undergoing something of a revolution. The year 1892 was a bench mark in American history: it was the last year the country had an unfavorable trade balance. By the middle of the nineties Pittsburgh began to undersell British steel in the world markets, and by 1898 the nation was exporting $600 million more of manufactured goods than it bought from abroad. Such an outpouring of native goods resulted in a steady purchase of foreign-held debt and in climbing exports of investment capital. By 1897 American investments abroad already totaled $700 million, a figure that was increased to $2.5 billion in 1908 and to $3.5 billion by the beginning of the First World War. The United States was still a debtor nation in 1900, but the gap between international debts and credits was being closed with amazing speed. By 1914 Americans owned about as much as they owed abroad.[5]

The trend of these salient figures did not go unnoticed. Already by the mid-nineties Brooks and Henry Adams were talking about the weakening in the position of the British Empire and cited the cheap Pittsburgh steel as irrefutable evidence that the scepter of world power had begun its transit from London to Washington. Already speculation in the nation's magazines centered about the question of just when New York would become the world's financial center.[6] Since in such things the appetite grows as it feeds, there was even more talk of how the nation could increase its exports, secure more sources of raw materials, and provide more places for investments. Three years

---

[4] Paul H. Douglas, *Real Wages in the United States, 1890–1926* (Boston, 1930), p. 39.

[5] *Historical Statistics of the United States, 1789–1945* (Washington, 1949), pp. 242–246.

[6] "The World's Financial Center," *World's Work*, IV (1898), 2040.

before the outbreak of the Spanish-American War the National Association of Manufacturers was organized for the specific purpose of promoting export trade. In 1898 the president of the American Bankers' Association exhorted his listeners to do even more: "We hold now three of the winning cards in the game for commercial greatness, to wit—iron, steel and coal. We have long been the granary of the world, we now aspire to be its workshop, then we want to be its clearing house." A short time later the impetuous Senator Albert J. Beveridge of Indiana voiced his blunt demand: "The trade of the world must and shall be ours." By 1901 McKinley was giving presidential blessings to the crusade for commercial dominance. Referring to "our increasing surplus" and to the "urgent" demand for foreign markets, the President stated a truism, not at all obvious to the less commercial-minded majority of the people, that "the period of exclusiveness" was past.[7]

Just as the manufacturer and the merchant had destroyed economic provincialism in the country, the imperialist, even more speedily, had engineered a revolution in the nation's world political position. Within two years, 1898–1900, the United States had acquired an empire the opposite ends of which stretched across almost half of the world's circumference. Explaining the acquisition of Cuba, Puerto Rico, Hawaii, and the Philippines, President McKinley observed that the nation "could not escape the duties imposed upon it by the Ruler of Nations." Whether the dynamics of empire were divine or mundane in nature may be debated. But it seems very unlikely that without the psychic and economic forces flowing from the new industrialism the train of events leading to the acquisitions could have been set successfully in motion. Whatever the explanation for imperialism, the taking of some 125,000 square miles of territory populated with a wide diversity of peoples with varied cultures, languages, and religions was to make a profound difference to Americans and to their relations with the rest of the world. For one thing the old, cherished concept of a republic equal in all of its parts was gone. There were to be gradations now in the status of territories and even in the legal status of men. The debates over imperial expansion had made clear that the

[7] James D. Richardson, *A Compilation of the Messages and Papers of the Presidents* (Washington, 1902), Supplement 1, pp. 294–295; John A. Hobson, *The Evolution of Modern Capitalism: A Study of Machine Production* (London, 1907), p. 84.

United States of 1900 had no intentions of making all of the territories free and equal participating states in the union. It was also clear that the citizens of the Philippines were not likely to be made citizens of the United States. In the Insular Cases the Supreme Court verified the doctrine that the common Constitution was no longer common but that parts of it could be applied to the new territories while other parts might be withheld.

Of even more importance perhaps was what the acts of imperialism did to the nation's relations to the rest of the world. By the acquisition of the Philippines the United States had interjected itself into the cockpit of the Orient, where Japan, Russia, Germany, Great Britain, and France were all contending for territorial and commercial supremacy. The Oriental struggle, moreover, was tied to the European balance of power by a system of world-girdling alliances. In the West the trade war between Germany and Great Britain had already excited comment; the German naval law of 1898 with its open challenge to Britain was already casting its long and ominous shadow before it. Reacting to the rising tensions in the world, the United States had by the end of 1900 taken part in an international expedition to quell the Boxers in China. And by virtue of John Hay's Open Door notes the nation had committed itself to the protection of China's territorial integrity against all comers. As years go, the period from 1898 to 1900 was a short time; but in the nation's world circumstance it represented the difference between relatively carefree adolescence and the beginnings of the burdens of maturity.

Even more impressive than industry's rate of growth were the momentous changes in the nature of its structure and control. The movement toward industrial combination had started years before 1900 and had indeed excited public opinion as early as the eighties. The word "trust" had long since become a part of the language. Technically a trust was a form of business organization not unsimilar to a modern holding company. But popularly the term was applied to any large industrial combination formed from many component companies and which dwarfed its competitors. In popular thinking, at least, its objectives were simple and clear: to lower wages, to raise prices and profits, and to run its competitors out of business.

Beginning with the Spanish-American War and continuing through the first decade of the new century, the rate of growth of these new combinations was nothing short of sensational. By the end of 1901 the national railroad network had virtually been consolidated into the hands of five or six groups of operators. The public at large learned about the development in February, 1902, when one of the more sober magazines carried a double-page map in color outlining the newly built railroad empires of Vanderbilt, Gould, Rockefeller, Morgan, Hill, and Harriman.[8] Paralleling this development in the carriers was the consolidation movement in industry. The three years following the war witnessed the formation of the Amalgamated Copper Company, the American Smelting and Refining Company, the Consolidated Tobacco Company, and the United States Steel Corporation. These were just the more spectacular among many less lusty combines. The census of 1900 reported the existence of seventy-three industrial combinations with a capital of more than $10 million each, many of which controlled 50 per cent or more of the production in their respective fields. Of these only twenty had been organized before 1898. Nor did the movement toward combination stop with 1901. Ten years later the Census Bureau again reported that, if anything, the rate of industrial consolidation had been stepped up. By 1909, 1 per cent of the total of industrial firms in the country was producing 44 per cent of the nation's manufactured goods.[9] In many areas the American industrial world was rapidly becoming highly differentiated, with a few extremely large and powerful national concerns looming over a great many small and relatively impotent local competitors.

This movement toward industrial aggrandizement did not stop at the sea but went on to the formation of even international organizations. By 1901 several American thread companies had joined with the British J. and P. Coats and Company to effect a near world monopoly. The following year Morgan and Company's International Steamship combine, incorporating both British and American companies, was referred to in the press as an "international trust." Two years later the United States Steel Corporation entered into a short-lived agreement with British, American, and Belgian firms to divide up the world market for steel rails. This was the logical conclusion of McKinleyism, Henry Adams later observed, a system of combinations, consolidations, trusts, "realized at home and realizable abroad." [10]

[8] M. G. Cuniff, "Increasing Railroad Consolidation," *World's Work*, III (1902), 1775.

[9] *Thirteenth Census of the United States*, 8, *Manufactures*, p. 180.

[10] *World's Work*, V (1902), 2704; Henry Adams, *The Education of Henry Adams* (Boston, 1918), p. 423.

Almost concurrently with the consolidation movement came a revolutionary change in both the nature and locus of control in large industry. In the fashioning of the new railroad and industrial combines the names J. P. Morgan and Company, Kuhn, Loeb and Company, Kidder, Peabody and Company, and Lee, Higginson and Company appeared with a frequency alarming to many. As the decade progressed, it became known that these great eastern investment banking houses were closely associated with the largest New York commercial banks, the leading insurance companies, and occasionally with an industrial giant like the Standard Oil Company, whose resources were equal or superior to those of many New York financial houses. Altogether they formed a pool of capital that virtually controlled the credit resources of the nation. As the chief inspirers, organizers, and financiers of the new industrial combinations, they almost inevitably took control of their creations. When the United States Rubber Company was formed from over a score of independent firms, three New York bank presidents and the president of the New York Stock Exchange sat on its first board of directors. Following the publication of John Moody's *The Truth About the Trusts* in 1904, and with the exposure of the New York insurance company scandals of 1905, the nation did not have to await the famous Pujo Committee report of 1913 to comprehend that there was a "money trust" whose lines of control ran out from New York and Boston to practically every major financial and industrial center in the country.[11]

The evolution of finance capitalism, as this banking control of industry was called, had a profound effect upon business life and upon the attitude of millions of Americans toward big business. By suppressing competition it assured a stabilizing effect upon the national economy. The economies inherent in its large operations gave a promise of real social savings. Through the sale of the new industrial securities it spread ownership over the country. But at the same time it concentrated a fearful power in the hands of a few, made the rough road to monopoly power easier, and, in the short run at least, further differentiated the economic world. The power and psychological gap existing now between this new financial-industrial captain and the small manufacturer or merchant was immeasurably greater than it

---

[11] See, for example, the graph of interlocking financial groups published by the *Literary Digest*, XXVIII (1904), 466; Harold U. Faulkner, *The Decline of Laissez-Faire* (New York, 1951), pp. 35–45.

had been even in the eighties, to say nothing of the more equalitarian pre-Civil War days. But far more important, the rise of finance capitalism had an immediate political effect. The men at the head of the new industrial apex were not primarily industrialists intimately connected with local communities or national sections. Instead they were eastern financiers as dissociated from particular regions as they were from industrial processes. Since their main interest was in marketing capital instead of goods, they became the target of an old American prejudice against the man who acquired wealth without producing tangible goods or services. The Kansas editor who growled that the way to cure the nation's problems was to seize these eastern gamblers, speculators, and manipulators and put them back to "honest work" was repeating an old refrain which still made sense in much of the country west of the Appalachians. Here the memory of card sharks, red-dog banks, land speculators, and the smooth-talking patent-medicine men had not entirely disappeared from the memory of the small manufacturer or the merchant. As he remembered them, most of such "transient trash" came from the East.[12]

The speed and size of the industrial combination movement so startled many people that even a conservative-dominated Congress felt called upon to investigate it. A joint commission of the Senate and the House was therefore created in June, 1898, to investigate the new contours of industrial life. Not many people read even a portion of the nineteen volumes produced by the commission. But a great many did follow the digests in the newspapers and magazines of its 1899 inquiry into the "trusts." From such reading the public learned that one of the primary reasons for the organization of the new combines was to avoid "intense," or "harmful," or "wasteful" competition; that the capital structure of the new organizations often amounted to two or three times the total sum needed to reproduce their constituent plants; that their organizers earned fantastic fees for their work and that their new executives were often paid fantastic salaries. Commenting a few years later upon the organization of the United States Steel Corporation, a conservative magazine, originally started "to record the advances and triumphs of American business," acidly observed that the total common stock of the new corporation was pure but needed water, which was sold to "dupes" throughout the country in order to

[12] Girard (Kansas), *The Appeal to Reason,* March 3, 1906.

provide a "rake-off" for the promoters, the size of whose fees had never been equaled "from the beginning of the world. . . ." [13]

Scattered through the report was rather conclusive evidence that the larger combines had placed the small producers of their raw materials into a state of semibondage; that their control often extended from the wholesaler to the retailers of their products; that by various practices they were able either to swallow or ruin effective competitors and to control consumer prices within certain limits. It came as no surprise then that the dividends of some of the more efficient and monopolistic firms were phenomenally high, those of the Standard Oil Company, for example, averaging a fat 40 per cent yearly throughout the decade. Nor did the census figures of 1910 contain startling news with their indication that in fifteen of the eighty kinds of manufacturers listed there had been an actual reduction in the number of individually owned and operated plants during the previous ten years. From the start of the ten-year period the implications for the old individualistic society of this new industrial collectivism had been all too plain. [14]

Collectivization seemed to be in the very air of 1900 America. Paralleling the rise of organized capital was the development of a strong nationally organized labor movement. Organized labor had been struck heavy blows in the late eighties and the early nineties. The collapse of the Knights of Labor, the defeat at Homestead, and the virtual destruction of Eugene V. Debs' National Railroad Union at Chicago had left the future of the movement in the hands of the crafts organized by the American Federation of Labor and the developing railroad brotherhoods. At the time of McKinley's first inauguration the A.F. of L. members numbered only some 250,000. But by 1900 that figure had doubled, and in 1904 the paid membership was up to an impressive 1,676,000.

Conscious of its increasing strength, labor became almost as militant as it had been during the early nineties. In 1900 it unsuccessfully tried to organize the steel industry and called a general strike in San Francisco. The following year the hatmakers of Danbury, Connecticut, instituted a national boycott in their attempt to win a closed shop from

[13] *United States Industrial Commission* (Washington, 1899), XIII, 107, 169, 177; *World's Work,* VII (1903), 4065.

[14] *Industrial Commission,* I, pp. 18, 21, 279–283, 689; *The Moody Manual* (New York, 1912), p. 3604; *Thirteenth Census of the United States,* 8 (1910), p. 182.

D. E. Lowe and Company. In 1902, as in 1900, the miners of Pennsylvania practically stopped the production of anthracite coal and precipitated a national crisis. Two years later a sizable portion of the state of Colorado was placed under martial law when the miners struck for an eight-hour day. In these and scores of lesser-known labor conflicts violence flared, resulting in death and injury to the partisans of both sides. During the thirty-month period following January, 1902, according to one recapitulation, 180 union men were killed, 1,651 injured, and over 5,000 arrested.[15]

Since the formation of the American Federation of Labor, Samuel Gompers, its perennial president, had steered the organization away from direct political action. Both the Populists in 1892 and Bryan in 1896 had wooed labor assiduously, but Gompers had remained disenchanted. Now despite the A.F. of L.'s official policy of hands off, labor was getting into politics at least by the back door. In December, 1898, James C. Chase, a Socialist, was named mayor of Haverhill, Massachusetts. The following year on the other side of Boston another Socialist, Charles H. Coulter, was elected mayor by the city of Brockton. Simultaneously two Socialists were elected to the Massachusetts state legislature. While organized labor took no official part in the campaigns, its name and its influence were willy-nilly thrown behind the Socialist candidates by local organizations. Directly as a result of the great strike of 1901 a hastily organized Union Labor Party took over the government of San Francisco in 1901, and within months the President of the Connecticut Federation of Labor was elected mayor of Hartford. By 1902 Bridgeport had a "stoker" mayor and Ansonia a "carpenter" mayor. Labor appeared to be on the march in the new century in both the political and economic arenas. And public opinion, at least in some urban districts, instead of condemning its activities as it had in the early nineties, seemed to support it.[16]

Labor militancy soon brought an industrial countermobilization which started not among the great national combines but, characteristically for the day, among small manufacturers and merchants in the inland cities. The first city-wide employers' association organized to defeat "restrictive" trade-union principles appeared in Dayton, Ohio,

[15] Slason Thompson, "Violence in Labor Conflicts," *The Outlook*, LXXVIII (1904), 969.

[16] George E. Mowry, *The California Progressives* (Berkeley and Los Angeles, 1951), pp. 25–26; *The Outlook*, LXX (1902), 938.

in 1900. The following years similar associations were organized in Chicago, Louisville, and Indianapolis. By 1903 this Middle Western movement was able to persuade the National Association of Manufacturers, originally organized to stimulate foreign trade, to organize the Citizens Industrial Association. In its published program of no closed shops, no restrictions of output, no limitation on the number of apprentices, and no sympathetic strikes, the national organization accepted the original Dayton program scarcely without embellishment. But within a month after the national action, eight hundred businessmen of Omaha, Nebraska, organized a local chapter whose stated purpose was to fight all forms of unionism whether restrictive or not. Soon many of the sixty-six state and local affiliates of the organization had followed the Omaha example by organizing a city-wide boycott of union "troublemakers" and by concluding understandings with local authorities which made the police virtual business auxiliaries during important strikes. During the year 1902 the antiunion movement was further accelerated by the formation of the American Anti-Boycott Association and by the determination of the National Association of Manufacturers to engage formally in national antiunion politics. President D. M. Parry reported to the 1903 convention that the association during the previous year had been influential in defeating both the federal eight-hour work bill and a bill limiting the issuance of labor injunctions by federal courts. Even more success, President Parry stated, had attended the association's "educational activities" among the several state legislatures. The following year the association publicly campaigned against the prolabor Senator L. C. McComas of Maryland and Congressman William Hughes of New Jersey. Neither man was elected.[17]

The rapid growth of organized labor and industry and their repeated violent clashes helped turn the attention of rural America again to the rapidly rising city. Actually 60 per cent of the American population in 1900 still lived on farms or in towns of less than 2,500 people. But by the end of the decade the figure had been reduced to 55 per cent and by 1920 the countryside and the small town had ceased to be the home of the average American. This development was clearly

[17] John Keith, "The New Union of Employers," *Harper's Weekly,* XLVIII (1904), 1422; *Literary Digest,* XXVI (1903), 640; Selig Perlman and Philip Taft, *A History of Labor in the United States, 1896–1932* (New York, 1935), p. 152.

anticipated in 1900 and there was much public discussion on the subject of whether the national character would not be drastically altered by this radical change in the nation's way of life.[18] Despite the steady population drift from the country to the city, a movement as old as the nation, the farmer retained a historic suspicion of the city and city ways, and the approaching point of urban dominance served to emphasize and re-excite a continuing prejudice.

The country distrust of the city was exacerbated further during the period by the nature of the growing urban population. Well over 40 per cent of the increase in urban population during the first decade of the twentieth century came from immigrant sources, whereas agrarian stocks probably accounted for something less than 30 per cent. During the fourteen years following 1900 over thirteen million immigrants entered the country. Furthermore, in its places of origins, purposes in coming, religious, cultural, and economic characteristics, as well as in its patterns of settlement within the United States, this "new immigration" was radically different from the older population. Continuing the trend, already obvious in the nineties, an increasing percentage of these new folk came not from the old familiar places of origin in western and northern Europe, but from Italy, Austria-Hungary, Poland, and Russia. In 1907, the year of the greatest influx, about 80 per cent of the total came from these four countries. Unlike the native population or the old immigration, the majority of these new peoples were either Roman Catholic or Jewish in religion, more than a third of them were illiterates, and their worldly possessions were indescribably meager. Over two-thirds of the new immigrants were males and a surprising number of them were, in the words of the day, "birds of passage," having no intentions of staying once they had made a sum sufficient to stake them to a better life in their old countries.[19]

Characteristically, this new and strange immigration settled in the cities, the census of 1900 indicating that over 80 per cent of the employed among them was engaged in industrial and commercial jobs. Thus, just at the time that it was becoming the dominant force in American life, the city was being rapidly differentiated from the rest

---

[18] See, for example, L. S. Rowe, "Political Consequences of City Growth," *Yale Review,* IX (1900), 20–32; and C. De Garme, "Can Education Restore What City Life Has Lost?" *Gunton's Magazine,* XXI (1901), 505–514.

[19] Earle Clarke, "Contributions to Urban Growth," *Publications of the American Statistical Association,* XIV (1915), 654–670; Jeremiah W. Jenks and W. Jett Lauek, *The Immigrant Problem* (New York, 1926), pp. 33–40.

of the nation by the growing ethnic, religious, and cultural differences. Later the process of acculturalization would make most of these new folk indistinguishable from the American mass. But now their strange ways and customs set them radically apart. Perhaps at no other time was the line of demarcation between urban and rural America so sharp as it was in the first two decades of the twentieth century. Beyond this distinction the city itself was being radically stratified on economic as well as ethnic lines. If the American city was to become the melting pot of the twentieth century, it was also first a veritable pressure cooker in which racial, economic, and psychic tensions bubbled and boiled to the consternation of the older American population.

Class and social differences, of course, had always existed in the United States since the day of its founding. At times distinction between various segments of its population had been extremely great. The social distance between the colonial aristocracy and the commonality and that between the southern manor house and the cottage of the poor white or the slave hut come to mind. But after Andrew Jackson's day in the North and after the Civil War in the South, the drift for a time seemed to be toward an undifferentiated society. With the rise of the great financiers and industrialists, however, a counter-wave had set in, and by 1900 it had reached a spectacular crest.

Huge profits flowing from corporate industry and from finance capitalism, together with a lack of graduated income or inheritance taxes, had created at the very top of economic society a small group of fabulously wealthy people. Their private railroad cars, yachts, stables, and monumental mansions were as conspicuous by contrast with the possessions of the average middle-class American as perhaps the feudal castles were in medieval Europe. On the bottom of society millions of native Negroes and millions more of foreign immigrants lived in almost indescribable squalor and poverty. In terms of sheer social power perhaps no other comparable group had so much influence as the nine or ten leading industrialists and financiers about the year 1900. And perhaps no other one man had as much solitary power as John Pierpont Morgan. By its control over finance and industry the firm of Morgan and Company, the Pujo Committee reported later,[20] could by its own actions virtually plunge the nation into a major financial panic and an industrial depression. Within a span of fifteen years Presidents of

[20] See the classic discussion of the Pujo Report in Louis D. Brandeis, *Other People's Money* (Washington, 1933), pp. 1–35.

the United States relied upon Morgan three times to save the nation from a major disaster. During the Panic of 1893 Cleveland negotiated a deal with the Lord of Wall Street in order to save the gold reserve. In the anthracite coal strike of 1902 Roosevelt was to deal in reality not with the coal operators but with John Pierpont Morgan. And in 1907, when the country was again wavering on the brink of a financial collapse, Morgan's agents came to the White House with a proposal whereby their firm might save the nation's financial structure. The tender was accepted.

The United States in 1900 was a highly stratified society, economically and socially. Serious fault lines ran between the large and small manufacturer, between capital and labor, between the masses of the new immigrants and the older population, between the city and the farm. Besides the southern Negro, two or three legal classes of citizens existed, one inside the country and the others with lesser rights in the newly acquired empire. Unless the trend were reversed it looked as if the nation were drifting toward a condition of fixed and highly differentiated classes, some highly privileged, some not having even the basic political rights guaranteed to all by the Constitution. The interclass strife, which so violently punctuated the early nineties, had disappeared temporarily during the Spanish-American War. But after 1900 the remobilization of labor and capital, the rising tensions between city and farm, and the strife between the native and the new immigrant threatened to imperil the nation's unity again. During the nineties, when Brooks Adams sought a historical period from which to draw his bead on the American future he chose as his example in *The Law of Civilization and Decay* the latter days of the Roman Empire. Granted, the comparison was at best vague and inexact. Still Adams, whose life span ran well back into the equalitarian-minded pre-Civil War period, was not writing entirely out of context with the facts of his own society.

CHAPTER 2

Intellectual Tides

JUST as the turn of the century ushered in a number of remarkable changes in the way the nation lived, so the new century marked a series of important changes in the way it thought. Among these, of basic importance, perhaps, was the shift in the cluster of attitudes held about man and his relation to society and to the universe. Nineteenth-century western thought had been dominated by a chain of deterministic formulations which on the whole denied to the animate world much of a part in the fashioning of its future. The classical economists, Hegel, Darwin, Marx, and Spencer, unquestionably inspired by the continuing scientific revolution, had looked for and found a series of overarching laws in the universe to which all life was subject and which were almost as rhythmic and predictable as the new machinery spawned by the Industrial Revolution. Central to the mechanistic thinking of such men was the assumption that life was the captive of a system of legal mechanics, the workings of which were beyond its reach either to influence profoundly or to alter. In the same way Darwin's organisms responded to the all-important physical environment, man responded to the sovereign law which lay beyond his grasp. For Marx, man was at best an agent and at worst a prisoner of the omnipotent movement in the techniques of production and was willy-nilly forced to march with the dialectic to an inevitable triumph of the classless state. For Spencer, it was true, he was more of a volitional being; but if his activities did not agree with the extrahuman laws of competition, his volition took him only to suffering and disaster. This sort of determinist thinking penetrated into most corners of life, and

16

in the novels of Zola even the individual was caught in an environmental trap which was almost as predictable as John Calvin's doctrine of predestination.

During the latter half of the nineteenth century, American thinking was perceptibly influenced by various strains of this kind of European thought. Eager to rationalize their unexampled wealth and power, the great industrialists seized upon Spencer's formulations after they had been brought to the United States by John Fiske, the historian. Spencer's "pure" competitive society, they argued, would produce by the workings of the natural law of the survival of the fittest the most progressive and abundant economy known to the world. Henry Adams, drawing his principle of historical phase from the works of his brother Brooks and from Kelvin's second law of thermodynamics, was far more pessimistic in his ideas of social cycles of acceleration, concentration, and ultimate diffusion. Neither the American followers of Spencer nor the Adams brothers believed that man could do much about the general drift of things. An ant might as well try to move a mountain, William Graham Sumner observed, as for man to attempt to modify the unchanging laws of political economy. But right in the midst of this emphasized determinism with its limiting view of man's ultimate power, some Americans caught the vision of another kind of a society and even a universe in which almost everything could be challenged and changed by man's growing intelligence. There might be a natural law for animals and a law for things which neither was able to transgress; but for man himself, both his society and the natural world were malleable and susceptible to change to suit his own convenience and interest. Implied in that vision was almost an act of creation, and thus a radical change in how man viewed himself in relation to the cosmos.

The reasons for this revolution in thought are complex and still greatly obscured. The rising appreciation of the principles of uncertainty and probability in the natural world toward which the American mathematician, Charles S. Peirce, contributed, the erosion of orthodox deterministic religious doctrines, the free will principles of radical Protestantism, all were factors. Perhaps as important were the applications of science to technology and industry. Ray Stannard Baker recalled that he and his contemporaries felt that they were living through the "Great American Renascence" during the years when the phonograph, the incandescent light, wireless telegraphy, the auto-mobile, moving pictures, the submarine, and the airplane were de-veloped. Such heady titles as "The Conquest of the Air" and "Space and Distance Annihilated" measured the rising crescendo of the new-found sense of power.[1]

The awesome assumption that man could control himself, his society, and his natural environment was, of course, not accepted everywhere, and the older varieties of determinism persisted and were even accentuated in the twentieth century by the initial impact of Freudian thought. Nor was the formulation exactly new to the twen-tieth century. Henry George had referred to man's "Godlike power" to modify his condition. The utopian novelists of the nineties had honored the fact, if not the theory. It was not, however, until the twentieth cen-tury that the view was precisely defined and accepted among some of the less conservative members of the nation's intelligentsia. In a series of lectures given in 1905, Simon Patten of the Wharton School made the unqualified prediction: "The recognition of man's power over heredity is equalled by the perception of his power over nature, as shown by his achievements in industry. . . . The final victory of man's machinery over nature's is the next logical step in evolution. . . ."[2] Within a short time such thoughts had escaped from academic halls. In 1914 Walter Lippmann produced *Drift and Mastery*. Lippmann's thesis was obvious from his significant title: scientific man had arrived at such a state of knowledge that he could now introduce his own plans where all before had been drift. True civilization, according to Lippmann, was the process of introducing plan where there had been clash, and purpose where there had been before only a "jungle of dis-ordered growth." This was now possible because of the rise of science, "the only discipline which gives any assurance that from the same set of facts men will come approximately to the same conclusion." Only in such a scientific world, where caste, church, and myth had been overthrown, and where "change became a matter of invention and deliberate experiment," could man master himself through the new psychology and true self-government be made possible. Science itself was the ultimate in self-government, and the scientific spirit "the

[1] Ray Stannard Baker, *American Chronicle* (New York, 1945), p. 83; Harry B. Haines, "The New Age," *World's Work*, XI (1906), 7346.

[2] Simon N. Patten, *The New Basis of Civilization* (New York, 1907), pp. 25, 205.

discipline of democracy, the escape from drift, the outlook of a free man." [3]

Deliberate social experiment and planning, of course, had not awaited a Patten or a Lippmann to call them into being. Frederick W. Taylor's achievements in scientific industrial management, George Harvey's manipulation of public opinion as a "public relations" agent for industrial corporations, city planning, resources conservation, and the birth-control movement were all previous practical emanations of the same spirit. By 1900 the phrase "social science," used to describe a group of new academic disciplines, had caught the public fancy, and the adjective "scientific" went far in ensuring any appeal to the public of at least an interested hearing. In 1899 the non-university-educated Eugene V. Debs asserted that socialism was the only political philosophy that was based upon a true social science. Two years later Vice-President Theodore Roosevelt called for "scientific management" of the tariff. [4]

Long before either Patten or Lippmann spoke, philosophy had also raised its voice in powerful support for the enfranchisement of man from a mechanistic universe. In 1897 William James published *The Will to Believe and Other Essays*. But by that time some generations of students had been indoctrinated with the principles of James's pragmatism, the one comprehensive American contribution to western philosophic thought. As developed by James and John Dewey, pragmatism attacked the fundamental concepts of the nineteenth-century mechanistic world in which man was a more or less controlled instrument of a Calvinistic scheme of predestination, a Hegelian or a Marxian dialectic, a Darwinian process of selection, or of Newtonian physics. Instead of this determined universe the world was an open one of constant but uncertain change in which man thinking and man acting could leave his mark. In this new world view there were few, if any, eternal verities, and no extrahuman road maps to security or victory for either man or animal. But there were also few, if any, final barriers. Provided man used his mind creatively and adventurously, was guided by his moral sense, and took courageous action, very little was impossible for the race. Beliefs, if held intensely, were in themselves instruments of creation. "Believe that life is worth living," James wrote in

[3] Walter Lippmann, *Drift and Mastery* (New York, 1914), pp. 266–273, 285, 333.

[4] Eugene V. Debs, *Writings and Speeches* (New York, 1948), p. 29.

"The Will to Believe," "and your belief will help create the fact." But
the value of a belief was not to be measured by the venerated affirmation of antiquity or even by its utility in the past. The real worth of an
idea was in its consequences. Thus man and society found what was
good by constant experiment, but the good thus found, since the world
was always in flux, was most often only relative to a particular time,
place, and condition. The price of success for man and society in such
a shifting world was constant thought, constant experiment, constant
"creative doing." This was a pluralistic, relativistic, and temporal doctrine; it was also idealistic and activistic. It presupposed a universe
which responded to man's creative intelligence. Its social implications
were plain: it was the negation of conservatism and a powerful instrument for the destruction of old faiths whether theological, economic,
or political.[5]

Between 1886 and 1890 at least five academic journals were founded
devoted to the new social studies. The *Political Science Quarterly*, the
Quarterly Journal of Economics, the *Annals of the American Academy of Political and Social Sciences*, the *Journal of Political Economy*,
and the *American Historical Review* all attested to the flourishing state
and growing influence of the social sciences. The names of some of the
journals also indicated the hopes of the founders to incorporate into
the new disciplines both the method and the spirit of the older physical
sciences. Even the historians, whose chief interest centered upon that
most variable of social factors, man, aspired to write "scientific
history."

For the most part the outlook of the early social scientists in America
was the outlook of Herbert Spencer. They found immutable laws in
the physical universe and correlated laws of social growth. Free competition and the survival of the fittest were just as basic for society as
they were for nature. Man might, of course, violate the laws, but he
could not change them. The academic high priest of this social
Darwinism was William Graham Sumner of Yale University. "The
truth," Sumner wrote, "is that the social order is fixed by laws of
nature precisely analogous to those of the physical order." Man's
attempts to reform, therefore, are attempts to reform the universe and
as puny and insignificant as the attempt of an ant to "deflect a mighty
river." Conceited and ignorant man, Sumner conceded, might momen-

[5] Henry S. Commager, *The American Mind* (New Haven, 1952), pp. 91–98.

tarily break nature's mandates, but in the long run only to the direful hurt of himself and his society.[6]

The first sustained theoretical attack against Sumner and his mentor Spencer came from a group of sociologists, including Lester Ward, Albion Small, Charles H. Cooley, and Edward A. Ross. Ward, the father of American sociology, was a paleobotanist for the government until 1906, at which time he accepted a professorship at Brown University. But as early as 1883 his *Dynamic Sociology* had challenged the philosophic heart of Sumner's doctrines. In this and subsequent books Ward argued that Sumner's long jump from nature to human society was utterly unsustained by both logic and fact. Social evolution was the result not of natural law but of "man's intellectual capacity" to conceive and produce change of infinite variety, and thus "to shape environmental forces to his own advantage." Man was not only the inheritor of change, Ward argued; he was also the creator of it, fully capable of "rational planning" and of "social engineering." [7]

Albion W. Small was the editor of the *American Journal of Sociology* for thirty years after its founding in 1895. His opening remarks in the first number of the journal argued his case for the gathering of "scientific knowledge of society" so that there could "be more effective research and action for the promotion of the general welfare." The entire spirit of sociology, he wrote later, is "a deep loyal impulse of social service. Its whole animus is constructive, remedial and ameliorative." [8] Certainly this was the spirit of most of the articles appearing in the journal under Small's editorship. At least seven articles on the subject of municipal reform appeared in the journal before 1902, the year Lincoln Steffens began to "muckrake" city government. Among these were some on political corruption, municipal socialism, and the evils of long-term utility franchises. In the same tenor numerous articles appeared on industrial conditions, rural life, the place of the church in modern society.[9]

[6] William Graham Sumner, *Selected Essays,* ed. Albert G. Keller and Maurice R. Davie (New Haven, 1924), pp. 245–246; Maurice R. Davie (ed.), *Sumner Today* (New Haven, 1940), p. 81.

[7] Lester Ward, *Outlines of Sociology* (Boston, 1898), p. 193; and *Psychic Factors of Civilization* (Boston, 1897), pp. 133–137, 260–280.

[8] Albion W. Small, *American Journal of Sociology,* I (1895), 1–15; and *General Sociology* (Chicago, 1905), p. 38.

[9] See, for example, Franklin MacVeagh, "Program of Municipal Reform," *American Journal of Sociology,* I (1895), pp. 551–563; and Charles R. Woodruff, "Philadelphia Street Railway Franchise," *ibid.,* VII (1902), 216–233.

During the 1880's an American university president observed that a belief in laissez faire was not a test for orthodoxy. "It was used to decide whether a man was an economist at all." [10] Sumner, Arthur T. Hadley, John Bates Clark, and J. Laurence Laughlin were the respected reigning conservatives. But as in sociology the revolution in economics was already under way. The credo, issued at the founding of the American Economic Association in 1885 by a "group of young rebels fresh from Germany," was a remarkable document. "We regard the state," it read in part, "as an educational and ethical agency whose positive aid is an indispensable condition to human progress." To Richard T. Ely, Simon Patten, and Henry C. Adams, man was no longer the passive recipient of change; he was the maker of it. Moreover, if these young economists were to have their way, change, i.e., progress, would be cut to the fashion of their ethical and moral views. Ely referred to himself and his colleagues as "the ethical school of economists"; they would direct, he promised, the growth of mankind toward "the most perfect development of all human faculties in each individual which can be obtained in harmony with the ethical ideal of Christianity." From that time on the published studies of the new organization were full of ethical measurement of what had hitherto been considered as natural economic propositions. Labor should be assured of an "equitable position," wages should be "fair," prices "just," and working conditions "decent." Economics, according to Professor E. R. A. Seligman, had become "the group of ethical up-building . . . the basis of social progress." [11]

Outside the circle of these young political philosophers, and difficult to classify, were the economist Thorstein Veblen and the jurist Oliver Wendell Holmes, Jr. Both men stood almost alone in their thinking, but both had a measurable influence on the intellectual currents of their day. Personally difficult and inconoclastic in his views, Veblen was no ethicalist. But his belief that man was not a prisoner of his environment and could shape society toward a better life is obvious in his *Theory of the Leisure Class,* published in 1899, and especially in his later works. Veblen's main contribution to the intellectual readjust-

[10] Cited in Arthur Mann, *Yankee Reformers in the Urban Age* (Cambridge, 1954), p. 105.

[11] Richard T. Ely, *Ground Under Our Feet* (New York, 1938), p. 121; Russel Nye, *Midwestern Progressive Politics* (East Lansing, 1951), p. 147; E. R. A. Seligman, *American Economic Association Publications,* 3rd Series, 5, 4, No. 1, 70.

ment in process was his sardonic and at times unfair analysis of the reigning social institutions. Once Veblen had formulated such concepts as "conspicuous consumption" and "pecuniary emulation," the old economic forms could never excite the solemn reverence they once did. Veblen's popular audience was neither wide nor significant. The man was too difficult to read and his ironic spirit too foreign to the day for that. But colleagues, students, and intellectuals were touched by his probing and original mind and reacted in ways unfavorable to the *status quo*.

In 1881 Oliver Wendell Holmes, Jr., published his *Common Law*. The book and Holmes's subsequent legal thought were to do in a way for jurisprudence what Ward was to do for the study of society and what the young economists were to do for economics. Both by taste and conviction Holmes was a conservative. But in his writings and in his decisions from the bench he contended against the long-held proposition that law was based upon nearly immutable principles and that it changed, if at all, by a process of rigorous logical extrapolations from such principles. Instead, Holmes held that the basis of law was human experience and man's total material and intellectual environment. Law then became one of "the felt necessities" of the times, "evolving from the prevalent moral and political theories, from economic rationalizations, and even from the unconscious prejudices which judges shared with their fellow men." But society, he recognized, was made up of conflicting groups of men, each contending for the supremacy of their own desires and prejudices. What then was truth? Simply what men could not help believing: "I therefore define truth," Holmes commented, "as the system of my limitations, and leave absolute truth for those who are better equipped." It followed that law was obviously the finely reasoned expressions of the truths or the limitations of the group or groups in power. In a democracy that seemed to mean the majority. And thus as power shifted in a state, as for example from a small farming class to the urban man, so did truth and eventually legal propositions. Holmes's emphasis upon man's inability to see beyond the prejudices of his own class hinted at a larger determinism that was almost absent from the thinking of the rebel economists or sociologists, and certainly from that of Patten or Lippmann. But the rest of his doctrine was consistent with the attack upon the mechanistic world of the nineteenth century. For if law came ultimately out of the total human condition, it was man-centered, temporal in character, pluralistic, and relative.[12]

Among the first institutions to feel the full impact of the new scientific spirit was religion. Darwin had been introduced into the country in the 1860's, and no matter what the rationalizations attempted, and there were many, orthodox religion was never the same thereafter. In 1883 existing religious beliefs had been struck two simultaneous blows. The year marked the publication of Professor Charles A. Briggs' *Biblical Study: Its Principles, Methods, and History*. This was the first comprehensive introduction of the results of German higher criticism, questioning many Biblical facts, especially those of the Old Testament. During the same year a suggested official creed for the Congregational Church contained neither a statement of original sin nor a formal doctrine of the Trinity. From that time on conservative theology was under almost constant attack. The result was a depreciation of the Old Testament, of original sin, supernatural redemption, and, in the more advanced churches, of hell itself and all supernaturalism. By 1902 the former clerical president of the University of Wisconsin, John Bascom, still thought that supernatural elements were essential to religious beliefs, but he noted that the subject was now "open to debate." Four years later a Christian, but not church-minded, editor asked whether it was possible that anyone in this enlightened world still believed in a "material hell, and everlasting physical torment." [13]

At the same time that basic theology was being seriously questioned in the nineties, the church as an institution was being attacked. One wave of criticism came from a small group of intellectuals who aimed their shafts at the cultural barrenness of the church. Harold Frederic's *Theron Ware* left the Methodist ministry in part because of its cultural bigotry. And Ellen Glasgow's pointed comment that the Episcopal Church was "charitable toward almost any weakness except the dangerous practice of thinking" reflected a feeling that was not confined to Virginia.

More serious to the future of the Protestant church was its desertion by social radicals and organized labor. Here and there individual

---

[12] For a broader interpretation of Holmes's impact upon American jurisprudence, see Commager, *The American Mind*, pp. 374–390.

[13] *Literary Digest*, XXV (1902), 46; *The Public*, October 7, 1905. For other treatments of the new criticism, see Orello Cone, *Gospel-Criticism and Historical Christianity* (New York, 1891); and Washington Gladden, *Who Wrote the Bible?* (New York, 1891).

ministers approached the social question with understanding and sympathy, and occasionally a Protestant cleric was outrightly prolabor. But the bulk of the Protestant ministry and the church seemed from the radical-labor viewpoint to be hostile. When Samuel Gompers was asked to name the religious groups in the order of their friendliness to labor, he listed in sequence ethical societies, Unitarians, nonbelievers, and Catholics. At the very bottom of his list were Protestants and ministers. Other radicals were more positive in their position. Although sincerely religious, Edward Bellamy never went into a church and forbade his family to go. Henry Demarest Lloyd was sure that he could do what ministers could not: "be right without being religious." Others were even more blunt, referring to ministers as "spiritual Pinkertons," whose main duty was that of "guarding the loot of the unrighteous rich." [14]

By 1900 the large groups of immigrants, preponderantly Roman Catholic, confronted American Protestantism with a major challenge. When the native laboring man continued his movement away from the congregations, the Protestant church, at first critical of the deserters, became increasingly anxious. In the nineties a leading Middle Western divine was obviously highly irritated and inclined to let "the atheistic and unreachable masses" sink into the depths of their own sinfulness. But with the situation more critical by 1900, the Reverend Charles Steltze was disposed to send out a nationwide questionnaire inquiring why workers did not go to church. He reported that the replies were almost unanimous: the Protestant church was being run by and for the rich; it sanctified the capitalistic ethic and damned labor unions and strikes as inventions of the devil. Almost at the same time three Methodist bishops called for a nationwide week of prayer to bring the erring laborers back to the fold. When such spiritual evocation failed of its mission, the church began to listen with more sympathy to the demand that it make itself useful to workingmen, not only spiritually on Sundays but also in a "far more material way," on every day of the week.[15]

---

[14] Nye, *Midwestern Progressive Politics*, p. 163; Aaron, *Men of Good Hope*, pp. 127, 140; James Dombrowski, *The Early Days of Christian Socialism in America* (New York, 1936), p. 8.

[15] Charles Steltze, "The Workingman and the Church," *The Outlook*, LXVIII (1901), 713; and "Decline in Methodism," *The Outlook*, LXIV (1900), 610–611; C. E. Ordway, "Will the Churches Survive?" *Arena*, XXIX (1903), 593.

As the new formulations of science and criticism struck at traditional Christian doctrines, Americans as usual responded in varied patterns. A cult of agnosticism, centering around Robert Ingersoll, appealed to an important group of young men which included Hamlin Garland, Edgar Lee Masters, Theodore Dreiser, Brand Whitlock, and Clarence Darrow. Some men saw a Deity not unlike Frank Norris's "prodigious mechanism of wheels and cogs," while others like Stephen Crane, whose father was a Methodist minister, saw God and his angels intrigued with man only to the extent of wondering why people went into a "fat church" and stayed so long. But most Americans, including the ministers who perceived the implications of the new science, preferred to modify their religion instead of discarding it.

In this process of modification most theologians saw in evolution and Darwinism a promise of spiraling change, but a spiral upward and not downward. As early as 1874, John Fiske had argued in his *Outlines of Cosmic Philosophy* that evolution was God's certain plan for achieving eternal progress. "On the whole," Washington Gladden, a proponent of the New Theology, remarked, "almost steadily, things get better." Since the new science and this new optimism clashed with both the facts and spirit of the Old Testament, this part of the Bible was under constant criticism and re-evaluation. After a long study, Lyman Abbott concluded "that the fall of man had much less importance in the Bible than it had been given by the theologians." Simultaneously the doctrine of original sin was attacked on more pragmatic grounds; it had, according to Rabbi Charles Fleischer of Boston, "tended to discourage men from trying to rise." A professor of theology agreed. Citing Emerson's denial of sin, George A. Coe of Northwestern University questioned whether the total conception of sin should not be vastly depreciated in Christian thought, since religion did not flourish "through a consciousness of guilt." [16]

But if man was not evil by inheritance, two questions arose: how did sin originate and how could it be ameliorated? The answer of the reformers was almost unanimous. Sin, or evil, was not theological but sociological; it had originated in man's actions toward man out of ignorance and fear, and the way to suppress it was for the good men to take action in the place where it arose and prospered, in society.

---

[16] Lyman Abbott, *Reminiscences* (Boston, 1915), ix; Charles Fleischer, "Education and Democracy," *Arena,* XXVII (1902), 496; *Literary Digest,* XXVII (1903), 231.

Three years before E. A. Ross, a professor of sociology, published his interesting study on sin, an article appeared in the *Arena* written by an unnamed minister arguing that, while sin was not an illusion in the modern world, it had been man-made and thus could be man-destroyed. Since the fall of man and original sin were intimately tied up with hell and the devil, these two ancient Christian concepts were likewise repudiated by the reformers. By the opening of the new century one of the leaders of the movement, Shailer Mathews, was defining hell as "an everlasting committee meeting on a good cause that could not be brought to pass." As for the devil, he was read out of existence by the same article in the *Arena* that had questioned the theological origins of sin.[17]

As the rebel theologians placed less faith in the doctrines of the Old Testament, they tended to emphasize the worth of the New. Christ, his life on earth, and his words, "Thy will be done on earth as it is in Heaven," became the cardinal principles of the new theology. In 1894 William T. Stead, the English journalist and reformer, came to Chicago. After a look at "the city of the hog butchers," he wrote the book *If Christ Came to Chicago.* On the cover was an angry Christ driving the money-changers from the temple. But the faces of the culprits, instead of being ancient Hebrew, were those of Charles T. Yerkes, the traction monopolist, and other leading municipal figures. Inside was a "map of sin" showing brothels in red and saloons in black, with their managers and their owners. The book was reputed to have sold seven thousand copies on its day of publication, with no estimates, of course, as to the purpose of the purchasers. Shortly after Stead's publication, a Kansas Congregationalist minister, Charles M. Sheldon, published *In His Steps,* an imaginative biography of a town trying to act as Jesus did. When the American Institute of Christian Sociology was founded in 1893, its first secretary, Professor John R. Commons, announced that its purpose was to "present Christ, the living Master and King, and Christian law as the ultimate rule for human society to be realized on earth." [18]

To abolish the devil and hell and deny original sin was an extra-

---

[17] Shailer Mathews, *New Faith for Old* (New York, 1936), p. 154; *Arena,* XXIV (1900), 76.

[18] Walter Peterson, "Some Aspects of Protestantism in the Midwest, 1870–1910," unpublished Ph.D. thesis, State University of Iowa, p. 23. Baker, *American Chronicle,* p. 28.

ordinary feat for this pious generation, but to obtain the Kingdom of
Christ on earth, to secularize heaven, was obviously an even greater
task. But the attempt was to be made in the name of the new movement referred to by its founders as "the social gospel," or social
Christianity. By 1885, the decay of the old orthodoxy among the
Boston Unitarian, Congregational, and Episcopal ministry was already
under way. Some Presbyterians and Lutherans resisted "modernism,"
but the great bulk of the remaining ministry was demanding "that
the church do its worldly duty." [19] By that time also the American
ministry was beginning to feel the influence of the British Christian
Socialists, Ruskin, Morris, and Kingsley (the Boston Society of Chris-
tian Socialists being organized by the Episcopalian minister Dwight
Porter Bliss in 1889). Prior to that date the Reverend Josiah Strong of
Cincinnati had organized a group of Congregational and Methodist
ministers to discuss the relation of "the church and the social issue."
This movement was led by Josiah Strong, Lyman Abbott, Washington
Gladden, and Professor Ely, and resulted in the formation of the Evan-
gelical Alliance in 1887 and subsequently in the Brotherhood of the
Kingdom. Abbott, Gladden, and Shailer Mathews, together with the
two laymen, Professors Ely and Commons, were to furnish the leader-
ship for the more moderate wing of the movement. Much further to
the left were George D. Herron, professor of Applied Christianity at
Iowa College until 1899, and Walter Rauschenbusch of the Rochester
Theological Seminary.

The more moderate wing of the social gospel movement was dedicated to comprehensive economic reforms, but not to the overthrow of
capitalism. What it objected to was not the institution but rather its
"excesses," "the excessive accumulation of wealth," "the rampant
materialism," the use of wealth "to corrupt people and politics," "antisocial competition," which set man against man and created the "un-
Christian disparities" of enormous wealth and deep and abiding
poverty. What it wanted was a "Christian capitalism" dominated by
moral considerations instead of laissez faire, in which prices would
be "just," wages "fair," and competition "ethical," and under which

---

[19] Arthur Mann, *Yankee Reformers* (Boston, 1954), p. 74. For a comprehensive view of the movement, see Charles H. Hopkins, *The Rise of the Social
Gospel in American Protestantism, 1865–1915* (New Haven, 1940); Aaron I.
Abell, *The Urban Impact Upon American Protestantism* (Cambridge, 1943);
and Henry F. May, *Protestant Churches and Industrial America* (New York,
1949).

men in the market place would act like "brothers" instead of "selfish animals." [20]

To accomplish these ends the moderates felt they had to change the church from being an apologist of wealth and power and its ministers from being dispensers almost exclusively of "orthodox theology and economics." Too many ministers, Shailer Mathews observed, were "cooperatively sustained private chaplains of well-to-do cliques." By dedicating the church to a social mission, the new ministry might hope to gain the confidence and the ear of the "unevangelized masses." After that it was just the matter of appeal to both "the heart and head" until the day when "the new morality" would dominate the ballot and day-to-day life.[21]

The more radical wing of the movement toward social Christianity was led by George D. Herron and Walter Rauschenbusch. Theoretically the various Christian Socialist groups should be included under this category. But often their doctrines and programs were so vague that, like the Boston society, they might be described as organizations "for the propagation of virtue in general." [22] Herron and Rauschenbusch, on the contrary, were painfully specific and militantly anticapitalistic. Herron wrote that the acquisition and possession of wealth were immoral and antisocial. To Rauschenbusch capitalism was "essential atheism." Both men believed that the abolition of private property and an equal division of wealth were necessities for the attainment of any real democracy.[23]

Whatever the feelings about capitalism, the right and the left of the social gospel movement were characterized by a burning desire to bring the ethics of the church down into the factory, the street, and the market place. As Washington Gladden wrote, the old individualistic pietism had no appeal for them. What they wanted was "a religion that laid hold on life with both hands." Seemingly something approaching a law of countervailing loyalties worked inside them. As

[20] See Washington Gladden, *The Church and Modern Life* (New York, 1908); Shailer Mathews, *The Social Teachings of Jesus: An Essay in Christian Sociology* (New York, 1897); and John R. Commons, *Social Reform and the Church* (New York, 1894).

[21] Shailer Mathews, *The Church and the Changing Order* (New York, 1907), p. 122.

[22] Mann, *Yankee Reformers*, p. 93.

[23] George D. Herron, *Between Caesar and Jesus* (New York, 1899), p. 107; Walter Rauschenbusch, *A Theology for the Social Gospel* (New York, 1917), p. 42.

their interest waned in the old orthodox dogma which Horace Bushnell called "immoral theology," their faith in the Christian ethic mounted. So did their zeal for applying those ethics to society. "Every Christian is a reformer," the minister of the New York Fifth Avenue Church declared, "if not, he is an infidel." [24]

The new social religion did not go uncontested. In many pulpits throughout the Middle West, as was probably also true of the nation, it was ignored. In others it met the most strenuous opposition on both theological and social grounds. But in the prewar twentieth century the intellectual and emotional tides of the age beat relentlessly against the old headlands of religious and social dogma. The total effect of the social gospel in creating a climate of reform is of course unmeasurable. An able American historian remarked in 1913, however, that it had been years since he had heard a sermon recalling those of his youth. "A new era," he observed, "has dawned in the history of human thought." Religion had joined scholarship and science in giving sanction for reform.[25]

When in 1900 William Dean Howells was asked what the upper- and middle-class Americans read, he is reputed to have replied, "The newspapers." Howells' ironic answer was not quite fair to the contemporary literary taste. Throughout the nineties and into the new century Americans were reading millions of solid books each year. Henry George's trenchant indictment of the new industrial society, *Progress and Poverty,* had already gone through a hundred editions. First published in 1879, this fervent volume mixing old American aspirations with the new single-tax doctrine was seminal to much of the reform thought for the next thirty years. Any one of two or three dozen urban-minded reformers in the new century might have uttered the words of Charles Edward Russell after first reading George: "I conceded the voice of ultimate wisdom and saw in Henry George the apostle of a new gospel." The guest list at a memorial dinner for George held in New York City, 1905, read like a roster of literary reformers and attested to his continued remarkable influence.[26]

By 1900 Edward Bellamy's *Looking Backward* had been read by

[24] Washington Gladden, *Recollections* (Boston, 1909), p. 63; and *The Public,* LX (1905), 25.

[25] James T. Shotwell, *The Religious Revolution of Today* (New York, 1913), p. 3 n.

[26] Charles Edward Russell, *Bare Hands and Stone Walls* (New York, 1933), p. 24; *The New York Times,* February 11, 1914.

countless Americans. Thousands of others had gone through Henry Demarest Lloyd's astringent *Wealth Against Commonwealth* and William Morris's *News From Nowhere*. As late as 1914 a reforming Congressman was advising his friends and supporters to read and absorb Morris's socialistic volume published a quarter-century before.[27] Howells was of course quite aware of the popularity and influence of such works. He had read *Progress and Poverty*, had been moved, and had written his own utopian protest against society. Howells had not been speaking of social studies and tractarian romances, but rather of literature. Here the record for men of letters was much more dismal. Of the thirty-seven "best sellers" published from 1898 to 1902, nineteen could be considered historical adventure fiction, the rest for the most part rural dialect tales, "pure" romances, and religious novels bearing little or no relation either to man's universal problems or to those of the American scene. It was probably true that in facing the disconcerting present the country needed the "nostalgic delights of a romantic past." But it was also true that the painful present was already producing its own reflection in American literature. For precisely at the time the literary review, *The Bookman*, was asking for a return to the "problem novel" and to "a degree of realism," Frank Norris, Theodore Dreiser, and David Graham Phillips had started works that in the opinion of the genteel magazine rather overshot the new mark. Some American novels, it was soon to complain, were "too real" in that "they show the nakedness of the human soul without the beauty and the romance which we demand in our fiction." [28]

The introduction of realism and of social problems in the American novel had, of course, antedated the Spanish-American War. William Dean Howells, Stephen Crane, Harold Frederic, and Hamlin Garland all had written with a realistic touch in the eighties and the nineties. But all had worked within a certain limited range. Subsequently the movement gained a real impetus and a much broader latitude. When Crane's *Maggie,* Frederic's *Damnation of Theron Ware,* and Norris's *McTeague* were published, both realism and the social problem had

[27] Ray Stannard Baker, "A Philosopher in Congress," *American Magazine,* LXXVIII (1914), 88.

[28] Alfred Kazin, *On Native Grounds* (New York, 1942), p. 53; *The Bookman,* XI (1900), 211; XII (1900), 511; *Literary Digest,* XXXVI (1908), 92. See also Frank Luther Mott, *Golden Multitudes* (New York, 1947); and James D. Hart, *The Popular Book: A History of American Literary Taste* (New York, 1950).

achieved status in writing of quality. Moreover, these three unsentimental (for the day) investigations into the lives of a slum girl, a minister, and a dentist opened the way for critical examinations of many other hitherto forbidden corners of American society. Norris's subsequent success with the subjects of California wheat, the Southern Pacific Railroad, and the Chicago Grain Exchange was followed by a spate of political and social investigations. As literary craftsmen Brand Whitlock, Alfred Henry Lewis, David Graham Phillips, and Winston Churchill were perhaps not too far above the level of the popular historical romancers; but their studies of contemporary politics, marriage, divorce, alcohol, religion, and kindred subjects, taken as a group, reached a much wider audience than books by abler writers.

This "new literature," as it was called by contemporaries, drew its strength and peculiarities from many sources. Zola and Tolstoy, whom Crane called the greatest living novelists, inspired it from abroad; and Howells, who likewise acknowledged a debt to the great Russian, gave it comfort at home. But Darwin and his omnipresent environment, the rising appreciation of science, the evolution of technology, and the growth of the city all had their weight in its making. Compared to the preceding literature, if it can be set apart, the new literature was more urban-centered, less limited to middle-class characters and themes, and more consciously environmental. Viewed from the rising pragmatic assumptions of an open universe, some of the best of this new literature was often in a way reactionary. For although the heroes of Frank Norris, Theodore Dreiser, and Jack London were strong, willful, and able men who appeared on the surface to be prime movers, the authors' strong attachment to nineteenth-century environmentalism and determinism made them more the instruments and less the fashioners of time, place, and change. But in the end, quantitatively at least, the new literature was indignant and had an immediate social purpose as one of its main reasons for being. Even Frank Norris was to succumb. Whatever reasons he had in mind for writing *The Octopus* and *The Pit,* shortly before he died he was encouraging young novelists to follow Strindberg's advice to become "a lay preacher," and plunge into politics, religion, and science.[29] Few of America's best writers were prepared to accept Hamlin Garland's Veritism, which held that fiction should reflect life and show its ugly sides to the end that society could

[29] Cited in the *Literary Digest,* XXV (1902), 378.

be changed. But a host of lesser talents, rushing in where the giants chose not to tread, joyfully added their strident voices for reform. As Alfred Kazin says, the history of realism in America after the Civil War has been "a history of grievances." [30]

At the end of the old century the university, the church, the bar, politics, and the world of literature were still overwhelmingly dominated by the male. But within a little more than a decade a rising and extremely self-conscious group of women began to play an important part in the fashioning of the twentieth-century mentality. Since the pre-Civil War feminist movement had disturbed masculine complacency, the status of women had changed greatly. By 1900 co-education through the college years had long been practically universal west of the Alleghenies and north of the Ohio. In the East the women's colleges founded after the Civil War had graduated thousands of well-trained women. Of the southern woman Ellen Glasgow could still write that she "was capable of dying for an idea, but not of conceiving one." But in the North and the West at least two generations of women had attended colleges and universities and were now demanding an outlet for their energies and their intellect.

Among the upper-class urban family the birth rate was rapidly dropping by 1900, leading Theodore Roosevelt among others to talk of "race suicide." Moreover, the rapidly growing wealth of such families and the introduction of new labor-saving devices provided this new upper-class woman with time and surplus energy that her sisters on the farm and in the village had never known. It was precisely this class of women that William Dean Howells described as "selfish by tradition," "generous by nature," and "infinitely superior to their husbands in cultivation." At the other end of the economic scale more and more women were entering industry and business. The advance of the machine put less of a premium on masculine muscle, and the presumed docility of women and their willingness to work for lower wages attracted industrial employers. The perfection of the typewriter and the rise of commercial education for women had meanwhile opened the doors to business offices. By 1900 one survey showed that 20 per cent of all women over the age of fifteen were gainfully employed; by 1910 the figure had risen to 25 per cent.

Along with this invasion of factory and office had come a good

[30] Kazin, *On Native Grounds*, p. 15 n.; see also Commager, *The American Mind*, pp. 108 ff.

many advances in women's social and legal rights. By 1900 women had been granted the suffrage by five western states.[31] The right of women to make a will was recognized by every state, their right to dispose of their own wages was secure in most commonwealths, and seven states had granted the right of equal guardianship in children. Legally, at least, women were also permitted to enter the learned professions. Despite these advances at the opening of the century the trained and educated woman still found precious few positions requiring more than manual skills actually open to her in professions, industry, and commerce. Tradition and masculine prejudice still confined her, in fact, to the "proper activities of the sex," which included education, charity, and the protection of women and children. Years before, the ambitious Frances Willard had blazed the path from teaching to the headship of the Women's Christian Temperance Union. Now, just as many of Edith Wharton's heroines revolted against the time-consuming and meaningless rites of high society, so their human counterparts followed paths to settlement houses, child welfare centers, consumers' leagues, and other such seemingly innocuous reform activities.

One of the longest steps taken by woman toward the center of the modern world was her organized attempt to educate herself in the issues of the day. By 1900, national women's clubs devoted to the study of social issues had become common. The number of women belonging to such clubs was perhaps larger then than the membership in the American Federation of Labor. The Association of Collegiate Alumnae, which later became the American Association of University Women, was already surprisingly strong. So was the National Council for Jewish Women. But perhaps the most important force in turning feminine attention away from the confining walls of the home was the General Federation of Women's Clubs. Founded in 1889, this "Middle-Aged Women's University" included in its "curriculum" matters far more mundane than polite literature. Observing that Dante had been dead for a long time, the new president in 1904 urged members to stop studying the *Inferno* and start an examination of their own social order.

To women like Emma Goldman, the anarchist, and labor's sainted Mother Jones, the implied comparison between Dante's hell and the modern world came as no shock. But for the gentler and more protected women who went down to the slums in the new century, the

[31] Wyoming, Colorado, Idaho, Utah, and Montana.

experience must have been both upsetting and illuminating. Jane Addams, Florence Kelley, Julia Lathrop, Lillian Wald, and Rheta Dorr all came from good upper-middle-class church families, and all but one had gone to college. (Miss Wald was refused admission to Vassar.) By the dictates of the masculine world these able women were practically forced to seek a professional career either in education or in charitable pursuits. By choice they elected the newly developing settlement houses usually set in the midst of the Chicago and New York slums. In administering to "the submerged tenth," they saw at firsthand the dichotomous character of late Victorian society: between the official statement and truth, as between progress and poverty, and between man and woman. Their real desire to help was soon accompanied by an even more ardent desire to reform.[32]

In one of Howells' novels a visitor from the utopian state of Altruria asked a matron whether she and her friends went to their husbands' clubs much. "Much!" Mrs. Makeley screamed. "They don't go at all! They can't. They won't let us!"[33] In this cultivated woman's shrill reply Howells was measuring the rising temper of her sex. After seeing the man-made world at firsthand with its slums, dives, crooked politics, and almost ubiquitous double standards, many women naturally accepted the belief that their sex alone was the guardian of "the sacred vessels that held the ancient sanctities of life." They were also convinced that the major reason for the existing moral chaos lay in the "lack of proper balance between feminine and masculine equality." Simultaneously among certain women there was a detectable rising dislike of the American male and a growing assumption of superiority. As a young woman, the journalist Ida Tarbell prayed to God to keep her from marriage. And after "objectively" surveying the state of the sexes, the author, editor, and popular sociologist, Charlotte Gilman, authoritatively described woman as "the highest human type."[34]

For the indignant and rebellious woman of the new century the route to equality lay along two possible directions. The first was to become like a male and practice the ethics of the masculine *status quo*. As the new century progressed, an increasing number of

[32] Anna Carlin Spencer, *Woman's Share in Social Culture* (New York, 1912), p. 122.

[33] *Through the Eye of the Needle* (New York, 1907), p. 43.

[34] Charlotte Perkins Gilman, *The Man-Made World* (New York, 1911), p. 83; Susan B. Anthony, "Woman's Half Century of Evolution," *North American Review*, CLXXV (1900), 810.

"emancipated women" quietly accepted the doctrines of equality more openly advocated by Rheta C. Dorr. Like some of Willa Cather's strong-minded frontier heroines, they simply cast aside Victorian morals. By 1912 Walter Lippmann noted that the pursuit of the single standard had created in quite a few instances a new sex, that of the "amateur male." [35] But for the great majority of woman reformers such a course was entirely repugnant. Their feet were too solidly planted in Victorian personal ethics for their heads to be turned by such immoral doctrines. What they wanted was equality, but an equality based upon a standard of feminine virtue instead of masculine sin. The new woman, Charlotte Gilman promised, would set the highest possible ethical standards and "draw men up to them." What was in store for the masculine world, at least for a generation, was indicated by one of the primary planks in this program of rehabilitation, "chastity for men." [36]

The influence of the reform-minded woman in the progressive period is self-evident in such matters as woman's rights, suffrage, the protection of minors, and in such moral crusades as those against liquor and prostitution. What is not so ponderable is the weight of their influence in the recasting of business and political ethics and in the age's general assault upon sin. That it was weighty few men would care to deny. But whatever woman's impact upon the new society, men had been largely responsible for it. The American upper-middle-class woman had been indoctrinated with the loftiest Victorian personal ethics. She had been well educated and at the same time denied the opportunity for the exercise of her new-found abilities, except for those open in the fields of charity and social service. These took her down to the slums, to a world of vice, immorality, and political corruption which all too often was connected with the males of her own upper-class circles. Her awakening to the disparities between man and woman, between the stated rules of the age and the actualities of the streets, called forth her demands for equality and reform which left an indelible mark upon the first two decades of the new century.

While America was rapidly changing its many material aspects around the turn of the century, it was also speedily altering many of its traditional beliefs and time-hallowed creeds. The new intellectual

[35] Lippmann, *Drift and Mastery*, p. 221.
[36] Gilman, *The Man-Made World*, p. 250; Rheta C. Dorr, *A Woman of Fifty* (New York, 1924), pp. 264–265.

trends in science, philosophy, the social sciences, jurisprudence, religion, and the arts started from varied sources about the same time. For a while they flowed separately. But the contours of the age brought them closer together, and somewhere around 1900 their confluence occurred. Reinforcing each other, these varying streams of thought formed a flood beating against the damlike structure of old ideas and conventions.

Central to this new intellectual formulation was the firm belief that to a considerable degree man could make and remake his own world. No longer was he simply an animate cog in a universal mechanism whose speed and direction were predetermined by extrahuman forces. Instead of this closed and confined world the new thought held out a vision of John Dewey's "perpetual open frontier" with its optimistic invitation for man to act creatively. The new thought also carried with it another burden of explosive freight. Both the rising social sciences and the new social gospel promised that basically men were more alike than different and that they were not evil by inheritance, but, if anything, were inclined by their own nature to be good. Unmitigated competition therefore, instead of selecting the best, as Herbert Spencer would have it, might reward the least ethical. At any rate, the great inequalities existing among them at the moment were not natural, and from the viewpoint of social peace and human welfare were decidedly bad. To this the educated upper-middle-class woman, acutely conscious of her second-class status in society, uttered a fervent affirmation, as did many another American suckled upon the more equalitarian doctrines of the past.

American society in 1900 was thus rent by two major forces propelling it in acutely different directions. Material changes and institutions were creating a highly differentiated society. Simultaneously the new intellectual and moral creeds were demanding a return to a more equalitarian life. Conflict between the two forces was inevitable, and, as usual in a democracy, the attempt at resolution was to take place first in the realm of politics.

CHAPTER 3

Political America

CONFRONTED with the turbulent world of 1900, fairly seething with economic and technological change, with strange new scientific and religious ideas, with the growth of giant industry and organized labor, and with the rapid and uproarious rise of "the alien city," thinking Americans divided politically into ideological groups which in their bewildering diversity almost defy analysis. At either end of the political spectrum the pattern was the classic one of conservative and radical, two strains that had much in common and were to alter very little in the first two decades of the new century. The middle ranges of political thought, however, were to feel the full impact of the new ideas and conditions, with the result that the old strains of agrarianism, individualism, and humanitarianism were disrupted and sharply altered. Collectively and inexactly labeled "liberalism," these traditions after strong infusions of the new thought underwent a process of mutation and hardened into a political creed that eventually became known as "progressivism." In this readjustment of political values many one-time conservatives became progressives or radicals, and some men, torn between old memories and loyalties and the new conditions and the impact of the new thought, never could decide just what they believed and why.

A few conservatives still clung to the classical European attitudes. Man was a frail vessel and indeed an evil one. His enemies within and without were numerous and tenacious, and thus society and civilization were infinitely perishable. With the present uncertain and the future unknowable, man had to cling to the time-tested and order-giving institutions of the past to prevent anarchy, chaos, and disaster. Elihu Root was convinced that society could not "trust the impulses of the human heart under temptation." Throughout even the most exuberant periods of the progressive belief in man, Paul Elmer More kept emphasizing "the impulse of evil in the heart of man" and insisting that the main virtue for society and individual alike was "the will to refrain." Even the subsequently progressive Frank Norris had been impressed in his earlier years with the persistence of evil in the human spirit. McTeague not only inherited his father's basic evil traits which led him to ultimate disaster, but such black spiritual genes could persist even to "the five hundredth generation." Against such forces man's moral sense, his reason, and his will to act were obviously puny. Life, to Edith Wharton, was not a matter of reason and of taking action; instead it was "a succession of pitiful compromises with fate, of concessions to old traditions, old beliefs, old charities and frailties." And the idealistic reformer who attempted to cut his way straight through the "tangled and deep rooted growth" that was society was destined to hear at the end of each stroke "the cry of the severed branch: Why woundest thou me?" [1]

Other conservatives saw society and the cosmos through the eyes of nineteenth-century mechanistic science as ruled by law which man evaded or broke at his own peril. Progress was possible within such a view, but only through "the working out," John D. Rockefeller believed, "of a law of nature." Whether such laws originated in a personal divinity or in the second law of thermodynamics, whether they were applied to prices by President William McKinley or to ethical considerations by Henry Higginson, man had nothing to do with their formulation. His power, such as it was, came only from his ability to discern such laws and abide by them. "God Almighty made men and certain laws which are essential to their progress in civilization," Henry Higginson wrote, "and Congressmen cannot break these natural laws without causing suffering." [2]

The great bulk of conservatives, including most of the practicing politicians, were not as pessimistic as Higginson either about man's

[1] Van Wyck Brooks, *The Confident Years* (New York, 1951), p. 293; Frank Norris, *McTeague* (New York, 1899), p. 117; Edith Wharton, *The Fruit of the Tree* (New York, 1907), p. 624.
[2] Henry Higginson to William Howard Taft, September 7, 1911, Taft MSS.; Russel Nye, *Midwestern Progressive Politics* (East Lansing, 1951), p. 24. (The specific location of all MSS. collections are indicated in the bibliography.)

opportunities to create or his chances for progress. Such diverse conservatives as Elihu Root, William Howard Taft, George F. Baer, and
George Harvey occasionally spoke in optimistic accents, at least in the
first decade of the new century. Caught up in the enthusiasm of the
Roosevelt years, Root once wrote that it was the citizen's duty to be
optimistic about man's chances for bettering himself and that pessimism was a "criminal weakness." Taft spoke of man as "perfectible,"
Baer referred to his primitive mandate to take dominion over the
world, and George Harvey once defined the American spirit as "a
species of restless energy . . . constantly urging humankind up and
along the path of progress and achievement." [3] But if progress was
possible, it was also painfully slow and not to be accomplished by
wholesale political methods. In his 1912 Nobel peace address Root saw
progress measured "not by days and years but by generations and
centuries in the life of nations." Moreover, Taft and Lodge agreed that
the onward process could scarcely ever be achieved by legislative fiat;
the political process was too rapid and superficial to achieve anything
of moment. Not even education, Lodge wrote, could change a man
quickly. It had taken six thousand years to make a Hindu and one
could not change him into an Anglo-Saxon simply by an Oxford
education. That was largely because the difference did not rest with
the intellect, the senator from Massachusetts argued, but rather with
a host of other factors over which "man in the mass" had little control.[4]

What progress had occurred in the past, according to the conservatives, had been achieved almost entirely without the aid of the masses
and often in spite of them. Few practicing politicians could afford to
air such sentiments publicly. One such courageous aspirant for governor who characterized the masses of the poor as "political junk"
constituting "a drag on the wheels of progress" was, not surprisingly,
defeated.[5] But something could be said by indirection. While still in
the Senate, Root referred to "the depravity of human nature" and

---

[3] Elihu Root, *The Citizen's Part in Government* (New York, 1907), p. 96;
William Howard Taft, *Present Day Problems* (New York, 1908), p. 246;
George Harvey, *The Power of Tolerance* (New York, 1911), p. 279; Baer, as
cited in Nye, *Midwestern Progressive Politics,* p. 130.

[4] Elihu Root, *International Subjects* (New York, 1916), p. 157; John A.
Garraty, *Henry Cabot Lodge* (New York, 1953), p. 143; William Howard Taft,
Liberty Under Law (New Haven, 1922), p. 43.

[5] Milwaukee *Sentinel,* June 2, 1910.

warned of the mass prejudice and frenzy carrying the nation "into those excesses which have wrecked all our prototypes in history." Lodge and Taft wrote repeatedly of the danger of mob passions. And to George Harvey, unconstrained to seek office, the phrase "the foolish multitude" came easily. While Harvey was willing to concede that most men were technically honest, he insisted that only the very few were really "honest in their minds." [6]

Throughout the period the conservative was far more interested in protecting the position of the exceptional man in society than he was in bettering the lot of the masses. Many conservatives, in fact, felt that even in the highly differentiated America of the early 1900's the "leveling process" had gone too far and had incorporated "the theory of mediocrity which instinctively hates ability and invariably seeks undue advantage." "The majority of men," George Harvey concluded, "still lead only automatic lives and contribute to progress only force, which serves no better than an idle engine unless directed." The true cornerstone of a democratic society, the President of Columbia University said, was "natural inequality," and thus the times had to be reversed or else the nation faced the loss of its heritage. Professor Woodrow Wilson of Princeton seemed to agree. In a magazine article predicting the triumphant return of Hamiltonianism, the author cited with enthusiasm the professor's statement that pure democracy was on the decline. And while still in the Senate, Elihu Root took comfort that the leveling age seemed to have lost its spark. "After many years of struggle for equality," the former Secretary of State wrote, "there is reason to think that mankind is now entering upon a struggle for the right of inequality." [7]

During the good days when Root was helping to guide the American government under Roosevelt, he spoke once of "the supreme governing capacity of America." But after the upsurging progressive movement had proposed such democratizing reforms as the direct election of United States senators, the direct primary, the initiative, the referendum and the recall, Root rapidly changed his mind. "The forces

[6] Elihu Root, *Men and Policies* (New York, 1925), p. 495; William Howard Taft, *Popular Government* (New Haven, 1913), p. 85; Harvey, *Power of Tolerance*, p. 66.

[7] Harvey, *Power of Tolerance*, p. 244; William Garrott Brown, *The New Politics and Other Papers* (Boston, 1914), p. 69; Philip C. Jessup, *Elihu Root* (2 vols., New York, 1938), II, 184. Wilson is cited in *Current Literature*, XXXI (1901), 14.

of evil," he said in 1913, "are as hard to control now as they always have been." And it was apparent that Root saw an unchecked and unenlightened democracy as one of the sources of evil. "An ignorant democracy," he later wrote, "leads directly to war." Most conservatives agreed with Root's fear of the crowd and what in the day was called a direct democracy. For President Butler of Columbia the crowd "with its well marked mental and moral peculiarities," the demagogue with his "hungry cries," and the resultant social disorder were in an inevitable symbiotic relationship. Given the crowd in power, the demagogue was bound to appear, and from the two disorder and chaos would inevitably follow. In arguing against direct democracy functioning through primaries, the initiative, and the recall, Taft appealed to Burke's ideal representative government, which would not reflect the combined will of the constituents but the welfare of the nation, something always more in total than the sum of the welfare of its living peoples. Many other conservatives were less subtle. They were "opposed to the abandonment of representative government" for one operated "by public clamor," of a government based "upon ideals and law" for an unworkable pure democracy in which the enthroned demagogues preach to the people and prey upon the commonwealth.[8]

Faced in 1900 with the growing popular resentment against the *status quo* and a rising desire for change—a desire that Root interpreted as one motivated by envy of the "one gallus fellows" against the cultured and the wealthy—the conservative had to contrive a way to enfranchise more completely the man of ability and at the same time check the rising political power of the masses. Since Lodge's much-beloved Hamiltonian "aristocratic republic" no longer existed, the task was to be difficult. One could exhort the public, as Root did, to "canonize the statutes of the past." Or one could appeal to a higher law against reform or revolution just as revolutionaries had once appealed to it against the dead hand of the past. "The principles of right and justice, and honesty and morality, are not merely conventional," William Howard Taft remarked in a lecture on democracy. They came from "a higher source" than a plebescite, the ex-President continued, from a "natural law" that was the best argument for God

[8] Richard Leopold, *Elihu Root and the Conservative Tradition* (Boston, 1954), p. 18; *The New York Times,* June 8, 1911; Taft, *Popular Government,* p. 29; Frank Short to Senator John D. Works, February 3, 1914, Works MSS.

since it worked "more accurately than any which can be devised by man." [9]

But such appeals to the canons of the past and to natural law were at best of little utility when the majority determinedly wanted change. What was needed was an effective institution to interpret this natural law and give it substance. Only then, said one eminent conservative, could the nation achieve the polity of justice that the first governor of colonial Massachusetts, John Winthrop, had envisioned, " a civil, a moral, a federal liberty, which consists in everyone's enjoying his own property and having the benefit of the laws of his country. . . ." Lacking a crown and an aristocracy, and with a clearly divided Church, one wing of which was ardently devoted to reform, the American conservative turned to the courts as the one instrument of government that would most likely preserve the saving order of the past. To Senator Carter the federal judiciary was "the sheet anchor of the Republic"; to Senator J. B. Foraker it was the one department of government from which the able man "in times of hysteria" could expect justice. To *The New York Times* it was by its very nature "the conservator of our institutions." And as the reform movement quickened its pace in the first decade of the new century, the conservative's admiration and devotion to the courts became almost mystical.[10]

While the conservative placed his confidence in the few rather than the many, this did not by any means signify a trust in an educated elite. Lodge's refusal to believe that an Oxford education could really change a Hindu was an oblique case in point. Root was more specific. "The great difficulty in the application of pure reason to practical affairs," he wrote to Professor George P. Fisher, "is that never in this world does the reasoner get all the premises which should affect the conclusions; so it frequently happens that the practical man who does not reason at all but who feels the effect of conditions which the reasoner overlooks, goes right while the superior intelligence of the reasoning man goes wrong." The college man, Root continued, was "peculiarly liable" to this sort of error when dealing with public affairs.[11]

[9] Root, *International Subjects,* p. 122; Taft, *Popular Government,* p. 188; Archie Butt, *Taft and Roosevelt* (New York, 1930), pp. 1, 212.
[10] Harvey, *Power of Tolerance,* p. 267; Thomas H. Carter to Charles G. Burk, July 2, 1910, Carter MSS.; J. B. Foraker to C. W. Fairbanks, June 20, 1912, Foraker MSS.; *The New York Times,* May 6, 1915.
[11] Elihu Root to George P. Fisher, January 25, 1904, Root MSS.

The doctrine that right action was more likely to come from the pores of experience rather than from the brain cells was one of the reasons the conservative was usually more congenial to change in the economic world than to its counterpart in the world of politics and public affairs. On one page William Howard Taft could argue against "radical and impractical changes in law and government by which we might easily lose what we have gained in the struggle of mankind for better things." On another Taft was sure that progress in history came largely from the quest for property. Often changes in education and intelligence, in art, morality, and religion, "simply proceeded as a corollary of the more material changes." [12] The conservative was also inclined to view economic change benevolently because the elite in the material world was not selected by the democratic process, but rather by a more aristocratic institution which he preferred to think was more accurate, just, and benevolent in equating rewards with ability. The millionaires, in Carnegie's thinking, "were the bees who make the most honey, and contribute most to the hive." If left alone by government, George Harvey was sure, the business mechanism would "confer upon the maximum of capacity the maximum of reward." The masses, operating through government or labor unions, were simply devices by which people and classes sought "to share property" which they had not created and ease "which they had not earned." [13]

The conservative saw not only a precise law of reward but also many another law operating in the practical world, giving it a symmetry and order entirely lacking in the area of democratic politics. The origins of such law might come from the natural order which, to George F. Baer, had given the able man a "primitive mandate" to conquer. Or they might ensue from the nicely mechanistic doctrines of the classical economists from which William McKinley could extrapolate: "Prices are fixed with a mathematical precision by supply and demand." Or they might have been handed down by the Deity himself, the cold omniscient God of the Calvinists, who had set the universe spinning with such logical injunctions that the lot of every man was predetermined. The irreverent reformer might jest: "Oh, I am the cause and the capital too, and the Lord's anointed as well." But George F. Baer, John D. Rockefeller, Henry Higginson, and their

[12] Taft, *Popular Government,* p. 236; *Present Day Problems,* p. 246.
[13] Nye, *Midwestern Progressive Politics,* p. 133; Harvey, *Power of Tolerance,* p. 265; *The New York Times,* May 4, 1911.

fellows believed. When Rockefeller felt called upon in 1907 to explain why he was staying in business, he issued a public statement through the Reverend Robert S. MacArthur of the New York Calvary Baptist Church. "I am a trustee of the property of others," his declaration read, "through the providence of God committed to my care. . . . Therefore, I feel it my duty to God and to the people whose money is invested in my company to continue active in its welfare." Only a man of certain faith could have made such a statement in 1907 and published it.[14]

Whatever the origins, the conservative thought he also saw law in the business world, and seeing it he was once again depreciating the power of man as an independent change-maker even in this field where he felt that progress might be made more rapidly. His strong decisive man of affairs and wealth was simply a man who more frequently than others discerned and abided by a higher law and was accordingly rewarded. He was in an ultimate sense an agent rather than a principle in a sphere which was more closed than open. Elsewhere throughout society the hope for man as a prime mover was even more bleak. For man was more evil than good, more weak than strong, a product of some thousand years of conditioning which neither intelligence nor reason could change vitally. Society itself was Edith Wharton's dark forest, "the tangled and deep rooted growth" which held him fast to his most imperfect past. If he moved forward at all he moved not so much by virtue of his own power but by the will of a benevolent providence or by abiding by the permissive dictates of a slow-moving but certain universe, predetermined or preordained.

Unlike the conservative, the American radical placed a premium on man acting in the political and social arena. Moreover, he saw nothing evil in basic human nature, and instead of being fearful about the future, he was supremely confident. But this optimism came not from a belief in the goodness of human nature or in the ability of the human mind to make intelligent and right decisions when confronted with a series of perplexing and open questions. Whether he was a Marxian or simply an economic determinist, the radical in theory at least tended to view original human nature as a *tabula rasa* which was neither inclined toward the good nor the bad, but was rather more like a

[14] James D. Richardson, *A Compilation of the Messages and Papers of the Presidents,* Supplement 1, p. 293. The Rockefeller statement is given in the Oakland (Calif.) *Tribune,* October 8, 1907.

mirror reflecting its environment. While even the most devout Marxists would admit that a variety of factors might influence the development of the individual personality, both the Marxists and economic determinists insisted that for all important purposes man in the group responded to but one dominant force in society, his material environment. And for the Marxists, at least, this material environment was governed by evolutionary law quite independent of and quite insensitive to man. Thus free will or ultimate choice in any important sense was an ontological fantasy. Man, Jack London wrote in one of his more socialistic moods, was "blind and helpless in the heritage of his age." His only real perception came from the knowledge of nature's laws; his only power came from his willingness to abide by them.[15]

Whether Marxian or revisionists, most of the Socialist leaders of the early twentieth century paid homage to the mechanistic birthright of their doctrines. Man was a creature of his economic class, which in turn was the product of the changing technology. Both evolved strictly according to "scientific laws of evolution." Capitalism, the "inevitable link" between feudalism and socialism, had automatically spawned "the two antagonistic economic classes," the wealthy exploiters and the radical working class. Between the two there could be no lasting peace or compromise because it was the "historic mission" of the working class to conquer and institute the classless socialistic society. Many conceivably could delay or speed the process, but the end was foreordained by the evolving means of production. "The Socialist program is not a theory imposed upon society for its acceptance or rejection," the Socialist party stated officially in 1904, "it is but the interpretation of what is sooner or later inevitable." [16]

There were fully as many kinds of Socialists in 1900 as there were varieties of Republicans and Democrats. And certainly most of the utopian, nationalist, Christian, and agrarian socialists had come to their position without the aid of the materialist interpretation of history. Eugene V. Debs himself occasionally referred to such mystical concepts as "the higher law of righteousness, of love and labor," which he saw as a "primal law" enacted long before the rise of Christianity. The Milwaukee revisionist, Victor Berger, was once willing to concede the possibility of moral concepts existing independently and out of

[15] Jack London, *Revolution and Other Essays* (New York, 1910), p. 57.
[16] National Convention of the Socialist Party, *Proceedings* (Chicago, 1904) p. 308.

context with the material environment. But for the most part the Socialist, whether Marxian or revisionist, believed in a nineteenth-century scientific teleology that went marching on impervious to man's will, want, or desire. Evolution, said Debs, is the order of nature, and "society, like the units that compose it, is subject to its inexorable law." The words "immutable," "inevitable," and "inexorable" appear as often in the Socialist vocabulary as the word "scientific." Despite Herbert Spencer's apotheosis of the competitive society, Professor Sidney Hook has noted, the Socialist was attracted to his works. That is not surprising. Both Spencer and the Socialist were evolutionists, both were materialists, and both saw an order in the economic world to which man must bow. The Marxian saw such genuflexion as inevitable; Spencer's only alternative was disaster.[17]

"Only the man whose hand never touches the realities of life," Senator Albert J. Beveridge of Indiana wrote in 1900, "despairs of human progress or doubts the providence of God." [18] Among the more important beliefs that set apart the progressive in 1900 from his more conservative fellow was his optimistic attitude toward the nature of the universe and man's place in it. A few progressives believed in a benevolent and purposeful God from whom a moral law flowed "as universal as the laws of electricity," by which man was assured of a constantly ascending future. The greatest virtue of Christianity, William Jennings Bryan believed, was that it gave to life the possibility of "an unending struggle upward, with no limit to human advancement or development." [19] In such a benevolent theological climate even a temporary defeat might be like one of Theodore Parker's falls, "a fall upward." The great majority of progressives, however, had no sense of an inflexible divine purpose. Even Bryan's Christianity seemed to imply a permissive rather than a mandatory guide to progress. A good many progressives, in fact, had lost most of their mystical religion. William Kent of California was so doubtful about the nature of the Divinity that he refused to express a preference between the many contending creeds. He was a member of no church, he wrote, "and was equally tolerant of all." His chief religious affiliation

[17] Eugene V. Debs, *Writings,* pp. 30–33, 119; *Social Democratic Herald,* April 21, 1900; Donald Drew Egbert and Stow Persons, *Socialism and American Life* (Princeton, 1952), p. 436.

[18] Albert J. Beveridge, *The Meaning of the Times* (Indianapolis, 1908), p. 246.

[19] William Jennings Bryan, *Speeches* (New York, 1911), XI, 326.

was with the Abraham Lincoln Center of Chicago, a social institution interested in ethical and not creedal matters.[20] Theodore Roosevelt once confided that his whole religious sense was confined in the verse of St. James: "I will show my faith by my works." [21] For most progressives the trouble with believing in the doctrine of automatic progress under divine inspiration was that it was too much of an open-and-shut affair in which man himself was all but excluded. For the progressive image of the universe was an open one in which a final score was never posted, and in which man himself was the main reactor and one of the ultimate causes of change. Such a view was as antagonistic to theological preordination as it was to a scientific or to an economic determinism. "Life," Theodore Roosevelt wrote—almost paralleling the very words of William James—"is a long campaign where every victory leaves the ground free for another battle, and sooner or later defeat comes to every man, unless death forestalls it. But the final defeat does not and should not cancel the triumph. . . ." [22]

Roosevelt, something of a Darwinist, was always a little more gloomy than the average reformer about the fate of both the individual and society, and as a consequence was just that much less a progressive. Throughout most of the rhetoric of progressivism, however, the hope for progress was as pervasive as it was perfervid. Phrases like "humanity's universal growth," "the upward spiral of human development," and "permanent progress" appeared again and again. Writing in 1909, Herbert Croly noted that whatever other gods had failed, Americans still had an intense faith in the future of themselves and their society. In the nondetermined world of the progressive mind, the persistence of this faith in fact needs explanation. Logically an open world, as James had said, meant both great opportunities and great dangers. But the difference between the progressive and James was in their estimate of man. James had thought well of him; the progressive believed him to be the hope of earth and heaven.[23]

In the last line of *The Gentleman from Indiana*, Booth Tarkington, Senator Beveridge's friend from Indiana, alluded to the men from the

[20] William Kent to Samuel A. Eliot, January 9, 1922; Memorandum, April 19, 1900, Kent MSS.

[21] Elting E. Morison (ed.), *The Letters of Theodore Roosevelt* (8 vols., Cambridge, 1951–54), III, xvi.

[22] Theodore Roosevelt to George Otto Trevelyan, March 9, 1905, Roosevelt MSS.

[23] Herbert Croly, *The Promise of American Life* (New York, 1909), p. 1.

midlands as "the beautiful people." About the same time Joseph Fels, the Philadelphia soap king, whose purse was usually available for progressive causes, denied any validity for the doctrine of "human cussedness." William Allen White of Emporia, Kansas, in one of his more optimistic moods, once wrote of "the essential nobility of man," and Tom Johnson, mayor of Cleveland, denied to a group of ministers that crime and vice were "the natural consequences of normal human impulses." "In the end the people are bound to do the right thing," Judge Ben B. Lindsey observed, "no matter how much they . . . fail at times." [24]

This generous estimate of humanity, so typical of the progressive mind, was, of course, based upon faith and not upon existing conditions. Theodore Dreiser once had such faith, but then, as he said, he saw Pittsburgh. The progressives were also familiar with Pittsburgh. They had also seen sin, corruption, and graft throughout the land and were quite aware that they were obliged to explain the pervasive existence of evil in the human act if not in the human mind and soul. Most all of the reformers were willing to admit that men had bad habits. One small wing of the reform movement, comprising the more emotional, doctrinaire, and scholarly individuals, felt that such habits were not so much intrinsic as social. "Far deeper" in the human spirit, economist Simon Patten wrote, were "noble instincts and swift accurate reactions to duty. . . ." The devil in the piece was not something inherent in human nature but rather in society. Evil and ugliness, according to Tom Johnson, were "largely, if not almost wholly, products of environment." Good men were driven out of the course they would naturally have followed because of "despair caused by inequality of opportunity and the hopelessness of an unequal struggle." That was the trouble with charity. While praising the generous impulse that prompted it, Johnson deplored its effect of keeping men "tinkering at a defective spigot" when the bunghole was wide open.[25]

An obvious corollary of the doctrine of the social origins of evil was that basically all men were alike. "The difference," Fremont Older

[24] Mary Fels, *Joseph Fels* (New York, 1916), p. 168; Joseph Fels, as quoted in the *New England Review*, XLIV (1911), 496; Fremont Older, *My Own Story* (New York, 1926), p. ix; *The Public*, February 3, 1906; Ben B. Lindsey to Rudolph Spreckels, November 3, 1909, Hitchborn MSS.

[25] Simon Patten, *The New Basis of Civilization* (New York, 1907), p. 205; Tom Johnson, *My Story* (New York, 1911), pp. 43–44.

of the San Francisco *Bulletin* wrote, "usually lies in what happens to them." Lester Ward, the sociologist, gave the assumption scholarly support. As far as he could see, ability, intelligence, and energy were all distributed about equally among men, and the near monopoly of these characteristics by the upper economic classes was due simply to their social advantages. If that was true, of course, there was rampant injustice in the world and rampant inefficiency. Remove the inequality and the major part of evil would be abolished. Man would then inherit his true estate. He would be the honest, aspiring, neighborly, affectionate, helpful, and capable individual that William Allen White so freely wrote about. Moreover, society would flourish because progress would then be almost automatic. "Nature will care for progress," Simon Patten promised, "if men will care for reform." [26]

The explanation for human evil as coming almost totally from the social environment has happily been called reform Darwinism by Professor Eric Goldman.[27] It was, of course, very closely allied with the social Darwinism of Herbert Spencer, William Graham Sumner, and Andrew Carnegie, and was the product of the same sort of thinking. Both hypotheses fully accepted Darwin's explanation of change in the natural world; both made the same assumption that the human and natural environments had much the same quality in their power to order animate life. The social Darwinists assumed that the fierce competition in nature was the natural and good thing for both animal and man. The reform Darwinists denied this was so for man, and although believing that man reacts to his environment much as ink does to a blotter, they still contended that by hook or crook some men at least could escape this fatal trap and by reordering the social environment change human nature.

Once in discussing the origins of evil William Dean Howells wrote: "We can't put it all on conditions; we must put some of the blame on character." This was the position of the great majority of progressives, and in particular that of the progressive politicians. Such diverse people as Theodore Roosevelt, William Jennings Bryan, and Woodrow Wilson all agreed with Howells' position without pressing too far its philosophic implications. The Californian, Chester Rowell, however,

---

[26] San Francisco *Bulletin,* May 11, 1914; Lester Ward, *Applied Sociology* (Boston, 1906), pp. 145 ff.; Merle Curti, *The Growth of American Thought* (New York, 1943), p. 578.

[27] Eric F. Goldman, *Rendezvous With Destiny* (New York, 1952), pp. 91–92.

further pursued the meaning of the doctrine for politics. There would always be temptation in society and men weak enough to fall for it, Rowell wrote, no matter how much effort went into reforming the environment. On the other hand, some men would not fall, "no matter how great the strain. Dealing with society, the task is to amend the system, but dealing with the individual man, the task is to reiterate forever 'thou shalt not steal,' and tolerate no exceptions, excuses or palliation." Rowell's major objection to unadulterated reform Darwinism obviously resulted from his dislike of its philosophical implications for the free man. He admitted it would not do to treat men entirely as "free moral agents" independent of the conditions surrounding them, but it was also repugnant "to treat them as puppets, the mere creators of environment." Rowell saw, as a good many other progressives sensed, that a complete environmental explanation of evil also meant a complete mechanistic explanation of good from which man himself was rigidly excluded as a prime force.[28]

The progressive so cherished the concept of the free individual that he could not agree to limit man even if it meant denying him the right to opt for evil. This firm belief of the progressive in man's choice of ways helps to explain the evangelical character of the movement, the constant stress on "the good man," the "moral position," "the right action." Perhaps no other American political movement had such a righteous tone about it. It was, as Elmer Davis has said, a political "carnival of purity."

Had the average progressive stopped with the assumption that inherently men were both good and bad, he would not have been too far away from the views of the more moderate conservative. What distinguished him was his conviction that human character was malleable and that through a strenuous process of moral and ideological training it could rapidly be changed. Although Theodore Roosevelt was more pessimistic about this point than most, he was still convinced that education was already responsible for making the average American much superior to the average Athenian in "moral cleanliness, family life and self-control." The moral objective, William Kent felt, could be reached by first educating and then letting the force of public opinion supply the necessary coercion. Through the two there was no natural compulsion in the average man that could not be overcome,

[28] Rowell to Lincoln Steffens, August 1, 1908, Rowell MSS.

"including the lust for blood, the savage passion of reproduction, the cruder forms of theft. . . ." Some of the more lyrical progressives felt that the work had mostly been done. There was no further need to voice Isaiah's lament: "Therefore are my people gone into captivity, because they have no knowledge." All that obstructed the march into Canaan was a silenced and muffled public opinion. Once it was free, money could not hold it; cunning could not baffle it. For, William Allen White wrote, public opinion was "God moving among men. Thus He manifests Himself in this earth. . . . the voice of the people, is indeed the voice of God." [29]

"I fear the plutocracy of wealth," William Jennings Bryan said, "I respect the aristocracy of learning, but thank God for the democracy of the heart." [30] Bryan's suspicion of contaminating wealth and his faith in the average man as a moral political agent, even when contrasted with the aristocrat of learning, was one of the more important beliefs of certain progressives that created almost a dogma about the democratic process. It was an old American faith, this belief in the reason of the heart solving problems and making right decisions. But the age's optimism and the introduction of some new democratic political devices so accentuated it that the very principles of democratic government became almost ends in themselves. Man, Lyman Abbott said, had an undeveloped capacity for chosing between right and wrong, and the capacity, when developed by education, carried "with it the right and duty so to choose—that is the right and duty of self-government." This postulation of an open society in which man was confronted with a series of never-ending choices had some of its seeds of course in radical protestantism. But it also reflected the revolt from the nineteenth-century determinism. Among some progressives, in fact, the right to choose was more important than even the ability to choose wisely. These men strenuously objected to Theodore Roosevelt's statement that the democratic process was just the means to the more important end of good government. "We would, if we had to choose," Charles D. Willard wrote to Roosevelt, "rather have bad government with democracy than good government without it." To Willard the right to be wrong was even more important than the

[29] Roosevelt to Raymond Robbins, March 3, 1914, Roosevelt MSS.; William Kent to John Phillips, May 26, 1908, Kent MSS.; William Allen White, *A Certain Rich Man* (New York, 1909), p. 326.
[30] Quoted in *The Public,* February 4, 1905.

ability to be right. "Democracy," Willard observed in a parting shot, "is a soul satisfying thing." [31]

This ardent belief in the right to choose carried with it some important corollaries. One of such even questioned the validity of representative government. The modern political problem, according to William Kent, was much like the one confronting the early Protestants of how to do away with the intermediaries between themselves and their God. "People," Kent wrote, "must get nearer the grub pile and nearer to their Governmental agencies." Bryan said much the same thing in denying that a representative had the right to defeat the will of the people who elected him. Moreover, if the voice of the people was the voice of God, then nothing should stand in its way, not a governmental agency, nor past experience, nor even the word of the expert. In fact, "the scientific soviet," as Bryan later labeled a part of the intelligentsia, was often a menace. So was a large consolidated and paternalistic government. The way to have the Golden Age, as one of the characters of William Dean Howells remarked, was "to elect it by the Australian secret ballot." [32]

Bryan's fear of an "aristocracy of learning" that would inspire action contrary to the will of the people was not without some grounds even as early as 1900. At the Chicago Trust Conference of 1899, and again at the 1900 meeting of the American Economic Association, the great majority of the economists agreed that business competition in the old sense had practically disappeared in many lines of American industry. While opposed to monopoly, they looked upon combination in both industry and labor as inevitable and indeed in the national welfare. The new movement, it was felt, would provide more goods at lower costs, ensure steadier and higher wages to workers, soften the impact of depressions by stabilizing the economy, and make the nation better able to compete on world markets. "Few, if any of us," a leading economist wrote, "would like to see a return to the era of the small shopkeeper and industrialists." [33]

[31] *The Outlook*, XCVI (1910), 618; Charles D. Willard to Theodore Roosevelt, (?), 1911, Roosevelt MSS.

[32] Kent to David J. Thompson, October 18, 1911, Kent MSS.; William Jennings Bryan, *Heart to Heart Appeals* (New York, 1917), p. 13.

[33] See Charles J. Bullock, "Trust Literature: A Survey and a Criticism," *Quarterly Journal of Economics*, XV (1900), 167, for a survey of professional opinion. E. S. Meade, *American Economic Association Publications*, 3rd Series, Vol. 1, No. 1, p. 183; *The Outlook*, LXIV (1900), 7.

But a return to the old competitive system of small units was precisely what a good many progressives wanted. The combination movement, they argued, was destroying the historic nation in which the small industrialist and shopkeeper, the farmer, and the laborer were free to be their own men and to change their station in life as their whim, or their abilities, and ambition warranted. The "curse of bigness" destroyed economic freedom and thus personal freedom. The United States, said the future justice of the Supreme Court, Louis D. Brandeis, was rapidly becoming a nation in which the privileged few at the top had great freedom and all the rest of the people were "more and more a class of employees." Granted, the new system might provide more goods, and even more of a chance to rise, but the way upward, expostulated one progressive, was only "by obedience." Moreover, this new industrial "military system" would become increasingly "oligarchical," and in the end threatened to become "monarchical, dynastic." [34] Clearly such men were not talking in terms of market conditions and price relationships, as were the professional economists, but rather about the conditions and relations of human freedom.

Most of the progressive politicians who opposed consolidated industrialism were, as could be expected, from the regions of farms and small towns in the South and the West. They were opposed to monopoly and power wherever found in capital or labor, or even in government. The closed shop they considered to be "a counter monopoly" of labor, a "trust of men as against a trust of capital." A government monopoly, i.e., the government ownership of railroads, the *California Weekly* proclaimed, would be the "worst bureaucracy and monopoly of all." [35] Since the transcontinental railroads obviously could not be reduced in size without impairing their efficiency, federal regulation seemed to be the only answer. But William Jennings Bryan, at least before 1906, fearing monolithic control, proposed that the federal government regulate only the railroads which were distinctly interstate in character, leaving the rest of the field to local action. As for the industrial problem, the West and the South were again chary of setting up a huge federal bureaucracy. One might as well talk of "controlling

---

[34] Louis D. Brandeis, *Other People's Money* (Washington, 1933), pp. 110 ff.; William G. Brown, *The New Politics and Other Papers* (Boston, 1914), p. 214.

[35] See, for example, *The Public*, July 29, 1905, and the remarks of Ernest H. Crosby in the New York *Daily News*, September 4, 1905; *California Weekly* (1905), 637.

burglary," Bryan said, as to talk of federal control of trusts. In 1900 both Bryan and Robert La Follette proposed that all interstate corporations be given a federal license, and when any business controlled over 25 to 30 per cent of the total in the region it be denied a further license to do business. The following year Governor Cummins of Iowa suggested that the protective tariff be abolished automatically on all trust-made goods. Such schemes, plus the vigorous use of the Sherman Antitrust Act, it was felt, would stop the movement toward industrial centralization without creating a centralized bureaucratic government. Governor John A. Johnson of Minnesota had both in mind when he called upon the Middle West to "overthrow the new paternalism and plunder. . . ." [36]

In 1911 Theodore Roosevelt deftly put his finger on one of the more basic fault lines running through the progressive mind, which threatened to split the whole movement and imperil its success. The progressives, Roosevelt lamented, had "gone to pieces" largely because they were at war with themselves over a basic economic program: "Half of them are really representative of a kind of rural toryism, which wishes to attempt the impossible task of returning to the economic conditions that obtained sixty years ago. The other half wishes to go forward along the proper lines, that is, to recognize the inevitableness and the necessity of combinations in business, and meet it by a corresponding increase in governmental power over big business; but at the same time these real progressives are hampered by being obliged continually to pay lip loyalty to their colleagues, who, at bottom, are not progressive at all, but retrogressive." [37]

Roosevelt's position on the industrial question was vigorously supported by a great many eastern progressives and intellectuals. Among the leaders of this group were men like Charles G. Bonaparte of Baltimore; George W. Perkins, the financier from the house of Morgan; the industrialist Andrew Carnegie, who by 1910 had changed his mind about Herbert Spencer and social Darwinism; Lyman Abbott, minister, editor of *The Outlook;* and the speculative journalists, Walter Lippmann and Herbert Croly. The new industrial consolidation, they argued, was "an inevitable feature" of modern civilization and government regulation of the industrial world, and perhaps ownership of monopolistic concerns was necessary. Democratic government would

---

[36] *The Public,* June 30, 1906; Nye, *Midwestern Progressive Politics,* p. 238.
[37] Roosevelt to Alfred W. Cooley, August 29, 1911, Roosevelt MSS.

have to destroy monopoly power by seizure, Herbert Croly stated, or else be destroyed by it. But far from being an evil, the new consolidation and the regulatory state would achieve, according to these men, a host of benefits. It would produce more goods, thus adding to the national power. This added production, when distributed in a "morally and socially desirable way," would cure poverty and all of its attending social ills. The new system would introduce a regime of co-operation between men instead of one based upon hostility and conflict. It would substitute intelligent planning for a policy of drift, and the government through its new-found strength could redivide the social surplus and shift economic power. A pre-established harmony would then exist "between the satisfaction of private needs and the accomplishment of a morally desirable result." [38]

Not content with holding forth glowing promises for the new organization, the theorists, but not the politicians, proceeded from there to attack the old competitive system and its attending individualism. Competition, George W. Perkins declared, had been mainly responsible "for the past horrors of the factory system." It had meant low wages, limited production, child labor, and "inadequate care for the safety of life and limb." It was a system characterized by "insufferable evils," said *The Outlook*, an economy, said Walter Lippmann, dominated by "the planless scramble of little profiteers." As for the pre-Civil War individualistic reform movement, it had been "meaningless," Herbert Croly wrote. It had sought to effect an "intellectual revolution without organizing either an army or an armament" and had failed because it had neither a collective purpose nor a discipline. Lippmann saw the main issue of the generation coming not from the evils of "crusted privilege" and authority, but rather from the weakness of the new freedom and from democracy. Lyman Abbott, close friend of Theodore Roosevelt, contrasted French democracy, which he said had started with the rights of individuals, most unfavorably with "Puritan Democracy," having its origins in divine morality. It was not strange that both Croly and Abbott questioned the worth of the new political devices for more perfectly registering the popular will. Critical of Thomas Jefferson for truckling to the crowd, Croly was for reducing the number of elected officials and predicted that the direct primary would increase the power not of the people but of the professional

[38] Herbert Croly, *The Promise of American Life* (New York, 1909), p. 22.

politician. These same voices that depreciated the "purposeless individual" and the "confused clamor of the crowd" logically celebrated
the rising power of the state. Both Croly and Abbott were for "a
strong and responsible executive." "The nation," Croly stated, "has
an individuality of its own " "It has a right," Abbott supplemented, "to
do whatever it finds to be for the interest of its self as a whole," provided it acts within the framework of divine sanction.[39]

A deep and significant ideological rift existed between the two wings
of progressivism represented by Louis Brandeis and William Jennings
Bryan on the one hand and by Herbert Croly and Lyman Abbott on
the other. The one school cherished the competitive system with its
individual values and feared the powerful state; the other welcomed
concentrated power whether in industry or politics, looked to a paternalistic state staffed by an educated elite for leadership, and depreciated individualism. A compromise position, of course, existed.
Henry Demarest Lloyd, for one, believed that it was possible to ag-
grandize the power of the individual simultaneously with the aggrandizement of the state so that the individual would remain in control of
the centralized political apparatus. And Walter Weyl hoped for a
socialization of industry without barring profits, and which would not
carry with it the "economic fatalism" of socialism that made society
everything and the individual nothing. There would still be room in
such a system, William Kent believed, for people like himself, "oppor-
tunists," who to the orthodox Socialists were "the ultimate of all evils."
This "New Individualism," Charles McCarthy of Wisconsin hoped,
would secure all the Socialist assets without sacrificing the individual
virtues.[40]

In 1900, and indeed even a decade later, it was too early to tell
which of these two contradicting progressive philosophies would establish itself as the dominant creed of the new movement, or whether an
acceptable compromise could be found. The ideological glue that held
the progressive position together as against either conservatism or

[39] *The New York Times,* May 8, 1911; Beveridge, *Meaning of the Times,* pp.
268–269; Croly, *Promise of American Life,* pp. 46, 317, 342, 423; Walter
Lippmann, *Drift and Mastery* (New York, 1914), p. 24; Lyman Abbott,
"Puritan Democracy," *The Outlook,* LXXIX (1905), 1006–1011.

[40] Henry Demarest Lloyd, *The Sovereign People* (New York, 1907), cited in
Aaron, *Men of Good Hope,* p. 163; Walter Weyl, *The New Democracy* (New
York, 1912), p. 276; William Kent to Edward M. Winslow, October 10, 1911,
Kent MSS.

socialism, however, was quite apparent. A belief in an open universe in which man was neither chained to the past nor riding on an automatic escalator into the future was central to the creed. Also at its heart was a belief in the doctrine of possible progress based upon the twin assumptions that man was more good than he was evil and that he had the power through his intellect and moral sense to change his environment. A devotion to Christian ethics, if not to Christian mysticism, and an ardent desire to apply such ethics to the daily life of the commonwealth, also motivated progressive thinking. When these principles were grafted onto the democratic and egalitarian doctrines of Jefferson, Jackson, Lincoln, and the Populists, the progressive was to stand clearly apart from his more conservative and his more radical fellow citizens. Just how far these principles could be translated into political achievements was partially dependent upon the progressive politician, who already by 1900 had made his appearance in city and state governments throughout the nation.

CHAPTER 4

The Cities and the States

THE LARGE city in the United States by the opening of the century had gained an unenviable reputation as the natural home of political corruption, crime, and vice. There was certainly much evidence to support Lord Bryce's often-quoted remark that it was one of the worst-governed units in the democratic world. From the Atlantic coast to the Middle West and on to the Pacific the city appeared to be the favorite haunt of the venal, where regularly "offense's gilded hand shoved by justice and the wicked prize itself bought out the law." In New York, Jersey City, Chicago, St. Louis, and Minneapolis, and in San Francisco and Los Angeles, the tale read much the same: city councils for sale and mayors protecting criminals; water, gas, and street-railway franchises granted for fifty years or more to private corporations with the legal right to charge exorbitant fees; police whose salaries were regularly enhanced by contributions from houses of prostitution and other noxious institutions; and politicians with such names as "Bath Tub" John Coughlin and "Hinky Dink" Kenna who methodically supplied the requisite votes on election day to keep the system operating. Meanwhile the ultimate victim of the graft, extortion, and jobbery saw his taxes mount, his water often contaminated, his sewage system fouled, his streetcars scheduled fortuitously, and his city adorned with ugly and ill-paved streets leading to noisome tenements.

Many descendants from the older stocks were quick to indict the new immigration for the unseemly conditions; but St. Louis with its long-settled Germanic population, Minneapolis with its Scandinavian

59

tradition, and that transplanted Midwestern heaven, Los Angeles, approached, if they did not equal, the normative corruption of the East. Obviously, the true explanation for urban misgovernment was much more complex. A part of the reason for the condition lay in the speed with which American cities grew. This rate of growth, perhaps then unmatched in the world, placed enormous pressures on city governments for the rapid creation and extension of a multitude of new services. The new utility, street, and transportation contracts, all political and many monopolistic by nature, offered great rewards for successful bidders. And just at the time when the demands on city government were the greatest, the peculiar and fragmented character of the cities' new population, largely recruited from the American countryside and from southern and eastern Europe, made efficient urban government impossible. Large-city life almost demanded a collectivist and planning point of view, but the rural Americans coming to the city were committed by tradition to a philosophy of individualism and private enterprise. The immigrants from southern and eastern Europe, desperately poor, often illiterate, and without a democratic heritage, were easy prey for the self-seeking boss. With added tensions centering around labor, racial, and religious questions, the result was chaos and corruption.

Even if the city had had a cohesive, intelligent, and interested citizenry devoted to the principle of urban planning, the path to efficient and honest government before 1900 would have been difficult. For few cities then had the power to grant franchises; in most instances that lay with the state governments. And in many commonwealths the ethics surrounding the statehouses were little better than those in the city chambers. Before the municipality could reform itself, it first had to cut the corrupt cord which led directly to the state capitals.

The multitudinous and pressing problems confronting the large city well before 1900 had not escaped critical citizens. Since the Tweed days Tammany Hall and its nefarious actions had excited sporadic and ill-sustained reform movements. Crime, vice, housing conditions, child labor, and the more prosaic subjects of sewage, transportation, and lighting facilities had all inspired citizens' investigating committees. But until the nineties little had been accomplished either in New York or in the rest of the country. What reform movements arose remained local in character and short-lived in time.

The defects in municipal life and government, however, became a subject of national discussion in the nineties. Within the five years after its founding in 1895, The *American Journal of Sociology* carried some thirteen scholarly articles dealing in a critical fashion with some phase of urban life. During the same period numerous questioning articles made their appearance in the more popular magazines. Dr. Albert Shaw's studies of English city governments in his *Review of Reviews* were objective and influential; a series by James D. Phelan in the *Arena* carried concrete suggestions for reformation by the practicing reform mayor of San Francisco. Phelan's demands for public ownership of municipal utilities, home rule, and provisions for direct legislation were elaborated in 1899 by Frank Parsons in his clinical and muckraking volume, *The City for the People*. A year later Gustavus Myers wrote *A History of Public Franchises in New York City* and followed it with *The History of Tammany Hall*.[1]

Meanwhile in dozens of the nation's major cities small groups of reformers had already come together, usually in nonpartisan organizations, to discuss possible cures for the ills of city life. Such a group in Chicago coalesced around the leadership of Charles R. Crane, Walter L. Fisher, Victor F. Lawson, and William Kent. Another such group was formed by Dr. John Randolph Haynes of Los Angeles to further the move for direct legislation. Haynes's organization soon became state-wide and elicited the support of such California reformers as James D. Phelan, Rudolph Spreckels, and President Jordan of Stanford University. In 1894 the National Municipal League was organized, and by the end of the century Municipal Ownership Leagues, City Clubs, and Direct Legislation Leagues spotted the land. All were nonpartisan; all were reform-minded.[2]

The accomplishments of these municipal reform organizations were not negligible. At a time when Bryan and his grass-rooted agrarian disciples were leading the national reform movement to defeat under the Democratic banner, these nonpartisan organizations were conducting a national campaign of education in street-corner politics. Here and there across the land they even succeeded in doing more than indoctrinating. After four unsuccessful attempts, San Francisco

---

[1] See, for example, James D. Phelan, "Municipal Conditions and the New Charter," *Overland*, XXVIII (1896), 104–111, in which Phelan cites the works of Dr. Albert Shaw.

[2] An interesting account of the formation of the Chicago reform group by William Kent is to be found in an undated manuscript in the William Kent Collection, Yale University.

achieved a new city charter in 1898, which permitted home rule, public ownership, and the establishment of a city civil service. The charter also strictly limited the conditions under which franchises were to be granted to utility companies.

Simultaneously other cities were putting pressure on their state legislatures for similar grants of freedom. By 1900 the movement was well under way, and by the opening of the First World War twelve states, ten of which were west of the Mississippi River, had passed general home-rule legislation. Once freed of the legislative incubus, municipalities began to experiment broadly with their governments. Within a decade Galveston, Texas, had adopted the commission form of government, and Staunton, Virginia, had pioneered the city-manager type. By 1910 over a hundred major cities were using either the commission or the manager type of government.[3]

During the quarter century after the Civil War the role of successful reform mayors is a short one. Grover Cleveland's career in Buffalo comes to mind, but few others. But beginning in 1889 a succession of colorful municipal leaders gained a national reputation for their work in urban politics. Hazen S. Pingree served four terms as mayor of Detroit before a grateful citizenry elected him governor of Michigan in 1896. A rich manufacturer, he gained a reputation during the depression days of the early nineties as a friend of the working class and as an opponent of business domination of civic utilities and politics. His personal war against long-term franchises and extortionate street-railway rates, and his "potato patch" plan for the unemployed, won national attention. Even more colorful was the career of a Toledo, Ohio, manufacturer, Samuel M. ("Golden Rule") Jones. A Welsh immigrant whose career began in the Pennsylvania oil fields, Jones gained a local reputation in Toledo for his labor policy. In his small but successful oil-equipment factory, he instituted profit sharing, the eight-hour day, a minimum wage, and paid vacations, and abolished the time-keeping system by permitting each workingman to keep his own time. An ethical anarchist, Jones fervently believed in the fundamental goodness of the human being, and deplored the crime of man's seeking power over other men. "I don't want to rule anybody," he remarked. "Each individual must rule himself."

[3] Dewey Anderson, *California State Government* (Berkeley, 1942), p. 196; "San Francisco's New Charter," *Forum*, XXVI (1899), 567–577; Benjamin Parke De Witt, *The Progressive Movement* (New York, 1915), p. 287; *The New York Times*, December 7, 1910.

Jones soon gained a national reputation when he was elected mayor as a fusion candidate of the Republicans and a local reform group, in 1897, only to repudiate the Republican machine that had supported him a short time before. Trouble developed when Jones refused to make the political payments expected by the regular politicians. What was worse, he insisted on infusing city government with his golden rule philosophy. One of his first deeds was to establish an open-air church where men of all faiths, including Jews and Catholics, preached and worshipped. Thereafter he took clubs away from the city police; established a free lodginghouse for tramps, free kindergartens, playgrounds, and night schools; constructed a municipal golf course; and set a minimum wage of $1.50 a day for municipal common labor when the prevailing wage was one dollar or less. Since every citizen of Toledo was a "member of the family," no man had the right, he declared, to enslave another by political or economic bonds. Jones soon came to believe that "of all forms of capital" public ownership was the only economic system consistent with Christian ethics, whose political expression was democracy. "Private ownership," he remarked, "is a high crime against democracy." Jones was quickly deserted by the regular politicians and their machines. In 1903 both major parties campaigned against him, and the three Toledo newspapers even refused to print his letter accepting the nomination by a group of independents. Nevertheless, he ran four times, won four times, died in office, and was succeeded by his disciple, Brand Whitlock.[4]

The same year that Toledo first elected "Golden Rule" Jones, San Francisco elected James D. Phelan mayor of San Francisco. Phelan, a wealthy banker, had been an anti-Bryan Democrat in 1896 at the same time he was allied with Rudolph Spreckels of the wealthy sugar family and the San Francisco Merchants' Association in a demand for the public ownership of the city's streetcar, telephone, water, gas, and electric services. During two years of effort San Francisco obtained a reform charter. But Phelan's administration and the businessmen's reform movement was abruptly ended by the famous strike of January, 1901, which resulted in the Union Labor party's victory of the following fall.

The reform spirit seemed to be moving rapidly in American cities in 1901. Seth Low, wealthy merchant, university president, and philan-

[4] *The Outlook*, LXXIV (1903), 73; Russel Nye, *Midwestern Progressive Politics* (East Lansing, 1951), p. 186.

thropist, was elected mayor of New York with the avowed purpose of divorcing municipal affairs from national politics. In Cleveland, Ohio, a millionaire streetcar magnate and former congressman, Thomas Lofton Johnson, was victorious on a program of public ownership. Mark M. Fagan, like Johnson a disciple of Henry George, won in Jersey City. And in St. Louis a young public attorney, Joseph W. Folk, was prosecuting election frauds committed by the machine that had supported him. Johnson had a particularly interesting career. Starting as an impoverished Southerner, he had accumulated a fortune in city street railways and in steel. According to his own testimony, he was converted to free trade and the single tax by reading Henry George's *Progress and Poverty*. After serving two terms in Congress in the nineties, Johnson was elected mayor of Cleveland in 1901, a position which he held until defeated in 1909. A Jeffersonian Democrat, Johnson invariably demanded in his campaigns home rule, equal taxation, and municipal ownership or the "three-cent fare." But probably his greatest contribution to municipal life was his eight-year campaign for the political education of the citizens of Cleveland. He attracted a remarkable group of educated and liberal-minded young men around him as subordinate administrators, and at the end of his political career he left Cleveland, according to Lincoln Steffens, "the best governed city in America." [5]

In 1902, the October issue of *McClure's Magazine* carried Lincoln Steffens' article "Tweed Days in St. Louis," which is usually cited as the start of muckraking, and which is often given credit for initiating a great wave of civic reform. The muckrakers obviously did not start the movement; it was well under way before their first articles appeared. It is probably more accurate to say that the reform spirit created the muckrakers and the muckrake magazines. Before 1890 the periodical field had been dominated by the traditional high-priced quality magazines, which devoted much of their space to literature, the arts, and polite fiction. After that date the rising curve of literacy and technical advance resulting in cheaper paper and printing first made possible real mass circulation. A number of periodicals selling for as little as ten cents appeared, but until 1902 their subject matter differed little save in quality from the older publications. After the appearance of Lincoln Steffens' article in the September *McClure's*

---

[5] Lincoln Steffens, *Autobiography* (New York, 1931), pp. 473–481. See also Tom Johnson, *My Story* (New York, 1911).

describing the corruption of the St. Louis government and another by Ida Tarbell the following month, originating a popular and sharply critical history of the Standard Oil Company, a revolution occurred in the periodical press. When *McClure's* sales soared skyward, *Munsey's, Cosmopolitan, Everybody's, Hampton's, Pearson's, Success,* and even some of the more elite publications sought to copy the same formulas. As the American appetite for the new literature appeared to be insatiable, a large group of the nation's first-rate periodical writers were attracted to the movement. In addition to Lincoln Steffens and Ida Tarbell, Upton Sinclair, Mark Sullivan, Ray Stannard Baker, David Graham Phillips, Charles E. Russell, Samuel Hopkins Adams, and a host of lesser talents joined the campaign of exposure. Collectively their articles pried into practically every political, economic, and moral problem of the age. They attacked the evils of city, state, and national government, labor unions, big business, Wall Street, life insurance, the press, the medical profession, the food industry, child labor, women's inequality, prostitution, and the drug trade. Heavily factual in content, critical in tone, and full of righteous but optimistic indignation, the average muckrake article presented no curative proposals, but simply sought to give the average citizen a scientific description of what was wrong with the varied sectors of American life. Taken as a whole, the impact of the muckrake literature was enormous. Before this journalistic crusade had run its course, few literate Americans could have any real feelings of complacency about their civilization. Steffens' painfully specific series of articles describing the wayward governmental operations of one major city after another, for example, was calculated to awaken even the most patriotic citizen to the evils in his home town. And a later series on urban reformers made him aware of what had been accomplished elsewhere. Within six years after Steffens' "Shame of the Cities" series had appeared, formidable reform movements had appeared in Philadelphia, Chicago, Kansas City, Minneapolis, Los Angeles, and San Francisco.[6]

Meanwhile, some of America's major cities had become the centers of another sort of reform activity, which had been inspired abroad. After visiting English settlement houses, Jane Addams came back to her native Illinois to establish, in 1889, Chicago's Hull House. Around

[6] Steffens, *Autobiography,* p. 365. See also Louis Filler, *Crusaders for American Liberalism* (New York, 1939); and Cornelius C. Regier, *The Era of the Muckrakers* (Chapel Hill, 1932).

this institution in the slums gathered a remarkable group of women. Julia Lathrop, the first woman member of the Illinois Board of Charities, was there, as was Florence Kelley, the first factory inspector of the state. Miss Kelley later went on to New York to become associated with Lillian Wald at the Henry Street Settlement. This energetic group of women and their associates were to be largely responsible for changing and broadening the old concept of wardship into a new police power which permitted the states to protect women and children at home and at work.

The rising tendency to throw the protective arm of the state around women and children also influenced the development of the juvenile court, which originated in an Illinois law of 1899 and soon spread across the country east to New York and west to Denver, where Judge Ben B. Lindsey became nationally known for his twenty-five-year effort to protect and reform wayward youth. Much of the same sentiment helped to inspire the New York Committee of Fifteen, organized in 1900 to investigate housing conditions in the "lower depths" of the city. The committee, which included among its members Jacob H. Schiff, John D. Rockefeller, Jr., and George Foster Peabody, soon extended its work into the associated areas of public health and prostitution. Its findings were partially responsible for the 1901 state building law, which included minimum standards for lighting, sanitation, and ventilation, and fire precautions.[7]

The role of the city as the inspirer of social democracy and as the originator of social regulation has been relatively overlooked in American history. The "gas and water socialism" of American cities during the first decade of the twentieth century persuaded many nonsocialistic Americans to accept the principle of limited public ownership. In 1896 less than half of the waterworks were owned by municipalities. By 1915 almost two-thirds of them were owned and operated by city governments. Less but still significant progress was made in the field of gas, electricity, and public transportation. In the local elections of 1911 it is interesting to note that the Socialist party carried eighteen cities in the country and almost won ten or a dozen more,[8] and this at a time when the Socialist vote in state-wide elections was all but

---

[7] New York Committee of Fifteen, 1900 (New York, 1902).

[8] Socialist mayors were elected in Schenectady, New York; Flint, Michigan; Butte, Montana; and Berkeley, California. Moreover, the party came within a few votes of carrying such major cities as Cleveland and Columbus, Ohio, and Los Angeles.

negligible. The city also either passed or inspired the passage of the first significant labor, housing, and public health legislation. Although the Grangers were responsible for the introduction of the regulatory commission, it was the city that first used it so effectively, on such a scale, and in such an intimate fashion that its virtues were brought home to the masses of the people. To a larger degree than has been

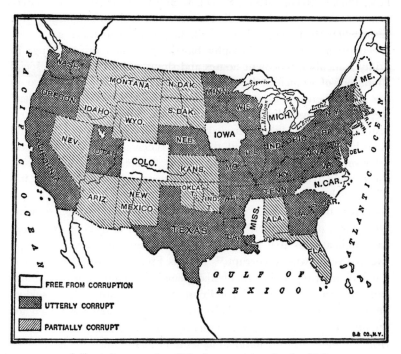

A French map of political corruption in the U.S.

recognized, it was the city that both blazed the way and supplied the pressure for the passage of much of the state regulatory enactments in the new century.[9]

In November, 1902, the Ohio legislature passed a new municipal code for cities with a population of over 5,000 people. The code took much of the appointive power away from mayors and placed it in the

[9] Harold U. Faulkner, *The Quest for Social Justice* (New York, 1931), p. 127; Henry F. Griffin, "The Rising Tide of Socialism," *The Outlook*, C (1912), 438.

city council or in the governor of the state. It was obviously aimed at Ohio's radical mayors.[10] Johnson and Jones found in Ohio what Mark Fagan and George Record found in Jersey City and what Joseph Folk encountered in St. Louis. Since the city was the servant of the state, urban control was not enough; to reform the city one had to reform the statehouse and the governor's mansion. Pingree, Jones, Johnson, Folk, Phelan, Record, Kent, Spreckels, and Crane carried their movements to the state, either leading a reform crusade or supporting one. Even when their personal stars fell, they carried to the state a new street-corner political philosophy based upon such urban things as utility franchises, tenement houses and slums, public health, the social conditions of women and children, factory legislation, and the war in the streets between capital and labor. George Record's "New Idea" Republicans never did obtain a majority in New Jersey, but as their historian has said, "the remarkable Wilson legislation of 1911 would have been impossible without them." [11] When this new middle-class, urban-minded reform strain was added to the older agrarian one, the existing political structure with its ideological and economic implications began to crumble.

A map of the United States appeared in France in 1905 showing "the stages of corruption" in each of the forty-five states. Six states were indicated as free from corruption, thirteen as partially corrupt, twenty-five as wholly corrupt.[12] To this French charge there were a few indignant replies but no blanket denials, for most informed Americans admitted the general condition. State legislatures have seldom been the focus of much public opinion. Their actions have been too remote from the immediate experience of the citizen and too divorced from the more exciting national issues to elicit sustained public interest. Legislative candidates, nominated by a party caucus in 1900, were usually unknown to the average voters. Neither their voting records nor their speeches were often carried in the average newspaper. Their actions obscured, state legislatures in the post-Civil War period fell prey to interested corporations and to political bosses. The diverse and often conflicting large economic interests in many of the states made a boss almost a necessity to act as an honest broker. General Brayton,

[10] *Literary Digest,* **XXIV** (1902), 543.

[11] Ransom E. Noble, Jr., *New Jersey Progressivism Before Wilson* (Princeton, 1946), p. 153.

[12] *Literary Digest,* **XXXI** (1905), 795.

"the blind boss of Rhode Island," boasted proudly that he never had to solicit any business. Since he ran the Republican campaign every year, he was in a position "to be of service to men all over the state," and thus both the corporations and politicians came to him to iron out their differences. Brayton, without a public office, had a room in the state capitol, which he held even after the election of a Democratic governor in 1903, who had charged him with wholesale corruption. Smilingly depreciating the power of the governor, the "general" admitted that he ran the state, but maintained that his power was necessary to make the processes of government work and "to look after the interests" of the corporations which had retained him.[13]

In some states the most powerful United States senator became the official arbiter and representative of corporate interests. Matthew Quay of Pennsylvania and Thomas C. Platt of New York held the dominant corporation voice in their respective statehouses for years at the same time they sat in the Senate at Washington. New Jersey was operated by a collegium. One of the senators, John Kean, specialized in independent city utilities; the other, John F. Dryden, was a director of the New Jersey Public Service Corporation and president of the Prudential Life Insurance Company. The chief justice of the state supreme court, the attorney general, the state comptroller, the commissioner of banking and insurance, and a majority of the state board of taxation were all former employees of the Pennsylvania Railroad. Except for an occasional conflict, this divided control apparently worked well for the few at the top. "We've got everything in the state worth having," Thomas N. McCarter commented, "except Trenton street cars and Elizabeth gas. . . ." McCarter was president of the New Jersey Public Service Corporation, a director of the Prudential Life Insurance Company, and one-time attorney general of the state and chairman of the Republican State Committee. At the time of the remark his brother, Robert H. McCarter, was attorney general as well as counsel for two important railroads.[14]

In the Middle West conditions were much the same. After a long career in state politics as a member of the inner group, United States Senator Isaac Stephenson wrote that he believed as true the boast of one of Wisconsin's chief corporation lobbyists that no bill "had passed

[13] New York *Evening Post,* March 25, 1903; *The Outlook,* LXXIII (1903), 746–747.
[14] Noble, *New Jersey Progressivism,* pp. 6–11.

for sixteen years without their approval." [15] Further to the west, where one or two corporations, usually railroads, towered above all their species, the state legislature and the dominant political machine became sort of ancillary bureaus to the main business offices of the firm. Sometimes such political power was so pervasive that it became vexatious. Collis P. Huntington, president of the Southern Pacific Railroad, observed bitterly that political matters often took more of his time than railroad operation. "If a man wants to become constable," he complained, "he thinks he has first to come down to Fourth and Townsend Streets to get permission." [16] But constables and other minor frustrations aside, the game seemed to be worth the candle for the interested corporations, the bosses, and the individual member of the legislatures. During the 1903 Folk investigation in Missouri, one insignificant member of the state legislature testified that he had received about $15,000 for his work in the session, getting $1,000 for voting for the school text bill, $500 for his vote on the St. Louis Transit bill, another $250 for voting no on a number of measures, and most of the rest as a salary from "the lobby" for taking care of the railroad. Where such sums of money originated was clear from the testimony produced in the New York life insurance investigations, one executive testifying that his company alone had spent close to a million dollars in five years stopping "undesirable legislation." But beyond such material matters there was also the question of power. During the same insurance investigations the young attorney Charles Evans Hughes asked railroad baron E. H. Harriman whether it was not true that through his connections with the New York boss, Odell, he had powerful political influence. Harriman indignantly denied the charge, observing that Mr. Odell had political influence because of his relations with him.[17] When Presley in Frank Norris's *Octopus* urged the farmers of Muscle Slough to use terror against the Southern Pacific Railroad and co-operating corporations because no other means of protest existed, there was some point to his peroration that these masters owned their homes, their legislature, their ballot boxes, and their courts. "We cannot escape them," he concluded, "there is no redress."

The pervasive and prevailing power of well-endowed corporations, political bosses, and corruptible legislatures had been scarcely chal-

[15] Isaac Stephenson, *Recollections of a Long Life* (Chicago, 1915), p. 212.
[16] San Francisco *Examiner*, April 10, 1890.
[17] *The Outlook*, LXXIV (1903), 201; LXXXI (1905), 948.

lenged during the late nineteenth century save for the rural areas dominated by the Populists. Here and there nonmachine reforming governors like John P. Altgeld of Illinois, Hazen S. Pingree of Michigan, and Theodore Roosevelt of New York made their appearance. Historians have had a tendency to deprecate Roosevelt's reform achievements in the Empire State from 1899 to 1901. But considering the short length of his term and the nature of New York politics, he was at least as successful as Altgeld or Pingree. The chief reform proposals of all three, however, were defeated by the power of the political opposition and public indifference. It was not until Robert La Follette defeated the Wisconsin regular machine in 1900 that the reform movement really got started. La Follette's election as governor seemed to start a chain reaction of revolt in the agricultural Middle West. A year afterward reform spread to Iowa, then to Minnesota and Missouri, and eventually down the entire tier of states immediately west, from North Dakota to Kansas.

The earliest and probably the ablest of these reform governors, La Follette, was also fairly typical. His family, from early farming stock, had moved west from Virginia to Kentucky, to Indiana, and then to Primrose, Wisconsin, where Robert was born. As a youth he attended the University of Wisconsin, where he fell under the intellectual influence of its ethically minded president, John Bascom. Within seven months after his graduation he was admitted to the bar, and in the same year, without consulting the local political boss, he announced his candidacy for district attorney. Although opposed by the machine, this young man in a hurry won the nomination and election. Four years later he announced his candidacy for Congress in the same fashion and was elected. During his three terms in Congress, from 1885 to 1891, he was a regular Republican, supporting high tariffs and the other party issues so effectively that he was placed on the powerful House Ways and Means Committee. He was defeated for re-election in the Democratic year of 1890 and, possibly because he had incurred the opposition of Senator Philetus Sawyer over a local issue, he was not supported by the party machine for renomination. Rebelliously declaring that he refused "to recognize the authority" of any set of men to decide his party status, he organized a campaign to support Nils P. Haugen for governor in 1894 against the regular Republican candidate. Haugen lost and La Follette himself tried in 1896 for the coveted office, and again in 1898, without success. By

1900 Sawyer was dying, and with him went most of the power of the old machine. After an understanding with the railroads and with the regular Republicans, La Follette was able to wage a successful "harmony" campaign and without serious opposition won the office that had eluded him for so long.[18]

When Robert La Follette first became governor of Wisconsin, he was forty-five years old. Short of stature, but with iron both in his hair and his character, and with little fun in his stern and rather dour nature, he was a born leader, especially of minority causes. La Follette once remarked that he could no more compromise than he could add twenty years to his life simply by wishing it. He fancied himself somewhat of an actor, and perhaps it is revealing that he was as happy lecturing on or reading one of Shakespeare's tragedies as he was leading an uphill political struggle or castigating the opposition from a public rostrum. A man of intense convictions, his life revolved around infallible principles instead of fallible men. By the end of his life he had quarreled with most of his close political associates, and it is doubtful whether outside of his family he ever had a close and warm friendship. Ambitious and almost inhumanly energetic, he and a few associates had built a political machine in Wisconsin based upon the small farmer in the interior and the laborer in the lake-shore cities. Never losing his conviction that he was the tribune of Wisconsin's small folk, he demanded obedience and unwavering support from his colleagues, and he usually saw in his opponents or competitors a willingness to sell out to the constant enemy, the large corporation, the great house of finance, or to concentrated and corrupting wealth. Throughout his life La Follette reflected the small and limited democratic folk aspirations of Primrose, Wisconsin.

Had the Republican majority in the 1901 Wisconsin state legislature passed the modest reform program promised in the platform, the history of the state, and perhaps that of La Follette, might have been somewhat different. But the regular wing of the party defeated both a direct primary proposal and a bill to regulate the rates of railroads. As always opposition seemed to stiffen the governor's moral fiber and to spur him to prodigious energy. He remarked once to a colleague that given the primary he and his associates could "hold this state for-

---

[18] Robert S. Maxwell, *La Follette and the Rise of the Progressives in Wisconsin* (Madison, 1956), pp. 18–21, 74; but for a different account, see Belle Case and Fola La Follette, *Robert La Follette* (New York, 1953), pp. 1, 105.

ever." After a long and grim struggle La Follette first succeeded in getting a reform majority in the legislature, and then in the course of three terms he inspired the most comprehensive reform program in the history of American state government down to 1933. Under his continuous demands and regular scoldings, the Wisconsin legislature enacted a direct primary law, established an efficient railroad rate commission, substantially increased taxes on railroads and corporations, and passed a civil service act, an antilobbying law, a conservation and water power franchise act, and a state banking control measure. Although not passed until after La Follette had gone to the United States Senate, a state income tax, the first of its kind, was due almost entirely to his support. By 1906 when La Follette left for the Senate, Wisconsin had earned the name Theodore Roosevelt later gave it: "the laboratory of democracy." And for the next forty years, whenever La Follette and his political legatees were in power, they gave the state the most efficient, honest, and progressive government it has ever had, before or since.

When La Follette went to the United States Senate in 1906, he was still a regular Republican. Throughout the early tempestuous years in Wisconsin he had remained steadfast in his support of the national Republican party. In 1896 he had supported McKinley for the nomination and campaigned for him against Bryan during the election. He did the same in 1900, defending both imperialism and the Dingley Tariff Act from the stump. But if he was still a regular Republican, he was an uncommonly independent one. And his Wisconsin governorship clearly foreshadowed what his relations to his party would be when once he took his seat in the upper house of the national government.[19]

Throughout the nineties the dominant voice in Iowa politics belonged to the railroads which fanned out from Chicago and ran west through the state. The Chicago, Burlington and Quincy, the Chicago, Milwaukee and St. Paul, and the Chicago and Northwestern railroads each had its individual political representatives; but because of his native ability Nathaniel W. Hubbard, representing the Northwestern Railroad, usually spoke on most important matters for the railroad community. Wherever Iowa politicians gathered, the remark was often heard that whoever was governor in name, the real governor in economic matters, at least, was Hubbard.[20] Until 1901 Hubbard had no

[19] Maxwell, *La Follette and the Rise of the Progressive*, p. 25.
[20] Cyrenus Cole, *I Remember, I Remember* (Ames, Iowa, 1936), p. 178.

more than the usual difficulties in coming to understandings with the reigning Iowa politicians. The incumbent governor at the time, L. M. Shaw, Senator W. B. Allison, and Speaker of the House D. B. Henderson, who collectively dominated the more formal politics of the state, were not unsympathetic to railroad interests. But in the autumn of 1901, Albert Baird Cummins, against the combined opposition of this triumvirate, the railroads, and the state's leading newspapers, was nominated and elected governor. Cummins belonged to one of the most important legal firms in the state, which had regularly represented the major railroads. But the politically ambitious Cummins had never been satisfied with the treatment he had received from the Iowa Republican machine. After gaining a popular reputation as the chief counsel in a legal battle against the so-called barbed-wire trust, he announced himself as a candidate for governor on an antimonopoly, antirailroad, low-tariff platform. Once governor, he rallied most of the dissident sentiment to his side and began battle against the reigning conservatives. For the next seven years he crusaded for the opening of "the channels of trade fairly and fully to all comers" and against the privilege of railroads "to sit in political conventions or occupy seats in legislative chambers.[21]

In Minnesota the dominant railroads shared political power with the milling and the brewing interests, but the result for the state was much the same as in Wisconsin and Iowa. Here again popular rebellion against corporate control appeared almost as soon as the Spanish-American War was finished. Although regularly supported by corporate groups in the state, Samuel R. Van Sant, governor from 1900 to 1904, felt the necessity to carry on an anticorporation canvass at every election. Tiring of the Republicans "talking sweet and acting sour," the state in 1904 elected a Democrat, John A. Johnson, who was anything but a radical. A former regular Republican, he had become a Democrat when offered the editorship of a Democratic paper. In 1896 he deserted Bryan to become a Gold Democrat. He wrote vehement editorials against the efforts of radicals to array class against class and was presented in 1907 to eastern Democrats as an anti-Bryan presidential candidate who was neither a reformer nor a "savior of society" but "a man of the people" who "looked well in

---

[21] Cole, *I Remember, I Remember*, p. 205; Benton Wilcox, "The Economic Basis of Northwestern Radicalism," unpublished Ph.D. thesis, University of Wisconsin, p. 104.

evening clothes." Nevertheless, in his two terms as governor, Johnson secured part of the program that La Follette and Cummins were advocating in Wisconsin and Iowa.[22]

Throughout the rest of the western Middle West the political pattern was much the same as it was in Wisconsin, Iowa, and Minnesota. W. R. Stubbs, a millionaire Republican businessman, engineered a successful revolt against the machine in Kansas in 1904. The same year Democrat Joseph Folk became the reform governor of Missouri against the combined efforts of the corporations and the party regulars, and Coe Crawford, running on a "La Follette program" in South Dakota, prepared the way for his successful race for governor in 1906. Crawford won in South Dakota, while John Burke, a Democrat, was elected governor of North Dakota to serve three terms filled with reform.

At almost the same time that the western portion of the Middle West was revolting against conservative corporation politics, a similar if not an identical movement was taking place in the agricultural South. In 1901 Jeff Davis won the governorship of Arkansas. Three years later James K. Vardaman upset the ruling political class in Mississippi to become governor, and in 1906 Hoke Smith was elected in Georgia. Following the pattern set by that unlettered son of the red soil, Benjamin R. Tillman of South Carolina, all of these men overcame the dominant corporation-minded conservative democratic machines by appealing to the "patched breeches and one gallus vote" of the poor whites. Vardaman campaigned in an eight-wheel lumber wagon drawn by numerous yokes of oxen, and Jeff Davis, it was said, was never once caught in certain parts of Arkansas with his coat on or his shoes polished. All of these rebels profited from the Populist antipathy toward the southern economic and cultural elite classes. Smith of Georgia, in fact, owed his election in part to the support of Tom Watson, Bryan's running mate on the Populist ticket in 1896 and one of the last of the Populists. They were also helped by the direct primary, or supported it vigorously once they gained office. But while they stood for the supremacy of the "red neck and wool hat" elements, they were united in curtailing the political rights of Negroes. During one of his many anti-Negro speeches, Vardaman shouted that "God Almighty had created the Negro for a menial." By the use of the

[22] Winifred G. Helmes, *John A. Johnson, The People's Governor* (Minneapolis, 1949), p. 238.

direct primary and devices like the grandfather clause, they were able to outvote the more cultured and moneyed classes of the South at the same time they were disfranchising the Negro.

Although many of the southern governors were well educated, they often adopted the manners and speech of their clientele. With their crude and impassioned tactics and their appeals to mob prejudice against both opposite ends of society, they set the pattern for the southern demagogue for half a century. But as they baited the wealthy and set back the Negro for a generation or more, they also secured real and lasting benefits for the South's other disinherited class, the poor white. Better educational facilities, antimonopolistic measures, stricter regulation of railroad rates, and laws prohibiting the leasing of convicts to private business were all a part of the pattern of their achievement. While governor of Arkansas, "Little Jeff" Davis virtually ran the insurance companies out of the state, secured better budgets for charitable institutions, and obtained the repeal of the fellow-servants rule which made it easier for injured workingmen to obtain compensation for their hurts. Hoke Smith, "the first insurgent governor of Georgia since Reconstruction," secured from a back-country legislature acts for the abolition of railroad passes, for a direct primary, for the abolition of corrupt political practices, and a measure controlling railroads and other public service corporations, which included a provision for the regulation of their securities.

Other southern states without the dubious benefit of the colorful demagogues were likewise responding to the reform spirit of the times. Led by Governor Charles B. Aycock of North Carolina, the drive for the improvement of public schools became an almost section-wide movement. Acts for the stricter regulation of railroads and other monopolistic corporations were passed in North Carolina, Alabama, and Texas. Anticonvict-leasing laws, as well as measures disfranchising the Negro, became rather general in the decade. But nowhere was there such a complete change in the class structure of political power as in Arkansas, Mississippi, and Georgia. Nowhere else did the middle elements of society draw the line more sharply between the upper and lower classes.[23]

[23] Dewey Grantham, "Hoke Smith: Progressive Governor of Georgia," *Journal of Southern History,* XV (1949), 425–440; C. Vann Woodward, *Tom Watson, Agrarian Rebel* (New York, 1938), pp. 370–395; Francis B. Simkins, *The South Old and New* (New York, 1947), pp. 438–441.

In the West the insurgent spirit was also evident. As soon as John F. Shafroth became governor of Colorado in 1910, he presented to a reluctant legislature a wide program of reform calling for the direct primary, the initiative and the referendum, the strict regulation of railroad rates, the creation of a public service commission, and the state insurance of commercial bank deposits. Shafroth, a silver Republican who had turned Democrat, resigned his seat in Congress in 1904 when he became convinced that many of the votes that had elected him were fraudulent. Back in Colorado, along with such men as Judge Ben Lindsey and Edward P. Costigan, he fought the regular state machine, which was tied in with both the Guggenheim mineral empire and the Rockefeller coal and iron interests.[24]

William S. U'Ren of Oregon was perhaps more responsible in an indirect way for influencing the political life of the several states than any other man in the nation. Although U'Ren held a minor office only once, Lincoln Steffens testified to his nationwide influence. In Oregon a contemporary observer was reported as saying that the state government was divided into four departments, "the executive, judicial, legislative, and Mr. U'Ren—and it is still an open question who exerts the most power." U'Ren, a blacksmith turned newspaper editor and lawyer, had been a member of the Farmers' Alliance. He became interested in direct legislation during the nineties after reading about its use in Switzerland. From that time on he devoted his life almost wholly to securing in Oregon and elsewhere the direct primary, the referendum, the initiative, and the recall. Largely through his efforts Oregon adopted the initiative and referendum in 1902, the direct primary in 1904, and the recall in 1910. Without these devices ensuring a better reflection of the will of the electorate, the reform movement almost everywhere would have encountered far more serious obstruction.[25]

The insurgent movement was evident in varying degrees of intensity in most states of the West. But throughout the mining and timber region its success was constantly threatened by the activities of radical labor and the conservative appeal to farmers and middle-class elements that an attack upon the existing political machine would open the way to victory for a radical and lawless left. Occasionally, as in Idaho, a

[24] Colin P. Goodykoontz, *The Papers of Edward P. Costigan* (Boulder, Colo., 1941), p. 146.

[25] Lincoln Steffens, *Upbuilders* (New York, 1909), pp. 286–309.

young reformer was able to make his opposition to labor radicalism so apparent that he could successfully cope with the reigning conservatives. The sometime progressive William E. Borah, who had won a wide reputation in prosecuting radical labor leaders, was sent to the Senate in 1907. But it was only in urban California, where a large middle class existed, that Far Western reformers could successfully challenge both the conservative corporate right and the radical labor left simultaneously. In winning their way to the statehouse, the California progressives, led by Hiram Johnson, smashed the long-dominant state-wide Southern Pacific Railroad machine in the statehouse and the Union Labor party's control in San Francisco. Later, when the Socialist party was a serious threat in Los Angeles, the reformers attacked the left with even more vigor and strength than they had marshaled against the right.[26]

In the East the new political spirit was never quite so spectacularly successful as it was in the Middle West, the West, and the South. The strong union movement in the section was not very cordial to middle-class reformers; Gompers himself pointedly remarked that most social advance was made solely by organized labor "without the sympathy, aid, or assistance of any other element in society. . . ." Other labor leaders were even more uncharitable: "Scratch a champion of the plain people," one of them remarked, "and you will find an aristocrat." [27] The large immigrant population often preferred to support organizations like Tammany rather than the progressives. Political action which did not promise an immediate improvement in the desperate economic lot of the immigrants was not too attractive, and reform centered upon Protestant moral values often positively repulsed the foreign-born. The direct primary and the prohibition of alcoholic liquors left the usual immigrant from southern and central Europe distinctly cold. Moreover, middle-class temper was never as anticorporation in the East as it was in the West and the South. A longer experience with large industry, job opportunities which the corporations offered ambitious men, and the rich returns made by their stocks and bonds had eroded away some of the more individualistic values still held dear in the less industrialized sections of the nation.

[26] George E. Mowry, *The California Progressives* (Berkeley and Los Angeles, 1951), pp. 23–56.

[27] *American Federationist,* XL (1904), 772; *Coast Seamen's Journal,* V (1906), 3.

Nevertheless the East, like other sections, distinctly felt the impact of the new politics. In 1905 a young, rather unknown lawyer became the leading counsel for the New York legislative committee investigating the nation's great insurance companies. The story that Charles Evans Hughes produced of corporate greed, illegality, and public faithlessness excited a wave of indignation against high finance only equaled by the feeling against the trusts. Even the New York *Journal of Commerce* described the testimony produced as a "remarkable record of turpitude," perhaps unequaled in the history of American finance. The investigation made financial reform almost inevitable. It also was largely responsible for electing Hughes governor of New York the following year on what, for this particular state, was a moderate reform program. Hughes' defeated opponent was William Randolph Hearst, the millionaire publisher, whom Theodore Roosevelt described as "a sinister agitator" similar to "the less worthy creatures of the French Revolution." Hughes was renominated again in 1908 over the strongest opposition of the New York regular Republican machine, and its continued hostility during his second term limited the legislative results of his four years.[28]

Even in traditionalist New England the reform movement left faint but still rather distinct marks. Following his election as governor of Vermont in 1908, George H. Prouty, a wealthy lumber manufacturer, insisted that the legislature create a public service commission. The resulting struggle started a split in the state Republican party that was not healed until 1916. With the support of Winston Churchill, the novelist, and other young reformers, Robert Bass two years later became governor of New Hampshire over the opposition of the regular machine and the Boston and Maine Railroad. Elsewhere in the section the rebel spirit was funneled off into the Democratic opposition. Both Rhode Island and Massachusetts elected Democratic governors, and thus foreshadowed the political reorientation of the two states in the second quarter of the century.[29]

No state in the East, however, had as long a rebellious tradition in the first decade of the century as New Jersey. The dereliction from

[28] *Literary Digest*, XXXI (1905), 1; Roosevelt to John St. L. Strachey, October 25, 1906, Roosevelt MSS.

[29] Winston Allen Flint, *The Progressive Movement in Vermont* (Washington, 1941), p. 48. See also Winston Churchill's novels *Coniston* (New York, 1906) and *Mr. Crewe's Career* (New York, 1908).

party regularity of Mark Fagan and George Record of Jersey City in the Democratic party was soon matched by that of Everett Colby in the Republican. Colby, son of a wealthy Wisconsin railroad executive, was apparently a not too unhappy regular Republican until 1904, when the utility, railroad, and insurance combine at the statehouse decided that he was much too unsafe to be made speaker of the Assembly. Thereafter, declaring himself a free lance, he sparked the formation of the "New Idea Republicans," dedicated to election reform, the removal of corporation influence from state politics, and the strict regulation of all public utilities, including municipal services. During the election of 1906 the Colby forces called themselves "Roosevelt Republicans"; three years later they changed their name to the Progressive Republican League and became known as "Progressive Republicans." [30]

Supporters of the federal form of government, as opposed to a consolidated national state, have usually argued that the system allows for more political experimentation as well as assures vitality for the processes of local democratic government. However torpid state government has been at other times, it was vital and experimental during the first dozen or so years of the twentieth century. Not only was state government alive and vigorous at the local level, but the states in fact were the original coiners of much of the reform legislation that subsequently was passed by the federal government. In no other period since the Civil War, perhaps, had state governments been so active and so creative.

In 1903 the novelist David Graham Phillips wrote to his friend Albert J. Beveridge that to succeed with his program the Indiana senator must support ways and means to reflect more clearly the will of the people in Washington. There must be, Phillips wrote, "no corrupt political priests between you and the people or between the people and their government." [31] In getting the people nearer the "grub pile," as William Kent put it, the reform movement in the states did quite well. The Australian secret ballot was not a progressive innovation; it had been first adopted by Massachusetts in 1888. But both the Populists and the Progressives gave the measure so much support that by 1910 every state in the Union had adopted the device to prevent the

[30] Noble, *New Jersey Progressivism,* pp. 48, 77; Steffens, *Upbuilders,* pp. 66–68.

[31] Phillips to Beveridge, (?), 1903, Beveridge MSS.

will of the voters being suborned at the polling places. Corrupt-practices acts limiting the amounts and uses of money in an election were also a favored progressive solution for limiting the power of corporations and money. By 1905 at least three relatively effective laws had been passed in the several states, and before a federal law was passed by the Sixty-first Congress practically every progressive-dominated state had such legislation on its statute books.

By the turn of the century five Rocky Mountain states had granted state-wide suffrage to women; by 1914 eight other trans-Appalachian states had followed.[32] But the record of the reform movement in the extension of the suffrage was a most uncertain one. Balancing the gains in the West was the steady curtailment of Negro suffrage in the South. Far more important in securing a better reflection of the people's will was the state-wide primary system, which abolished the party caucus for the selection of party nominees. Wisconsin led the way in 1903, and by the close of 1912 state-wide primary laws were in operation in thirteen of the forty-eight states. In addition five of the southern states operated a primary election under the rules of the Democratic party. Accompanying the spread of the primary system was the simultaneous move for popular nomination of United States senators, which had the effect in most states of making the subsequent election by the legislature almost a *pro forma* action. By 1909 twenty-nine states selected senatorial nominees by the popular ballot, although in a few the vote was advisory and not conclusive. Thus the United States Senate's reluctant action in submitting a constitutional amendment to the states in 1912 for the direct election of senators was an act of recognizing the inevitable. Sometimes the direct primary and the popular election of senators worked in an opposite way from that hoped for by its supporters. In Wisconsin's first general primary election La Follette's candidate for governor lost to James Davidson, who became a standpatter. But in most instances during the first two decades of the century the reform forces gained by the adoption of the devices.

The progressive belief in pure democracy, emphasizing as it did the conviction that the masses of the people were fully capable of settling the most complicated state questions, was nowhere better illustrated than in reform support for the initiative and referendum instruments, which made it possible for an electorate to initiate and

---

[32] The eight were Washington, California, Arizona, Kansas, Oregon, Illinois, Nevada, and Ohio.

pass legislation without reference to a legislature and to veto a legislative measure by a majority vote of the people. By 1912 twelve states west of the Mississippi had adopted these two devices. In the same year seven states, again all of them west of the Mississippi, had adopted the recall, whereby an elected officer could be recalled from his office at any time a sufficient number of the voters so expressed a desire. The definite geographical pattern of the states adopting the initiative, the referendum, and the recall may be explained by the tolerance to change and experimentation of a youthful West. But it may also point out another of the ideological fissures that separated urban and rural progressivism. To the extent that the more rural and traditional progressives distrusted a state bureaucracy and the expert, they relied upon the ethical and intellectual qualities of the masses.[33]

Although the democratization of the election machinery was to some reformers almost an end in itself, most of them considered it simply a means to attain more significant objectives. Foremost among these objectives was the better regulation of railroads and the control of the great industrial combines, popularly called trusts. A major item in the program of almost every progressive governor was a demand for either the institution of state railroad or utility commissions, or their reinvigoration where they already existed. The powers of such bodies were rapidly extended not only to include the setting of firm rates but also to base such rates on physical evaluations of the assets of corporations. Power to prohibit rebates, unequal rates, and variations in rates between long and short hauls was also given to many of the state bodies, as well as the power to supervise the issuance of railroad securities. Many of the state commissions were given regulatory power over all other types of common carriers as well as over telegraph, telephone, and electric power companies. So comprehensive was the total of these regulations that scarcely a major provision of either the federal railroad acts of 1906 and 1910 had not been first tried out in the states.

Attempts by the states to curb monopoly and to regulate large industrial concerns likewise preceded the progressive period. But here again a remarkable flowering of statutes and administrative regulations on the subject took place under the progressive governors. Since the publication of Henry Demarest Lloyd's *Wealth Against Commonwealth,* the Standard Oil Company had come to represent to the

[33] Frederic Austin Ogg, *National Progress* (New York, 1918), pp. 162–165.

American public the personification of the word *trust*. Inherent in its operations, according to public belief, were the illegal practices of all other industrial combines, practices threatening the position of small business, labor, and the consumer. And although the Standard Oil Company was but one of the many national industrial combines attacked by the states during the period, no other company's difficulties with state legislatures and courts so caught public attention. Almost as soon as the new Kansas antimachine governor had taken power in 1904, the state's long fight against Standard Oil Company was accelerated. Similar action was soon taken by Governor Hadley in Missouri, and thereafter the movement spread rapidly from state to state. By 1905 the Kansas legislature had defined petroleum pipelines as common carriers, and as such under the regulation of a state commission. The legislature also approved a bill to provide for the construction of a publicly owned refinery. In retaliation the Standard Oil Company suspended all operations within the state. Soon Texas started proceedings to prohibit a Standard subsidiary from doing business under a law prohibiting the selling of trust-made goods within the state. Shortly afterward the Supreme Court of Missouri barred Standard Oil of Indiana from operating within that commonwealth. By 1907 nearly one thousand legal indictments against the Standard Oil Company stood in as many cities across the country.[34]

Long before Theodore Roosevelt's trust-busting program had caused much anguish among large industrialists, state legislatures and state courts were striking such telling blows that an inclination arose among corporation executives to ask for quarter. In 1905 Senator John F. Dryden of New Jersey, president of the Prudential Life Insurance Company, amazed a portion of the business world by asking for federal regulation of insurance companies. While he was opposed to government regulation of business, the senator explained, he considered the proposed federal action infinitely preferable to "the intolerable supervision" of fifty state insurance departments.[35] Similar sentiment was to grow, and by such indirection the states contributed to the extension of the federal regulatory power.

The governments of the several states were actively creative in still another sphere, namely, in the broad field of social legislation. Of particular concern to them were the working conditions for women

[34] *Literary Digest,* XXX (1905), 271; XLIII (1907), 195.
[35] *World's Work,* X (1905), 6782.

and children. Legislation prohibiting night work, setting a maximum number of hours and minimum wages, and raising the required age level was common. So were laws providing a state pension to husbandless women with dependent children. Following the lead of New York in 1910, some twenty-five states passed employers' liability acts before 1914. By the same time five of the commonwealths had limited the issuance of labor injunctions, and numerous others had passed weekly pay laws and mechanics' lien laws, giving a preferred status to wages in the collection of debts from a bankrupt person or concern.

The geographical pattern of state social legislation is an interesting one. Before 1914, for example, nine states had passed minimum wage laws for women: California, Colorado, Massachusetts, Minnesota, Nebraska, Oregon, Utah, Washington, and Wisconsin. Before the federal provision in the Clayton Act was passed, five states had limited the rights of courts to issue labor injunctions: California, Arizona, Kansas, Iowa, and Oregon. Of the twenty states providing pensions by 1913 to unsupported mothers with dependent children, sixteen lay west of the Alleghenies and all, save Missouri, north of the so-called border states.[36] With certain exceptions, most of this type of legislation was passed in agrarian states where the need for it was far less pressing than in the more industrially mature commonwealths. Obviously, progressivism in the states cannot be explained alone in terms of industrial evolution. It was much more than a simple response to material conditions. If it is to be fully and properly understood, one has to turn to an examination of the mentality of its leaders and to a consideration of what made such leaders react the way they did.

---

[36] Faulkner, *The Quest for Social Justice*, pp. 64–65.

CHAPTER 5

The Progressive Profile

A S A group, the reform mayors and governors, their prominent supporters, and the muckrakers were an interesting lot. Considering the positions they held, they were very young. Joseph W. Folk was only thirty-five when elected governor, Theodore Roosevelt forty, Charles Evans Hughes and Hiram Johnson forty-four, and Robert La Follette forty-five. The average age of the important progressive leaders who upset the Southern Pacific Railroad machine in California was a little over thirty-eight. The tale of a rather typical young reformer was that of Joseph Medill Patterson of the Chicago *Tribune* family. Patterson's grandfather founded the *Tribune,* his father was general manager of the paper, and his cousin was Robert McCormick, who controlled the paper for over thirty years. Patterson sharply reacted against the reigning conservatism by winning a seat in the Illinois legislature at the age of twenty-four on a platform advocating the municipal ownership of all city utilities in the state. Two years later he resigned from the Chicago Commission of Public Works to become a Socialist because, he announced, it was impossible to reform the city and the country under capitalism. In 1906 he published a diatribe against wealth in the *Independent* entitled "The Confessions of a Drone," and followed it two years later with a book of similar tone.[1] Obviously, this was a period, like the ones after the War of 1812 and in the 1850's, when energetic and incautious youth took

[1] George E. Mowry, *The California Progressives* (Berkeley and Los Angeles, 1952), p. 87; *The Public,* April 8, 1905; *Independent,* LXI (1906), 493–495; Joseph Medill Patterson, *Little Brother of the Rich* (Chicago, 1908).

command. And in each instance the departure of the elder statesmen portended great changes.

Some of these reformers, like Golden Rule Jones, Charles Evans Hughes, and Tom Johnson, were self-made men, although Hughes's father was a minister, and Johnson's, a Confederate colonel, had come from the upper stratum of Kentucky society. A surprising number of them came from very wealthy families, with names like du Pont, Crane, Spreckels, Dodge, Morgenthau, Pinchot, Perkins, McCormick, and Patterson. The quip was made that this was a "millionaire's reform movement." But the great majority of the reformers came from the "solid middle class," as it then was called with some pride. That their families had been of the economically secure is indicated by the fact that most of them had had a college education in a day when a degree stamped a person as coming from a special economic group. It is interesting to note that most of the women reformers and social workers had gone to college. Occupationally also the reformers came from a very narrow base in society. Of a sample of over four hundred a majority was lawyers, as might be expected of politicians, and nearly 20 per cent of them newspaper editors or publishers. The next largest group was from the independent manufacturers or merchants, with the rest scattered among varied occupations, including medicine, banking, and real estate. A statistical study of sixty of the wealthier reformers reveals that the largest single group of twenty-one was manufacturers or merchants, ten lawyers, six newspaper publishers, while nineteen more had inherited their wealth. Quite a few among the latter group had no definite occupation save that of preserving their family fortune and indulging in reform. Of the sixty only about half attended college, a figure much lower than that for the entire group of reformers. Of this number just 50 per cent came from three institutions, Harvard, Princeton, and Yale.[2]

If names mean anything, an overwhelming proportion of this reform group came from old American stock with British origins consistently indicated. Except for the women, who were predominantly Midwestern, the reformers' places of origin were scattered over the country roughly in proportion to population densities. Practically all of them by 1900, however, lived in northern cities, most of the Southerners having left their section during early manhood. Religious affiliations

[2] These statistics and the ones following came from a series of studies in the writer's seminar. The figures were rechecked and are in the author's possession.

were surprisingly difficult to get, and no really trustworthy national sample was obtained. The figures collected were not at all consonant with national church membership statistics. Representatives of the Quaker faith bulked large among the women reformers, as did members of the Jewish religion among the very wealthy. But for the group as a whole the religious descendants of Calvin and Knox predominated, with the Congregationalists, Unitarians, and Presbyterians in the vast majority. Thus it seems likely that the intellectual and religious influence of New England was again dominating the land.

Whether Democrats or Republicans, the overwhelming number of this group of twentieth-century reformers had been conservatives in the nineties. If Republican, they had almost to a man followed the way of Theodore Roosevelt, Robert La Follette, Lincoln Steffens, and William Allen White to support William McKinley. Most of the progressive Democrats had not been supporters of Bryan, but, like Woodrow Wilson, John Johnson, and Hoke Smith of Georgia, had either followed the Gold Democratic ticket or had remained silent during the election of 1896. Yet from four to six years later most of these men were ardent advocates of municipal gas and water socialism, and were opposed to their regular party machines to the extent of leading either nonpartisan movements in the municipalities or rebellious splinter groups in the states. Moreover, the new century found most of them, except on the currency issue, supporting many of the 1896 Populist and Bryanite demands. Before the Progressive years were finished they and their kind had not only secured the inception of a host of the Populists' reforms, but had contributed a few of their own.

Obviously, a good many questions arise about the motivation of this economically secure, well-educated, middle-class group. On the surface it looked as if the progressive movement was simply a continuation under different leadership of the Populist cause. According to William Allen White, Populism had "shaved its whiskers, washed its shirt, put on a derby, and moved up into the middle class. . . ." But White's remark scarcely probed beneath the surface. Populism arose from farmer distress in a period of acute depression. Its reforms were belly reforms. The movement was led by angry men and women not too far removed from the Grange hall. Except for the western silver men, they were incensed at the mounting figures of farm foreclosures and a withering countryside. To the contrary, progressivism arose in a period of relative prosperity. Its reforms were more the results of the heart and the head than of the stomach. Its leaders were largely recruited from the professional and business classes of the city. A good many were wealthy men; more were college graduates. As a group they were indignant at times, but scarcely ever angry. What caused them to act in the peculiar way they did? A part of the answer lies in the peculiar economic and social position in which this middle-class group found itself at about the turn of the century, a part in the intellectual and ethical climate of the age, a part in the significant cluster of prejudices and biases that marked the progressive mind.

"The world wants men, great, strong, harsh, brutal men—men with purpose who let nothing, nothing, nothing stand in their way," Frank Norris wrote in one of his novels. This worship of the strong man, so characteristic of the age, produced a cult of political leadership with ominous overtones for later years. Tempered at this time with the ethics of the social gospel, the cult produced an image far less frightening: an image of men dedicated to the social good, an image approximating the hope of Plato for his guardians. These strong good men, "the changemakers," Harold Frederic wrote, were the protectors of morality, the originators of progress. They were ambitious men and ruthless, but only ruthless in their zeal for human advancement. They were supremely alone, the causative individuals. Far from being disturbed when isolated, David Graham Phillips's hero Scarborough was only concerned when he was "propped up" by something other than his own will and intelligence. "I propose," he commented, "never to 'belong' to anything or anybody." [3]

In 1872 a future progressive, Henry Demarest Lloyd, confessed that he wanted power above all things, but "power unpoisoned by the presence of obligation." That worship of the unfettered individual, the strong pride of self, the strain of ambition, and the almost compulsive desire for power ran through progressive rhetoric like a theme in a symphony. From Frank Norris's strong-minded heroes to Richard Harding Davis's men of almost pure muscle these feelings were a badge of a restless, sensitive, and troubled class. They were never far below the surface in the character of Theodore Roosevelt. Robert La Follette knew them, and Woodrow Wilson had more than his share of them. While still a scholar and teacher, Wilson poured out his

[3] Frank Norris, *A Man's Woman* (New York, 1900), p. 71; David Graham Phillips (Indianapolis, 1904), *The Cost,* p. 17.

frustration with the contemplative life: "I have no patience with the tedious world of what is known as 'research,' " he wrote to a friend. "I should be complete if I could inspire a great movement of opinion. . . ." [4]

A few progressive leaders like William Jennings Bryan and Golden Rule Jones really thought of themselves as servants of the people,[5] and almost completely identified themselves with their constituents. But most progressives set themselves apart from the crowd. Mankind was basically good and capable of progress, but benign change scarcely issued from the masses. Rather it was only accomplished through the instrumentality of a few great and good men. Woodrow Wilson believed that efficient government could come only from "an educated elite," William Kent thought that progress never came from the bottom, and Roosevelt often spoke of government as the process of "giving justice from above." Occasionally, when the electorate disagreed with them, the progressives contented themselves with the thought that truth "was always in the minority" and a possession alone of the "few who see." In 1912 Walter Lippmann wrote that since men could do anything but govern themselves, they were constantly looking for some "benevolent guardian." To the progressive politician that guardian, of course, was patterned after his image of himself.[6]

"I am so sick of fraud and filth and lies," David Graham Phillips plaintively wrote to Senator Beveridge in 1902, "so tired of stern realities. I grasp at myths like a child." The myths Phillips reached for were the supposed realities of an older day, a day when the individual presumably had been able to make his way to the top by the strength of his abilities, and yet a day when there was enough opportunity left at the bottom so that mass poverty, slums, and crime were never evident enough to assault either the eye or the conscience of the successful. Things were different now even in the Valley of Democracy.

The Indiana town where Booth Tarkington's Magnificent Amber-

[4] Quoted in Daniel Aaron, *Men of Good Hope* (New York, 1951), p. 139; Richard Hofstadter, *The American Political Tradition and the Men Who Made It* (New York, 1948), p. 243.

[5] Frances G. Newlands, *Public Papers* (New York, 1932), p. 311.

[6] Theodore Roosevelt, "Who is a Progressive?" *The Outlook*, C (1912), 2; *The Public*, April 18, 1903; Walter Lippmann, *Drift and Mastery* (New York, 1914), p. 189.

sons had benevolently ruled from their big house on Amberson Boulevard had now become a city. In the process of growth spanning the lives of just one generation, the fortunes of the Ambersons had declined until the grandson George was working as a clerk in a factory. As all the young George Ambersons set about to reassert their rightful power and prestige, they were confronted both by enormous and monopolizing wealth and by the rising labor unions. The United States, it seemed, had become almost what Bellamy's historian in *Equality* called it, a world of organized degraded serfs run by a plundering and tightly knit plutocracy. The continual clash between the serfs and the plutocrats engulfed almost everyone. It was enough to disenchant the bystander whose loyalties were neither to the plunderers nor the plundered, but rather to an older America where such social extremes, it was felt, had not existed. Morosely, Professor Barett Wendell observed that America had sold her democratic, equalitarian birthright and was becoming "just another part of the world." Europe no longer learned at America's feet, Walter Weyl, the economist and publicist, wrote with an air of nostalgia, but rather in some respects had become "our teacher." Obviously something needed to be done. Should it be the "return or reversion . . . to certain elementary doctrines of common sense" and the simple rural institutions of the past, as some progressives hoped, or a going forward to something approaching Howells' utopia, which combined the new urban industrialism and a concern for human values in a new type of ethical socialism? [7]

A small reform-minded minority in 1900 was outspoken in defense of the large industrial and commercial city as the creator of the good life. Some of them saw the city as a place of refuge from an ugly countryside and from a hostile natural environment. Remembering his own bleak and lonely boyhood on an upstate New York farm, the novelist Harold Frederic condemned a daily communion with nature that starved the mind and dwarfed the soul. Theodore Dreiser bluntly described the natural processes as inimical to man as a species. Others felt the fascination of the city, a place of excitement and of opportunity. Lincoln Steffens recalled that he felt about the concrete canyons of New York as other youths felt about the wild West. For people

[7] Walter Weyl, *The New Democracy* (New York, 1912), p. 2; Colin P. Goodykoontz, *The Papers of Edward P. Costigan Relating to the Progressive Movement in Colorado, 1902–1917* (Boulder, Colo., 1941), p. 17.

like Jane Addams, Jacob Reis, and Hutchins Hapgood the city offered a place to work and an avenue to opportunity.

For the great majority of the new century's reformers, however, the city contained almost the sum of their dislikes. It was a "devilsburg of crime" sucking into its corrupt vortex the "young, genuine, strong and simple men from the farm." There, if successful, they became "financial wreckers" who made their money strangling legitimate enterprises and other human beings. If they were failures—that is, if they remained factory workers—they gradually became like the machine they tended, "huge, hard, brutal, strung with a crude blind strength, stupid, unreasoning." At the worst such unfortunates became the flotsam of the slums, making the saloon their church and the dive their home. The native American lost not only his morals in the city but also his talent for creative work and his sense of beauty. "Sometimes, I think, they'se poison in th' life in a big city," Mr. Dooley remarked, "the flowers won't grow there. . . ." If a man stayed in the city long enough, one of David Graham Phillips' characters remarked, he would almost inevitably lose those qualities that made him an American: one had to go West to see a "real American, a man or a woman who looks as if he or she would do something honest or valuable. . . ." [8]

With such intense antiurban feelings, it is small wonder that the United States began to romanticize its pioneer past and its agrarian background. Following the Spanish War historical novels fairly poured from the publishers. The public appetite for western stories had one of its periodic increases, and the virtues of the countryside were extolled in even the best literature. In one of Ellen Glasgow's first novels the country, "with its ecstatic insight into the sacred plan of things," is contrasted with the city's "tainted atmosphere." Almost repeating William Jennings Bryan in 1896, Miss Glasgow wrote that the country was the world as God had planned it, the city as man had made it. The cult of the frontier, first introduced into historical scholarship by Frederic Jackson Turner in 1890, and the new emphasis upon agrarian virtues were zealously reflected by the more sensitive poli-

[8] For varied expressions of this antiurbanism, see Irving Bacheller, *Eben Holden* (Boston, 1900), p. 336; Alice H. Rice, *Mrs. Wiggs of the Cabbage Patch* (New York, 1901), p. 29; Winston Churchill, *The Dwelling-Place of Light* (New York, 1917), p. 79; Finley Peter Dunne, *Mr. Dooley in Peace and War* (Boston, 1898), p. 125; D. G. Phillips, *Golden Fleece* (New York, 1903), pp. 57–58.

ticians. William Jennings Bryan, Theodore Roosevelt, Robert La Follette, and Woodrow Wilson all showed to varying degrees this national nostalgia, this reactionary impulse. Roosevelt in particular saw the great city as the creator of national weakness and possible disintegration, and the countryside as the nation's savior. It was the man on the farm, he wrote, who had consistently done the nation the "best service in governing himself in time of peace and also in fighting in time of war." Dangerous elements to the commonwealth lurked in every large city, but among the western farmers of the West "there was not room for an anarchist or a communist in the whole lot." What Professor Richard Hofstadter has called the agrarian myth, but which might better be called the agrarian bias, was one of the more important elements that went into the making of the progressive mind.[9]

A part of the progressive's romantic attraction to the countryside at this particular time can be explained by the alien character of the urban population. In 1903 the Commissioner of Immigration reported that the past year had witnessed the greatest influx of immigrants in the nation's history. But far from being pleased, the Commissioner was plainly worried. An increasing percentage of these newcomers, he pointed out, belonged to an "undesirable foreign element," the "indigestible" aliens from south Europe. The public was neither surprised at the figures of the report nor shocked by its adjectives. It had been made increasingly sensitive to the changing patterns of immigration by numerous periodical articles and newspaper items calling attention to the alien nature of the eastern seaboard cities. As the immigrant tide welled stronger each year, the nativist spirit that had been so obviously a part of the mental complex leading to the Spanish War increased in intensity. Throughout the decade editors, novelists, and politicians competed with each other in singing the praises of the "big-boned, blond, long-haired" Anglo-Saxon with the blood of the berserkers in his veins, and in denigrating Jack London's "dark pigmented things, the half castes, the mongrel bloods, and the dregs of long conquered races. . . ." In Frank Norris's novels the really despicable characters run all to a type. Braun, the diamond expert in *Vandover;* Zerkow, the junk dealer in *McTeague;* the flannel-shirted

---

[9] Ellen Glasgow, *The Descendant* (New York, 1897), p. 254; Roosevelt to George Otto Trevelyan, March 9, 1905, and to Kermit Roosevelt, January 1, 1907, Roosevelt MSS.; *The Public,* November 14, 1903.

Grossman in *The Pit;* and Behrman in *The Octopus* were all of the same religion and approximately from the same regions in Europe. One of the themes in Homer Lea's *The Vermillion Pencil* was the extranational loyalty of the Catholic bishop who intrigued endlessly for the Church and against the State. Although Chester Rowell frankly admitted that California needed "a class of servile labor," he was adamantly opposed to the admission of Orientals, who were dangerous to the state and to "the blood of the next generation." [10]

The progressives, of course, had no monopoly of this racism. Such conservatives as Elihu Root, Henry Cabot Lodge, and Chauncey Depew, and even radicals like Debs, shared their views to a degree. But for one reason or another neither conservative nor radical was as vocal or as specific in his racism as was the reformer. No more eloquent testimony to the power of racism over the progressive mind is evident than in the writings of the kindly, tolerant Middle Westerner William Allen White. In a book published in 1910 White explained nearly all of America's past greatness, including its will to reform, in terms of the nation's "race life" and its racial institutions, "the home and the folk moot." Nor would this genius, this "clean Aryan blood," White promised, be subjected to a debilitating admixture in the future despite the incoming hordes. "We are separated by two oceans from the inferior races and by an instinctive race revulsion to cross breeding that marks the American wherever he is found." [11] Such diverse reformers as Theodore Roosevelt, Albert J. Beveridge, Chester Rowell, Frank Parsons, Hoke Smith, Richard W. Gilder, and Ray Stannard Baker, with more or less emphasis, echoed White's sentiments.

The attitude of the progressive toward race, religion, and color, and his attending views of the great city, was to have profound effects on both internal and external policy. Its consequences were already obvious by 1905 in the South; it was to provoke an international storm in California, and it was to keep alive and possibly nourish a strain of bigotry that was to bear bitter fruit for the United States after the First World War and for the entire world in post-depression Germany. But this is far from saying that the progressive was a

[10] *Literary Digest,* XXVII (1903), 158; Jack London, *The Mutiny of the Elsinore* (New York, 1914), pp. 197–198. See also John Higham, *Strangers in the Land, Patterns of American Nativism, 1860–1925* (New Brunswick, N.J., 1955), pp. 131 ff.

[11] William Allen White, *The Old Order Changeth* (New York, 1910), pp. 128, 197, 253.

spiritual father of either the Ku-Klux Klan of the twenties or the Nazi of the thirties. He might well have been anti-immigrant, anti-Catholic, and anti-Jewish, and he might have thought of himself as one of the racial lords of creation, but he was also extremely responsive to the Christian ethic and to the democratic tradition. It was just not in his character to be ruthless toward a helpless minority, especially when the minority was one of his own. The progressive's response to the big-city slum was the settlement-house movement and housing, fire, and sanitary regulations, not the concentration camp. It was probably not entirely politics that prompted Theodore Roosevelt to invite the first Negro to lunch in the White House or to appoint people of Jewish or of Catholic faith to the Cabinet. Roosevelt thoroughly sympathized with California's Oriental problem. But he insisted that the state live up to the nation's international agreements and to the Constitution in its treatment of American Orientals. True, he was worried about Japan's reaction, but elsewhere in international politics he was not so careful of the sensibilities of other nations.

The progressive had reasons beyond racial ones for disliking the big city. For him the metropolis was the home of great wealth, and excessive wealth was as much an enemy to civilization as excessive poverty. A surprising number of very wealthy men supported the progressive cause, and their feelings toward their wealth produced a most interesting psychic state. Taken together, their statements sounded something like those in a confessional session of an early Puritan congregation. Explaining that he had acquired his wealth by "special privilege," Joseph Fels sought expiation by proposing "to spend the damnable money to wipe out the system by which I made it." Medill Patterson and William Kent produced similar variations on the same theme, and Tom Johnson repeatedly used coups from his own career of money-making to illustrate the social viciousness of the system he was contending against in Cleveland. Professor Hofstadter has ascribed this sense of guilt to the Protestant mind as it made the transit from rural and village life to the urban world where great extremes of economic circumstance were the common condition. It is also probable that as the Protestant upper middle class lost its mystical religion, it compensated by more fiercely adhering to Protestant ethic. It may be of note that the very wealthy who maintained their belief in a mystical religion were never as earnest in social well-doing as their erring brothers. If no one is as zealous as a convert, then perhaps no one conserves what is left of his ideological inheritance more than the man who has lost part of it.[12]

The less well-circumstanced progressive was just as critical of great wealth as his more fortunate colleague. Theodore Roosevelt, who had been left a comfortable but not a great fortune, disliked the American multimillionaire and felt that a society that created an ideal of him was in a very "rotten condition." Bryan once declared that great wealth and personal goodness was something of a paradox. And a reforming journalist from the midlands raised the question whether a man could honestly earn more than a few million dollars in one lifetime. By 1913 Walter Lippmann noted that great wealth, along with "the economic man of the theorists," was in public disrepute.[13]

The reasons for this antimaterialist crusade of the progressive are an interesting study in complex human motivation. Some of the sentiment undoubtedly came from personal frustration and personal envy. Perhaps to the point is Lincoln Steffens' experience with the stock market. In 1900 he wrote his father that the boom in stocks had made him considerable profits and that he was joining the Republican organization in his district. A year later, after some reverses, he insisted that character was the important desideratum for a young man and not wealth, which often meant the loss of character. The rising intensity of competition for the small merchants and industrialists also played a part in the attack on great wealth. Occasionally one found a reformer who had lost his business. But more often than not in the new century such men were moderately prosperous. Their resentment, if it arose from economic causes, came not from despair but from other feelings, from their sense of lessened power, perhaps, from their regard for their good name, from their sensitivity to the opinion of their fellows. Their relative status and power in society had been going down consistently since the rise of the economic moguls following the Civil War. The gap between them and the Morgans and the Rockefellers had been steadily increasing, and their hopes for attaining the top of the economic heap were progressively dimming. As one com-

[12] Joseph Fels, "Mr. Fels' Own Story," *World's Work*, XXIII (1912), 566; *San Francisco Bulletin*, January 14, 1910; Joseph M. Patterson, *A Little Brother of the Rich* (New York, 1906); Richard Hofstadter, *The Age of Reform* (New York, 1955), pp. 203–206.

[13] Roosevelt to Cecil Arthur Spring-Rice, March 19, 1904, Roosevelt MSS.; *The Public*, February 4, 1905; Lippmann, *Drift and Mastery*, pp. 28–30.

mentator noted, the ambitious middle classes in society had "suffered a reduction less in income than in outlook." [14]

This reduction in outlook that Walter Weyl perceived was even more acute for another class, the old American elite whose wealth, family, name, and social power had been secure long before the rise of the relatively new multimillionaires. The Adamses, the Lodges, the Roosevelts, the Bonapartes, and their local counterparts in the hinterlands were a self-consciously proud group. Although Theodore Roosevelt was well down academically in his 1880 Harvard class, he observed that "only one gentleman stands ahead of me." The turbulent and revolutionary waves of the new industrialism and finance had washed up on such polished shores some exceedingly rough gravel. The Rockefellers, the Hannas, and the Harrimans, to say nothing of the Jay Goulds, had not importuned for power in either industry or politics; they had seized it. As their names dominated the newspaper headlines and their ladies laid violent siege to formal society, old families and old ways seemed to have been forgotten. To the recent plutocrats, Henry Cabot Lodge acidly observed from the historic shores of Nahant, "the old American family" and society's long-tested "laws and customs" meant nothing. And far to the west in Cincinnati, it was reported, a social war had broken out between "the stick-ems" and "the stuck-ems." The first group was a "barbarous new class" of millionaires, just risen from the packing industry, who had assaulted an older class of "thousandaires," who had inherited their wealth made two generations before in the same industry.[15]

In the nineties New England's Brooks Adams had written a book about the fall of Rome. The volume contributed little to historical scholarship, but it revealed with remarkable clarity one facet of the American patrician mind at the end of the century. Fundamental to the work was a hypothesis that human history moved in a two-staged evolutionary scheme. The first stage was one reminiscent of the early days of the Republic, of an expanding progressive society dominated by a military, religious, and artistic mind with an emphasis upon

[14] Lincoln Steffens to Joseph Steffens, November 11, 1900, Steffens to William F. Neeley, January 14, 1901, in Ella Winter and Granville Hicks (eds.), *The Letters of Lincoln Steffens* (2 vols., New York, 1938), I, 1, 136, 143; Weyl, *The New Democracy*, p. 249.

[15] Theodore Roosevelt, quoted in Arthur Mann, *Yankee Reformers in the Urban Age* (Cambridge, 1954), p. 103; John A. Garraty, *Henry Cabot Lodge* (New York, 1953), p. 226; Weyl, *The New Democracy*, p. 242.

loyalty to the state and containing a superstitious strain, which led the adventurous spirit to the creative act. A second stage of decay, clearly identified with Adams's own day, was characterized by an acquisitive, greedy, and feminine personality which resulted in a static and defensive upper class and a sullen, idle mass below, whose loyalty to the state was as uncertain as its livelihood.[16]

In 1905 a young hunchbacked Californian, Homer Lea, decided that a local Los Angeles reform movement was too tame for his impetuous, adventurous spirit. Lea dropped politics to sail to the Orient, where he eventually became a general in the Chinese revolutionary armies and military adviser to Sun Yat-sen. During his short, incredible career Lea wrote two books, the first of which indicted commercialism as "the natural enemy" of national militancy. Pure industrialism Lea approved of as "incidental to national progress." But industrialism as a vehicle of "individual avarice" was a national cancer because it tended to destroy "the aspirations and world-wide career open to the nation." Herbert Croly, sometimes described as the theorist of the progressive movement, echoed Lea's sentiments a few years later. Modern democracy, unlike economic individualism, he argued, impelled men to forget their self-interest and to transfer their devotion away from acquisitiveness toward "a special object," the nation-state and its "historic mission." This distrust of materialism and emphasis upon romantic nationalism were reflected in a good many progressives, especially those with more collectivist inclinations. It was almost completely absent in the thinking of such Midwesterners as Robert La Follette and George W. Norris. But something of the same spirit had sent Theodore Roosevelt to the Cuban shores in 1898 and something akin to it perhaps was to lead Woodrow Wilson into his great crusade for international idealism in 1917.[17]

The idea that value was created only by the production of things or in rendering service, and that there was something dishonest in making money on other men's products, was an old American one. In part it stemmed from religious origins, in part from an unsophisticated system of agrarian economics. It was implicit in the thought of Henry George; it was basic to the progressive attitude toward great wealth. In apologizing to his constituents for his wealth, the progres-

[16] Brooks Adams, *The Law of Civilization and Decay* (Boston, 1895).
[17] Homer Lea, *The Valor of Ignorance* (New York, 1909), pp. 26–27; Croly, *The Promise of American Life*, p. 418.

sive Congressman William Kent admitted that he was not entitled to
the money he had made out of speculation. Andrew Carnegie, who
late in life became something of a progressive, agreed with the attitude. It was time, he felt, that the honest businessman, who made
money "legitimately," should refuse to recognize those of his fellows
who made money and rendered no value for it. Speculators, to the
progressive, were immoralists, men with fat hands sitting in ma-
hogany offices who had acquired the dishonest art of taking money
away from the earth's real producers. They believed, said the hero
of one of Winston Churchill's novels, that "the acquisition of wealth
was exempt from the practice of morality." [18]

In reviewing Professor Seligman's *The Economic Interpretation of
History,* the editors of *The Outlook* vehemently denied that progress
primarily depended upon materialist forces. The history of society,
they argued, was like the history of individuals, composed of a struggle
between the moral and the material forces, and "only through the
subordination of material ends to moral ends has humanity advanced."
There was something corrosive about great wealth, the progressive
believed, and in acquiring it a man usually had to sacrifice moral
values to overriding material ambitions. In the world of progressive
fiction this sloughing off of morality usually produced the hero's economic collapse and his return to morality. But in the less well-ordered
practical world the progressive was sure that the multimillionaire remained unredeemed, trapped by the very ethics he had used to acquire
his fortune. The world of the great rich was usually an idle one, a
sensuous one, and often a vicious one. The lives of its people, Theodore Roosevelt observed, often "vary from rotten frivolity to rotten
vice." The way to rescue them from their state of moral degradation, a
Midwest editor wrote, was "to put them to work." [19]

Since the progressive usually came from a comfortable part of
society and a general attack upon property was usually furthest from
his mind, this assault upon great wealth put him in a rather ambiguous position. The one way out of the paradox was to draw a line be-

---

[18] William Kent, quoted in the San Francisco *Bulletin,* June 14, 1910; *The
Public,* April 13, 1907. For literary expressions of the view, see Churchill, *The
Crisis* (New York, 1901), p. 345, and *Mr. Crewe's Career* (New York, 1908),
p. 392; Robert Grant, *Unleavened Bread* (New York, 1900), p. 392.

[19] *The Outlook,* LXXIII (1903), 216; Roosevelt to Cecil Arthur Spring-
Rice, July 30, 1901, Roosevelt MSS.; Girard (Kansas), *The Appeal to Reason,*
March 3, 1906.

tween good and bad wealth. For some the limit of private fortunes was the total that man could "justly acquire." For others the measurement was made in terms of service to society. Tom Johnson, for example, believed that the law could be so drawn that men would be able "to get" only the amount "they earned." Still others argued that there must be a point where additional money ceased to be salubrious for a man's character and became instead a positive evil force. Wayne MacVeagh, Garfield's Attorney General, suggested that all people could be divided into three classes: those who had more money than was good for them, those who had just enough, and those who had much less than was morally desirable. Just where the exact lines should be drawn, most progressives would not say. But the imputation that the state ought to redivide wealth on a morally desirable basis found a receptive audience. To George F. Baer's claim that coal prices should be the sum of "all the traffic will bear," the editors of *The Outlook* replied that property was private not by any natural right but by an "artificial arrangement made by the community." "If under those artificial arrangements," the editorial continued, "the community is made to suffer, the same power that made them will find a way to unmake them." Thus in the progressive mind the classical economic laws repeatedly described in the past as natural had become artificial arrangements to be rearranged at any time the community found it morally or socially desirable. Admittedly the formulations of new ethical standards for a division of national wealth were to be extremely difficult. But once the progressive had destroyed the popular sanction behind the "laws" of rent, prices, and wages, there was to be no complete turning back. A revolution in human thought had occurred. Man, it was hoped, would now become the master and not the creature of his economy. And the phrases punctuating the next fifty years of history—the "square deal," the New Deal, the Fair Deal, the just wage, the fair price—attested to his efforts to make the reality square with his ambitions.[20]

After revisiting the United States in 1905, James Bryce, the one-time ambassador from Great Britain, noted that of all the questions before the public the ones bearing on capital and labor were the most insistent and the most discussed. Certainly for many a progressive the

---

[20] *The Public,* September 23, 1905, and February 3, 1906; Wayne MacVeagh, "An Appeal to Our Millionaires," *North American Review,* June, 1906; *The Outlook,* LXXVI (1904), 240.

rise of the labor union was as frightening as the rise of trusts. True, he talked about them less because nationally they were obviously not as powerful as were the combines of capital. But emotionally he was, if anything, more opposed to this collectivism from below than he was to the collectivism above him in the economic ladder.[21]

"There is nothing ethical about the labor movement. It is coercion from start to finish. In every aspect it is a driver and not a leader. It is simply a war movement, and must be judged by the analogues of belligerence and not by industrial principles." This statement by a Democratic progressive illustrates the ire of the small and uncertain employer who was being challenged daily by a power he often could not match. In their lawlessness and in their violence, remarked another, unions were "a menace not only to the employer but to the entire community."[22] To the small employer and to many middle-class professionals unions were just another kind of monopoly created for the same reasons and having the same results as industrial monopoly. Unions, they charged, restricted production, narrowed the available labor market, and raised wages artificially in the same manner that trusts were restricting production, narrowing competition, and raising their own profits. "Every step in trade unionism has followed the steps that organized capital has laid down before it," Clarence Darrow observed in a speech before the Chicago Henry George Association. The ultimate direction of the two monopolies was as clear to the individual entrepreneur as it was to Darrow. Either trade unionism would break down, a Midwestern editor argued, or it would culminate in "a dangerously oppressive partnership" with the stronger industrial trusts. The end result was equally obvious to such men: a steady decrease in opportunity for the individual operating as an individual, an economy of statics, an end to the open society. The burden of the industrial evolution, Darrow said in concluding his speech, "falls upon the middle class."[23] And Howells' traveler from Altruria put the case even more graphically: "the struggle for life has changed from a free fight to an encounter of disciplined forces, and the free fighters that are left get ground to pieces between organized labor and organized capital."

On the whole, the average progressive preferred to talk in moral

21 James Bryce, "America Revisited," *The Outlook*, LXXIX (1905), 848.
22 *The Public*, June 13, 1903; *The Outlook*, LXVIII (1901), 683.
23 Chicago *Record Herald*, June 26, 1903; *The Public*, June 11, 1903.

rather than in economic terms. Orally, at least, he reacted more quickly to appeals based upon abstractions than the usual ones connected with day-to-day livelihood. Characteristically, he denounced more vehemently the philosophic overtones of unionism than its pragmatic economic gains. He was almost obsessed with the class consciousness implicit in unionism and flaunted by the more radical parties of the left. Almost to a man the progressive fervently agreed with one of Harold Frederic's heroes that "the abominable word 'class' could be wiped out of the English language as it is spoken in America." [24] Sociologists, economists, preachers, politicians, and publishers all joined the chorus. Economic classes, according to the sociologist Cooley, were characterized by a "complacent ignorance." Other progressives regarded them as "greedy," "arrogant," "insolent," "ruthless," "unsocial," and "tyrannical." Morality did not know them, declared one editor, because morality could only come from the individual who had not succumbed to "the economic temptation" manifested by the class. But the ultimate in the way of devastating criticism of the class spirit came from Ray Stannard Baker. Although sympathetic with the economic plight of the garment workers, Baker observed that in devotion to their class they were "almost more unionists than Americans."

" 'I am for labor,' or 'I am for capital,' substitutes something else for the immutable laws of righteousness," Theodore Roosevelt was quoted as saying in 1904. "The one and the other would let the class man in, and letting him in is the one thing that will most quickly eat out the heart of the Republic." Roosevelt, of course, was referring to class parties in politics. Most progressives agreed with Herbert Croly that a "profound antagonism" existed between the political system and a government controlled by a labor party. [25] In San Francisco in 1901, in Chicago in 1905, and in Los Angeles in 1911, when labor used or threatened direct political action, the progressive reacted as if touched by fire. Chicago was a "class-ridden" city, remarked one

---

[24] Harold Frederic, *The Lawton Girl* (New York, 1890), p. 444.

[25] Charles H. Cooley, *Human Nature and the Social Order* (New York, 1902), p. 72; Ray Stannard Baker, "The Rise of the Tailors," *McClure's*, XXIV (1904), 14. For other expressions of the same spirit, see Simon Patten, *The New Basis of Civilization* (New York, 1907), p. 84; John N. McCormick, *The Litany and the Life* (Milwaukee, 1904), p. 93; H. B. Brown, "Twentieth Century," *Forum* XIX (1895), 641; *The Public*, November 26, 1914; Jacob A. Riis, "Theodore Roosevelt, The Citizen," *The Outlook*, LXXVI (1904), 649; Croly, *Promise*, p. 129.

progressive journal, which would not redeem itself until the evil pretensions of both organized capital and labor had been suppressed. In Los Angeles, where a Socialist labor group came within a hair's breadth of controlling the city, the progressives combined with their old enemies, the corporation-dominated machine, to fight off the challenge, and as a result never again exerted the power they once had in the city. Apropos of that struggle punctuated by a near general strike, dynamite, and death, the leading California progressive theorist, Chester Rowell, expostulated that no class as a class was fit to rule a democracy; that progress came only from the activities of good citizens acting as individuals. Class prejudice and class pride excused bribery, mass selfishness, lawlessness, and disorder. This class spirit emanating from both business and labor was "destroying American liberty." When it became predominant, Rowell concluded, American institutions would be dead, for peaceful reform would no longer be possible, and "nothing but revolution" would remain.[26]

At various times and places the progressive politician invited the support of organized labor, but such co-operation was almost invariably a one-way street. Somewhat reminiscent of the early relations between the British Liberal and Labor parties, it worked only if the progressive rather than the labor politician was in the driver's seat. In Maine, for example, when labor attempted to lead a campaign for the initiative and referendum, it was defeated in part by progressives, who two years later led a successful campaign on the same issues.[27] In the progressive literature the terms "captain of industry" and "labor boss" were standard, while "labor statesman" was practically unknown. Roosevelt's inclination to try labor lawbreakers in a criminal court is well known; his administration's failure to indict criminally one corporation executive is eloquent of the limits of his prejudice. Progressive literature contained many proposals for permitting corporations to develop until they had achieved quasi-monopoly status, at which time federal regulation would be imposed. No such development was forecast for labor. Unions were grudgingly recognized as a necessary evil, but the monopolistic closed shop was an abomination not to be tolerated with or without government regulation. In the Chicago team-

[26] *The Public*, May 13, 1905, and June 17, 1905; Fresno *Republican*, November 20, 1911.

[27] J. William Black, "Maine's Experience with the Initiative and Referendum," *Annals of the American Academy of Political Science*, XLII, 164–165.

sters' strike of 1905 Mayor Dunne ordered the city police to be "absolutely impartial" toward both capital and labor. But he also insisted that the strikers not be allowed to block the teams of nonunion men or the delivery of nonunion-marked goods.[28]

A few progressives, of course, hailed the rise of labor unions as an advance in democracy. But the majority, while sincerely desirous of improving the plight of the individual workingman, was perhaps basically more hostile to the union than to corporate monopoly. If the progressive attention was mostly centered on the corporation during the decade, it was largely because the sheer social power of the corporation vastly overshadowed that of the rising but still relatively weak unions. When confronted with a bleak either-or situation, progressive loyalties significantly shifted up and not down the economic ladder.

Emotionally attached to the individual as a causative force and to an older America where he saw his group supreme, assaulted economically and socially from above and below, and yet eager for the wealth and the power that flowed from the new collectivism, the progressive was at once nostalgic, envious, fearful, and yet confident about the future. Fear and confidence together for a time inspired this middle-class group of supremely independent individuals with a class consciousness that perhaps exceeded that of any other group in the nation. This synthesis had been a long time developing. Back in the early 1890's Henry George had remarked that the two dangerous classes to the state were "the very rich" and "the very poor." Some years afterward a Populist paper referred to the "upper and lower scum" of society. At about the same time the acknowledged dean of American letters had inquired just where the great inventions, the good books, the beautiful pictures, and the just laws had come from in American society. Not from the "uppermost" or "lowermost" classes, Howells replied. They had come mostly from the middle-class man. In the first decade of the twentieth century the progressive never questioned where ability and righteousness resided. Nor was he uncertain of the sources of the nation's evils. "From above," one wrote, "come the problems of predatory wealth. . . . From below come the problems of poverty and pigheaded and brutish criminality." [29]

[28] *The Public*, April 15, 1905.
[29] Aaron, *Men of Good Hope*, pp. 84, 193; Jackson (Michigan) *Industrial News*, March 8, 1894; *California Weekly*, December 18, 1908.

As the progressive looked at the sharply differentiated America of 1900, he saw "pyramids of money in a desert of want." For William Allen White the world was full of "big crooks" and the "underprivileged." The polar conditions of society assaulted the progressive conscience and threatened progressive security. Supremely individualistic, the progressive could not impute class consciousness, or, as he would have phrased it, class selfishness, to himself. His talk was therefore full of moral self-judgments, of phrases like "the good men," "the better element," "the moral crowd." From the Old Source, he paraphrased, "Thou shalt not respect the person of the poor, nor honor the person of the great; in righteousness shalt thou judge thy neighbor." His self-image was that of a "kind-hearted man" dealing in justice. William Kent publicly stated that he could not believe in the class struggle because every great reform of the past had been wrought by men who were not "selfishly interested." "I believe," he concluded, "altruism is a bigger force in the world than selfishness." [30]

Since the progressive was not organized economically as was the capitalist and the laborer, he chose to fight his battles where he had the most power—in the political arena. And in large terms his political program was first that of the most basic urge of all nature, to preserve himself, and secondly to refashion the world after his own image. What the nation needed most, wrote a Midwestern clergyman, was an increase in the number of "large-hearted men" to counteract the class organization of both capital and labor. "Solidarity," Herbert Croly stated, "must be restored." The point of reconcentration around which the hoped-for solidarity was to take place, of course, was the middle class. It was to "absorb" all other classes, thought Henry Demarest Lloyd. It was to be both the sum and substance of the classless state of the future. [31]

The progressive mentality was a compound of many curious elements. It contained a reactionary as well as a reform impulse. It was imbued with a burning ethical strain which at times approached a missionary desire to create a heaven on earth. It had in it intense feelings of moral superiority over both elements of society above and

<hr/>

[30] William Allen White to Henry J. Allen, July 28, 1934, in Walter Johnson (ed.), *Selected Letters of William Allen White, 1899–1943* (New York, 1947), p. 348; San Francisco *Bulletin*, September 8, 1911.

[31] William J. McCaughan, *Love, Faith and Joy* (Chicago, 1904), p. 206; Croly, *Promise of American Life*, p. 139; Aaron, *Men of Good Hope*, p. 160.

below it economically. It emphasized individual dynamism and leadership. One part of it looked backward to an intensely democratic small America; another looked forward to a highly centralized nationalistic state. And both elements contained a rather ugly strain of racism.

The progressive mentality was generated in part from both a fear of the loss of group status and a confidence in man's ability to order the future. Had progressive militancy come in a more despondent intellectual and ethical climate and in a bleaker economic day, group fear might have won over group hope. Its more benign social ends might then have been transmuted into something more malignant. But in the warm and sunny atmosphere of 1900 the optimistic mood prevailed. For the year marking the beginning of the new century was a year of progressive success in the cities and the states. And within another year, by the ugly agent of an assassin's gun, Theodore Roosevelt had become President. With the shot in Buffalo, progressivism achieved a spokesman in the White House.

CHAPTER 6

Roosevelt: The First Year

WHILE attending the Pan-American Exposition at Buffalo, New York, William McKinley was shot on September 6, 1901, by an anarchist. For a week the President hovered between life and death, and then on September 14 the Vice-President, Theodore Roosevelt, became President of the United States. For the moment most of the nation's thoughts centered upon McKinley's assassination. But then as politicians and men of affairs turned their attention from the dead to the living, it was apparent that they approached the subject of Roosevelt's succession with a troubled mind. The new President's first official words that he would "continue absolutely unbroken" the policies of his predecessor were of some comfort. Despite this assurance, an obvious nagging doubt existed about what the new and untried chief executive would do. Conservative men both in Washington and New York openly hoped for the best. But privately they agreed with Mark Hanna that practically anything could happen now "that damn cowboy" was in the White House. Underneath they sensed that things had changed and the comfortable days under McKinley had ended. For one thing, the new President was not true to the type that had been almost standard for nearly a hundred years. Instead of being self-made and coming from the people of the West, Roosevelt was from an old eastern patrician family of moderate wealth. Not being self-educated, as Lincoln or Cleveland were, nor coming from a "log-cabin college," as many of the others had, he attended Groton, the nearest American equivalent to the aristocratic English public schools, and then had gone on to Harvard. Moreover, he had traveled extensively in Europe and was interested in such strange things as art, literature, and birds. Perhaps even more strange, the new President had written books not in any way related to politics. One had to go back almost a century to John Quincy Adams to find someone near his kind. And while this last of the cultivated fathers of the early Republic was still orally honored occasionally in Washington, most 1900 businessmen and politicians would have found Adams' company uncomfortable, if not downright embarrassing.

Many other things about Roosevelt troubled the professional politician and the practical men of affairs. He was only forty-three years old, certainly young to be in charge of grave national affairs. He had not climbed up the political ladder slowly as most of the seasoned veterans had, maturing on the way, but had shot up to the nation's highest office with amazing and impetuous speed. He was impulsive, often embarrassingly so in both word and deed. Had he not talked about lining up some of the nation's radicals back in the nineties and shooting them? And then, as if to balance matters somewhat, he had spoken about the need for chastising corporations and their executives. It was well known in Washington that during the time he was Assistant Secretary of the Navy he had given critical orders to the fleet without the knowledge or consent of his superior, Secretary Long. He had quit his position to go riding off to the Spanish War with a group of college graduates and cowboys. Despite his assurances that he would not rock the official boat, almost anything could be expected from such a man, and many feared the worst. Commenting upon his accession, the friends of the incumbent Secretary of State, John Hay, agreed that the national situation, on a most conservative estimate, was "big with possibilities of change." [1]

Had the disturbed men looked less at Roosevelt's personal deeds and more at his official political acts, they would have been somewhat comforted. For however bizarre Roosevelt's crowded young life was after leaving Harvard, punctuated with a near duel for his first wife's favor, and the ranching episode in the badlands, his official actions were far more discreet. True, he had captured public attention by his war on graft as a member of the New York state legislature, and he had sounded like a reformer again as a New York City police commissioner and as a member of the United States Civil Service

[1] Tyler Dennett, *John Hay: From Poetry to Politics* (New York, 1933), p. 343.

Commission. But aside from administrative reforms his talk had always promised more than his acts performed. On economic questions he was as sound as McKinley. During his three terms as a member of the New York legislature he voted against a teachers' pension act and labeled a law limiting the hours of streetcar conductors to twelve as "socialistic." Moreover, he was a party man. He had proved that in 1884 after the Blaine nomination. He had considered Blaine the worst possible choice. But instead of supporting Cleveland and his reform record, as Henry Cabot Lodge and so many young men of Roosevelt's social group had, he had remained silent for a time and then had vigorously supported the knight from Maine with the somewhat bedraggled plumes.

Roosevelt's record of party loyalty, as well as his war-born popularity, stood him in good stead in 1898 when Boss Tom Platt and Chauncey Depew of the New York Central Railroad were looking for a respectable Republican candidate for governor of New York to cover up a party record of graft and corruption. After Roosevelt had promised the "Easy Boss" that he would not disturb the state machine, he was duly nominated. The following campaign, carefully contrived to keep fresh the public's memory of the Rough Rider and his charge up San Juan Hill, was not just a formality. The party's record was bad and the opposition formidable. Roosevelt covered the entire state, occasionally speaking about the need for civil service reform and confessing once that in the past he had been a little too severe with labor. But most of his speeches were full of the sounds of marching men and references to the glories of far-off empire. His pounding fist, waving arms, and his staccato-like denunciation of the Democrats for opposing the war and being false to the nation's imperial destiny did the rest. He was elected by a small majority of less than 18,000 votes.

While he was governor, Roosevelt was able to secure from a reluctant legislature a measure taxing corporation franchises and, over the opposition of his own party, a good civil service law. He was also instrumental in the passage of measures outlawing prize fighting and protecting the state's wild game. His appointments to state offices were of a much higher caliber than those of previous governors, and in a successful fight to discharge the Superintendent of Insurance for corruption he established in the public mind that he was not Boss Platt's creature. True, he had lived up to his pledge that he would not try to alter the hold of the Republican machine on the state.

More often than not, behind the scenes, he found ways to support the machine and still live comfortably with his lively conscience. But in the two years he held office he was so troublesome to Platt that the "Easy Boss" took pains to see that he was nominated as McKinley's running mate in 1900. Roosevelt accepted the dubious honor in part because he was maneuvered into it and in part because he realized that his renomination and re-election as governor were not at all assured.[2]

Theodore Roosevelt was unhappy both as the vice-presidential candidate and then as the incumbent. His real desire was for the Presidency, and he acutely realized that historically the second office had usually been a way station on the road to oblivion. After the inauguration he wrote to Leonard Wood that he had "taken the veil" and revealed his plans for studying law on the side or perhaps becoming a scholar, although he indicated he would prefer "a more active life." But Roosevelt was not the man to permit present despondency to obscure future possibilities. Soon he was writing discreet letters to possible supporters in 1904 and was able to report to his friend Senator Henry Cabot Lodge that he was receiving back "what might be called conditional offers of friendship." [3] The shot at Buffalo made further discreet letters unnecessary. Roosevelt was President.

Few Presidents have evoked more contradictory emotions and conflicting judgments among his fellows than Theodore Roosevelt. The man simply inspired strong words. To an adoring William Allen White he was a paragon of moral and intellectual values. Henry Adams assigned to him "the singular primitive quality . . . that medieval theology assigned to God—he was pure act." Others spoke in angry tones of his "ambitious, imperious and arrogant" character, full of "brutal fury and coarse violence." During his lifetime an English journalist nominated him along with William II of Germany as the two world rivals for being the omniscient and omnipotent "masters of the obvious." Henry Demarest Lloyd called him an "atavism . . . with much the same appetite for the spread of ideas by explosion which Napoleon had." [4]

[2] Henry F. Pringle, *Theodore Roosevelt* (New York, 1931), p. 222.

[3] Roosevelt to Leonard Wood, March 27, 1901; Roosevelt to Henry Cabot Lodge, June 29, 1901, Roosevelt MSS.

[4] William Allen White, *Autobiography* (New York, 1946), p. 297; Henry Adams, *The Education of Henry Adams* (New York, 1918), p. 417; William G. Brown, *The New Politics and Other Papers* (Boston, 1914), p. 142; *Literary*

Theodore Roosevelt was so many things to so many men because he was also many things to himself. The trouble was that the emotional and the intellectual man refused to add up to any round and consistent sum. Many of his dominant impulses were matched by their opposites. But instead of creating an equilibrium within the man, these antipodal feelings sometimes impelled him to go hurtling off, first in one direction and then in another. Roosevelt loved life in all of its phases with a ferocious intensity, and he was not so constituted that he could enjoy any portion of it as a bystander. The quip about him at a wedding that he wanted to be the preacher, the bride, and the bridegroom revealed more possibly than the quipster understood. Roosevelt once remarked that man's mission in life could be summed up with the words "work, fight, and breed." A natural competitor and combatant, he was happiest when testing his powers against those of other men or of the universe. Killing a grizzly bear with a hunting knife, he wrote about a prospective hunting trip, "would be great sport." Yet despite this love for the strenuous life Roosevelt had yearnings for the quieter career of science and scholarship. His first ambition was to be a naturalist. He produced more than one creditable work of history, and at times thought of being a professor. His favorite American Presidents showed something of the cleavage within the man. On the one hand he admired the reflective, compromising, and patient Abraham Lincoln, on the other the impetuous, headstrong, and trigger-quick Andrew Jackson.[5]

Roosevelt was possessed both of a burning urge to excel and a deep social consciousness. He was quite aware that he belonged to a very special social group. And he easily and superciliously divided men, races, and nations between those few who counted in his eyes and the many who belonged to the "junk of history." After his graduation from Harvard, he resolved to belong "to the governing class and not to the governed." As a youth he had been trained to the manners of a gentleman, but in a contest he was the ancient man ready to clutch at any

Digest, **XXX** (1905), 174; Daniel Aaron, *Men of Good Hope* (New York, 1951), pp. 251–252.

[5] Roosevelt to Helen K. Johnson, January 10, 1899; Elting E. Morison (ed.), *The Letters of Theodore Roosevelt* (8 vols., Cambridge, 1951–54), II, 904; Roosevelt to Philip B. Stewart, June 10, 1901, Roosevelt MSS. (Not a few of the Roosevelt letters cited on subsequent pages may also be found in Morison. But I prefer to cite my own notes made years before the Morison volumes were published.)

convenient club. Elihu Root once observed that he was essentially a fighter who in a struggle was "completely dominated by a desire to destroy his adversary." At such times he could be cruelly unfair, especially to an outmatched opponent. The word "liar" and worse came readily to his lips. Despite his strong competitive urge, Roosevelt was a warmhearted, kindly man with a deep sense of obligation for the downtrodden and the unfortunate. For the Latin-American "banana republics" and the "inferior races" of south and central Europe he had an easy scorn. But once the people of these countries joined the immigrant groups in the eastern cities of the United States, he was genuinely concerned with their material and civil condition.

Intellectually and morally Roosevelt was as multifaceted as he was emotionally. He was a Darwinist who believed that man and the higher anthropoids had developed from creatures which originally possessed "only such mental attributes as a mollusk or crustacean of today." Identifying man with the entire living kingdom, he suggested to the naturalist John Burroughs that the higher animals thought and trained their young, endowing them with both "intellectual and moral traits." He was disinclined to talk about mystical religion, and repeatedly stated that his religion consisted of "good works." But this Jamesian doctrine scarcely suggested immortality to him. He went to church, not because he felt he needed it, but to "set an example." Loving life as he did, he felt that death was the "final defeat," "a going out into the darkness," "when all things are the same to everyman." Possibly because of his religious views Roosevelt shared the same intense moral sense of his fellow progressives. His Secretary of the Interior once told him that legally he could not bar the re-entry into the United States of an alien who had gone to Canada with a woman not his wife. Despite the law Roosevelt insisted that the man should not be allowed to re-enter the country. This strict sense of personal morality and his willingness to measure other people by it in a public fashion often put him into an untenable position. In his private life he was impeccably consistent with his code. The ends of politics and public life often constrained him, however, to forget about the means. Amos Pinchot once wrote him that he had to be either a great politician or a great moral teacher; he could not be both. But Roosevelt simply had to be both, and thus his public actions often belied his private but highly publicized ethics. So strong was this moral sense that he found it necessary to justify even his most realistic actions in the highest moral terms, and the results at times made him look like a first-class hypocrite.[6]

Although Roosevelt believed in human progress, he was not under the delusion that progress came automatically to everyone. Just as there were inferior races, there were also inferior individuals, and progress came only to those men and nations who proved themselves superior in the world's ceaseless competition. Change was inevitable, but benevolent change came only to those men and nations who exerted all of their intellect and energy to effect it. For the slothful, the ignorant, and the complacent, change meant only a decline and perhaps eventual disappearance from the earth. Roosevelt's evolutionary patterns of thought seem to link him with nineteenth-century determinism. In his youth, it is true, he appeared to be an ardent believer in social Darwinism. But as soon as he entered practical politics he found out, he later confessed, that "the economic man of most textbooks simply did not exist. . . ." Roosevelt had too much faith in individual determination and power to effect change to be a determinist of any variety. Had he not changed himself from a sickly and weak child to an athletic and pugnacious adult? He approved of Lord Acton's treatise on liberty because freedom gave the individual and the nation a chance "to remold themselves." Admitting that the direction of human affairs was often shaped by "great blind forces" over which no man or nation had sovereignty, he did not share to this extent the confident belief of the more naïve reformers of his day that man could entirely remake himself and his society. But he was convinced that there were margins between such forces, and rather large ones, where the person and the state could make significant changes. Taft once wrote him that he had never met a man "more strongly in favor of strong government" and more confident that government intervention in society's troubles would prove efficacious for the state and the individual alike. Roosevelt's 1912 program for sweeping reform, which looked forward to a future Roosevelt New Deal, was neither a bastard political creation of the moment nor entirely the ideological child of Herbert Croly. The New Nationalism

[6] Roosevelt to John Burroughs, May 29, 1905, Roosevelt MSS.; Oscar S. Straus, "Diary" (manuscript), pp. 108, 202; Roosevelt to Taft, August 28, 1908, Taft MSS.; Roosevelt to Oliver Wendell Holmes, December 5, 1904, Roosevelt to George Otto Trevelyan, March 9, 1905, Roosevelt MSS.

came from a natural wedlock between a specific political situation and some of Theodore Roosevelt's basic beliefs.[7]

"At times I feel an almost Greek horror of extremes," Roosevelt wrote to an English friend. To his more politically cautious allies, especially when he was doing something radical, Roosevelt often described himself as a conservative. At times he was inordinately critical of the "impractical reformers" who were pushing him past the point he wanted to go. Throughout his life he considered the farmers, the small businessmen, and the upper-class mechanics his "natural allies." When his morality did not interfere with desirable public policy, he was perhaps more interested in the processes of government rather than its ends, and as a gradualist he had a reverence for social order and historical continuity. For these and other reasons he has been called a conservative by some very able contemporary historians.[8]

Measured against the world-wide socialism of today perhaps Roosevelt was a conservative. What American statesman would not be? But in the context of American history and of his own times his conservatism, to say the least, was a most peculiar type. So was that of his political supporters, the farmers, the small businessman, and the upper-class mechanics. If occasionally he felt a horror of extremes, that did not stop him at other times from going a long way toward the polar positions when public ends and personal ambition were pushing him. If at times he criticized radicals, he was also vociferous in his criticism of conservatives. The truth is that Roosevelt, the politician, often called himself a conservative when he was going in a radical direction and a radical when he was headed the opposite way. Likewise, when writing to his more conservative friends, he was a conservative, and to his more progressive supporters he was a progressive. To the middle he was usually the practical man dealing in justice.

However traditional his code of personal morality, Roosevelt was far more libertarian in other areas. His preference for functionalism and simplicity in public architecture was far advanced for his day and in sharp contrast to the traditional taste for structures after the Greco-

[7] Roosevelt to Arthur J. Balfour, March 5, 1908, Roosevelt MSS.; William Howard Taft to Roosevelt, July 16, 1907, Taft MSS.; Roosevelt to F. J. Ranlett, June 24, 1907, Roosevelt to John St. L. Strachey, September 16, 1908, Roosevelt MSS.

[8] Roosevelt to John St. L. Strachey, March 8, 1901, Roosevelt MSS.; John Blum, *The Republican Roosevelt* (Boston, 1954), pp. 5–6, 55; Morison (ed.), *Roosevelt Letters,* VI, 910.

Roman mode. If a building was functional but lacked distinction, he wrote, it was at least "never ridiculous" as were some of the copies of old-world castles which dotted the American pioneer earth. When he was a young man he preferred the sensuous prettiness of Jean Baptiste Greuze to the more realistic efforts of other artists. But his review of the radical 1913 New York Armory show, while critical, was far more sympathetic than those of the more established critics of the day. He praised the paintings of Charles Sheeler and John Sloan, and commented in their defense that there existed "forces which cannot be ignored in modern life." [9]

Roosevelt had a deep reverence for traditional moral law. But he showed no such fondness for historic economic and political institutions. In the areas of economics and politics he was often a modifier and an innovator. In 1895, when his judgments were still relatively free from the expediency and the push of office, he remarked that in the last analysis every government was "a system of mixed individualism and collectivism." And then the real Roosevelt emerged. "Political expediency," he concluded, "draws the line." Years later one of the shrewdest minds of his generation appraised him, perhaps a bit unfairly. Justice Oliver Wendell Holmes described him as "a very likeable, a big figure, a rather ordinary intellect, with extraordinary gifts, a shrewd and I think pretty unscrupulous politician. . . ." [10]

Whether Roosevelt was a conservative or a radical depends largely upon one's yardstick, and how one measures the man. His intellect and emotions were often at odds. So were his deeds and words. In some things he was a traditionalist and in others a reformer. Most of his beliefs and prejudices reflected the beliefs and prejudices of the middle register of Americans, and in that sense he was a progressive. But most of all he was a skillful broker of the possible, a broker between the past and the present, between the interest groups pushing the government one way and the other, between his own conscience and his opportunities. An able, ambitious nondoctrinaire, a moralist with a deep

---

[9] Roosevelt to Corinne Roosevelt, June 16, 1881, Morison (ed.), *Roosevelt Letters*, I, 49; Albert B. Hart (ed.), *Theodore Roosevelt Cyclopedia* (New York, 1941), pp. 25–26; *The Works of Theodore Roosevelt* (20 vols., New York, 1926), XII, 149; J. Mellquist, "The Armory Show Thirty Years Later," *Magazine of Art*, XXXVI (1943), 300.

[10] Theodore Roosevelt, "The City in Modern Life," *Atlantic Monthly*, LXXV (1895), 371; Catherine D. Bowen, *Yankee From Olympus* (Boston, 1944), p. 371.

love for his country and an abiding sense of responsibility, he was of that *genus sui generis,* a democratic politician.

When Theodore Roosevelt became President, both houses of Congress were dominated by solid Republican majorities, and in each case these majorities were almost totally conservative.[11] Somewhere in the years prior to Roosevelt's accession, a subtle but decisive change had taken place in the Republican congressional leadership. For one thing, power had shifted radically from the House to the Senate since the days when Thomas B. Reed, William McKinley, and Samuel J. Randall had directed the proceedings of the lower house. Secondly, the character of Senate leadership itself had changed. Until the issue of imperialism had divided Republicans, the voices of Reed, and those of senators like George F. Hoar of Massachusetts and William E. Chandler of New Hampshire, had been weighty in party councils. Such men were conservatives, but their conservatism stemmed from an older, more individualistic day before the power of the new industrialism had left its imprint upon Congress. Adamant in their protection of property rights, the sympathies of Hoar and Chandler, however, lay more in the direction of the individual than with artificial personalities called corporations, and their devotion to human rights, possibly reflecting their Civil War background, was as ardent as it was sincere.

During McKinley's first administration a new controlling group arose in the Senate. By 1901 the power of Nelson W. Aldrich of Rhode Island, John C. Spooner of Wisconsin, Orville H. Platt of Connecticut, and William B. Allison of Iowa was practically unchallenged in Congress. Aldrich had started life as a delivery boy and had acquired a modest fortune as a wholesale grocer. But after going to the Senate in 1881 he rapidly became a multimillionaire through the manipulation of street railways and franchise politics. In 1901 his only daughter married John D. Rockefeller, Jr. Since the time he had opposed the interstate commerce bill in 1886, big business and finance had considered him their most trustworthy representative in the capital, and it is doubtful whether he ever wholly violated their trust. In his politics Aldrich was almost a pure Hamiltonian. That wealth should rule the country was almost axiomatic to him; otherwise all security would depart and the hope for progress end. Since manufacturing was the

[11] The Fifty-sixth Congress was made up of 197 Republicans and 151 Democrats in the House and 55 Republicans and 31 Democrats in the Senate.

greatest producer of wealth, its interests and welfare should be protected at all costs. To the general commonality Aldrich gave scant consideration. "Most people," he often scornfully observed, "don't know what they want." Aldrich rarely took the floor of the Senate in a debate; his work was usually done behind the scenes. An imposing figure of a man, with a first-rate if rather an uncultivated mind, and supported by his unseen but powerful constituency, Aldrich was the leader of the four and until 1910 deserved his title "boss of the Senate." [12]

John Coit Spooner came from early New England stock. As a brilliant young lawyer in Wisconsin he soon made his way to the top of the Wisconsin bar. As counsel and legislative representative for two of the largest railroads in the state he earned the title "chief of the corporation lobbyists" and the confidence of the regular Republican machine. Elected to the Senate in 1885, he became a brilliant debater and later served as floor leader and constitutional adviser of the dominant four. Platt of Connecticut was the faithful supporter of Republican Presidents, the elder statesman and adviser of the four, and Allison of Iowa became the group's fixer and conciliator. Just as conservative as the other three in his basic views, Allison was sensitive to the agrarian unrest in his home state and consequently was always a little more willing to bend before a storm of popular protest.[13]

Other men of considerable power sat in the Senate chamber and occasionally challenged the four on a particular measure. The cultured Matthew Quay, boss of Pennsylvania since 1885 and conscienceless political manipulator, defied Aldrich on a statehood bill and defeated a currency proposal close to the Rhode Islander's heart. Henry Cabot Lodge of Massachusetts sometimes went his own way in foreign politics confident in his superb intellectual powers and in the support of his lifelong personal friend in the White House. Eugene Hale of Maine, New York's "Easy Boss," Thomas C. Platt, and relative youngsters like Boies Penrose of Pennsylvania and Joseph Benson Foraker of Ohio all made their individual weight felt at times. And until 1904 there was Marcus A. Hanna, always an independent force in the party because of his power with the Republican organizations in the South and West and his influence with Wall Street.

[12] Nathaniel W. Stephenson, *Nelson W. Aldrich* (New York, 1930), pp. 41, 136.

[13] Walter Wellman, "Spooner of Wisconsin," *American Monthly Review of Reviews,* XXVI (1902), 167.

At the very start of the Roosevelt years the shrewd Matthew Quay sensed trouble ahead since there were two "Executive Mansions," one at the White House and the other presided over by Mark Hanna in the Senate. And at times there was even trouble between the four, as on the ship subsidy measure when Allison was listening to the West and not to the party directorate in the Senate. But except for such differences on peculiarly sectional measures and those arising from personal ambitions, an over-all harmony existed under the leadership of the four because of an almost complete identity of economic and social viewpoints. In the Ohio campaign of 1902 Hanna, with his eyes on the White House, asked his constituents to "stand pat and continue Republican prosperity." Scarcely a Republican senator would have found such remarks objectionable. Even the younger men from the West who would later split radically away from Republican orthodoxy were in 1901 contented with both the dogma and its four leading expositors. Allison's protégé, Jonathan P. Dolliver, wrote to a protesting constituent that as "a straight and strict Republican" he could only admire Aldrich. And the ambitious Albert J. Beveridge was jubilant that Aldrich and his associates had acknowledged his basic "conservatism" by placing him on the Senate steering committee. Meanwhile, in Wisconsin, Robert La Follette had just won an election with the support of Spooner.[14]

Until 1903 the House of Representatives was little more trouble to the four than the Senate. Since Thomas Brackett Reed's day the House under an able Speaker could be managed against anything but a major rebellion. David B. Henderson, the Speaker from 1901 to 1903, was not a strong man. But save for higher Civil War pensions, which he incessantly supported, he thoroughly agreed with the Senate cabal and was content to follow their lead. As often as not high policy was worked out by the four to be subsequently presented to Henderson. Only in the matters of tariff revision and corporation policy was the House, with its heavier representation from the farming country, apt to cause difficulties, and even these were more vocal than substantive. In December, 1902, a change occurred in the House when Henderson resigned as Speaker because, he announced, he was absolutely opposed to the rising sentiment in his home state of Iowa for tariff revision as

[14] Everett Walters, *Joseph Benson Foraker* (Columbus, Ohio, 1945), p. 200; Jonathan P. Dolliver to James D. Hall, October 9, 1901, Dolliver MSS.; Beveridge to J. C. Shaffer, February 7, 1902, Beveridge MSS.

a cure for the trust evil. "Not one revision" in any schedule, Henderson observed on parting, would affect the trusts an iota, while any revision would introduce a noxious "free trade poison" into the arteries of industry.[15]

Joseph G. Cannon, the newly elected Speaker, was a man of far different kidney from Henderson. A rough and able politician, Uncle Joe, as he was called, assiduously cultivated the arts of potation, profanity, and poker. But under his free and easy backwoods manner was a determination to regain for the House some of the prestige it had lost under Henderson. Ruthlessly using the Speaker's great powers, he rapidly organized the House after his own preferences, and until the 1910 rebellion he ruled the chamber as few Speakers have. Soon the senatorial four were by necessity seriously listening to his advice. Aldrich, Spooner, Allison, and Platt, Roosevelt wrote, had been at the White House the previous night to discuss financial legislation. But, the President was careful to state, no decisions were made since they desired to find out Cannon's views before even formulating their own. A short time later Root noted that any bill before the House was likely to pass in the form Cannon approved, and pretty sure to be defeated if he disapproved.[16]

If the senatorial four had to be more diplomatic with the sensibilities of the Speaker and the House after Cannon's rise, their general philosophic outlook was safer in the hands of Cannon than it had been in Henderson's. When first rounding up votes to support his candidacy for Speaker, Cannon had written that his politics could be summed up in the phrase "stand by the status." In assigning new members to House committees in 1902 he frankly admitted that his intention was to choose "judicially minded men" who would lessen the danger of "class and local legislation." It was not long before the quip was being passed around Washington that the new Speaker was so conservative that had he been in on the Creation he would have voted against the Lord for chaos.[17]

The Democratic congressional delegation was quite unable to offer any effective opposition to the reigning Republican conservatives. It was not only a badly outnumbered minority, but worse, a minority

[15] *Literary Digest,* XXV (1902), 367.

[16] Roosevelt to Cannon, August 13, 1903, Roosevelt MSS.; Root to John L. Cadwallader, January 22, 1904, Root MSS.

[17] Joseph G. Cannon to William H. Moody, November 11, 1902, Moody MSS.; *The Outlook,* LXXV (1903), 865.

without cohesion. The pugnacious and erratic Joseph W. Bailey of Texas, minority leader of the House under McKinley and elected to the Senate in 1902, seemed to be the congressional heir apparent to the Bryan tradition of agricultural reform. But Bryan had been soundly beaten for the Presidency in 1900 and his radical western congressional following had dwindled. The young and able Francis J. Newlands entered the Senate from Nevada in 1903, but after the 1900 elections the western congressional delegation was largely Republican.

In the South the forces of poor-white radicalism were gathering, but with the exception of Senator Benjamin Tillman of South Carolina this small farmer group was still without important leaders in Washington. The southern congressional delegation in 1901 was on the whole conservative. But here again the South could not unite even in its conservatism. For one wing of southern conservatism was represented by the new minority leader of the House, John Sharp Williams of Mississippi. Brilliant, unconventional, and amiable, Williams was the essence of cotton-planting traditionalism, an ardent advocate of states' rights, and one of the last of the Jeffersonians. Far removed from Williams in their thinking were such Democrats as Senator Arthur P. Gorman of Maryland, considered a serious candidate for the presidential nomination in 1904, and Senator John Lowndes McLaurin of South Carolina. After the tradition of Sam Randall, Gorman was a high-tariff, industrially minded Democrat. McLaurin was even closer to the Republicans. Speaking in 1901, he denounced Bryanism as "the first step toward revolution," and defended the expansionist, protectionist, and subsidy policies of the McKinley administration.[18]

In the North and East the party was even more of an ideological patchwork quilt. At one corner was the wealthy August Belmont and his conservative coterie dedicated to defeating Bryan in 1904. At the other was the rapidly rising journalist William Randolph Hearst, avidly hungry for any important office and ready to go far to the left in impassioned radical appeals to gain his ambition. In the center stood Tammany, its power based upon an old Irish minority and upon recent immigration, possessed of the only sizable northern Democratic congressional delegations and mostly indifferent to ideology provided offices and spoils could be won. From such a party little responsible and consistent opposition could be expected. Consequently in 1901 conservative Republicanism, save for an internal schism, had little to

[18] *The Outlook,* LXVIII (1901), 68.

fear. And so imposing was the alliance of power constructed by Aldrich, Spooner, Platt, Allison, and Cannon that such a development, at least in Congress, seemed improbable. Just one possible source of danger was apparent to the conservative coterie in 1901 and 1902: the young and inexperienced man in the White House already had a reputation for doing the unusual. And Platt, the man who of the reigning four probably knew him best, observed to Aldrich that the President and his ideas had a tendency to wander. He advised Aldrich to keep in close touch with Roosevelt, else time might find him "working against what we think is right." [19] Noting the comforting thought that Roosevelt had promised not to alter McKinley's economic policies, conservative newspapers nevertheless expected changes in the general Washington climate. They were not to be disappointed. As the Brooklyn *Eagle* pointed out, "the velocity of Administration" had suddenly been stepped up. The supervision of lower offices became more taut; more politicians came to the White House in the mornings and early afternoons; groups of strange people, including poets, labor leaders, naturalists, and prize fighters came to lunch; and by midafternoon Washington high officialdom was quite often seen strenuously exercising in the company of the new President. "Under the new administration," Secretary of War Root wrote to Senator Lodge, "horseback riding is the order of the afternoon." It was not long until many an ambitious statesman was really perspiring from exercise for the first time in his adult life. Senator Beveridge did not like riding and did not want to buy a horse, he confided to a friend, but if one wished to gain the ear of power there was nothing else to do.[20]

If Roosevelt made rapid changes in the social life of the White House, he was exceedingly cautious in these early days about his politics. Except for Lyman J. Gage, Secretary of the Treasury, who resigned for personal reasons, and Postmaster General Charles E. Smith, whose resignation the President requested, McKinley's Cabinet was kept intact. Both replacements for these officers, Governor Leslie B. Shaw of Iowa and Henry C. Payne of Wisconsin, moreover, were standpatters. Roosevelt's most trusted Cabinet advisers during his first administration were Secretary of War Elihu Root and the Attorney

[19] Platt to Aldrich, August 17, 1903, Platt MSS.
[20] *Literary Digest*, XXIII (1901), 333; Root to Lodge, November 5, 1901, Root MSS.; Beveridge to George W. Perkins, November 11, 1901, Beveridge MSS.

General, Philander C. Knox. Both men had been confidants of Mc-Kinley and both were thoroughly sympathetic to the conservative point of view. When Root resigned in 1904 Roosevelt called him "the ablest, most generous, and most disinterested friend and adviser that any President could hope to have. . . ." [21]

The President's first message to Congress in December, 1901, was also hailed by contemporaries as a safe document. It contained no "fireworks," reported the New York *Evening Post*, and might have come from "a man of sixty, trained in conservative habits." It was a long message of over thirty thousand words, and it roundly denounced assassins and anarchists, called for both educational and economic tests for would-be immigrants, described the growth of great corporations as a "natural" phenomenon, stressed the need for expanding foreign markets, supported the existing tariff schedules, and asked for a sub-sidized merchant marine. But on careful reading Roosevelt's first message does not appear as conservative as either his contemporaries thought or as subsequent historians have judged. [22] In the first paragraph addressed to the trust question Roosevelt stated without equivocation that the old laws and customs regulating the accumulation and distribution of wealth were "no longer sufficient." Subsequently he spoke of the "real and grave evils" of large industry, particularly of overcapitalization and its "baleful consequences." [23] The President called for "practical efforts" to correct these evils, and specifically for national supervision of corporations and the amendment of the Inter-state Commerce Law to ensure equality of railroad rates and facilities to all shippers. He also asked for reciprocity tariff treaties and a large national program of conservation and reclamation. Although Roosevelt was careful in every instance to surround and qualify these suggestions with much cautious talk, the central fact is that many of the seeds of his future legislative program can be found in this first message to Congress.

The equivocal yes-and-no qualities of Roosevelt's first effort with Congress reflected his ambiguous political position as well as his simple lack of understanding of many of the basic issues facing the country.

[21] Roosevelt to Theodore Roosevelt, Jr., February 6, 1904, Roosevelt MSS.
[22] New York *Evening Post*, December 3, 1901; James D. Richardson, *A Compilation of the Messages and Papers of the Presidents* (Washington, 1902), Supplement 1, pp. 313–354.
[23] Henry F. Pringle states that after a talk with Hanna, Roosevelt cut the references to overcapitalization from his message. *Roosevelt*, pp. 245–246.

But his equivocation also arose from his realization that unless he co-operated with the forces led by Aldrich, little if any legislation could be won from an overwhelmingly conservative Congress. An outright struggle with the Senate leadership also would have imperiled his nomination and re-election in 1904, a consideration that was never far from his mind during the next three years. Before writing his first message, he cordially invited Aldrich, Spooner, Platt, and Allison to go over the chief issues with him. Hanna saw the message before it was put into final form, as did Root and Knox. This consultation set a pattern that lasted for the next three years and more. When Joseph Cannon became a power as Speaker of the House, his advice was also carefully solicited and reflected in Roosevelt's legislative policy.[24]

In the spring of 1903 William Howard Taft wrote the President bitterly criticizing Aldrich, a criticism which by implication included Roosevelt for his co-operation with the Rhode Islander. Characteristically Roosevelt replied with a defense of Aldrich and himself. Although he had had a "stand up fight" with Aldrich over trust policy, he had come to have great respect for him and his conservative associates, including Cannon. These men were "the most powerful factors in Congress" and were far more satisfactory to work with than the "radical reformers." The query might be raised, what radical reformers? The fact was that they did not exist in Congress in any significant number. Roosevelt was simply working with what was at hand, and after the fact defending his actions. Whatever his inclinations toward reform, the President was thoroughly aware that the support of the congressional party was a necessity for any legislation he might care to pass and probably for his nomination and election in 1904. An adept and ambitious politician, he was prepared to pay the price for such support.[25]

[24] Roosevelt to Aldrich, September 30, 1901; Roosevelt to Spooner, September 30, 1901, Roosevelt MSS.

[25] Taft to Roosevelt, February 11, 1903; Roosevelt to Taft, March 19, 1903, Roosevelt MSS.

CHAPTER 7

The Square Deal

THEODORE ROOSEVELT'S legislative requests from the Fifty-seventh and Fifty-eighth Congresses were extremely modest. In his annual message of December, 1901, he had featured the trust issue by giving it the first place in his list of recommendations. Specifically, he had asked for the creation of a new Department of Commerce with a Bureau of Corporations to collect and publicize information about interstate industry, an act to expedite antitrust prosecutions, and a railroad bill barring the giving of rebates on freight shipments. Under his so-called commercial policy he recommended the passage of the Aldrich proposal for the expansion and contraction of the currency, a reciprocity tariff measure with Cuba and the Philippines, a ship subsidy bill, construction of the Panama Canal, and major additions to the Navy. A group of miscellaneous measures included Elihu Root's plans for reorganizing the Army, new immigration restrictions, and the creation of a permanent census bureau.

The so-called Expedition Act, which added two assistant attorney generals to the government payroll and expedited the trying of suits under the Sherman Law, met little opposition. The Elkins Act of 1903, forbidding railroads from giving rebates to large industrial companies, and thus providing them with a substantial advantage over their competitors, won the support of both conservatives and liberals. Subsequently the charge was made by Democratic Senator Augustus O. Bacon of Georgia that the Elkins Act was first drawn up by an attorney for the Pennsylvania Railroad. In denying the charge, Senator Foraker answered that Bacon was confused, since he had reference only to the first Elkins bill, introduced in an earlier session. Since both proposals were substantially the same, it is clear that by 1901 the railroads no longer wanted the privilege of granting rebates to large shippers.[1]

The Department of Commerce bill, however, was a horse of another hue. A reluctant Aldrich had agreed to support the proposal for a *quid pro quo,* but a good portion of the business world and many members of Congress were openly or secretly opposed to the measure. The conservatives did not object to the creation of a new governmental department to aid and assist commerce. But the bill as amended in early January of 1903 included a provision for a Bureau of Corporations to collect and supply the President with information about interstate industrial undertakings and with the same power to subpoena and compel attendance and testimony as possessed by the Interstate Commerce Commission. So strong was the opposition being led by Senator Matthew Quay and the Pennsylvania House delegation that Senator Beveridge doubted at times whether it would even come to a vote. When the chances of the bill seemed darkest, the President released to the press a threat that unless the bill was passed he would call a special session of Congress. Then he told the newsmen that John D. Rockefeller was leading the secret opposition and had been deluging Congress with telegrams. The President purported to give even the text of the telegrams. On both the origin and the wording of the telegrams Roosevelt was wrong; obviously he had not seen copies, for the sender was John D. Archbold of the Standard Oil Company and not Rockefeller. But in the spirit of the story, if not in its details, he had been substantially correct. In the ensuing uproar from the country both the House and the Senate quickly passed the measure with the corporation bureau included.[2]

The President also exerted himself for the Newlands reclamation measure and Root's Army reorganization bills. During the summer of 1901 thirty senators and representatives of the seventeen western states, meeting at Cheyenne, Wyoming, had approved a plan drawn up by Senator Francis G. Newlands of Nevada whereby a proportion of the receipts from public-land sales in these states would be utilized for the purpose of constructing dams and reclamation works. Leading the op-

[1] *Congressional Record,* 57th Congress, 2nd Session, pt. 3, pp. 2778 ff.; Memorandum, February 6, 1903, Foraker MSS.

[2] Albert J. Beveridge to George W. Perkins, January 8, 1903, Beveridge MSS.; Roosevelt to Lawrence F. Abbott, February 3, 1903, Roosevelt MSS. See also Henry F. Pringle, *Theodore Roosevelt, A Biography* (New York, 1931), p. 341; and L. White Busbey, *Uncle Joe Cannon* (New York, 1927), p. 417.

position to the measure was Joseph G. Cannon, who, speaking for eastern and middle-western agriculture, charged that the effect of the bill would increase the amount of agricultural goods at a time when they were already in oversupply. The President refuted the charges, and a combination of western Republican and Democratic votes passed the bill with Roosevelt's substantial help.[3]

Elihu Root, Roosevelt's most trusted adviser, had been appointed to the Cabinet by McKinley. As Secretary of War, Root brought order out of the military chaos of the Spanish-American War. Afterward he devoted much of his time to improving the antiquated military organization, and fully deserves the title of father of the modern American Army. Shortly after Roosevelt took office, Root had instituted the Army War College, and in 1902 he presented to Congress a comprehensive plan for modernizing the Army's creaking administrative machinery. Among his most important reforms were the proposal to create a general staff after European precedents, the incorporation of the state militia into the regular Army, and the institution of physical and other tests required for the promotion of officers. Root's proposals met immediate and wide opposition. His chief opponent was Nelson A. Miles, Commanding General of the Army, who had already crossed swords with Root and Roosevelt in the Schley-Sampson naval affair and in the Philippine Army scandals. The latter resulted in the court-martialing of General Jacob H. Smith for the use of brutal methods in putting down the insurrection. Supporters of a separate state militia joined Miles in denunciation of the scheme as imported "Prussian militarism." After Miles had been gauchely treated by the administration, the G.A.R. came to his support, an act which Roosevelt at least interpreted as a sure indication that Miles was campaigning for the coming Democratic presidential nomination. For over a year, despite all the pressure Root and Roosevelt could bring, a reluctant Congress refused to move. Then after Miles' retirement in the fall of 1902, and after Root had dropped his plan for the incorporation of the state militia, the Army reform bill was passed. Subsequently, a National Guard Act was approved that provided some, but not by any means all, of the co-ordination with the regular Army that the Secretary of War desired.[4]

[3] Roosevelt to Cannon, June 13, 1902, Roosevelt MSS.; Francis G. Newlands, *Public Papers* (2 vols., Boston, 1932), pp. 67–69.
[4] Root to J. B. Bishop, April 10, 1902; Root to C. W. Bowen, May 21, 1902;

In his first annual message to Congress, Roosevelt had also called for a merchant marine subsidy program and the passage of a currency bill sponsored by Senator Aldrich. The original subsidy measure had been introduced by Mark Hanna before the death of McKinley. Defeated in its original form, it was modified sharply and reintroduced again in December, 1901. Even so, this more moderate act, providing for the government payment of only $9 million a year, met the sharpest opposition of the South and the West. Both Allison of Iowa and Spooner of Wisconsin voted against the measure in the Senate, and a substantial negative vote in the House finally killed it. The Aldrich bill to permit a moderate contraction and expansion of the currency met a similar fate. With Roosevelt's concurrence Aldrich had opposed an omnibus statehood measure sponsored by Senator Matthew Quay of Pennsylvania which would have permitted the admission of Oklahoma, Arizona, and New Mexico. The admission of these three presumed Democratic states, Roosevelt felt, would "complicate" the 1904 election. But for some unknown reason, Quay was highly miffed at Aldrich's opposition to his statehood proposal and in return effectively blocked the currency reform, even though Roosevelt had indicated repeatedly that he desired some "remedial," but "not too far-reaching," legislation. Significantly, the President was not too downcast at the defeat of either the subsidy or the currency measure. Never once in the history of either bill had he exerted himself as he had in the Bureau of Corporations fight. In his annual message of 1903 he passed by both proposals with a few meaningless phrases and eventually concluded that no real need existed for either bill.[5]

The President was also lukewarm on a more critical issue that threatened to disrupt the Republican party. Ever since the Spanish War certain groups in the party had demanded tariff revision. During the summer of 1900 and again a year later the National Association of Manufacturers asked for the negotiation of reciprocity trade agreements as an outlet for the nation's "excess production." In his last address McKinley had favored the mutual lowering of rates with foreign countries as a way to obtain "more markets" abroad. A year later Senator Beveridge told the Indiana State Republican Convention that

Root to Grenville Dodge, January 22, 1903, Root MSS.; Roosevelt to Oswald Garrison Villard, March 22, 1902, Roosevelt MSS.

[5] Roosevelt to James Stillman, August 22, 1903; Roosevelt to Cannon, August 13, 1903, Roosevelt MSS. Beveridge to Roosevelt, September 5, 1902; Beveridge to J. C. Schaffer, March 19, 1902, Beveridge MSS.

the reciprocal lowering of tariff rates was a necessity: "The great problem of the hour is to find markets where the American people can sell their surplus. Daily the surplus grows . . . and failure to sell it means ruin." The problem was made more acute in 1902 because of foreign reaction to the Dingley Tariff rates. In reply to American advances, Russia had raised its rates on American machinery, Switzerland was considering doubling her rates against all American goods, and the year's statistics showed that, though the internal trade was good, exports were falling.[6]

Meanwhile the corn and wheat belt was demanding tariff revision for totally different ends. Partly for health reasons both Germany and Hungary had recently restricted entry of American plants, fruits, and meats, an action helping to send farm prices down in the United States at a time when the prices of manufactured goods were climbing. Many farmers ascribed this unequal movement of prices to the monopolistic practices of the trusts and hoped that a general tariff reduction would provide more markets abroad for foodstuffs and at the same time reduce the American prices on manufactured goods. In 1901 Governor Albert B. Cummins proposed his "Iowa Idea," the burden of which was simple: to cure the monopoly problem the governor suggested that all tariff protection be abolished on all trust-made products. In considerable part the "Iowa Idea" accounted for Cummins' popularity in Iowa, and the proposal caught on in neighboring states with amazing speed. In the House, Representative Babcock of Wisconsin offered a bill putting on the free list all iron and steel goods made by a trust in the United States. In 1902 the Idaho State Republican Convention endorsed the idea, as did party representatives in Minnesota and Nebraska. By the fall of 1903 the stanchly Republican St. Paul *Pioneer Press* stated categorically that the only way to keep the Northwest Republican was through a radical and thorough revision of the tariff.[7]

But the tariff problem, as both the President and Congress were painfully aware, was exceedingly complicated. The great bulk of manufacturers still sold almost exclusively to the domestic market. For such people high tariff rates were a part of the Republican ark in covenant. Moreover, western demands for radical reduction as an instrument

6 "Tariff Reciprocity," *World's Work*, II (1901), 1248; *The Outlook*, LXXI (1902), 2; *Literary Digest*, XXIV (1902), 420.

7 Albert B. Cummins to James D. Hall, April 4, 1901, Cummins MSS.; *The Outlook*, LXXII (1902), 99, 428, 452; St. Paul *Pioneer Press*, October 14, 1903.

against the trusts so frightened the East that some of the more internationally minded producers tended to rally around the existing custom rates. Among others, the American Iron and Steel Institute, the Boston Home Market Club, and the Manufacturers Club of Philadelphia excitedly petitioned Congress to ignore the pleas for reduction and preserve the Dingley rates even for the newly acquired empire and Cuba.[8]

After a careful count of noses, the conservative leaders of Congress, with the exception of Iowa's Senator Allison, agreed that any general reduction of rates might be politically disastrous. If only a very limited reduction could be achieved, "a bill that could be passed before breakfast," Cannon was willing to "go along." When the subject was once opened up, however, the future Speaker doubted that limited action would be possible. Any general revision, whether up or down, Cannon believed, would result in the party's losing the next election. Aldrich agreed and advised Roosevelt to omit all references to the tariff in his first message. After some pondering, the President replied that except for mentioning McKinley's reciprocity treaties he would follow Aldrich's advice exactly.[9]

Roosevelt was in a quandary. As a young man he had been a low-tariff disciple, and as Vice-President he had written Taft that he was inclined theoretically to support reciprocity, but he recognized that any attempt to change the existing rates might open the door to "all sorts of changes." He was to continue that yes-and-no attitude throughout his two administrations. In part his position came from political caution, in part from his own indecision on the question. He was frankly not sure what rates were best for the country as a whole. The setting of exact schedules, he wrote, was after all a matter of "expediency and not of morality." There was nothing intrinsically right or wrong with either 40 or 60 per cent rates. The danger existed that a radical revision might "bring on a panic." And he was aware that widespread feeling existed both for and against reduction; any move might "split the party." That settled that. Whenever Roosevelt could argue himself into believing that morality was not involved in a question, the right thing to do was usually the expedient thing; and in the general tariff issue, by far the most expedient thing was to do nothing.[10]

[8] *World's Work,* XXIV (1902), 1248–1249.
[9] Cannon to William H. Moody, November 11, 1902, Moody MSS.; Busby, *Cannon,* p. 211; Roosevelt to Aldrich, November 16, 1901, Roosevelt MSS.
[10] Roosevelt to Taft, July 15, 1901; to Nicholas M. Butler, August 12, 1902; to Joseph B. Bishop, April 17, 1903, Roosevelt MSS.

Although Roosevelt was chary about a general tariff revision, he was insistent in his demands for a reduction of duties on Cuban and Philippine goods. The economy of Cuba depended upon sugar, and the health of the sugar industry largely depended upon its American market. In inducing the Cuban Constitutional Convention to accept the Platt Amendment, both McKinley and the American commander in Cuba, General Leonard Wood, promised to support special tariff rates for Cuban sugar. Roosevelt not only felt morally obligated to carry out the promise; he was also convinced that a rate reduction was necessary to the stability of Cuba and to continued good relations between the two countries. National interest, he argued, also made it necessary for the United States to give the same preference to Philippine goods. Philippine reciprocity, he remarked to Lodge, was "only less important than the currency bill." [11]

The great difficulty in securing lower rates for Cuba and the Philippines came not from the friends of high protection in the East but from the advocates of general tariff revision in the South and the West. Here the tobacco farmers, the cane growers, and the sugar-beet producers protested so violently that Roosevelt was soon wishing that Cuba "grew steel and glass" instead of agricultural products. Spooner of Wisconsin pointed out that a reduction in raw-sugar duties would aid the Cubans, the eastern manufacturers seeking markets in the islands, and the American sugar refineries, already collectively referred to as the "Sugar Trust." It was a nasty situation for the President, alleviated only by the promise of support from Aldrich, Platt, Hanna, and Foraker. Even so, the Cuban bill failed to pass in 1902. Finally in 1903, after a planning conference at Aldrich's home and after the President had called a special session of Congress, the Cuban bill was passed, providing a 20 per cent reduction on Cuban products in return for a 20 to 40 per cent reduction on American products entering Cuba. The Philippine bill, however, was lost to a combination of western Republicans and southern Democrats. By the vagaries of internal sectional politics, an integral part of the empire was denied concessions granted to an independent state.[12]

As a whole the nation's press was not too impressed with the achievements of either the Fifty-seventh Congress, which adjourned in March,

[11] Roosevelt to Henry Cabot Lodge, February 24, 1903, Roosevelt MSS.
[12] Roosevelt to Nicholas M. Butler, February 4, 1902, Roosevelt MSS.; John C. Spooner to Wayne MacVeagh, June 24, 1902, Spooner MSS.

1903, or with its successor. The general conclusion was that during the first session under Roosevelt the struggle between "an aggressive administration and a reluctant Senate" had resulted in a legislative draw without too many benefits for the country. During the second session both the administration and Congress, the press asserted, had done little save play politics with an eye to the coming election and spend money.[13] From this meager congressional record, from the cordial letters between Roosevelt and Aldrich, and from the substantial record of co-operation between them, some historians have concluded that Roosevelt was in fundamental agreement with Aldrich, and that his policy differed from that of the conservative congressional leadership only in the noise made for public consumption. Citing one important legislative conference held at Roosevelt's Oyster Bay home on September 16, 1902, which Aldrich, Hanna, Platt, Allison, and Lodge attended, one historian has stated that the full agreement there signaled the formation of a party within the Republican party, "the Conservative Party." That substantial agreement existed between Roosevelt and his congressional leaders during his first administration cannot be denied. But the suggestion that a "conservative party" was formed is totally unwarranted. The Roosevelt agreement was one of expediency and convenience rather than in the spirit of holy wedlock. It reflected Roosevelt's willingness to compromise with power and not his basic ideas, and it extended to legislative matters only and not to executive affairs. Twice during 1902 the President acted on most important matters of domestic policy without previous consultation with the leaders of either the Senate or the House. In both the Northern Securities affair and the famous anthracite coal strike of 1902 his need and will to co-operate with Congress were minimal. And in both cases the results were not too acceptable to conservatives either inside or outside the legislative halls.

On February 19, 1902, the Attorney General, Philander C. Knox, startled the country and threw the financial world into a state of consternation. At the request of the President, Knox announced, the government would soon start a suit under the Sherman Act to dissolve the Northern Securities Company. A good portion of the country cheered the news, but New York and the stock market were temporarily demoralized. Not since the day of McKinley's death, the New York *Tribune* stated, had the market had such "a sudden and severe shock."

[13] *Literary Digest,* XXVI (1903), 373; XXVIII (1904), 650.

On the following day Theodore Roosevelt, for the first of many times, became the target of an angry Wall Street. The President's "thunder-bolt out of a clear sky" was variously described as "unreasonable" and "beyond comprehension." [14]

The Northern Securities Company was a giant holding company for three large northwestern railroads, the Northern Pacific, the Great Northern, and the Chicago, Burlington and Quincy. The company's architects, J. P. Morgan and Company, the Rockefeller interests, James J. Hill, and E. H. Harriman, were the very Sanhedrin of the nation's railroad and financial oligarchs. This first true holding company had been put together to create a transportation monopoly in the North-west, and according to the Attorney General it had practically achieved its purpose. Thirty per cent of its capital stock of $400 million was pure water, Knox estimated, a sum representing both an "unwar-ranted profit" to its organizers and an index to its expected need to overcharge the public.[15]

The magic names of Morgan and Rockefeller involved in the Northern Securities suit and the secrecy of its preparation—apparently no one save Roosevelt and Knox had prior news of it—account for the nation's excited reaction to its announcement. A trust-conscious coun-try, fearful of complete domination by further conquests of the New York financial and industrial oligarchy, was cheered by this sudden and energetic use of the long-moribund Sherman Law. When a federal court a year later held the Northern Securities Company illegal and ordered its dissolution, a decision later sustained by the Supreme Court, there was general exultation. No longer was there a question, one jour-nal declared rather optimistically, over whether the giant corporations controlled the people or the people the corporations. "Even Morgan no longer rules the earth," declared another, "and other men may still do business without asking his permission." [16]

The promise in the Northern Securities Case for further action under the Sherman Law was not unfulfilled. In the following seven years the Roosevelt administration started similar actions against forty-four cor-porations, including some of the largest industrial combines in the nation. During the remainder of 1902 only one such suit was orig-

[14] New York *Tribune,* February 20, 1902; *Literary Digest,* XXIV (1902), 277.
[15] "The Northern Securities Case," Memorandum, April, 1902, Knox MSS.
[16] *The Outlook,* LXXIII (1903), 892; *Literary Digest,* XXVI (1903), 565; XVIII (1904), 6.

inated, that against the so-called beef trust, an action which delighted both the western farmers and the consumers in the city. During 1903 and 1904, an election year, a lull occurred. But in 1905 the antitrust program was once again accelerated, reaching a crescendo in 1906 and 1907, when suits were started against the Standard Oil Company, the American Tobacco Company, the New Haven Railroad, and the Du Pont corporation.

Roosevelt's antitrust activities earned him the name of the "trust buster." At his death in 1919 the Democratic New York *World* suggested that his greatest public service had been rendered when he demonstrated that "the Government of the United States was more powerful than any aggregations of capital. . . ." [17] It is one of history's small ironies that Roosevelt never once in his public life argued that trust busting would cure the industrial problem. As a matter of record, from the time he was governor of New York to the end of his life he believed in government regulation and not dissolution of giant corporations. He stated his position clearly in his first message to Congress, reaffirmed it at Pittsburgh on July 4, 1902, and again all across the country in the campaign of that fall. At Pittsburgh he declared that the growth of large industry was natural, inevitable, and beneficial, and that the nation could no more turn it back by legislation than it could turn back the Mississippi spring floods. But, the President added, we can "regulate and control them by levees." [18]

Why then did Roosevelt launch his attack against monopolies in 1902 and why did he keep at it intermittently during the rest of his administration? There is little direct evidence in the Roosevelt manuscripts to answer the question, but something can be implied.

At a very early age Roosevelt shared the progressives' fear of the rising commercial and industrial oligarchy and its political pretensions. Speaking of labor's misdeeds in 1894, he said that the bankers and railroad men also needed "sound chastisement." In his *Autobiography* he stated bluntly that "of all the forms of tyranny the least attractive and the most vulgar is the tyranny of mere wealth. . . ." Early in Roosevelt's Presidency J. P. Morgan came to see him to talk over commercial policy. Roosevelt was beside himself at the tycoon's attitude. Morgan had treated him as he might a rival businessman "who either

[17] January 7, 1919.
[18] *The New York Times*, July 5, 1902; see also his speeches at Fitchburg, Massachusetts, September 2, 1902, and at Cincinnati, September 20, 1902.

intended to ruin all of his interests or else could be induced to come to an agreement to ruin none. . . ." [19] Here was a challenge to the President and the nation that Roosevelt had to meet. Roosevelt knew that to attack the trust problem was the one action calculated to win the admiration and support of middle-class America. He was also aware that the conservative-dominated Congress would not pass the required legislation for any effective program of control. Even for his limited 1902 objectives of inspection and publicity he had a "stand-up fight" with Aldrich in early 1903 before he obtained a promise of necessary support. What he had paid for that support is obvious from a memorandum in the manuscripts of Attorney General Knox. The Knox memorandum of February 15, 1903, states that Senator Aldrich had that day brought a note from the President asking Knox to make a public statement on the trust problem, including the statement: "Congress has now enacted all that is practicable and all that is desirable to do." Knox's statement was published the following day, and Congress received no more requests for trust regulation during Roosevelt's first term. [20]

With the path to effective regulation blocked by a stubborn, conservative Congress, the only way for Roosevelt to bring the arrogant capitalists to heel was through the judicious use of the antitrust laws. The Northern Securities suit, involving Morgan, Rockefeller, and Harriman, was natural for his purpose. During 1903 and 1904 his campaigning against the trusts lagged, but after his re-election he returned to his demands for regulation. In his 1904 annual report, Commissioner of Corporations James R. Garfield, one of the President's bright young men, argued that the only valid way to meet the threat of monopoly was through federal regulation and recommended that all interstate business be licensed by the federal government with a requirement that the licensees be obligated to report annually on the kinds and amounts of business done, together with profits earned. Back in 1903, after he had made his agreement with Aldrich, Roosevelt had called a similar proposal by Senator Hoar "idiotic." But in 1906 and again in 1907 he asked Congress to pass such supervisory legislation. Again Congress

[19] Roosevelt to J. Brander Matthews, December 9, 1894, in Elting E. Morison (ed.), *The Letters of Theodore Roosevelt* (8 vols., Cambridge, 1951–54), I, 410; Theodore Roosevelt, *An Autobiography* (New York, 1921), p. 425; Bishop, *Life and Letters*, I, 184–185.
[20] Roosevelt to Taft, March 19, 1903, Roosevelt MSS.; Memorandum, February 15, 1903, Knox MSS.; New York *Herald*, February 16, 1903.

refused and again the antitrust campaign seemed to be stepped up. There was something almost contrapuntal in Roosevelt's use of the Sherman Law and his demands for federal supervision. Long afterward Roosevelt stated that his antitrust campaign had given the government the power to suppress monopolies and to control holding companies. This was not altogether true, and it is doubtful whether Roosevelt when in office really believed what he was to write in his *Autobiography*. His real views to the contrary were expressed many times. During the campaign of 1908 he argued that the only effective action was to increase greatly "Federal control over all combinations engaged in interstate commerce, instead of relying upon the foolish anti-trust law. . . ." [21]

Some months after Roosevelt's spectacular action against the Northern Securities Company, the administration was confronted with a labor crisis of major proportions which, had it been handled badly, might have endangered its political future. In May, 1902, over fifty thousand anthracite coal miners enrolled in the United Mine Workers walked off their jobs in northeastern Pennsylvania, demanding a 10 to 20 per cent increase in pay, recognition of the union, an eight-hour day, and other fringe benefits. A similar strike in the preceding election year of 1900 had won a settlement granting a 10 per cent increase, due largely to the mediating influence of Mark Hanna. Hanna had been disturbed by the possible effect of the strike on McKinley's election prospects, and had persuaded the reluctant operators that four more years of McKinley Republicanism was worth a 10 per cent wage raise.

From 70 to 80 per cent of the anthracite fields were owned by six railroads crisscrossing the region. The rail presidents, headed by George F. Baer of the Reading and W. H. Truesdale of the Lackawanna, insisted that this time there should be no political compromise. Relying upon the fuel needs of the seaboard cities from Boston to Washington, they closed down the mines, rejected all offers of negotiation, and waited for the union to crack. Led by the able John F. Mitchell and financed by contributions from the soft-coal miners, the United Mine Workers held their ranks through July, September, and into October. As winter approached even schools and hospitals had empty coalbins, and the public temper became increasingly ugly. Senator Lodge re-

21 Roosevelt to Joseph B. Bishop, February 17, 1903, to Joseph M. McCormick, July 14, 1908, Roosevelt MSS.; Roosevelt, *Autobiography*, p. 469.

ported that civil commotion was imminent in Boston, and the President felt that there was real danger of riots in New York City.

By September it was obvious that the bulk of press opinion was opposed to the stand of the mine operators. Some of the more conservative journals, it was true, labeled the strike as an "insurrection" and demanded that force be used against the unions. Occasionally an eminent individual like the newly elected president of Princeton University defended capital's side of the argument. Woodrow Wilson interpreted the strike not as one over wages and hours but as a union attempt "to win more power. . . ." [22] But the weight of opinion was with the unions. Labor's orderly conduct of the strike during its first three months, and its repeated willingness to arbitrate the issues, were in favorable contrast with the intransigent stand and the incredibly foolish statements of the operators. To a proposal that the dispute be referred to Archbishop Ireland for arbitration, George F. Baer replied, "Anthracite mining is business and not a religious, sentimental or academic proposition." A month later he claimed that the Deity had conferred the large property rights of the country exclusively upon the Christian men who now directed the nation's corporations, a divine-right property doctrine which President W. H. Truesdale of the Lackawanna Railroad promptly supported.[23]

Such paleolithic statements elicited public protests even from conservative sources, and as the viewpoint of the operators remained unchanged, public opinion rapidly hardened against the coal roads. By early September not a few of the country's leading newspapers were tentatively suggesting government ownership of the mines, while others demanded compulsory arbitration. "The economic harmonies of free contract," one paper commented, "were no longer working in the coal fields." Others vigorously asserted the "paramount rights of the public welfare" to any and all considerations of private property. In October an action of the New York Democratic State Convention recalled the days of the Populists and the bad times of the early nineties. "We advocate," the platform stated, "the national ownership and operation of the anthracite coal mines." [24]

As early as the middle of June, Roosevelt had sent the Commissioner

[22] Wilson is cited in *World's Work*, IV (1902), 2479. See also *Literary Digest*, XXV (1902), 399.

[23] *Literary Digest*, XXIV (1902), 824; *The Outlook*, LXXI (1902), 1035.

[24] *Literary Digest*, XXV (1902), 307, 513. Governor William A. Stone of Pennsylvania, a Republican, also advocated compulsory arbitration.

of Labor into the coal fields to investigate and propose a solution in the event the strike was not soon settled. But despite the almost unanimous approval of the press for government intervention, Roosevelt refused to act during July and August. Since Knox, Root, and Lodge all advised that the government was without constitutional power to intervene, the President found himself at his "wit's end." The whole affair proved to him again that it was necessary to have government supervision over big corporations.[25] As September rounded into October, as temperatures fell and the public pressure mounted, Roosevelt determined to intervene, advice or no advice. On October 1, telegrams went out from the White House inviting the chief coal operators and the union leaders to a conference on October 3. Exactly what took place at the day-long conference has in the past been guessed at. Apparently, Loeb, the presidential secretary, took notes, but the notes have never been unearthed. Among the papers of Philander C. Knox, however, a long unannotated memorandum, hitherto undetected, gives a purported blow-by-blow account of the day's events. According to the Knox memorandum, Roosevelt opened the short morning session at eleven with the disclaimer that he "had any right or duty to intervene in this way on legal grounds." The urgency of the situation and the national interest, however, made his intervention necessary. Mitchell spoke first for the miners. They were prepared to meet the operators at any time to adjust their differences. If such a meeting was not agreeable, the union was willing to accept the findings of an arbitral commission appointed by the President, provided that the operators also agreed to accept its awards. Roosevelt then asked both parties to think over the offer and adjourned the meeting until three o'clock.

At the afternoon session Baer and his colleagues ignored the labor leaders completely and adamantly refused to talk with the unions either directly or indirectly. What the President was asking them to do, John B. Markle said, was "to deal with outlaws" who were responsible for the "existing anarchy." Baer then started a long diatribe against the unions, accusing them of daily violence against the fifteen to twenty thousand peaceful miners who wanted to work. If the power of the state of Pennsylvania was not sufficient to meet the challenge to peace, it became the duty of the President to restore order. "Free government," he concluded, was "a contemptible failure if it can only protect

[25] Roosevelt to Lodge, September 27, 1902, Roosevelt MSS.

the lives and property and secure comfort of the people by compromise with the violaters of law and instigators of violence and crime." After much the same line had been taken by E. B. Thomas, chairman of the board of the Erie Railroad, and by Markle, representing the independent coal operators, David Wilcox, vice-president of the Delaware and Hudson, charged specifically that the miners had committed twenty murders. Mitchell immediately objected that the charge was false and offered to resign his position if the operators would name the men responsible for the alleged murders and show that they were guilty as charged. Ignoring Mitchell's interruption, the operators demanded that a permanent injunction be granted against the strikers and that the President "put an end to the anarchy in the coal fields" by using the Army, if necessary, as in the Pullman strike, and by starting an immediate suit against the unions under the Sherman Law. When the President finally asked the operators whether they would agree to Mitchell's proposal for arbitration, he was met with a blunt refusal. Upon his further inquiry whether the owners had anything else to suggest, they replied they had no other proposal except that the miners should return to their jobs and leave the determination of their grievances to the decision of the judge of the courts of common pleas in the districts where the mines were located. After twice "insulting" the President and the Attorney General, the operators left the conference without once addressing a word directly to the union representatives. Three days later the Attorney General received a formal petition from the general attorney of the Delaware, Lackawanna and Western Railroad, asking that an injunction be issued against the strikers for interference with interstate commerce and that federal troops be sent to Pennsylvania to restore order. The miners, Knox was told on the same day by the vice-president of the Delaware and Hudson Railroad, should be proceeded against as Eugene Debs was proceeded against in Chicago some ten years before.[26]

During and after the conference Roosevelt was beside himself at the operators' "arrogant stupidity." But the meeting had given him one constructive idea. Suggesting to Root and Knox that they could write letters of protest if they desired to disclaim responsibility, he indicated

[26] Memorandum, October 3, 1902, Knox MSS.; Roosevelt to Robert Bacon, to Mark Hanna, and to Grover Cleveland, October 3, 1902, Roosevelt to Murray Crane, October 22, 1902, Roosevelt MSS.; Walter W. Ross to Knox, October 6, 1902, David Wilcox to Knox, October 6, 1902, Knox MSS.

that he was prepared to send ten thousand federal troops to dispossess
the operators and produce coal. By previous constitutional interpretation the President had the authority to send federal troops into a state
to assure the exercise of duly authorized federal powers or when they
were requested by a governor or a state legislature to preserve peace

With all his faults we love him—still.

and order. Nowhere was the right to seize and operate private property
even hinted at, much less specified. Nevertheless, the President talked
with General J. M. Schofield and through Senator Mathew Quay ar-
ranged for the governor of Pennsylvania to request the intervention of
federal troops. Spurred by this terrible specter of state socialism, the
friends of capital began to move fast. On October 8, Senators Quay
and Penrose held a conference with John Mitchell. Two days later,

together with Senators Odell and Platt, they met with Baer. On October 11, with Roosevelt's blessing, Root journeyed to New York for a secret conference with J. P. Morgan. The "Great Mogul of Wall Street" was induced to put pressure on the railroad presidents, and at a White House conference on October 13 the groundwork for a compromise was worked out between the President and agents of the acknowledged autocrat of American finance and industry, Morgan. The miners were to go back to work, and a five-man commission appointed by the President, consisting of one Army engineer, a mining engineer, a "businessman familiar with the coal industry," a federal judge, and an "eminent sociologist," was to arbitrate the points at issue. Subsequently the commission was raised to seven members, and the President, in order to meet labor's objections to the one-sided nature of its personnel, agreed to appoint E. E. Clarke, president of the Brotherhood of Railroad Conductors, as the "eminent sociologist." In March, 1903, the commission made public its awards: the miners were given a 10 per cent raise on the average, working hours were reduced in some cases to eight and in most to nine, recognition of the union was not conceded, and the traditional manner of weighing coal was to be continued. The commission also recommended a 10 per cent increase in the price of coal, a proposal of which the operators quickly availed themselves.[27]

During the presidential campaign of 1904 Roosevelt described his actions in the coal strike as simply giving both labor and capital a "square deal." The phrase was to stick in public memory as so many of Roosevelt's did, and perhaps it started the twentieth-century fashion of likening national political programs to phrases in an ethically operated game of chance. The President's actions during the strike set many important precedents. For the first time in a labor dispute representatives of both capital and labor were called to the White House, where the influence of the government was used to obtain a negotiated settlement. For the first time the President had appointed an arbitral board whose decision both sides promised to accept. In order to obtain capital's consent to arbitration, Roosevelt, for the first time in Ameri-

[27] Good summaries of the complex maneuvers that preceded the settlement are to be found in Pringle, *Roosevelt*, pp. 268–278, and Philip C. Jessup, *Elihu Root* (2 vols., New York, 1939), I, pp. 275–276. The whole story must be pieced together from the hundreds of letters dealing with the strike in the manuscripts of Roosevelt, Root, and Knox.

can history, had threatened to use troops to take over and operate a major industry. Whether he would have gone that far or not is problematical. As Root said later, the President was "a bit of a bluffer" at times. But both by his actions and threats Roosevelt had moved the government away from its traditional position of isolation from such economic struggles. The government, by precedent if not by law, had become a third force and partner in major labor disputes.[28]

As if to balance his threatened action in 1902, Roosevelt did use federal troops a year later, but this time in the interest "of peace and order." During a mine strike in Morenci, Arizona, the governor of the territory asked for federal troops. Roosevelt sent them quickly but withdrew them after eight days when it appeared that there was little need for them beyond their possible effect of cowing the strikers, mostly Mexicans, into submission. A year later the governor of Colorado requested federal troops to quell a labor disturbance at Cripple Creek. Serious trouble started when the Western Federation of Miners struck and the Mine Owners' Association answered with a counter-campaign of terror. Governor James Peabody, a stanch friend of the owners, thereupon declared martial law and virtually ordered the militia to set about destroying the miners' organization. During the course of this work the militia violated most of the basic civil rights of the strikers, even ignoring writs of the state courts. In a subsequent report, William Howard Taft remarked that in their zeal to destroy the unions the mining corporations had "possessed themselves of the executive and the party and seem to have gone to great lengths in reaching for the bench." [29] At this juncture, just before the election of 1904, the miners petitioned the President for troops. Roosevelt denied the requests from both sides in Colorado, claiming that neither side had clean hands. But four years later, on the request of the governor of Nevada, he ordered federal forces into Goldfield, only to reverse the order a short time later when he found that the troops were being used to guard against potential instead of actual trouble. In effect the troops were used to quell union opposition to a campaign, inspired by the governor and the mine owners, to drive all the union members out of the state.[30] In both the Colorado and Nevada affairs the President was bitterly criticized for taking an antiunion position. He was also

[28] Root to Philip C. Jessup, cited in Jessup, *Root*, I, 275.
[29] Taft to Roosevelt, July 13, 1905, Roosevelt MSS.
[30] *Literary Digest*, XXXVI (1908), 39.

roundly condemned by the friends of organized labor for his actions in both the Steunenberg murder case in Idaho and the 1910 bombing of the Los Angeles *Times*. In both instances members of labor unions had resorted to violence against long-time foes of labor, and in both instances Roosevelt's reaction was a well-publicized, speedy, and harsh criticism of unions, as well as the individual perpetrators of the violence, before the courts had delivered judgment. When in 1906 organized labor attempted to defeat Governor Frank R. Gooding of Idaho, who had supported the prosecution of the unionists, the President extended himself to support Gooding, even sending Cabinet members to campaign in the state.[31]

From the total of these incidents many contemporaries and historians have concluded that Roosevelt was a friend of capital and a foe of labor. As usual the truth is more complex than any such simple statement conveys. Unquestionably, the President believed in an open shop, but this meant a shop open to union men as well as nonunionists. "I would guarantee by every means in my power," he wrote Carroll D. Wright, his labor commissioner during the Colorado strike, "the right of laboring men to join a union, and their right to work as union men without illegal interference from either capitalists or nonunion men." He applied this principle also to nonunion men. Roosevelt was opposed to the labor boycott and he was powder-quick to oppose union intervention in politics and the use of force during strikes. His acceptance of substantial sums of money from corporation representatives in the election of 1904 and his refusal to condemn publicly the use of illegal force by the mining corporations in Colorado, although he criticized them privately, indicate his fundamental bias, a bias he shared with most progressives.[32]

Roosevelt's position on labor, as that of most progressives, was a distant one from the usual conservative stand. Big labor, like big capital, he remarked, was one of the laws of the social and economic development of the age. Unions, he believed, contributed to the general welfare. Writing to his son at school, he cautioned young Theodore not to attack the principle of unions, which was "beneficial," but rather

[31] Roosevelt to Calvin Cobb, June 16, 1906, Roosevelt MSS.; Taft to M. J. Hill, October 20, 1906, Taft MSS.

[32] Roosevelt to Carroll D. Wright, August 13, 1904, Roosevelt MSS.; Roosevelt to Calvin Cobb, June 16, 1906, copy in Taft MSS.; Roosevelt to George B. Cortelyou, June 4, 1903, Root MSS.; Oscar S. Straus, "Diary" (manuscript), p. 170.

their "abuses" of power. As a New York City police commissioner and later as governor, he was always willing to meet with union leaders and consider their viewpoints. During his Presidency he carried an honorary membership card in the railroad brotherhoods, and when the famous English liberal, John Morley, visited him at the White House, among the guests for luncheon were the presidents of three labor unions. During the Miller affair, in which Roosevelt insisted on the open shop in government, numerous business leaders protested against the President's holding a conference in the White House with Samuel Gompers and John Mitchell. Roosevelt replied that as President he could not fail to give anyone a hearing.[33]

Some of Roosevelt's concern for labor was undoubtedly political, as was some of his concern for big business. Some of it came also straight from the heart and the mind of the man. How else is one to explain his long, cautionary letter to Knox, his former Cabinet member, who had become the senator-elect from Pennsylvania? Roosevelt had just announced that he would not again run for the Presidency. Therefore his views were not colored by considerations of popular support four years later. Roosevelt urged Knox to study labor and find out what it wanted. He also exhorted him not to adopt the views of the reactionary wing of the party lest the Republicans go down some day "before a radical and extreme democracy" with a crash which would be disastrous to the nation. "We must not only do justice, but be able to show the wage workers that we are doing justice." Beyond this long-time political consideration, other less material ends were to be achieved: "The friends of property must realize that the surest way to provoke an explosion of wrong and injustice is to be shortsighted, narrow-minded, greedy and arrogant, and to fail to show in actual work that here in this republic it is peculiarly incumbent upon the man with whom things have prospered to be in a certain sense the keeper of his brother with whom life has gone hard."[34]

Like so many progressives, Roosevelt believed that a superior station in life entailed superior responsibilities, both to the more unfortunate individual and to the state. Strangely enough, neither Roosevelt nor many of his fellow progressives carried this sense of *noblesse oblige* across national boundaries into the realm of foreign politics.

[33] Roosevelt to Theodore Roosevelt, Jr., June 29, 1904; to John Morley, October 25, 1904; to Henry Cabot Lodge, September 30, 1903; Roosevelt MSS.; A. B. Hart (ed.), *The Theodore Roosevelt Cyclopedia* (New York, 1941), p. 290.

[34] Roosevelt to Knox, November 10, 1904, Knox MSS.

PRESIDENT McKINLEY speaking at San
ose, California

*All photographs in this section are from
rown Brothers)*

WILLIAM JENNINGS BRYAN returning from
urope in 1908

3. ORVILLE H. PLATT of Connecticut   4. NELSON W. ALDRICH of Rhode Island

THE REPUBLICAN BIG THREE OF THE SENATE 1900-1904

5. WILLIAM B. ALLISON of Iowa

PRESIDENT THEODORE
ROOSEVELT in the early
years of his first term

7. ROBERT MARION LA FOLLETTE
of Wisconsin

8. ELIHU ROOT, SECRETARY OF WAR, 1902

9. SPEAKER OF THE HOUSE, JOSEPH CANNON in 1908

MAKERS OF REPUBLICAN POLICY

11. SENATOR HENRY CABOT LODGE of MA-SACHUSETTS

10. SENATOR MARCUS A. HANNA of Ohio

12. Lower East Side, New York, about 1900

13. SENATOR JOSEPH BAILEY of Texas

14. REPRESENTATIVE JOHN SHARP WILLIAMS minority leader of the House

LEADERS OF THE DEMOCRATIC MINORITY

15. SENATOR ARTHUR P. GORMAN of Maryland

16.   Japanese workmen in the orchards of California

17.   Immigrants at Ellis Island about 1907

18. Ida M. Tarbell

19. David Graham Phillips

THE MUCKRAKERS

20. Lincoln Steffens

. PRESIDENT ROOSEVELT
ith the Russian and Japa-
ese peace-conference dele-
tes

2. ROOSEVELT at Culebra
ut in Panama in 1906

23. Samuel M. Jones of Toledo, Ohio 24. Thomas L. Johnson of Cleveland, Oh

THREE REFORM MAYORS

25. Seth Low of New York

26. J. P. MORGAN, SR.

27. EDWARD HENRY HARRIMAN

BIG BUSINESS

28. JOHN D. ROCKEFELLER

29. SENATOR JONATHAN P. DOLLIVER of Iowa

30. REPRESENTATIVE GEORGE W. NORRIS of Nebraska

MIDDLEWESTERN PROGRESSIVE LEADERS

31. SENATOR ALBERT J. BEVERIDGE of Indiana

32. PRESIDENT THEODORE ROOSEVELT speaking

33. HIRAM JOHNSON of California

34. JOSEPH W. FOLK of Missouri

THREE PROGRESSIVE GOVERNORS

35. WOODROW WILSON of New Jersey

. SAMUEL GOMPERS, President, the Ameri-
n Federation of Labor

37. WILLIAM "BIG BILL" HAYWOOD, or-
ganizer of the Industrial Workers of
the World

THREE FROM LABOR

38. EUGENE V. DEBS, quadrennial candidate of the Socialist party

39. WILLIAM HOWARD TAFT as a candidate for the Presidency

CHAPTER 8

Hemisphere Diplomacy

WHILE considering the advisability of Cuban intervention in 1906, Roosevelt remarked to Taft that he would "not dream" of asking congressional permission for the venture. Since a legislative body was "not well fitted for the shaping of foreign policy," he felt himself obliged to act and to establish precedents "which successors may follow even if they are unwilling to take the initiative themselves." [1] Roosevelt was definitely not among the unwilling. On foreign policy matters he consulted Congress when he was legally obligated to consult, but in most other cases he used the executive power to its limits, and sometimes perhaps beyond. The President's foreign policy was peculiarly a personal one. Until July 1, 1905, the gifted John Hay, whom Roosevelt had inherited from McKinley's Cabinet, was Secretary of State. Hay was not the nonentity in foreign policy that Roosevelt later remembered him to be. But during his later years he was ill much of the time and away from office. Elihu Root succeeded Hay, and his influence, especially on Latin American and Oriental policy, was substantial if not always decisive. During Roosevelt's two administrations most of the nation's major foreign policy actions were the result of executive direction without congressional consent, and a surprising number of them were sired in the fertile presidential head.

The international world which Roosevelt confronted as he became President was one dramatically punctuated by rivalry and tension. The United States, Germany, and Japan, all rapidly rising industrial powers, were laying zealous siege to Britain's no longer secure commercial

[1] Roosevelt to William Howard Taft, September 17, 1906, Taft MSS.

dominance. Each of the three was rapidly building navies to project its power from home shores, and each had already joined the race for world empire. Since by 1901 the unallocated colonial world was already in short supply, the competition between these vigorous newcomers and the older expansionists, Great Britain, France, and Russia, took on a frantic quality which meant increasing conflict both abroad and at home. In seizing the Philippines and Puerto Rico and in "liberating" Cuba, the United States in fact had helped set a new fashion in empire building. Prior to 1898 the imperial process had evolved mostly at the expense of non-Europeans or distinctly unadvanced peoples. But the United States had profited from attacking an old empire controlled by peoples with a historic culture. The new example was not to be lost in the years ahead.

Roosevelt saw the world as one trifurcated between a few great and wealthy powers, the smaller "civilized states" of Europe, and the remaining nations and races of the world, which he thought of as occupying distinctly lower positions on a scale of desirable qualities. Among all nations he saw a constant conflict for supremacy, in which force was the ultimate ratio dividing the successful from the defeated and the destroyed. But this unrestrained international competition was not at all, in his thinking, divorced from justice. The great powers were the civilized powers, the purveyors of enlightenment and culture, the protectors of law, order, and liberty, and to a lesser extent the practitioners of democracy. In his first message to Congress the President noted that the wars between the "civilized powers" seemed to be lessening in frequency. Although the conflicts between civilized nations and "the semi-barbarous peoples" were still numerous, they were of "an entirely different category, being merely a most regrettable but necessary international police duty which must be performed for the sake of the welfare of mankind." [2]

In this precarious world Roosevelt was thoroughly at home, as were many progressives who supported him. For the nationalist and collectivist impulse that prompted one wing of progressivism to rely upon the federal state for the solution of most internal problems reflected itself also in foreign affairs. Senator Beveridge, the brothers Abbott, William Allen White, and Herbert Croly were all preaching in the first decade of the new century the doctrine that Roosevelt had once re-

<hr>

[2] James D. Richardson, *A Compilation of the Messages and Papers of the Presidents* (Washington, 1902), Supplement 1, p. 338.

ferred to as the "ultra-American spirit of patriotism." Without such a spirit, Roosevelt wrote, no man could achieve anything worth while. Beveridge placed its value second only to the religious sense, and without it Homer Lea predicted the nation would die.[3] At the heart of this new patriotism was a mystical concept of the state as an organic unity, Croly's nation of the past and future "organized for its historic mission." Individualism in such a state was often the enemy of national purpose. Croly, quoting John Jay Chapman, argued that modern democracy insisted that every man should think first of the state and next of himself.[4]

Progressivism had other ideological ties with the rising expansionism and belligerency in the world. The confidence in progress, the emphasis upon accomplishment for the sake of accomplishment, and the almost evangelical belief in the ethical, political, and cultural mission of the United States all contributed to a more energetic and ambitious foreign policy. By some dimly perceived organic law Roosevelt saw the nation compelled to exert its rising power in the "larger world life, in which, whether we will or not, we must take an ever increasing share." [5] Nature's categorical injunction to man was to work, fight, and breed; it was the same for nations, if one substituted the word "expansion" for "breeding." And while Lyman Abbott's hearty belief in "manifest destiny" was couched in more ethical and religious terms, it resulted in much the same activity. At the identical time Senator Beveridge was making a trip through eastern Siberia and Manchuria looking for additional markets for American goods, Abbott was writing that American expansion was not imperialism, but rather the denial of it. As Anglo-Saxon democracy with "its roots in the Hebraic Commonwealth" had advanced over the world, imperialism had decayed: "this international unity, this combination of union with self-government which is the ultimate goal of social progress, is further advanced toward its ideal in the United States of America than in any other form of world Empire." The end of this divinely inspired movement was clear to Abbott. It was nothing less than the world "brotherhood of

[3] Roosevelt to Osborne Holmes, May 5, 1892, in Elting E. Morison (ed.), *The Letters of Theodore Roosevelt* (8 vols., Cambridge, 1951–54), I, 278; Albert J. Beveridge, *The Meaning of the Times* (Indianapolis, 1908), p. 234; Homer Lea, *The Valor of Ignorance* (New York, 1909), pp. 10–11.

[4] Herbert Croly, *The Promise of American Life* (New York, 1909), p. 418.

[5] Richardson, *Messages and Papers,* Supplement 1, p. 338.

man founded on justice and liberty, which is the kingdom of God." [6]

There were, of course, more practical considerations prompting a militant American policy. The newly acquired empire had to be protected. This almost automatically meant supremacy in the Caribbean, a new emphasis upon the Pacific basin, and an isthmus canal so that naval power could be efficiently transferred from one ocean to another. "I wish to see the United States the dominant power on the shores of the Pacific Ocean," Theodore Roosevelt announced to receptive Californians in 1900. A little more than a year later, in his first message to Congress he stated that no other single work on the continent was more important to the American people than the building of an isthmian canal. [7]

Beyond the Caribbean and the projected canal lay South America. Months before the enunciation of the Roosevelt Corollary to the Monroe Doctrine, but after the 1902 European intervention in Venezuela, an American magazine pointed out that Argentina, Brazil, Venezuela, and in fact all of South America had everything that Germany and Italy lacked: unpopulated land, plentiful resources, and immeasurable opportunity for exploitation. "The pressure of the whole organized world," the journal warned, "toward these fertile and unused territories is becoming exceedingly strong." The President, John Hay, and Elihu Root had already come to the same conclusion. As early as 1896 Roosevelt was not only thinking in terms of protecting South America from a possible European thrust but was also advising the adoption of a policy which would remove the European nations from the colonies they then held in the Western Hemisphere. A part of Roosevelt's 1896 dislike for the existing arrangements in the hemisphere came unquestionably from a suspicion of Great Britain's intentions in Venezuela. But persistent British friendship during the Spanish-American War and afterward had so changed Roosevelt's views that by the time he became President he envisioned no serious trouble with Britain in South America or elsewhere. By 1901 Germany had become the chief

[6] Claude G. Bowers, *Beveridge and the Progressive Era* (New York, 1932), p. 152; Lyman Abbott, "The Rights of Man," *The Outlook*, LXVIII (1901), 487, 450–451. See especially William E. Leuchtenberg's extremely perceptive article, "Progressivism and Imperialism: The Progressive Movement and American Foreign Policy, 1898–1916," *Mississippi Valley Historical Review*, XXXIX (1952), 483–504.

[7] Howard K. Beale, *Theodore Roosevelt and the Rise of America to World Power* (Baltimore, 1956), p. 76; Richardson, *Messages and Papers*, Supplement 1, p. 337.

and possibly the only great troublemaker. In 1901, while still Vice-President, Roosevelt made an analysis of future world politics from an American viewpoint for English friends. Since the progress of the Slav was slow, Russia's day was "yet far off." Japan was too engrossed in becoming a modern nation to cause much trouble. Though there was great vigor in the English race, he did not expect difficulties from that quarter since fundamentally the two nations were very much alike. The great formidable rival in both trade and war was Germany. Germany was the only power in the immediate future, he wrote to Lodge, that constituted a "menace." The German military classes were evidently intent upon taking "a fall out of us," and Roosevelt thought that the specific locale of the fall might come in the West Indies or in South America.[8]

Roosevelt was not alone in his suspicion of Germany. Hay was also distrustful, as were Taft and Root. And while such attitudes were bound to fluctuate over the changing years with the character of foreign politics, the distrust, and at times even a fear, of Germany was almost a constant in Washington during the next decade and a half. Dr. Albert Shaw summed up the American case against Germany as early as 1903. Germany was "cocky," guilty of "bad manners" and "militarism," apparently intent upon a trade and tariff war with the United States, and, perhaps most serious of all, she had much to gain by disturbing European and world peace. With German naval power yearly on the upswing, Shaw pointed out something that was never far from official thinking, the potential German threat to Latin America.[9]

The possibility of German pressure in the world was partially responsible for the growing Anglo-American friendship. It probably also helped in Roosevelt's formulation of a principle that eventually created a revolution in American foreign politics. In 1898, the year of the first great German naval law and before Dewey fought at Manila, the former Secretary of State, Richard Olney of British-baiting fame, spoke at Harvard of the "patriotism of race as well as of country" to which both the British and the Americans responded.[10] Two years later Theodore Roosevelt indicated that he was quite aware that a large

[8] *World's Work,* V (1903), 3040; Roosevelt to John St. L. Strachey, March 8, 1901, to Cecil Arthur Spring-Rice, March 16, 1901, to Henry Cabot Lodge, March 27, 1901, Roosevelt MSS.

[9] *World's Work,* V (1903), 3044, 3153–3154.

[10] Richard Olney, "The International Isolation of the United States," *Atlantic Monthly,* LXXXI (1898), 577.

part of the explanation for the unhindered development of the Western Hemisphere lay in the European balance of power between British sea strength and the continental armies. A zealous defender of the Monroe Doctrine, Roosevelt had few illusions about how it had been maintained in the past. While still governor of New York he wrote to Root in anger against those Americans who wanted to see British strength reduced. If that eventuality came about, he predicted, "It may very well be that within a few years we shall be face to face with the question of either abandoning the Monroe Doctrine and submitting to the acquisition of American territory by some great European military power, or of going to war. . . ." There was little doubt in Roosevelt's mind what the choice must be. "If England should fail to preserve the European balance of power," he continued, "the United States would be forced to step in to re-establish it, no matter against what countries our efforts would have to be directed." As an afterthought he added, "we ourselves are becoming, owing to our strength and geographical situation, more and more the balance of power of the whole globe." [11]

When thoroughly implemented, the new Rooseveltian doctrine would mean a decided break with the nineteenth-century doctrine of isolationism. Roosevelt's future actions at Portsmouth and at Algeciras were to constitute important steps along the new way. But his complete formulation constituted too sharp a break with traditional thought to gain any immediate widespread support from either Congress or the people. In an ethically minded age it was couched in much too materialistic and selfish terms for public acceptance. Nine years later, however, the sentient mind of Herbert Croly was to give a new twist to the doctrine of world intervention which would make it a good deal more palatable to the progressive faithful. "It looks as if at some future time," Croly wrote, "the power of the United States might well be sufficient, when thrown into the balance, to tip the scales in favor of a comparatively pacific settlement of international complications. Under such conditions a policy of neutrality would be a policy of irresponsibility and unwisdom." [12] When the objective of world peace was added to the factor of American security, the resulting compound of idealism and self-interest was to become a heady brew.

While Roosevelt's public foreign policy statements were characteristically burdened with moral strictures and appeals to ethics, the

[11] Roosevelt to Root, January 29, 1900, Root MSS.
[12] Croly, *The Promise of American Life,* p. 312.

President fully understood that the major determinant in the international world was power. Since to be as rich as the United States and yet to be weak in war was "to invite destruction," he was determined to construct a Navy equal to the protection of American interests at home and commensurate with his new objectives abroad. In his first message to Congress he spent more time on proposals to strengthen the Navy than on any other single subject. By the end of his second term, thanks largely to his continual prodding of Congress, the Navy had been substantially doubled in actual strength. When the Panama Canal was completed, its potential power in any one spot in either ocean was again to be sharply increased.[13]

Roosevelt was not responsible for originating the diplomacy with Great Britain which cleared the way for the final critical negotiations with Colombia regarding the canal. The credit for securing the second Hay-Pauncefote Treaty, which allowed the United States to build the canal and to fortify it, belongs mostly to John Hay. But from that time on the President became the major force in the spinning out of subsequent dramatic events. It is interesting to note that as governor of New York he advised Hay to ignore the Clayton-Bulwer Treaty and to proceed with the construction of the canal with or without Britain's consent, arguing that "a nation has the right to abrogate a treaty . . . for what she regards as sufficient cause." [14]

The second Hay-Pauncefote Treaty was ratified by the Senate on December 16, 1901, just a few weeks after Roosevelt had become President. There followed a long dispute in Congress and the press over the choice of routes. Was the canal to be built in Panama or Nicaragua? While the Panama way was the shortest and possibly the cheapest to construct, it involved a lock canal, whereas in Nicaragua the construction of a sea-level canal was perfectly feasible. Complicating the question were two other factors: the interests of the old French Canal Company whose charter from Colombia had a few more years to run, and the respective attitudes of the Colombian and Nicaraguan governments. After reversing itself, Congress on June 28, 1902, passed the Spooner Bill, directing the President to negotiate with Colombia for the construction of a Panama canal, provided perpetual control of the

[13] Richardson, *Messages and Papers*, Supplement 1, p. 314; Roosevelt to Theodore E. Burton, February 23, 1904, Roosevelt MSS.

[14] Roosevelt to John Hay, February 18, 1900, Hay MSS.; Roosevelt to Arthur H. Lee, March 18, 1901, Roosevelt MSS.

canal was obtained and the French company could deliver a clear title to its equity, the whole to be secured within a "reasonable time" at "reasonable terms." If these specific conditions were not met, the President was instructed to start negotiations with Nicaragua and Costa Rica for the use of the alternative route. Previous to the passage of the Spooner Bill, the French Canal Company had reduced its price for its holdings from over $100 million to $40 million, which Roosevelt and Hay decided was reasonable. Pursuant to congressional instructions Hay thereupon concluded a draft treaty with the Colombian ambassador in Washington, Tomás Herran, which granted the United States the right to construct a canal as well as control in perpetuity over a three mile strip on either side of the waterway. In return Colombia was to receive $10 million and an annual rental of $250,000. While Colombian sovereignty in the zone was to be theoretically respected, American courts were to function throughout the six-mile-wide strip. The agreement contained one other most curious clause, which forbade Colombia from conducting negotiations with the French Canal Company, obviously meant to prevent Colombia from securing any of the $40 million to be paid to the company.

When the Hay-Herran agreement reached Colombia, her government refused to accept the document. Instead, a new Colombian representative in Washington proposed several alternative agreements, by one of which Colombia was to receive $20 million from the United States and $10 million from the French company. In addition, Colombian sovereignty was to be specifically acknowledged and further strengthened by the maintenance of Colombian police and sanitary commissioners in the zone.[15]

Instead of negotiating further, however, Roosevelt became increasingly indignant at the Colombians. Casting aside Hay's suggestion to open negotiations with Nicaragua as a "feint" to bring Colombia to her senses, the President relied upon more direct diplomatic pressure. Despite all the weight Washington could bring to bear on Columbia, its government refused to accede to the Hay-Herran agreement, and there the matter rested until October, 1903. By that time Roosevelt had lost all patience with the "homicidal corruptionists" in Bogotá who, he declared, were trying to "blackmail" both the government of the United States and the French company. By September the exasperated President concluded that only two alternatives remained: one, starting the

Nicaragua canal that winter; the other, interfering in Panama "so as to secure the Panama route." Meanwhile the President had acquainted a good many important people with the course of his thinking and occasionally had added wistfully that it would be most convenient if Panama were an independent state. He could not make such views public, he cautioned, lest they be taken "as an effort to incite an insurrection in Panama." If the President felt himself constrained to silence, other people had no such compunctions. In August *The Outlook,* whose editor was a very close personal friend of Roosevelt, was suggesting that Panama "might secede." If this happened, the editorial concluded, "our recognition of the republic would probably give it political standing with the rest of the world, and a treaty with it would be quickly ratified." [16] The suggestion caught on and within days a host of journalistic voices had approved of a revolution in Panama. By the middle of September the American press evidently had discovered a promising revolutionary movement in Panama. "Many public men of prominence," the anti-imperialist New York *Evening Post* stated, are "in favor of intimating to the Panama revolutionists that if they will maintain resistance long enough . . . this government will see to it that they are not run over by the superior forces of Colombia." [17]

In early October Roosevelt prepared a draft of his annual message to Congress. In it he recommended that the nation take possession of the isthmus "without any further parley with Colombia" and complete the canal.[18] But this part of the message was never sent, nor was there need for it. On November 3 a revolution broke out in Panama, financed and inspired by a junta in New York City headed by Philippe Bunau-Varilla and William Nelson Cromwell. The United States aided and protected the revolution during its short career, and within hours after it had ended blessed it by officially recognizing the new government. An American warship, the U.S.S. *Nashville,* conveniently put into Colón on the evening of November 2 and on the following days prevented Colombian troops from reinforcing their outnumbered forces on the isthmus. By an old American-Colombian treaty both countries had guaranteed the right of transit across the Isthmus, and by an

[16] Roosevelt to W. H. Taft, September 15, 1903, to Jacob H. Schurman, September 10, 1903, Roosevelt MSS.; *The Outlook,* LXXIV (1903), 961.
[17] Cited in the *Literary Digest,* XXVII (1903), 341.
[18] Roosevelt to Albert Shaw, October 7, 1903, Roosevelt MSS.

astonishing feat of definition the United States interpreted the movement of Colombian troops as constituting a threat to free transit.
Shortly after the new republic had been proclaimed, the Panamanian
government signed a treaty granting the United States canal rights in
return for the $10 million originally offered to Colombia.[19]

The names of William Cromwell and Philippe Bunau-Varilla, the
impresarios of the isthmian revolution, appear throughout the story of
Panama with a strange and startling persistence. Bunau-Varilla came
to the United States as an agent of the French Canal Company. Cromwell had contributed heavily to Mark Hanna's Republican campaign
chest of 1900. Hanna later persuaded the Panama Railroad Company
to appoint him as its attorney, and subsequently he became the chief
American attorney for the French Canal Company. During 1901 and
1902 Cromwell and Bunau-Varilla were often in Washington urging
Congress to accept the Panama rather than the Nicaragua route. The
final decision to accept Panama was due in no small part to the leadership of Cromwell's friend Mark Hanna in the Senate. Both Cromwell and Bunau-Varilla had easy access to the State Department and
to the President. As Professor Dennett points out, one draft of the
Hay-Herran Treaty containing the clause forbidding Colombia from
attempting to squeeze additional money from the French company was
written in Cromwell's hand.[20] Throughout the summer of 1903 Cromwell repeatedly urged Roosevelt to adopt a stiff policy toward Colombia. Unquestionably the United States government was supplied
with the details about a possible revolution in Panama. Roosevelt later
denied that he had inspired the revolution, but he also commented
that Bunau-Varilla would have been "a very dull man" had he not
guessed what American policy would be once the revolution broke out.
But it could be argued that the coincidence of the arrival of the
U.S.S. *Nashville* at Colón and the planned opening of the revolution
was one of the best guesses in all American history. Bunau-Varilla was
rewarded for his part in the affair by being appointed the first Panamanian representative in Washington. As such he negotiated the treaty
which granted the Canal Zone to the United States and made possible

[19] For more detailed accounts of the Panama affairs, see Tyler Dennett,
John Hay (New York, 1933), pp. 380 ff.; Henry F. Pringle, *Theodore Roose-
velt, A Biography* (New York, 1931), pp. 301 ff.; H. C. Hill, *Roosevelt and the
Caribbean* (Chicago, 1927); W. D. McCain, *The United States and the
Republic of Panama* (Durham, N.C., 1937).

[20] Dennett, *Hay*, p. 380.

the payment of $40 million from the treasury to the French company. Cromwell later sent a bill to the French company for over $600,000 as repayment for his efforts. During the following years charges were made in Congress and the press that a portion of the sum paid to the French company found its way into American hands, thus by inference explaining why the United States government had been so solicitous in protecting the interest of the French Canal Company at the expense of Colombia. But neither a Congressional investigation, a search by the New York *World,* nor a libel suit instituted by the President against the *World* revealed exactly where and to whom the money was paid. In answer to one charge the President stated on December 1, 1908, that the United States had "not the slightest knowledge" as to the particular individuals to whom the sum was distributed. But either then or a few days later Roosevelt had in his possession, as did Philander C. Knox, a list furnished by Cromwell showing the names of stockholders in the French Canal Company as of 1900 and again as of 1902.[21] Neither Roosevelt nor Knox made the names public, and the lists have disappeared from both men's manuscripts. In 1904 a series of messages had been sent by Knox to the American envoys Day and Russell in Paris concerning the payment of the money to the French company and the securing of the deed to its property in Panama. On Knox's instructions the details of the transactions were to be kept "permanently secret" to prevent Colombia, he said, from taking legal action against the company. There was much about the Panama affair that was secret and much that was obscure, and it is doubtful whether all the secrecy and the obscurity will ever be lifted.[22]

Six years after the remarkable events on the Isthmus, Roosevelt claimed the total responsibility for American actions in the Panama affair. "The vital work, getting Panama as an independent Republic . . . was done by me without the aid or advice of anyone . . . and without the knowledge of anyone." Of no accomplishment was Roosevelt prouder and at times more boastful; and about no other was he more sensitive to the charge that he had acted in a lawless and an unethical manner. In defending his action to Congress he wrote that "every" single action in the affair had been "carried out in accordance with the highest, finest and nicest standards of public and govern-

[21] Knox to Cromwell, December 8, 1908; Roosevelt to Knox, December 10, 1908, Knox MSS.

[22] Knox to Day and Russell, April 6–21, 1904, Knox MSS.

mental ethics." But in 1911, glowing with enthusiasm for his own accomplishment, he told a university audience at Berkeley, California, "I took the Canal Zone." [23]

Roosevelt defended his actions by stating that the construction of the Canal was in the "vital interests of civilization," prompting one critic to suggest that he had announced a new American doctrine of eminent domain for the Western Hemisphere. The President was also aware that the newly acquired empire plus the rising tensions in the world made the Canal vital for American security. But obviously, neither the interest of civilization nor American security required the exact actions Roosevelt took; there were numerous alternatives. The Canal could have been built through Nicaragua, or the United States could have met Colombia's price, since the addition of fifteen or so million dollars was an insignificant sum compared to the total cost of the project. Or the two countries might have come to an agreement at the expense of the French Canal Company since its equity was obviously worthless without being used and since its charter had so little time to run. But after Colombia's refusal to accept the first agreement, Roosevelt and the American government became increasingly inflexible in their demand that the canal be dug where they wanted it to be dug and at the exact price they wanted to pay and in the immediate future. Moreover, the President and the government, on the record, were far more eager to protect the rights of the French stockholders than they were to observe the national rights of a friendly sovereign state. In view of the role William Cromwell played in the drama, Roosevelt's heated indictment of the Colombians as "corruptionists" looks most peculiar. This is not to suggest that the President was himself implicated in any corruption, but it is perhaps significant that afterward Roosevelt had "a most uncomfortable feeling" about Cromwell and his part in the Panama affair.[24]

The President denied repeatedly that he had participated in any way in starting the Panama revolution. But there is no question that he let important people know that he would be happy with a revolution and that these wishes were reflected in the American press as well as known to the Panama conspirators in New York. The presidential

[23] Roosevelt to Henry Cabot Lodge, January 28, 1909, Roosevelt MSS.; *Papers Relating to the Foreign Relations of the United States,* Washington, 1903, p. 275; *The New York Times,* March 25, 1911.

[24] Roosevelt to Taft, June 3, 1905, Taft MSS.

invitation to revolt by indirection, the remarkable split-second timing of the U.S.S. *Nashville's* arrival in Panama, the utterly indefensible interpretation of the transit treaty with Colombia, and the indecent haste in the recognition of the new Panama Republic made Roosevelt a moral accomplice both before and after the act. The whole affair suggested that for Roosevelt ethics stopped at the tidewater beyond which lay a moral jungle where power was the only rightful determinant. Apparently, the American people held the same view. Even the judicious Elihu Root defended Roosevelt's actions both publicly and privately. Above the sovereignty of Colombia, Root declared, there existed a "higher right." Not even the Democratic opposition challenged the President immediately after the event. Senator Gorman's plea to disapprove the treaty was ignored. Instead, the Louisiana legislature by a unanimous vote approved the treaty and congratulated the President. So did the great majority of newspapers and periodicals. International law, *The Outlook* observed, was sometimes based "upon a sense of justice but quite as much on national convenience. . . ." [25]

The taking of the Canal Zone was just one manifestation of a much larger interest the United States had taken in the Latin-American world following the Spanish-American War. The basic formulations of a new Caribbean and Latin-American policy had been worked out by McKinley, Hay, and Root before 1902. But under Roosevelt the new policy was greatly extended and given a precision which it had hitherto lacked. Before Roosevelt took office, John Hay, fearing the possible establishment of a German naval base off the American coast, had started negotiations to purchase the Virgin Islands from Denmark. A draft treaty of purchase was worked out in January, 1902, which Denmark eventually repudiated because of German pressure, or so it was thought at Washington. The new President eagerly supported the proposal to purchase, as he did various other attempts to buy Margarita Island, the Cocos, and the Galápagos. In the fall of 1902 Roosevelt also urged Hay to let Cuba know definitely that, irrespective of the fate of the pending reciprocity tariff treaty between the two countries, the naval stations promised in the Platt Amendment were to be ceded "and in the near future." [26]

[25] Root to Horace Porter, December 15, 1903, and to J. C. Carter, February 25, 1904, Root MSS.; *The Outlook*, LXXVI (1904), 248–249. See the *Literary Digest*, XXVII (1903), 649, 689, for a survey of press opinion.

[26] Roosevelt to Hay, October 23, 1902, Roosevelt MSS.

But what concerned Washington just as much as the Caribbean islands controlled from Europe were the independent republics of South and Central America whose weak governments and chaotic finances constituted a standing invitation to European intervention. In 1902 and 1903 the danger of intervention was sharply presented to

The uneasy lid.

the American government by affairs in Venezuela. The facts of the case were fairly common ones to the area. The inevitable dictator, one Cipriano Castro, had borrowed heavily in Europe and then had refused to pay. In December, 1902, Great Britain, Germany, and Italy, seeking to extract payment for their nationals, blockaded five ports and bombarded the Venezuelan forts at Puerto Cabello. Both Great Britain and Germany had informed Washington of their intended action; but since both had explicitly rejected the principle of seeking territorial compensation, the American government interposed no objection.[27] When Venezuela on December 13 asked the United States for arbitration, the government sent the request to London and Berlin without comment. Upon the request of the two countries that Roosevelt act as arbiter, a conference was held in Washington in January. Up to that time the American press had been extremely moderate in its opinions, pointing up the adamant refusal of Castro to pay his legally contracted obligations. But during the arbitration conference American opinion became inflamed when a German warship bombarded Fort Carlos and the surrounding Venezuelan village. "Worse international manners than Germany has exhibited," *The New York Times* declared, "have rarely come under observation of civilized man. . . ." Roosevelt himself was incensed at the German action even though he thought of Castro as an "unspeakable villainous little monkey." Later, when Germany showed a reluctance to accept a proposal to refer the dispute to the Hague Court, the President was further annoyed and probably increasingly suspicious that Germany was seeking more than monetary compensation. Germany, he wrote his son in February, "takes an impossible stand."[28] Eventually Germany was to give way, and the case was arbitrated by the Hague Court.

Years later Roosevelt was to remember that in the course of the controversy he had delivered an ultimatum to Germany stating that Dewey's naval squadron would sail for Venezuela if an agreement to arbitrate was not forthcoming. Whether Roosevelt issued such an ultimatum or not is still the subject of a lively historical controversy. Whatever the truth, there can be little question that the Venezuela episode made him extremely suspicious of German designs on American territory and set him to thinking about how to reconcile the possibility of future European intervention and American security.[29]

[27] Roosevelt to Albert Shaw, December 26, 1902, Roosevelt MSS.

[28] *The New York Times,* January 26, 1903; Roosevelt to Theodore Roosevelt, Jr., February 9, 1903, Roosevelt MSS.

[29] For various views on the Venezuela affair and the alleged ultimatum, see Dennett, *Hay,* pp. 390–92; Dexter Perkins, *A History of the Monroe Doctrine* (Boston, 1955), pp. 216–227; John M. Blum, *The Republican Roosevelt* (Boston, 1954), p. 128; S. W. Livermore, "Theodore Roosevelt, the American Navy and the Venezuela Crisis," *American Historical Review,* LI (1946), 452; and Beale, *Roosevelt and the Rise of America,* pp. 143–146.

In his December, 1901, message to Congress, Roosevelt defended the traditional interpretation of the Monroe Doctrine with reference to Latin America. We would permit no territorial aggrandizement, he emphasized, but this did not mean that "we would guarantee any state against punishment" if it misconducted itself. But in his private correspondence the President was already wondering just how far the United States should interfere with the affairs of the Latin-American nations and just how much we could "with justice prevent interference by others. . . ." [30] By the next February, months before the Venezuela incident, Elihu Root had expressed in general terms the principles which were to undergird the famous Roosevelt Corollary to the Monroe Doctrine. Writing to Andrew Carnegie, Root insisted that future American policy "must certainly bring the West Indies, from the point of Florida to the gateway of the Isthmian Canal, under the political and naval control of the United States, and must with equal certainty create special economic relations between them and the United States quite different from those which they or we bear to the rest of the world. Speaking in a broad way the first is our interest; the second is theirs." During the following summer, in a speech at Pittsburgh the President underscored Root's observations. [31]

The events of the year 1903 vastly accelerated the administration's formulation of a new Latin-American policy. Following the Venezuelan incident the Canal Zone was taken. And hard upon the creation of Panama a revolution in Santo Domingo demanded attention. There the already familiar story had reoccurred. A profligate dictatorship had left the country bankrupt and unable to meet its foreign obligations, while a revolution had destroyed all semblance of order. In the early winter of 1903 France, Germany, and Italy were threatening intervention. By the end of the year it was rumored that a German naval squadron was on its way across the Atlantic. And eventually, in order to protect himself against both the revolutionaries and the intrusive foreigners, President Morales asked the American government to assume a protectorate over his hapless country. There were many pressures on Roosevelt to act. Throughout January, 1904, German newspapers were firmly supporting their government's intention to protect "intimate German interests" in the Caribbean. Contrariwise,

[30] Roosevelt to Edward E. Hale, December 17, 1901, Roosevelt MSS.
[31] Root to Carnegie, February 8, 1902, Root MSS.; *The New York Times,* July 5, 1902.

British journals had already argued that if the United States were to protect Latin-American countries from foreign intervention, then in the name of logic it must assume some responsibility for their actions. In 1903 the chief of the Bureau of Navigation had requested the stationing of a permanent fleet in Haitian waters. Across the country newspapers were beginning to raise a familiar cry for action in "insufferable Santo Domingo" to bring order "out of the black chaos and cruelty." [32]

But Roosevelt was cautious in 1904; it was an election year. He had no more desire to annex the island, he wrote with rather a curious choice of words, "than a gorged boa constrictor might have to swallow a porcupine wrong-end to." For a year he held off official action by the compromise of sending an "unofficial" mission headed by Admiral Dewey to Santo Domingo and used the time to test public sentiment on a revolutionary extension of the Monroe Doctrine. On May 20, at a Cuban anniversary dinner in New York, Root read a letter from Roosevelt concerning relations of the United States to the Latin-American republics. There should be no interference, the President wrote, with a country conducting itself "with decency in industrial and political matters," provided it kept order and met its international obligations. But "brutal wrongdoing, or an impotence which results in a general loosening of the ties of civilized society, may finally require intervention by some civilized nation, and in the Western Hemisphere the United States cannot ignore this duty. . . ." In much the same words the President officially proclaimed the doctrine to Congress in December. The Roosevelt Corollary, as it became known, patently arrogating to the United States international police power in the hemisphere, altered Monroe's doctrine from one denying the right of European intervention in the Americas to one sanctioning the process when conducted by the United States. [33]

With the elections safely out of the way, application of the new principles proceeded rapidly. On the suggestion of the State Department an "agreement" was forced upon the Dominican government in January, 1905, which called for the appointment of an American as the collector of Dominican customs and director of national finance.

[32] H. C. Taylor to W. H. Moody, December 30, 1903, Moody MSS.; *Literary Digest*, XXVI (1903), 350; XXVIII (1904), 24; *World's Work*, VII (1904), 4501.

[33] Roosevelt to Joseph Bucklin Bishop, February 23, 1904, Roosevelt MSS.; Roosevelt to Root, May 20, 1904, Root MSS.

Under this executive agreement 45 per cent of the total receipts were to be allocated to the Dominican government for operating expenses, the rest to be placed in a trust fund for the settlement of outstanding international obligations. A future development in the scheme was foreshadowed when the new director, Colonel George R. Colton, proposed in 1906 that a large American bank be called in to consolidate and take over the European-held debt, which, of course, would have obviated the occasion for future European concern and intervention.[34]

Trouble appeared when the new agreement was presented to the Senate for its ratification. Both the Roosevelt Corollary and the first application of it had occasioned criticism at home and abroad. Continental newspapers were almost united in denouncing this "grafting of Caesarism upon Republican institutions." German journals in particular interpreted the doctrine as a fruitless effort of the United States to hold Latin America "against the expanding colonial urges of Europe." Abroad only the British press generally approved of the doctrine. At home some journals also challenged the advisability of this new departure; but surprisingly, the majority of the once formidable anti-imperialist press was silent, while a good many newspapers actually advocated outright annexation of the Dominican Republic.[35]

Notably rising support for the creation of the new financial protectorate came from large financial circles in Boston and New York. Some of it came directly from American holders of Dominican bonds, some because of the implied promise of direct State Department support for American business interests throughout Latin America, a promise that Elihu Root guilefully held forth to numerous interested people. Writing to the capitalist H. M. Flagler, Root argued that the building of the canal required the United States to police the surrounding premises. "In the nature of things trade and control, and the obligation to keep order which go with them must come our way. . . ." A short time later Root supported the effort of a New York banking group so to word an agreement to refund the Costa Rica debt that, if the interest were not paid, the United States would be able to protect the American bondholders. Forwarding the agreement to Secretary of State Hay, Root observed that it seemed very important to have Costa

[34] Root to Taft, January 8, 1906; George R. Colton to Taft, February 15, 1907, Taft MSS.

[35] *Literary Digest,* XXVIII (1904), 319; XXX (1905), 151, 319; XXXI (1905), 995.

Rica "under the financial control of Americans, with a power of ultimate control by the United States rather than have it vested in any foreign power." After surveying the "Venezuela mess" and other imperiled American interests throughout Latin America, Albert Shaw, editor of *World's Work*, wrote to Senator Beveridge that it seemed most likely "that substantial American interests will have to be protected by the government." The term "dollar diplomacy" was obviously being honored in word and act some years before it was given a precise definition by the Taft administration.[36]

Despite the cogent reasoning of the administration and the powerful support of the financial community, the United States Senate took another view of the agreement with Santo Domingo. Arguing that "the flag should not follow every contract" abroad, the Democratic minority led by Senator Rayner was almost unanimously opposed. Surprisingly, the minority was joined by enough Republicans first to amend the treaty out of recognition and then let it die without action. The Senate's obvious antagonism to the President's independent course in developing novel foreign policy greatly contributed to the treaty's defeat. And Roosevelt's later action in implementing his Dominican policy by executive agreement without benefit of consent was scarcely designed to assuage senatorial anger. The Dominican agreement was in operation for over two years before the Senate reluctantly approved it with some modification in 1907.[37]

With the death of John Hay in July, 1905, Elihu Root became Secretary of State, and subsequently Roosevelt's aggressive Latin-American policy was tempered by Root's caution and respect for constitutional procedures. Twice in 1908 Roosevelt might have embarked upon other Caribbean adventures in Venezuela and Haiti. But in each instance Root advised patience and delay, in part because he felt that neither Congress nor the American people would "sustain the administration in making war." Root spent most of his term, in fact, in attempting to win the good will of Latin America, and except for the 1906 Cuban intervention the United States position in Latin America was consolidated instead of aggressively extended.[38]

The Roosevelt administration faced one other vexing problem in the

[36] Root to H. M. Flagler, January 3, 1905, to John Hay, January 7, 1905, Root MSS.; Shaw to Beveridge, September 21, 1905, Beveridge MSS.
[37] *Congressional Record*, 59th Congress, 1st Session, Vol. 40, pt. 1, pp. 793 ff.
[38] Root to Whitelaw Reid, May 22, 1908, Root MSS.

Western Hemisphere in which, while the real interests were rather insignificant, the results were important and could have been infinitely more so had they evolved differently. The controversy over the Alaskan boundary began after gold was found in northwestern Canada. The major point of issue was whether the boundary line was measured from the heads of the inlets on the deeply scarred coast or from the headlands of the many peninsulas. If the United States claims were valid, then the Canadian gold fields had no outlet to the sea; if the Canadians were right, then the United States stood to lose a sizable area of the wild and practically uninhabited southernmost coast of Alaska which it had claimed and occupied for many years. By a temporary settlement in 1899, Canada was granted the use of the head of the Lynn Canal, which ran some eighty miles into the interior. What reprovoked the controversy was the reported findings of gold in 1902 near the Lynn Canal. Roosevelt, who had already made public his refusal to budge an inch on the American case, recognized the possibility of trouble among the rough mining population. He ordered the Army to reinforce the troops in the area and asked for a report on any improper actions by the population on either side of the border.[39]

From available evidence it appears as if the American claims were supported by the weight of both the historical and legal arguments advanced on the case. Even the Anglophile John Hay felt strongly that the Canadian claims, first advanced after the gold discoveries, were thoroughly unjustifiable, as did practically every American conversant with the facts of the dispute. This prompted Roosevelt's consistent refusal to arbitrate the matter, since, he explained, arbitration usually ends "in splitting the difference," a procedure which in this instance, he felt, would have been grossly unfair. An agreement to negotiate over the boundary came only when Canadian officials indicated that they wished to save face publicly and that if the United States agreed to arbitrate, the final decision would approximate the American position. Grumbling about the necessity for saving the public dignity of the "foolish Canadians," Roosevelt accepted the arbitral agreement, which, as he understood it, excluded arbitration. The arbitral instrument called for the appointment of six "impartial jurists," three representing the United States and three Canada and Great Britain. But the conditions under which it was accepted by the United States probably explain the President's explicit direction to the three American com-

[39] George B. Cortelyou to Root, March 27, 1902, Root MSS.

missioners, Root, Henry Cabot Lodge, and ex-Senator George Turner of Washington, not to deviate one jot in upholding the American case. It also explains his independent warnings to London through Associate Justice Oliver Wendell Holmes, Jr., that if the American case was not supported he would order the United States Army to survey the boundary line independently and afterward defend its findings. The President's mood probably also prompted his appointment of such intense partisan commissioners even though the agreement had called for the selection of impartial arbiters. As a matter of fact, he first offered the positions to two Supreme Court justices, who refused the honor, and he secured Root's acceptance only by what that unhappy man called a process of draft, impressment, and shanghaiing.[40]

The Canadian public was incensed at the obviously partisan character of the American commissioners, as were some Americans. Canadian opinion became more inflamed when the British representative on the commission, Baron Alverstone, consistently, except on two minor points, voted to support the American contentions. Canadians were quick to charge that Alverstone had sacrificed Canadian interests for British world policy.[41] Whatever the truth of the charge might be— and it is quite conceivable that Alverstone simply voted his judicial convictions—it was quite true that the dispute, which might have had a most deleterious effect on Anglo-American relations, instead nurtured a growing agreement between the two English-speaking countries that was already taking on the spirit, if not the legal apparatus, of an international entente.

It is illuminating to contrast the Roosevelt operating in the realm of foreign policy with the Roosevelt who dealt with Congress. The latter was cautious, conservative, and even timid at times. The first was bold, creative, and often ruthless in his use of power against the weak and helpless. If one measure of a civilized democratic state is the restraint with which it treats its unwanted classes of social and physical unfortunates, its criminals, and its subversives, then another might be the way it treats its weaker foreign neighbors. Should such a measure

[40] Roosevelt to Elihu Root, H. C. Lodge, and George Turner, March 17, 1903, to Oliver Wendell Holmes, Jr., July 25, 1903, Roosevelt MSS.; Root to Taft, August 11, 1903, Taft MSS.

[41] For a survey of Canadian opinion, see *Literary Digest*, XXVI (1903), 279. Beale, *Roosevelt and the Rise of America*, pp. 114 ff., and John A. Garraty, *Henry Cabot Lodge* (New York, 1953), pp. 242 ff., contain excellent elaborations of the dispute.

also be used to gauge a President's real inclinations toward the ruthless use of power against people whom he dislikes or with whom he fundamentally disagrees? If so, the Roosevelt of 1901–1905 would scarcely have won a *cum laude*.

The Roosevelt of the Northern Securities Case and the coal strike was in some ways also a strikingly different man from the President who carefully calculated his relations with Aldrich and Cannon. It might be argued that he was something of a prisoner of the reigning conservative ideologues in Congress because of his need for their support then, and in the coming nominating convention and the elections. It might also be suggested that his actions in the coal strike and the Northern Securities Case were simply prompted by an equal need for mass approbation and votes. Or Roosevelt might be pictured, as he has been in the past, as either the conservative who willingly co-operated with Congress or a sincere progressive frustrated by the congressional conservative majorities. Some better answers to these vexing questions may be gained after Roosevelt's second term, when the complexion of Congress had been changed somewhat and when there was no election to be won or lost in 1908. But there was no question about Roosevelt's thirst to win the Presidency on his own. This ambition certainly was not the primary factor in all the actions he took as the Chief Executive during his first three years. But the contest of 1904 was never very far from the surface of his thoughts, and the beguilement of future victory was probably as important as his principles in many of his crucial decisions.

CHAPTER 9

Trial and Triumph

THEODORE ROOSEVELT had scarcely been in office a month when he created a furor throughout the South by inviting the Negro educator Booker T. Washington to lunch at the White House. "The most damnable outrage," "a crime equal to treason," were among the more printable remarks from the South. "No Southern woman with proper self-respect," a Memphis paper fumed, "would now accept an invitation to the White House." The President was to tilt with southern racialism again when he appointed Dr. William Crum, another Negro, as collector of customs at Charleston, and again over his selection of Mrs. Minnie Cox as postmistress of Indianola, Mississippi. Roosevelt kept Crum in office by interim appointments after the Senate refused to concur in his selection, and closed the Indianola office temporarily when the town forced Mrs. Cox to resign.[1]

The Booker T. Washington incident made Roosevelt appear as a champion of the Negro. He had opposed antiminority activities in the nineties. He wanted very much to see the Negro advance economically. He could not support Negro suffrage, he wrote, but he did hope that the honest and intelligent members of the race would be afforded a "chance to have a little reward, a little respect. . . ." Of Roosevelt's sincerity in this matter there can be little doubt, but his southern appointment policy was scarcely aimed at these particular objectives. As far as the President had any distinctive Negro appointment policy in

[1] Memphis *Commercial Appeal,* cited in *Literary Digest,* XXIII (1901), 523.

the South, Root wrote, it had operated to reduce the number of Negro appointments.[2]

The principal aim of Roosevelt, the politician, during his first term was to be nominated and elected in 1904. Unerringly, he concluded that his main rival for the honor was Marcus Alonzo Hanna, the man who had made McKinley President and who was now senator from Ohio and national chairman of the party. Hanna had secured McKinley's nomination in 1896 in part by destroying ex-President Harrison's hold over the southern Republican "black and tan" machines. He had accomplished this feat by building up the power of the contesting "lily white" Republicans who controlled the party organization and the patronage when Roosevelt became President. Now Roosevelt reversed the process, and southern patronage was taken away from Hanna's loyal liege men and given to people who were trusted to vote right in 1904. In the 1900 South this meant granting the patronage either to the "black and tan" Republicans or to the Gold Democrats who had refused to return to their traditional party. The career of Dr. Crum was a case in point. For many years Crum had been the Republican county chairman of the Charleston district. He had been appointed collector of the port by Harrison but had lost the position when the Hanna "lily white" faction of the party triumphed. Now he was reappointed by Roosevelt and kept in office despite the Senate's refusal to concur. Eventually the President was to replace almost two-thirds of the federal officeholders in some of the southern states with his own black and tan Republicans and Gold Democrat partisans. Booker T. Washington had a wide acquaintance in the South with both educated whites and Negroes. He was invited to the White House to discuss southern patronage, not southern sociology, and he continued to act after the famous luncheon as one of Roosevelt's chief advisers on such matters. The President's purposes in the South were not related to color but to politics, something which he never cared to admit. Years later, in 1912, Roosevelt found that his own carefully constructed black and tan machines were then supporting the incumbent President, William Howard Taft. In seeking to win the Republican nomination from Taft, Roosevelt had to double back on his tracks in

2 Roosevelt to Owen Wister, April 27, 1906, Roosevelt MSS.; Root to Elihu Root, Jr., January 21, 1903, Root MSS.

the South. The Louisiana Roosevelt delegation to the Republican National Convention of 1912 was solidly lily white in character.[3]

Roosevelt came to office with the reputation of being a firm friend of the civil service principle. Many of his appointments during his first term, however, were to sadden his more idealistic reforming friends. Henry C. Payne of Wisconsin, "an old guard machine politician," was made Postmaster General. Leslie M. Shaw, the standpat governor of Iowa, became Secretary of the Treasury. Most shocking of all, James S. Clarkson of Iowa was appointed surveyor of the customs at New York. Back in 1891, Clarkson as Harrison's Assistant Postmaster General had dismissed 15,000 fourth-class postmasters, and as a result had had a first-class row with the Civil Service Commissioner, Theodore Roosevelt. Now Clarkson was of the anointed, as were Senator Matthew Quay of Pennsylvania and the members of the notorious Addicks machine in Delaware. Collectively their virtue lay in their local political power and their opposition to Mark Hanna. For the moment that was enough for Roosevelt. Reformers might find his appointments "disconcerting" and "inexplicable"; for Roosevelt they were the means to the end of nomination and election. In other ways he more than balanced the score. After Clarkson's appointment he cautioned him not to get into any trouble with the Civil Service Commission. In a strenuous fight with Congress in 1902 the President secured a permanent Census Bureau without blanketing all of its old politically appointed employees under civil service as Congress desired. Finally Roosevelt brought to the public service a host of young, energetic, and educated men from some of the better eastern universities whose like had possibly not been seen in such numbers before. Lord Bryce, the British ambassador in Washington, remarked of the Roosevelt appointments that he had never encountered "a more eager, high-minded, and efficient set of public servants. . . ."[4]

The administration was to stand in need of able men. Almost at its inception several vexatious administrative problems appeared, the mis-

[3] John M. Blum, *The Republican Roosevelt* (Boston, 1954), pp. 41–43; see also the characteristically perspicacious note on the Booker T. Washington affair in Elting E. Morison (ed.), *The Letters of Theodore Roosevelt* (8 vols., Cambridge, 1951–54), III, 181; George E. Mowry, "The South and the Progressive Lily White Party of 1912," *Journal of Southern History,* VI (1940), 237–247.

[4] Quoted in Gifford Pinchot, *Breaking New Ground* (New York, 1947), p. 229.

handling of which might cost many votes in the coming presidential contest. The most important of these, perhaps, concerned the Philippines, where the ugly revolt for independence of American rule still went on. The continuing need for men and money to suppress the rebellion had begun to disenchant many voters about the advisability of remaining in the islands. In February, 1902, Nelson A. Miles, Commanding General of the Army, created a sensation by making charges that the American commanders in the Philippines were guilty of widespread brutalities in their attempt to put down the native uprisings. Already in opposition to Root's plan for the reorganization of the Army, Miles demanded that he be sent to the Philippines with discretionary powers to attempt a settlement. A short time later the inspired publication of an order by one of the American field commanders in the Philippines "to kill and burn and make a howling wilderness of Samar" threw further fat in the fire. Afterward a congressional investigation disclosed the fact that the order had been carried out literally on Samar and to a lesser degree on the island of Leyte.[5]

Originally Roosevelt had a share of the responsibility for the taking of the Philippines and then had vigorously supported the retention of the islands under American rule. After the Philippine rebellion he had his private doubts about the wisdom of his position. When Vice-President, he wrote that he had "varied very much in his feelings" about the islands and expressed a hope that "events will speedily justify leaving them." But reacting to the 1902 attacks by Democrats and anti-imperialists, he became characteristically uncompromising and belligerent in his public statements. "The Republic has put its flag in those islands," he told the Sons of the American Revolution, "and the flag will stay there." [6] In the midst of excited public debate the Philippine Government Act was approved on July 1, 1902. Among the provisions of the act, which had largely been inspired by Elihu Root before Roosevelt became President, were ones for the organization of an elected assembly and many measures for the social and economic welfare of the Filipinos. Under the act, on July 4, the President abolished the office of Military Governor and gave full powers to the civilian Governor William Howard Taft, and proclaimed a general amnesty

[5] Miles to Roosevelt, February 17, 1902, Roosevelt MSS.; Roosevelt to Root, February 18, 1902, Root MSS.; Luke E. Wright to Taft, April 19, 1902, Taft to Root, September 13, 1902, Taft MSS.

[6] Roosevelt to Frederic R. Coudert, July 3, 1901, Roosevelt MSS.; manuscript of speech in Roosevelt papers.

and an end to the insurrection except in the Moro districts. As some cynics pointed out, the official end of the rebellion as proclaimed by Roosevelt must not have impressed many Filipinos, who went on fighting. The proclamation and the Philippine Government Act did, however, serve to still public criticism, as did the testimony before the congressional committee of Secretary of War Root and Governor Taft, who had been in Washington since January aiding the administration on Philippine problems.[7]

From Washington, Taft went to Rome, where he was to initiate extremely touchy political negotiations with the Vatican on the disposal of Church lands in the Philippines. A vexing situation had arisen when some 60,000 tenants of three friar orders had expelled the friars and had seized the lands, claiming that the rents they had been forced to pay were exorbitant. To restore the land to the friars, Taft wrote, would precipitate another revolution. Yet the United States had by the treaty of cession with Spain guaranteed all existing property rights. Apparently, the American Catholic Archbishop John Ireland first suggested that the government arrange for the transfer of the lands by dealing directly with the Vatican. After Root had opened the negotiations, Taft and the American Bishop O'Gorman concluded the discussions which eventuated in the sale of over 400,000 acres of land paid for by the bonds of the new Philippine government. The negotiations at Rome were complicated by the desire of the American hierarchy to replace the Spanish clergy in the Philippine Church with Americans—a program that Taft supported—and by the efforts of the friars to break up the negotiations for the sale of their former lands by protesting against the Vatican's use of the money involved. But Taft's tact and Root's patience finally triumphed. As Root wrote, there was no need to be troubled either by the "friars' sharp practices" or by the length of time the negotiations took. "We have got the money, the Filipinos have the land, the Pope has got a lot of worthless friars on his hands, and the friars have got nothing." No political capital could be made of the situation, he concluded, if they persisted in treating the Church "fair and kindly." [8]

The political capital Root referred to reflected the administration's

[7] For the best discussion of the thorny Philippine government problems, see Philip C. Jessup, *Elihu Root* (2 vols., New York, 1938), I, 363 ff.

[8] Of the very many letters on the friar land situation, see especially Root to Taft, September 5, 1901, and August 11, 1903; Taft to Root, April 7, May 21, and July 22, 1902; Taft to Magnus Larsen, October 9, 1908, Taft MSS.

fear that both Protestant and Catholic voters in the United States would be alienated by the delicate negotiations. When Taft's visit to the Vatican was announced, a number of American Protestants heatedly protested against this "political recognition" of the papacy, protests which were only partially stilled by the Washington announcement that Taft's mission was concerned with a "real estate deal" and had no political implications. As late as 1908 Taft was still receiving censorious letters for his Roman excursion. Some Catholics were also critical, fearing that the government was subjecting the Church to political pressure. This criticism increased when Father Aglipay broke away from the Roman Church in the Philippines and set up his own independent institution. The Vatican asked that the United States refuse to recognize the splinter group and demanded the return of Church property. "It would be a fatal mistake," Cardinal Merry del Val wrote, "to give equal rights or support in the Philippine Islands to Aglipay or any other stray adventurer who for one reason or another rebels against his legitimate superiors. . . ." If the government continued to support the hierarchy in the islands, the Church would find it "comparatively easy to guide the Philippinos from a religious and moral point of view and make them loyal American citizens. . . ." But if the contrary were true, "dissensions and factions of all kinds would arise" and the United States might have to govern by force. While insisting that the United States could not discriminate between any religious groups, Taft did recognize the property rights of the Church.[9]

The administration faced another potentially serious political situation in the summer of 1903, when it became generally known that widespread fraud had been discovered in the Post Office Department. The President was particularly vulnerable to the charge of fraud in his administration because of his self-assumed position of being the nation's number one expounder of morality. Tom Read jested once that he was delighted to hear that Roosevelt had rediscovered the Ten Commandments. Another quipster remarked that the President was the kind of a person who, upon reading a child's essay on ethics, would mount a horse and ride ten miles at breakneck speed to tell his neighbor the news. In December of 1902, Postmaster General Payne reported to Roosevelt that corruption did exist and the President, waiting until

---

[9] Taft to Roosevelt, November 9, 1903, Roosevelt MSS.; Cardinal Merry del Val to Taft, August 29, 1904, Taft MSS.

after Congress adjourned, appointed an investigating committee headed by the fourth Assistant Postmaster General, Joseph L. Bristow. The Bristow report was made in November, 1903. Only a summary of it was made public; the rest, including much of the evidence, was suppressed. Acting upon a letter from the President, the Attorney General had issued forty four indictments against government employees. Four high officers in the Post Office had resigned and thirteen more had been removed from office.[10]

Meanwhile the reason for the suppression of parts of the Bristow report had been whispered around Washington: a good many important members of Congress were implicated, the names of Hanna, Cannon, Lodge, and Beveridge given prominence, and even some members of the administration. A report of the Civil Service Commission in June, 1903, had hinted at these connections. Despite Postmaster General Payne's attempt to conceal the matter, the news leaked out in March, 1904, that the Bristow report named some 150 members of Congress in leasing buildings to the Post Office Department for high rents and in obtaining "unwarranted" raises in pay for postmasters of their districts by placing pressure on the department. For a time very strained relations existed between the White House and Congress, but then a special committee of the House found that although some members had not acted properly, none was guilty of fraud. Roosevelt and Payne were first unfairly charged with responsibility for the corruption, but since most of the indicted men had been appointed by the previous administration, the charge failed to stick. The President's quick action in ordering an investigation and the congressional connections with the matter all helped to remove any possible stain on the President's reputation. The association of Hanna's name with possible wrongdoing, in fact, aided Roosevelt in his campaign for nomination, and there were some people who saw a connection between the publicity given to Hanna and the coming events of 1904.[11]

It is almost impossible to say with certainty what Hanna's plans for 1904 were. He was not a man to wear his intentions on his sleeve. One can guess that he wanted the Republican nomination. At least, many important Republicans wanted it for him. A most important element

[10] *The New York Times,* November 24, 1900; Roosevelt to Knox, July 22, 1903, Knox MSS.

[11] Congressional Record, 58th Congress, 2nd Session, pt. 5, p. 4721; *Literary Digest,* XXVIII (1904), 393; Dorothy G. Fowler, *The Cabinet Politician, The Postmaster General, 1829–1909* (New York, 1943).

in the party, the business and financial people, one Republican paper stated, would "acquiesce in the nomination of Roosevelt rather than welcome it." Among such people, according to the journal, Hanna was clearly the favorite. As late as June, 1902, *The New York Times* ventured the opinion that Hanna was a far more likely winner than Roosevelt.[12]

As national chairman of the party, Hanna was not without influence among the local professional politicians who often determine a nomination. But the patronage belonged to the President, and through its judicious use Roosevelt by the opening of 1903 had destroyed most of Hanna's strength in the South. There was little that the Senator could do to restore it. Even Hanna's home state of Ohio had become uncertain in its loyalty as Senator Joseph Benson Foraker, backed with presidential patronage there, was busily sapping the strength of the Hanna-McKinley machine. So far the contest between the President and the Senator had been conducted privately and decently behind the scenes. But in May, 1903, the issue burst out into the public view. Just prior to the meeting of the Ohio State Republican convention, Senator Foraker publicly demanded that the meeting endorse the President for the coming nomination. Hanna objected, arguing that it was against the Ohio tradition to pledge the party so far in advance. But he felt it necessary further to explain his position by telegram to the President, then campaigning for delegates in the Northwest. Roosevelt replied in an abrupt and graceless fashion to the effect that he was not asking anyone to support him, and that he assumed those for him would be for him in the coming meeting and those against him, against him. Hanna's telegram had been private, but the substance of the President's angry reply was made public. The following day, in a speech at Butte, Montana, Roosevelt made the charge that the "class of criminal rich" was organizing to defeat him. After that double volley Hanna gave ground and announced that he would not stand in the way of the Roosevelt endorsement. Then and later Hanna refused to make a positive statement supporting the President, but his partial capitulation in Ohio was considered as a major defeat by the public. Roosevelt thoroughly understood this. He had been feeling jaded, but the incident gave him "a new lease on life." [13]

[12] Cited in *Literary Digest*, XXVI (1903), 452.

[13] Roosevelt to Lodge, May 27, 1903, in Lodge, *Letters*, II, 18–20; *The New York Times*, May 26, 27, 1903.

When Roosevelt returned from his long campaign trip to the Pacific coast in the late spring of 1903, his nomination and re-election looked almost inevitable. Then near-disaster struck in the form of a sharp but short financial panic. The year 1902 had been a prosperous one for the American economy. Exports had fallen somewhat, but the domestic markets had bounded upward. Six thousand miles of new railroads had been built, employment rates were good, wages increased, and the corporate dividends were the highest on record. But during the summer of 1903 a curious fiscal movement occurred. While crop prices remained high and manufacturing was steady, the stock market went into a steep decline, wiping away over $2 billion in security values. As credit became increasingly stringent, business failures rose alarmingly. The great nabob of Wall Street, J. Pierpont Morgan, publicly blamed the financial panic on the amount of "undigested securities" then in the market. But other financial authorities, speaking less elliptically, called it the result of the President's harassment of business. Only a few conceded that the panic was due to an inflexible monetary structure and to the spectacular overcapitalization of trusts like the United States Steel Corporation.[14]

By late summer Roosevelt admitted that the financial situation looked very "ugly." He was not sure whether to blame the panic mostly on the wild and reckless speculation among the capitalists or upon the sinister and shortsighted wrongdoing of the labor leaders. But he had heard, he told Root, that "certain of the big men" in Wall Street were not at all reluctant to see the panic get worse, so as to discredit the administration and "to force the Republican party back into the paths of conservatism. . . ." The most obvious conservative Republican candidate, of course, was Hanna.[15] In November the Ohio senator made national headlines by his sweeping victory over the liberal Democrat, Tom Johnson, mayor of Cleveland. The White House became increasingly sensitive in December to Hanna's refusal publicly to endorse the President's cause and to his efforts in Ohio to secure delegates to the national convention. With a note of desperation Lodge wrote to Root in January of the new year asking him to see Hanna and get a public commitment. It was asking too much of the President, Lodge contended, to expect him to support Hanna in Ohio or be neutral when Hanna was actively opposing Roosevelt's friend Foraker. People were

[14] *Literary Digest*, XXVII (1903), 183.
[15] Roosevelt to Root, October 3, 1903, Root MSS.

"talking and spending money in New York" in activities which would not defeat Roosevelt but would certainly "hurt the party." "What we want," Lodge expostulated, "is just one word in public." But that word never came. Instead, Root reported that the pro-Hanna, anti-Roosevelt campaign among the "substantial men" of New York was being received with enthusiasm at the Union League Club, of which Root was president.[16]

Apparently fearful of a Wall Street-Hanna coalition, the administration exerted itself in the fall and winter of 1903–4 to counteract the supposed opposition. No disturbing legislative proposals came from the White House. Instead, cordial letters went out to J. P. Morgan, H. L. Higginson, and E. H. Harriman, asking their advice on financial legislation. Root journeyed to the Union League Club in January, where he made a speech designed "to cut the ground from under the Roosevelt people." Some of the President's journalistic friends prepared articles to indicate the administration's concern for the business world and businessmen. One such article, written by Ray Stannard Baker on the suggestion of Gifford Pinchot, carried the title "The Business Achievements of the Administration." And then Mark Hanna was struck down with typhoid fever. Roosevelt's worry about any dangerous opposition for the nomination was all but ended. From then on his pro-business moves were made for the sake of obtaining the necessary funds to conduct a proper campaign. Roosevelt was insistent that a friend of business be made national chairman of the party. When Cornelius Bliss refused to act, even after the President had assured him that he would become "one of the trusted and intimate advisors in all matters . . . for the next four years," the plum went to George B. Cortelyou, the President's private secretary, a relatively unknown man, but one who was to become increasingly acceptable to the eastern conservative wing of the party. Bliss then accepted the position of treasurer. By September, 1904, a friend reported to Taft that an "entente cordiale" seemed to exist between the White House and the house of Morgan.[17]

Even after Hanna's death and the conversion of the business community, a few problems, more vexatious than important, needed to be confronted before Roosevelt was satisfied with the prenomination cam-

[16] Lodge to Root, January 17, 1904; Root to John St. L. Strachey, March 23, 1904, Root MSS.

[17] Gifford Pinchot to Ray Stannard Baker, January 11, 1904, Pinchot MSS.; Roosevelt to Bliss, May 6, 1904, Roosevelt MSS.; Clarence R. Edmonds to Taft, September 20, 1904, Taft MSS.

paign. A "very, very ugly" situation had developed in Wisconsin, where the La Follette forces won a majority in the state convention. The regulars bolted, and under the leadership of Senator Spooner and Postmaster General Payne held a rump convention to select Roosevelt delegates to the national meeting. The President chose to go along with his proved friends and the word went out that the minority delegation was to be seated in the coming meeting, an action that some historians have interpreted as indicating Roosevelt's basic hostility to both reform and reformers. The President's decision, of course, indicated nothing of the sort. Roosevelt was interested in just two things, the nomination and the maintenance of party harmony. He could scarcely have repudiated his Postmaster General without creating a party row in Wisconsin. Simultaneously with his decision against La Follette he was urging the Republican State Chairman of Missouri not to nominate a candidate against the liberal Democrat, Joseph W. Folk, running for governor. Folk, of course, had no votes in the Republican convention.[18]

A similar quarrel between Senator Platt and regional boss Benjamin B. Odell threatened the peace and harmony of the New York party. Here Root negotiated an armistice. Astonishingly, Congress had to be reminded of the critical political situation. It had failed to act on an administration-inspired measure to designate all Civil War veterans who had arrived at the age of sixty-two as half-disabled and thus eligible for a pension. In April, the Pension Commission, spurred by a presidential request, was delighted to find that the congressional oversight could be remedied by an administrative ruling, and that henceforth all Union veterans aged sixty-two or more were entitled to a sum of $5 a month. The President was highly irritated when uncharitable critics imputed that the order was based less on medical facts than upon political anticipations. He contended that it was nonsense to say that at sixty-two the average man had not had his capacity for physical labor "impaired at least one-half." [19]

Few national political conventions have been so carefully planned as the Republican meeting of 1904; few have offered less surprises. Root was Roosevelt's choice for temporary chairman, Cannon for permanent chairman, and Lodge for head of the Committee on Platform. All the important speeches had been written weeks before the

[18] Roosevelt to Nicholas Murray Butler, May 21, 1904; Roosevelt to Thomas J. Atkins, April 5, 1904, Roosevelt MSS.
[19] Roosevelt to Root, May 5, 1904, Root MSS.

body met, and each had received the careful review of the President. Even the seconding speeches were scrutinized, and one unhappy southern delegate was abruptly requested to throw away his overlong speech and write another one "seconding a nomination." Except for a suffrage plank, the platform, conservative, noncommittal, and undistinguished, was passed substantially as the President desired it. Weeks before the convention assembled, Senator Charles W. Fairbanks of Indiana had been agreed upon as the vice-presidential candidate. Roosevelt would have preferred Congressman Robert R. Hitt of Illinois, but the party professionals insisted upon Fairbanks' obvious suitability: he was wealthy, conservative, and Indiana was always a doubtful state. Roosevelt agreed. Among the least surprising actions of the convention was the unanimous nomination of Roosevelt. The meeting adjourned as it had opened, in an air "of feigned enthusiasm punctuated with indifference." According to one journalist, the delegates "all knew why they had been invited to Chicago, and they had done it." [20]

An important element of Republican strength lay in the chaotic condition of the Democratic party. After the defeat of 1900 various conservatives in the party started a movement to wean it away from Bryanism. Among the leaders in this campaign for a "sensible candidate" in 1904 and "a good old-fashioned platform" were Richard Olney, Secretary of State under Cleveland; the perennial upstate New York boss, David B. Hill; the financier, William C. Whitney; and the conservative Senator Gorman of Maryland. Supporting the reorientation were some of the most important party newspapers of the East and the South. The aging ex-President Cleveland became the temporary rallying point for the anti-Bryanites. In June, 1902, he called for a marshaling of the party "outside the shadow of predestined defeat." Eight months later at a testimonial banquet Cleveland described the laissez-faire program which he hoped the party would adopt in 1904: a reduction in the tariff, support of the gold standard, strict government economy, freedom for the Philippines, and finding a solution to the trust problem in the common law and the wisdom of the state legislatures.[21]

[20] *The New York Times,* June 22, 23, 24, 1904; Roosevelt to Theodore Roosevelt, Jr., May 14, 1904, and to Harry S. Edwards, June 8, 1904, Roosevelt MSS.
[21] *The New York Times,* June 20, 1902; *Literary Digest,* XXVI (1903), 417.

Since Cleveland was obviously too old to be considered a serious candidate, gradually and almost by default of other likely choices the conservatives of the party began to support the candidacy of Judge Alton B. Parker of New York. Parker was almost unknown outside of his home state. There he had been a successful organization Democrat, working hard for the party and asking little in return. In 1885 he had managed the successful campaign of David B. Hill for governor, and in return had been appointed to an unexpired term of the State Supreme Court. He refused the party nomination for the governorship, but had been eminently successful on the court, where, probably because of his liberal labor record and his refusal strictly to limit the legislative power, he had been returned in the Republican year of 1897 by a remarkable popular vote. Parker had steadfastly refused to participate in inner party quarrels, and in 1896 and 1900, instead of joining the Gold Democrats, he had supported Bryan. His consistent refusal in 1903 and early 1904, because of his judicial office, to take any public position on the nomination or on political questions won public respect. When the New York State Democratic Convention in April, 1904, pledged him its support, despite Tammany opposition, he became the national hope of conservative and eastern Democrats.

By his attacks upon Cleveland as an ex-Democrat and upon party conservatism, Bryan made it known early that he was willing to run for the third time. But even Bryan's western friends were not able to muster enough support to overcome the stigma of his two successive defeats. The radicals widely acknowledged that the only hope for victory lay in the person of the bizarre millionaire newspaper owner, William Randolph Hearst. Hearst's public service consisted of a single term in Congress, during which he had rarely occupied his seat. Consequently, his record was most evident in his newspapers, which already dotted the country from New York to California. Everywhere the units of the Hearst chain were uniformly characterized by the same formulas of belligerent nationalism, bloody crime, and blatant sex, all presented with culminating paragraphs seeping with rectitude. Editorially the papers were devoted to local crusading, real and fancied, together with an anticorporate, prolabor viewpoint. Also in question during Hearst's campaign was his most unconventional private life, which the New York *Post* described as "a sewer laid open." [22]

With such qualifications Hearst came to the convention supported

[22] New York *Post,* quoted in *Current Literature,* XXXVI (1904), 382.

by the Pacific coast and much of the intermountain region. But despite Bryan's support he was defeated by Parker on the first ballot, 658 to 200. The Democratic platform was a little more successful than the Republican document in refusing to meet the issues of the day, its most distinguished characteristic being an omission of any mention of the currency question. Parker, however, wired the convention that he believed the gold standard to be inalterably "established" and invited it to nominate another candidate if it did not agree with his views. Whereupon the convention added a gloss to the platform, stating that it saw nothing in the document that would not coincide with the candidate's views and prevent him from accepting the nomination.[23]

The presidential campaign of 1904 was almost as dispirited as the two conventions. A careful, cautious, lackluster man, Parker won a certain respect from the public but scarcely enthusiastic devotion. Possibly to distinguish himself from the peripatetic Bryan, he chose to stay at home during most of the campaign and make speeches only to visiting groups. Since the President by tradition was restrained from campaigning, the battle for the most part was fought out at long distance. And since both men were attempting to appear as conservatives, the issues advanced were not calculated to raise the public blood pressure. Parker did protest against "the rule of individual caprice," the presidential "usurpation of authority," and the "aggrandizement of personal power." But his more positive proposals were so backward-looking, as for example his proposal to let the state legislatures and the common law develop a remedy for the trust problem, that the New York *World* characterized the campaign as a struggle of "conservative and constitutional Democracy against radical and arbitrary Republicanism." [24] Roosevelt, remarkably restrained, countered with an appeal for "the traditional Republican doctrines" that had worked so well for so long. Considering the rising progressive spirit in the cities and the states, it was a strange campaign.[25]

Only in its last few weeks did the contest take on something of the air of a normal presidential canvass. On October 1 *The New York Times* charged that the Republican National Chairman, Cortelyou, had collected vast sums of money from large industrial trusts by methods almost approaching blackmail and was using it virtually to purchase the

[23] *Official Report of the Proceedings of the Democratic National Convention* (New York, 1904), p. 277.

[24] New York *World*, August 1, 1904.

[25] "Mr. Roosevelt in a Safe and Sane Role," *Literary Digest,* August 6, 1904.

election. Parker on a short campaign trip took up the charge, and during October made "Cortelyouism" the leading issue of the contest. Cortelyou's reply that the funds at the party's disposal were not as large as those that McKinley had in 1896 or Cleveland in 1892 neither answered the charges nor satisfied Roosevelt. On November 4, just before the election, the President answered in a characteristic fashion. The statements made by Parker, Roosevelt heatedly declared, were "unqualifiedly and atrociously false." This categorical statement was to trouble its author a good many times in the future. During the insurance investigation in 1905, again in 1907 during the Harriman controversy, and later in 1912, it was unmistakably shown that large corporations or their executives had contributed a large portion of the more than $2 million the National Republican party had at its disposal in 1904. Moreover, it is practically certain that Roosevelt at the time knew a portion of the truth and suspected a good deal more. It is true that he peremptorily asked Cortelyou to return the $100,000 contributed by the Standard Oil Company, a request ignored by the party treasurer, Cornelius Bliss. He did so, however, only after the issue had been raised by a newspaper reporter. Significantly, he did not raise the issue of other corporation gifts with Cortelyou. And when in October he was informed that E. H. Harriman of the Union Pacific Railroad desired to make a "sizable contribution" to the New York State Republican Campaign fund, Harriman was quickly invited to the White House. It was during the course of these Roosevelt-Harriman negotiations that the President wrote his much-regretted phrase, "Now my dear sir, you and I are practical men. . . ." But in November, 1904, Parker could not produce the proof for his charges, and Roosevelt's righteous blast was enough to convince an already biased public in favor of the trust buster.[26]

More than a week before the election Roosevelt wrote to his son that he was practically sure of two hundred electoral votes and probably of thirty-eight more, one less than needed to elect. The odds, he said, seemed to be with him, but he would not grumble if things went wrong, since he had had "three good years." Very early on election night it was obvious that the nation had voted him four more. The national Republican ticket had been astonishingly successful everywhere save

[26] *The New York Times,* November 5, 1904; Whitelaw Reid to Theodore Roosevelt, September 15, 1904, Roosevelt to Reid, September 16, 1904, Roosevelt to Harriman, October 10, 14, 1904, Roosevelt MSS. But see Morison, *Roosevelt Letters,* IV, 995–996, for a different interpretation.

in the South. Roosevelt had carried even West Virginia and Missouri on the border, and most of the old Bryan states in the trans-Missouri West. The combined Republican majority in the Senate and the House was the largest since the Civil War. The President was elated by "the

"What are you doing here?"

sweep" and on election night issued the famous statement that he had prepared mentally some weeks before. The three and a half years he had already served, he stated, constituted his first term; and since he found the custom wise which limited the President to two terms, he would not run again. "Under no circumstances," the fateful statement concluded, "will I be a candidate for or accept another nomination." [27]

[27] *The New York Times,* November 10, 1904.

CHAPTER 10

The Orient and the World

MONTHS before the presidential election of 1904, the United States was deeply involved in the Russo-Japanese War, the outcome of which, the government realized, would profoundly influence the future of the Orient. The quickening interest in the Far East flowed naturally from the imperialist spirit of 1898, the taking of the Philippines and Hawaii, and the intention to construct an isthmian canal. In 1900 Alfred Thayer Mahan published a volume of collected magazine articles entitled *The Problem of Asia and Its Effect Upon International Policies.* Arguing for an Anglo-American-Japanese understanding to balance Russia's growing power in north China, Mahan took for granted that the United States would become a great Pacific and Asiatic power. Congratulating Mahan on his work, Vice-President Roosevelt entirely agreed with the need for Anglo-American naval co-operation in the Orient. As President, two years later, Roosevelt was even more expansive. "America's geographical position on the Pacific," he told a San Francisco audience, "is such as to insure our peaceful domination of its waters. . . ." Sometime later he wrote that the nation's future would depend more on "our position on the Pacific facing China than on our position on the Atlantic facing Europe." [1]

When Roosevelt became President the nation was already deeply committed in East Asia. John Hay had expanded his Open Door policy from its original commercial objective to one of preserving the territorial integrity of China. In 1900 the nation had joined the inter-

[1] Roosevelt to Mahan, March 18, 1901, to Benjamin Ide Wheeler, June 17, 1905, Roosevelt MSS.; *The New York Times,* May 14, 1903.

national military expedition to rescue the besieged foreign legations in Peking. By 1902 America's economic stake in East Asia was large and rapidly expanding. Exports to Asia, where the largest customers were China and Japan, were approximately double those to South America. Among the more powerful private American groups interested either in trade or investments in China were the Standard Oil Company and the American China Development Company, a railroad construction syndicate headed by J. P. Morgan, E. H. Harriman, and Jacob Schiff.

The Chinese political situation was a complicated one. The corrupt and dying Manchu dynasty had neither the power to repulse Western European imperialism nor to stop the rise of a weak but growing revolutionary, nationalistic movement aimed at the destruction of both the existing government and constantly increasing foreign intervention. From the enfeebled Manchus the British had already seized the dominant economic power in the south, the Russians held parts of Manchuria, and Japan, repulsed on the Liaotung Peninsula in 1895 by a European concert, was recouping her loss in Korea. Germany and France, by the extraction of treaty ports, had also joined the race for Chinese trade and territory. Russian pressure on both Manchuria and Tibet was responsible for the Anglo-Japanese alliance in 1902. The rapidly growing grand alliances in Europe further confused the already complex rivalries. At times Roosevelt was tempted to use outright force in China to obstruct the gains of other powers and grab economic and possible territorial concessions for the United States. But his doubt that the American people would support an aggressive Asia policy and his fear of how the other European powers would react persuaded him to fall back on John Hay's Open Door formulation, which sought to maintain Chinese territorial integrity and guarantee an equality of trade and investment opportunity there for all nations. Short of the application of force, such a policy, ensuring the continuance of American commercial interests, could be maintained only by the balancing of power between the various other national contestants.

Until 1902 Roosevelt was not worried about Russia's threat to China. In the long run he was sure that no European power could contest Russia's control of Asia. The day of the Slav was "far off," but Russia's refusal to honor its 1902 agreement with China by withdrawing its forces from Manchuria and its persistent efforts to close Manchuria to American trade changed his opinion. "I wish, in Manchuria, to go the very limit I think our people will stand," he informed his Secretary of State, John Hay. Keenly aware of what the American people would not stand, he turned to Great Britain and Japan as a counterpoise against Russian encroachment. Covertly the government and the press openly welcomed the Anglo-Japanese Alliance of 1902. It was "a shaft aimed at Russia," one New York journal announced; a treaty, a second declared, assuring the Open Door and thus agreeing with our policy. Throughout 1903, as Russia kept Chinese ports closed and resisted the establishment of American consulates in Manchuria, anti-Russian sentiment grew steadily in Washington and in the nation's press. The "mendacity of the Russians" was something appalling, Roosevelt commented. The bad feature of the situation was "that as yet it seems we cannot fight to keep Manchuria open." [2]

In February, 1904, Japan did what Roosevelt wanted to do theoretically but felt he could not—attacked Russia by staging a torpedo-boat raid on the Russian fleet anchored at Port Arthur. This initial Japanese success was shortly followed by others on both land and sea. By the following summer the Japanese had practically destroyed Russian naval strength in the Pacific and had won important land victories at Port Arthur and Mukden. Assailed by a revolution at home and confronted with the loss of Manchuria and a possible conquest of Siberia, the Czarist government seemed to be tottering.

It was no secret at the start of the war that American official and public sympathies lay with Japan. The danger existed, of course, that a Japanese victory would eventually result in a Manchuria exclusively dominated and exploited by Japan. But the President commented that in balancing "the certainty of immediate damage against the possibility of future damage," he would have to prefer the latter. In most of his correspondence the President was far more pro-Japanese. Japan was "playing our game," he told his son. He was pleased with the Japanese naval victories and wrote to his Secretary of State that the United States could possibly be of great service if Japan won the war by "preventing interference to rob her of the fruits of her victory." So open was America's stand, in fact, that at the beginning of the war continenal papers took it for granted that an Anglo-American-Japanese "concord" existed and wondered whether the agreement was not of

[2] Roosevelt to John Hay, May 22, July 29, 1903, Roosevelt MSS. For a survey of American press opinion on the Anglo-Japanese Alliance, see *Current Literature*, XXXII (1902), 257.

a more formal kind. There appears to be no evidence, however, to support Roosevelt's later statement that he warned both France and Germany that the United States would act if the two nations combined against Japan.[3]

While American opinion at the start of the war was decidedly partial as Japan's series of victories continued, serious questions were raised about her future intentions in the Orient. In June, 1905, a magazine edited by a confidant of the President carried two articles, one by J. Gordon Smith, called "Japan's Closing the Open Door"; the other, by John Hays Hammond, an important Republican who had mining interests in China and Korea, more ominously entitled "The Menace of Japan's Success."[4] Roosevelt had foreseen the possibility that the war might substitute one monopolistically inclined power for another in the Orient. As early as March, 1904, he had voiced the rather wistful hope that Russia and Japan might fight on until both were exhausted. In that event the peace would not create "either a yellow peril or a Slav peril." For the next fifteen months he repeatedly stated confidentially that he would be sorry to see Russia driven entirely out of East Asia. If Japan were thoroughly successful and reorganized China, he observed to Spring-Rice, there would result "a real shifting of equilibrium as far as the white races are concerned."[5]

Even before the war broke out the President had suggested mediation to both sides, and he continued his efforts throughout the summer of 1904 for a compromise agreement that would leave both powers facing each other with unimpaired strength. Since neither side was yet convinced that a complete victory was impossible, both refused his confidential suggestion. Then in an amazing series of adroit, complex, and supersecret moves, the President personally carried through his program for a peace which would re-establish a balance of power in China. A close personal friend of the President replaced the incumbent American ambassador at St. Petersburg. Roosevelt dealt directly with Japan through the friendly Japanese ambassador at Washington, Takahira, and through a Harvard classmate, Baron Kaneko. His per-

[3] Roosevelt to Spring-Rice, June 13, 1904; to T. Roosevelt, Jr., February 10, 1904; to John Hay, July 26, 1904, Roosevelt MSS. For a survey of American and Continental press opinion on the war, see *Literary Digest*, XXVIII (1904), 101, 487.

[4] *World's Work*, X (1905), 6267.

[5] Roosevelt to Spring-Rice, March 19, 1904, and to Whitelaw Reid, June 5, 1905, Roosevelt MSS.

sonal friends in the British and German diplomatic corps were also used when necessary. And without the knowledge of the Cabinet or Congress, or even most of the State Department, the President finally won consent from both powers to meet in a peace conference at Portsmouth, New Hampshire. Aiding Roosevelt were some exceedingly fortunate circumstances. By the summer of 1905 Russia was disastrously defeated and was also faced by a revolution at home. Japan, on the other hand, as her Washington envoys revealed to Roosevelt, was at the point of financial collapse. But fortune is often a necessary ingredient for the success of such complicated maneuvers, and the favor of chance should not detract from Roosevelt's outstanding achievement. As Professor Beale has shown, the Peace of Portsmouth resulted in good part from the President's patient, tactful, brilliant diplomacy.[6]

Before the opening of the Russo-Japanese War, Roosevelt had hoped the quarrel might be settled by granting Manchuria without Port Arthur to Russia, Korea to Japan, and a pledge from both to preserve the integrity of China and the Open Door throughout their newly won territory. The actual settlement at Portsmouth was even more favorable from America's point of view. Port Arthur and the Russian-controlled railroads in Manchuria were turned over to Japan, as was the southern half of Sakhalin. Russia recognized Japan's "predominant" interests in Korea, but Manchuria was left as a part of China where officially the nationals of all countries could trade and invest. Thus the Open Door was guaranteed in Manchuria. Russia was not liquidated as an Asiatic power and was left, in Roosevelt's words, "face to face with Japan so that each may have a moderative action on the other." [7]

Until the last moment of the Portsmouth conference the Japanese had demanded a huge war indemnity which Russia refused to consider. In capitulating on the point, the Japanese government ran afoul of popular criticism at home, some of which was turned against Roosevelt and the United States as being partially responsible for the failure to secure the payment. The Japanese government, however, was quite content with American policy at Portsmouth because that policy also included American recognition of a Japanese Korea. By June, 1905,

[6] Roosevelt to Lodge, June 5, 1905, Roosevelt MSS.; Howard Beale, *Theodore Roosevelt and the Rise of America to World Power* (Baltimore, 1956), pp. 272 ff.

[7] Roosevelt to Lodge, June 16, 1905, Roosevelt MSS.

sixty thousand Japanese soldiers were in Korea protecting a huge prewar commercial invasion of that ancient kingdom. On his way to the Philippines in the summer of 1905, Taft stopped at Tokyo, and in a conversation with the Japanese foreign minister unofficially expressed his views that Far Eastern politics would be further stabilized if the United States recognized Japan's right to take over Korea in return for a Japanese promise not to imperil the Philippines. Taft communicated his talks to both Roosevelt and Root, and on August 7 wrote to the Japanese Foreign Minister that he was empowered by the President "to confirm in every respect" the statements made by him in their conversation. In November, 1905, after Japan had indicated her desire officially to take over Korea, Secretary of State Root withdrew the American legation at Seoul. Despite the protests of Koreans in Washington, including that of a young man by the name of Syngman Rhee, the United States refused to interfere, and Korea disappeared as a nation. As early as January, 1905, Roosevelt had decided that "we could not possibly interfere for the Koreans against Japan." The Open Door in Asia, as he was later to point out, was a good policy as long as it could be maintained with something less than military force.[8]

Far more disturbing to Japanese-American relations than the Japanese resentment over the war indemnity was the question of Oriental immigration to the West Coast. Congressional action in 1902 excluding Chinese laborers from entering the United States for an indefinite period, and continuing discrimination against even educated Chinese, had brought on a serious boycott of American goods in China. The President agreed that Chinese coolie labor should be barred from the country, but he felt "everything should be done to encourage [the coming of] Chinese businessmen and students." Therefore, while increasing pressure was put on the Chinese government to order off the boycott, the administration sought to eliminate the discourtesies afforded to Chinese travelers and students. When, however, the Chinese government proved itself reluctant to proceed in the face of the impressive popular demonstration, Roosevelt talked for a time of a military expedition against Canton, suggesting to Taft that fifteen thousand troops be used in the attempt to gain "equal rights for Americans within China." Fortunately, the boycott movement weakened, and

---

[8] Taft to Roosevelt, July 31, 1905, to Count Katsura, August 7, 1905, Taft MSS.; Roosevelt to John Hay, January 28, 1905, Roosevelt MSS.

the quarrel tended to be overshadowed by the far more heated dispute with Japan.[9]

The Japanese problem on the West Coast was a relatively recent one. In 1890 only some 2,000 Japanese lived in California. Ten years later there were 24,000. In January of 1900 the governor of California referred publicly to the "Japanese menace," and in August of the same year the State Department concluded an agreement with Japan whereby the Tokyo government promised not to grant passports to Japanese laborers seeking to emigrate to the United States. The Japanese immigration to Hawaii, Mexico, and Canada continued, however, and the illegal sale of passports in Japan helped to swell the Japanese population on the West Coast. In 1904 a San Francisco newspaper printed a series of inflammatory articles on the Japanese influx; the following year a Japanese and Korean exclusion league was organized in California. During 1905 the California legislature debated an all-inclusive Oriental exclusion bill, and on October 11, 1906, the San Francisco School Board placed all Japanese, Chinese, and Korean children in a segregated school. The following year anti-Oriental riots occurred all along the West Coast from Vancouver, Canada, to Los Angeles.[10]

The Japanese pride, increased by the recent victory over Russia— incidentally, the first Oriental triumph over the white race in modern times—was touched to the quick by this continued insult. After a sharp Japanese protest at the School Board action, Roosevelt promised that he would try to remedy matters, at the same time pointing out the difficulties placed in his way by the federal structure of the United States. The President acted quickly. He proposed naturalizing all Japanese then in the United States. He sent a Cabinet member from California to intercede with the state legislature and personally communicated with both the governor and members of the San Francisco School Board. Meanwhile he had instructed the American ambassador in Tokyo to assure the Japanese government that the United States had not "the slightest sympathy with the outrageous agitation against the Japanese. . . ."[11]

[9] Roosevelt to Cortelyou, January 25, 1904; to Victor H. Metcalf, June 16, 1905; and to Taft, January 11, 1906, Roosevelt MSS.

[10] See Thomas A. Bailey, *Theodore Roosevelt and the Japanese American Crisis* (Palo Alto, 1934), for the best account of the controversy.

[11] Oscar S. Straus, "Diary" (manuscript), March 23, September 10, 1907;

Roosevelt was indeed angry at the Californians. While perceiving the reasons for organized labor's objections to free immigration, he found the discrimination against Japanese residents and the use of force against them incomprehensible. He served notice on the "idiots of the California legislature" that he would use force to ensure the basic rights of all Americans, and angrily told Root that refusing to restrain any Japanese immigration would treat the San Franciscans "just as they deserve." But he also observed that this would not settle the grave problem, which he was afraid might drift to a crisis. The Hearst newspapers and some of the lesser incendiary sheets were already mentioning a possible war against Japan. Roosevelt's first thought was to pass a national immigration law barring the entrance of all common laborers of any nationality. When Congressional opposition made that impossible, he proposed a mutual Japanese-American treaty barring the passage of workingmen both ways. A partial solution was finally worked out by another visit of Taft to Tokyo and by a series of notes from Secretary of State Root. Japan, Taft cabled Root, was willing to make almost any concession except "one which would admit the inequality of the Japanese people with the other peoples of the world." By the so-called Gentlemen's Agreement, specifically not dignified by a formal treaty, both governments consented to stop all unwanted traffic between the two countries.[12]

At the height of the tension over the West Coast immigration problem a good many people were predicting an American-Japanese war. Senator Perkins of California argued that the conflict between the "two irreconcilable races" was inevitable, and Captain Richard Hobson of Spanish-American War fame predicted that when the war broke out Japan would take both the Philippines and Hawaii. In Japan the opposition party in the Diet was likewise talking about war. But perhaps this was more for domestic politics than it was to influence national policy. An American survey made in 1907 reported that the Japanese press was far less belligerent than its American counterpart.[13] President Roosevelt himself was apparently worried about the possibilities of a conflict in the spring and early summer of 1907. He spoke to Taft of the obvious "Japanese intention to force a war with us";

Roosevelt to George Keenan, May 6, 1905, to Lloyd C. Griscom, July 15, 1905, and to James N. Gillett, March 9, 1907, Roosevelt MSS.

[12] Roosevelt to Root, March 10, 1907, Root MSS.; Taft to Roosevelt, October 5, 1907, and to Root, October 18, 1907, Taft MSS.

[13] *Literary Digest,* XXXIV (1907), 193, 283; XXXV (1907), 598.

reported to Root that German, English, and French authorities all thought that the Japanese would resort to arms; and was particularly despondent over the fate of the Philippines. Roosevelt could not see that the Philippines were of any physical value to the nation then or in the future. Instead, they were "our heel of Achilles," the one element that made the current situation with Japan dangerous. Underlining Roosevelt's deep pessimism was his remark that the United States should be prepared to give the Philippines independence at a very early moment. He would be glad to see the islands made independent with "an international guarantee," because he would "rather see this nation fight all of her life than to see her give up to Japan or any other nation under duress." [14]

Just how much these expressions of pessimism reflected Roosevelt's considered view of Japanese-American relations is problematical. Both Root and Taft felt that there was no likelihood of war, a view which Taft confirmed when he stopped in Japan in October. He was given a remarkable reception, he wrote, and was "feted all over the place." Throughout 1907 Roosevelt was worried about Congressional disinclination to support the naval building program that he felt necessary for the future security of the country. Roosevelt may have been emphasizing the difficulties with Japan for its effect upon Congress. If he did believe that war was likely, then his own secret plans, made in the summer of 1907, to sail the American battle fleet around the world are almost incomprehensible. Had Japan attacked the fleet in Tokyo Bay without warning as it had the Russian fleet, or had it attacked the Philippines and Hawaii while the fleet was in the Mediterranean, the advantage would have been all Japan's. Roosevelt's naval *beau geste* might then have proved to be one of the more disastrous moves in the history of naval warfare. As it turned out, the fleet was received in Japan with warm welcome, and relations between the two countries improved remarkably.[15]

A month after Taft's Tokyo visit the Japanese ambassador in Washington approached the President with a proposal for a common declaration of friendly intent and co-operation. Out of this conversation grew the Root-Takahira agreement of November, 1908. By the agreement both nations promised to support the *status quo* in the Pacific,

[14] Roosevelt to Root, July 26, 1907, and to Taft, August 21, 1907; Taft to Roosevelt, August 26, 1907, Roosevelt MSS.

[15] Taft to Roosevelt, October 4, 1907, and to Charles P. Taft, October 10, 1907, Taft MSS.; Roosevelt to Root, July 13, 1907, Roosevelt MSS.

respect each other's territory, observe the Open Door in China, and protect Chinese territorial integrity. If documents can accomplish such things, the Root-Takahira agreement should have answered practically every doubt the United States had about Japanese expansion in the Pacific. But simultaneously with the final negotiation of the Root-Takahira agreement, Roosevelt, in quest of two more battleships from Congress, was eager to spread the word of Japan's belligerent attitude. Temporarily the agreement was played down and the existing tensions emphasized. As Professor Morison suggests, he "manufactured" another war scare with Japan and obtained his coveted ships.[16]

Roosevelt's "balance of power" in East Asia was not too successful in stimulating American commercial interests there. A number of causes led to the disappointing condition. One was the disinclination of American capitalists to risk large stakes in the uncertain area. Even before the end of the Russo-Japanese War the American China Development Company had its concession to construct a Canton-Hankow railroad canceled by the Manchu government. Despite Roosevelt's pledge to J. P. Morgan that the government would "stand by" the company and do all in its power to see that it suffered no wrong, Morgan was reluctant to enter into a struggle with the Chinese government and finally gave up the concession. A part of Morgan's disinterest may have resulted from the attitude of the new Secretary of State, Elihu Root. Cautious and conciliatory, Root was never happy with too close a connection between the government and corporations operating in foreign areas. He was opposed to government officials using the political power of the United States to obtain contracts for private business. The United States, he wrote, "expects its agents to be scrupulous in avoiding any appearance of soliciting favors for Americans or American corporations."[17]

But the major reason for the lack of business success under the Roosevelt Asiatic balance was that the balance did not exist very long. In 1907 and again in 1910 Japan and Russia came to an understanding blessed by their alliance partner, Great Britain, who undertook to divide between them most of North China, Mongolia and Korea, from which spheres of influence they hoped to exclude the nationals of all

[16] Philip C. Jessup, *Elihu Root* (2 vols., New York, 1938), II, 34 ff.; Elting E. Morison (ed.), *The Letters of Theodore Roosevelt* (8 vols., Cambridge, 1951–54), VI, 1342 n.

[17] Roosevelt to Morgan, July 18, August 17, 1905, Roosevelt MSS.; Root, Memorandum, cited in Jessup, *Root*, II, 55.

other nations. It is not remarkable that in both Korea and Manchuria American business was soon complaining that there was less respect for the Open Door than had existed before the Russo-Japanese War.[18] To a Russian claim that railroad control in Manchuria conveyed sovereignty of the territory the road served, Root strongly objected and wished that Britain might soften the attitude of both Russia and Japan with a mild word. Mildly or otherwise, the British word was never spoken to her two alliance partners. While Root maintained that we did not intend to give up "our treaty rights" in China, he also was emphatic that this nation did not want to be "a protagonist in a controversy in China with Russia and Japan or with either of them." The difficulty was that to maintain the one the nation had to be the other. With the Roosevelt Asiatic balance of power destroyed, there was nothing left with which to counter Japan and Russia but power, and that the American people, as the State Department knew, were loath to use. The paradox was to dog American policy in the Orient for the next thirty years.[19]

The President's handling of the Japanese crisis of 1907 indicated a softening of the berserker spirit that had at times dominated the man in his earlier years. Nowhere is this better indicated than in his efforts to promote arbitral agreements with other nations. From Roosevelt's actions in Panama it might appear as if he were scarcely the person to support arbitration. But Roosevelt's definition of what was arbitral always excluded the nation's vital interest. He would, of course, have put Panama in that category. Previous to 1905 Secretary Hay had negotiated arbitration treaties with nine foreign countries, treaties which called for a special executive agreement before proposed arbitral procedure could be put into effect. The understandings permitted the President to initiate arbitration without the consent of the Senate. When the treaties were considered by the Senate, however, that body substituted "special treaties" for "special agreement," thus requiring Senate action before every case of arbitration. Roosevelt was beside himself with this display of senatorial prerogative. The treaties, he wrote sharply to his friend Lodge, were now nothing but a "sham." If the Senate refused to take this "very short but real step" toward settling international disagreements in a legal fashion, he preferred to recall the treaties and make it known to the country that the Senate

[18] *Literary Digest*, XXXIII (1906), 252; John Hays Hammond to Taft, May 6, 1908, Taft MSS.
[19] Root to Whitelaw Reid, May 22, July 31, 1908, Root MSS.

was "hostile to arbitration." The 1905 treaties were dropped. But three years later Root, getting senatorial approval before he negotiated, signed such instruments with twenty-four nations. The treaties, relating to all matters except "the honor, independence, and vital interests" of the contracting nations, were to be operative only if two-thirds of the Senate agreed to a special treaty concerning the specific dispute.[20]

The Roosevelt administration was also interested in furthering the cause of arbitration at the Second Hague Conference, the American delegates being instructed to work for a model arbitration treaty and the conversion of the international panel of judges set up by the first conference into something approximating a permanent international court of justice. Both objectives failed of achievement, as did a third American proposal to grant immunity to private property on the sea in time of war. The President's chief interest was in naval armament limitation. In 1906 Great Britain unquestionably possessed the strongest navy in the world, and the United States, perhaps, the next. Roosevelt did not wish to diminish either Britain's or America's strength in ratio to that of other powers. By that time the British were developing the dreadnought class of capital ships which threatened to antiquate all existing battleships. If Roosevelt's proposal to freeze the navies at their existing strength and also freeze the size of ships had been accepted, the relative Anglo-American strength would have been maintained without an increase in the American naval appropriations. Since Germany, Russia, Austria-Hungary, and Italy were all opposed to the principle and the British were only "lukewarm," the plan was doomed. Thereafter, Roosevelt rapidly lost interest in the Hague Conference, in part because of the failure on naval limitations, in part because he had become engrossed in the much more portentous Moroccan affair.[21]

By 1905 competition between France and Germany for commercial and political dominance in Morocco brought Europe to the edge of war, a war which Roosevelt later said "would probably have extended to take in a considerable portion of the world." In 1880 fourteen nations, including the United States, had signed the Madrid Convention,

[20] Roosevelt to Lodge, June 6, 1905, Roosevelt MSS.; Richard Leopold, *Elihu Root and the Conservative Tradition* (Boston, 1954), p. 57.

[21] Root to Whitelaw Reid, October 24, 1906, and to Edwin D. Neade, June 19, 1907, Root MSS.; Roosevelt to Whitelaw Reid, August 7, 1907, Roosevelt MSS.

which guaranteed all the signatories an equality of commercial opportunity in the backward country. After 1900 France, by a series of secret treaties with Italy, Spain, and Great Britain, prepared the way diplomatically for French hegemony, and in 1904 the French government announced its intention to intervene in Morocco's political life. This brought an immediate response from Germany in the form of a defiant speech from the German Emperor at Tangiers in March, 1905, a gesture culminating in a German demand for an international conference to settle the fate of Morocco. Tensions grew rapidly as the French Foreign Office refused to consider a meeting, and Europe was on the brink of a major catastrophe.[22]

At this juncture the German Kaiser appealed to Roosevelt, asking him first to support the Open Door in Morocco and second to persuade Great Britain to cease her support of the alliance partner, France. At first the President declined to intervene in the affair, citing America's negligible interests in Morocco and the known antipathy of Congress to any European political adventure. He did not care to take sides between France and Germany, he wrote Taft, who was acting in his stead during April and May while Roosevelt was on vacation. "We have other fish to fry and we have no real interest in Morocco." As the international tension grew to the point where the press on both sides of the Atlantic was by the middle of May freely predicting a war, Roosevelt reversed his position. He first instructed Taft to talk to Great Britain about the affair and then, cutting short a Rocky Mountain vacation, he took over the negotiations himself. Thereafter, in a series of extremely secret and delicate moves he persuaded both sides of the controversy to meet in a conference to which the United States would be a party, scheduled to open at Algeciras, Spain, on January 16, 1906. Aiding Roosevelt in securing agreement to the conference was the Kaiser's alleged promise as conveyed by the German ambassador at Washington that in case of a serious disagreement at the meeting he would abide by what Roosevelt thought was practicable and fair. It is reasonable to suppose that the French knew about the German promise; they certainly were aware of Roosevelt's basic prejudice in their favor. A short time after the conclusion of the negotiations Roosevelt wrote that whereas von Sternberg, the German ambassador, had simply acted as the "mouthpiece" of the Kaiser, he and Jusserand,

[22] Roosevelt to Jean J. Jusserand, April 25, 1906, Roosevelt MSS.

the French ambassador, had been able to go over the whole matter and had finally worked out an entirely satisfactory conclusion.[23]

On August 23, 1905, Roosevelt told Henry White, the American delegate to the coming conference, that while he wanted to remain on good terms with Germany his sympathies had "at bottom" been with France, and he supposed they would remain so. Just a short time before the President had observed that he wanted "to stand by France" but at the same time "keep on fairly good terms with Germany." This thinly veiled partiality was carried into the conference itself. In Root's opening instructions to White he admitted that American interests in Morocco were "very general." White was instructed to concern himself with the plight of the Jews in Morocco, as the American Jewish community was then "much excited" over the anti-Semitism in Russia. He was also directed to prevent any "discrimination against American trade." But America's interests at Algeciras were not in Moroccan affairs; rather, they centered in the European national power pattern. In a letter to Joseph H. Choate, Roosevelt had disclaimed any prejudice in the immediate quarrel between France and Germany, "save the interest of trying to keep matters on an even keel in Europe." In Root's instructions to White, however, it was obvious that to America the "even keel" meant the continuance of the Anglo-French Entente. White was instructed to keep on friendly terms with Germany. But Root added, "we regard as a favorable condition for the peace of the world and, therefore, the best interests of the United States, the continued entente cordiale between France and England, and we do not wish to contribute towards any estrangement between these two countries."[24]

White did not disobey his instructions at Algeciras. Throughout the conference America's vote on most crucial issues was steadily cast with the French and the British. The President himself played an important part in the decisive matter of policing Morocco by recalling to William II his alleged promise to abide by Roosevelt's decision on contested matters, and by proposing a plan to police Morocco, which was essentially the one adopted. The President's policy at Algeciras helped France win a major diplomatic victory at Germany's expense and ex-

[23] Roosevelt to H. von Sternberg, April 20, 1905; to Taft, April 20, 1905; to Lodge, July 11, 1905; and to Whitelaw Reid, April 28, 1906, Roosevelt MSS.

[24] Roosevelt to Henry White, August 23, 1905, and to Joseph H. Choate, August 16, 1905, Roosevelt MSS.; Root to Henry White, November 28, 1905, Root MSS.

treme discomfort. It also contributed to the closing of the Open Door in Morocco and it may have delayed the opening of the First World War by a matter of some nine years.[25]

As was expected, the announcement of the government's intention to participate in the Algeciras Conference brought on a storm of criticism from both Congress and the press. American political interest in Morocco was nil and her economic concern not much larger, it was asserted. Roosevelt's decision to intervene was a case of international "meddling" at a most dangerous time, since the chances for war, if the conference was not successful, were great. The Democratic minority in the Senate pointed out that Roosevelt's actions violated the long-standing American diplomatic position of isolation from Europe's political quarrels; charged the President with trying to be a "World Caesar" at the expense of American security; and demanded that the Chief Executive produce the diplomatic papers leading up to America's participation in the conference. In defense of the President, *The New York Times* and the Senate majority, led by Lodge, argued that intervention at Algeciras had simply thrown America's moral weight on the side of peace and had not constituted a break with the traditional policy of isolation. The Senate ratified the agreement with the proviso that the United States was under no obligation to enforce its provisions.[26]

Despite the disclaimer of everyone connected with the Algeciras intervention that the action in no way violated the nation's isolation, the episode was eloquent testimony to Roosevelt's growing appreciation that the frontiers of twentieth-century American security often lay along the Yangtse and the Rhine, at Algeciras and Rome and Paris, and in a host of other places, some of them unknown or obscure even to members of Congress. The Algeciras affair also highlighted the growth of another very important development, the increasingly close Anglo-American understanding which was to become one of the dominating factors of world politics for the next half-century at least.

Like most Anglo-Saxon institutions, the Anglo-American agreement was not born of formal protocol or nourished by precisely stated obligations and privileges; it just grew from the soil of a common past and, more often than not, common purposes. In such fertile earth the

[25] Roosevelt to William II, March 7, 1906, Roosevelt MSS.
[26] *Literary Digest*, XXXII (1906), 96, 112, 329; *Congressional Record*, XL, 59th Congress, 1st Session, pp. 792, 2139 ff.

immediate seed was first planted perhaps by Great Britain during the Spanish-American War. British indulgence in the Hay-Pauncefote negotiations, the amicable conclusion of the Canadian boundary dispute, and the obvious understanding in the Caribbean furthered the development. The growing threat of Germany and the increasing American comprehension of the part British sea power had played in the protection of the Western Hemisphere constrained both nations to focus less on the inevitable small irritants and more on the mutual benefits of co-operation. Secretary of State Hay was unquestionably an unregenerate Anglophile. With far less intensity, so were Root and Taft. One can trace Roosevelt's growing appreciation of Britain in his correspondence. In contrast to his belligerent anti-British days of 1895, he wrote to an English friend in 1901: "Fundamentally our two nations are very much alike." "In keeping ready for a possible war," he observed in 1905, "I never even take into account war with England. I treat it as out of the question." By 1911 he was to remark, apropos of Taft's arbitration treaties, that the only country with which he would be willing to sign a total arbitration agreement was Great Britain.[27] So closely were the two nations co-operating by 1905 that Sir Charles Dilke proposed a formal alliance, a proposal that won immediate assent on this side of the water from the choleric New York *Sun*. It is interesting to note that London furnished Roosevelt a draft of the Anglo-Japanese treaty of the same year before the agreement was operative. At the same time, *Kokumin*, the recognized Japanese government organ, in summarizing the Taft talks about Korea, said they amounted to a United States-Anglo-Japanese Alliance and predicted that the United States would join the existing alliance formally in the immediate future. Roosevelt's Algeciras venture helped to cement the understanding by showing that the rewards of co-operation could flow both ways. Congress and the American people, of course, would never have agreed to a formal alliance. Roosevelt and Root understood as much and gave up the formalities for the substance. In forsaking the principle of isolation and in steadfastly supporting the Anglo-French Entente, the American policy makers at Algeciras were reaching out to the future when twice the power of the New World was to move to redress the balance of the Old.[28]

[27] Roosevelt to John St. L. Strachey, March 18, 1901; to Arthur H. Lee, June 6, 1905, and August 22, 1911, Roosevelt MSS.
[28] *Literary Digest*, XXX (1905), 104; *Kokumin* Memorandum in Taft MSS.

CHAPTER 11

Roosevelt: The Final Years

JUST before his inauguration, March 4, 1905, Theodore Roosevelt was alleged to have said: "Tomorrow I shall come into my office in my own right. Then watch out for me." Somehow the words do not ring quite true. Authentic or not, Roosevelt had been acting in their spirit since his victory of November, 1904, and he would continue to do so throughout his second term. His message to Congress in December, 1904, was significantly without most of the equivocations of the past. Over half the document was given over to proposals for new economic and social legislation. Among the measures devoted to labor were an employers' liability act for federal employees and federal contractors, a limitation of the working hours for railroad labor, and the required institution of safety devices throughout the nation's railroad network. Turning to the relations between society and corporations, the President listed many of the well-known corporate abuses, adding at the end that it was "an absurdity" to expect to eliminate such abuse through state action. As remedial measures he proposed that Congress grant the Interstate Commerce Commission power to establish reasonable railroad rates once existing schedules were challenged by shippers, that a forthcoming proposal of the Bureau of Corporations to license all interstate business be passed, and that the insurance business be placed under the investigative powers of the Bureau. Arguing that the District of Columbia should be made into a model of social welfare practices as a guide for state action in spheres where the federal power did not reach, the President called for the enactment of child labor, compulsory school attendance, factory inspection, slum clearance, and juvenile court legislation.[1]

Roosevelt also included in the message calls for a statehood measure for the southwestern territories of Oklahoma, New Mexico, and Arizona, and the reduction of the tariff on Philippine products. He was earnestly to support all of these measures, but his heart was foremost with the railroad rate bill. The railroads had been a prime target for reformers since the Granger days. Their inherently monopolistic characteristics, their exceedingly dubious financial record, their near control of politics in many cities and states, and their abiding inclination to flaunt the law had increasingly cost them the support of reformers and conservatives alike. Since the 1890's, moreover, the consolidation movement which culminated in five large corporate groups controlling a great part of the nation's total railroad mileage had increased their monopolistic aspects. By 1905 the Interstate Commerce Commission had had its power so shorn by the Supreme Court that it was not much more than a statistical bureau. Despite the energetic attempt of the Roosevelt administration to enforce the anti-rebate act—by 1904 some fifty-nine suits had been instituted—rebating went merrily on.[2] Writing anonymously, one executive of a large railroad charged that the violation of the anti-rebate law was "open and notorious" and estimated that if the rebates granted by American railroads in one year were collected they would increase the total revenues of the roads by a figure approximating 15 per cent.[3]

By 1905 railroad rate regulation had become a major issue over the nation. In the Middle West the rise of the state reform movement had given a new intensity to the section's old antirailroad bias. Governors La Follette in Wisconsin, Cummins in Iowa, and Johnson in Minnesota, already successful in intrastate regulation, united in a petition to the President for the effective regulation of interstate rates. An interstate commerce convention meeting in St. Louis asked Congress for similar action. These sentiments, according to one survey, were supported by a great majority of the Republican newspapers throughout the whole region from Illinois to the Rocky Mountains. In the South both the old Jeffersonian wing of the party and the new rising

---

[1] James D. Richardson, *A Compilation of the Messages and Papers of the Presidents* (Washington, 1902), Supplement 2, pp. 828 ff.

[2] Memorandum, March 3, 1904, Knox MSS.

[3] "Railway Rebates and Preferences," *The Outlook*, LXXX (1905), 577.

leaders appealing to the poor-white elements were anticorporation by faith. Even some of the more intelligently conservative elements in the East agreed that the time for federal regulation had come. Supporting the railroad concentration movement as necessary for efficiency, the *Wall Street Journal* declared that sooner or later in the interests of the public welfare the railroads would "have to surrender their ratemaking power to the government." In December, 1904, the most conservatively inclined Attorney General, Philander C. Knox, advised the President that regulation was "inevitable." Roosevelt, never one to delay the inevitable, especially when it was supported by what looked like a majority of the country, demanded action.[4]

In response to Roosevelt's request a number of regulatory measures were introduced in the House, including the presidentially blessed Hepburn Bill. But the Hepburn measure, providing for a new commerce court, lost out to the more stringent Esch-Townshend bill, which was passed by an amazing bipartisan vote of 326 to 17. The measure was given a different reception in the Senate. There the Committee on Interstate Commerce conducted long public hearings, mostly given over to the opposing testimony of railroad executives. Although the four conservative Republican members of the committee were not able to win over a western Republican-Democratic coalition, they did manage to waste enough time to kill consideration of the bill before the summer recess. Meanwhile the railroads had launched a nation-wide publicity campaign against both the Esch-Townshend bill and the principle of rate regulation.[5]

None of the President's recommendations was given much consideration in the 1905 congressional sessions. By the end of the short session Congress had succeeded in passing a pork-barrel rivers and harbors bill and a measure to pay members of the House expenses to and from their homes during the "constructive recess" between sessions, a recess that actually lasted for a few hours at the most. By summer vacation time little more of national import had been accomplished. The session, one newspaper wryly observed, "was not a brilliant one" and distinguished only by the ingenious activities of the "pickpockets" in the House.[6]

The President tried desperately to inspire action from a lethargic

[4] *Wall Street Journal,* April 2, 1902; Philander C. Knox to Roosevelt, December 19, 1904, Knox MSS.

[5] *The New York Times,* April 27, 1905.

[6] *Literary Digest,* XXX (1905), 352.

Congress. Immediately after the election in November he had talked freely about an attempt to revise the tariff, and actually proposed calling an extra session for the purpose of tariff revision to Speaker Cannon. But after a good many conferences he admitted defeat. To Nicholas Murray Butler, whom he had previously written that he had started his "campaigning to revise the tariff," he now confessed that an immediate revision was not possible.[7] As Professor Blum has pointed out, Roosevelt may have been using the tariff issue as trading goods. He certainly capitulated to Cannon's high-tariff views in January, 1905. It is also remarkable that Cannon, standpatter that he was, did not oppose either the Esch-Townshend rate bill nor the Hepburn bill of the following year. Still, the President never gave up entirely on the tariff issue. From time to time during the next three years he proposed the possibility of tariff revision, though he was always more optimistic about revision in his letters to the standpatters than he was to the proponents of reduction. Thus on August 15, 1906, he wrote to Cannon that while he believed in protection, he stood ready to revise any schedule or the whole rate structure when the need for it arose. Yet only one week later he told Senator Beveridge he sympathized with his revisionist views, but did not see how a reduction could be accomplished "just at this time." Even if the President's lack of any real interest in the custom rates is taken into account, his occasional thrusts at the conservatives seem to be more in the nature of counterpunching than of shadowboxing.[8]

The President threatened to call an extra session of Congress if railroad legislation was not passed in 1905. Neither the possible tariff bargain nor the threat of an extra session, however, seemed to intimidate the Senate. The White House was already having trouble with the upper house over the Dominican treaty, and when it showed no inclination to act on the rate bill Roosevelt's ire arose. Men of the mind of Spooner, Hale, and Foraker, he wrote a friend, were "a curse" and he suggested to another that he would be glad to lend to

[7] Roosevelt to James A. Tawney, November 17, 1904; to Cannon, November 30, 1904; and to Butler, November 10, 1904, and December 9, 1904, Roosevelt MSS.

[8] John M. Blum, "Theodore Roosevelt and the Legislative Process: Tariff Revision and Railroad Regulation, 1904–1906," in Elting E. Morison (ed.), *The Letters of Theodore Roosevelt* (8 vols., Cambridge, 1951–54), IV, 1333–1342; Roosevelt to Cannon, August 15, 1906, and to Beveridge, August 23, 1906, Roosevelt MSS.

the Russian government several eminent statesmen if they could guarantee to place them where a bomb was most likely to go off. The President left the capital during April and May for a long vacation in the West, and it was whispered around Washington that he had backed up on the subject of rate regulation. A blast from Chicago put the country right. Speaking before the Iroquois Republican Club, Roosevelt went all the way toward a rate-making commission. He now demanded that the I.C.C. have "ironclad powers" to set rates, which were to be suspendable by the courts only if they could be proved confiscatory.[9]

During the following summer and fall the President said very little about railroad or any other type of regulation. But his December message to Congress shattered the calm. On rate-making powers he retreated somewhat to his previous position; nevertheless he insisted that the services of railroads and private-car lines be afforded to all on an equal basis at "reasonable and just rates." To that he added a demand that railroads be prevented from giving any favors to anyone, including the issuance of free tickets and passes. More importantly, he suggested that the books of railroad corporations be opened to inspection by the Interstate Commerce Commission. This revolutionary suggestion was just the start of a series of unusual proposals. Discussing the relations of business and government, the President remarked that the fortunes of the great corporations had become "so great" and their power "so vast" that effective public supervision of their corporate use was now a necessity. The great social evil of large interstate industry was that it was a subject "without a sovereign." The time had come "to assert the sovereignty of the National Government by affirmative action." To do so railroad rates should be equalized and justified, the overcapitalization of corporations stopped, interstate insurance transactions supervised and regulated by the Bureau of Corporations, corporations prohibited from contributing to political campaigns, and the interstate shipment of misbranded and adulterated foods regulated, if not suppressed. Turning to labor and society in general, the President reiterated his legislative requests in his previous message and added other demands calculated to curl the hair of industrialists. During every great labor disturbance, Roosevelt declared, there were three interested parties: the employer, the employee, and the "general public." In the interest of protecting all three the President recom-

[9] Chicago *Tribune*, May 11, 1905.

mended that every strike involving interstate commerce be "investigated by the Government and the facts officially reported to the public." [10] In issuing labor injunctions, some judges had "misused" their power, Roosevelt admitted, a misuse that promoted requests for the abolition of the injunction. Such a total limitation of the equity powers of the courts would be unwise, the President believed. The remedy was to "regulate the procedure" by which labor injunctions were granted.

Three of the most cherished powers of private business had been the right to set its own prices for services, the right to maintain its books and records in secrecy, and the right to negotiate with labor without interference by a third party. The President's 1905 message challenged the exclusiveness of all these rights and proposed their severe limitations. The reaction of the press to the challenge was instantaneous and violent. The message was "the most amazing program of centralization" ever proposed, declared one newspaper. It was a call for the regulation of every social evil, a second stated, an attempt, said a third, to "subvert the American tradition." Subsequently ex-Governor Odell of New York charged the President with trying to wreck the Republican party, and Senator Spooner in a public speech accused him of attempting to abolish the states.[11]

The President still had other arrows for his bow pointed at the railroads. During the fall of 1905 and the following winter the Attorney General was suspiciously active in launching suits against railroads and other corporate groups for the giving and receiving of rebates. The Chicago and Alton, the Great Northern, and the Burlington were indicted during December, and then, in the following March while the railroad debate still went on, the greatest combination of them all, the Standard Oil Company, felt the heavy hand of a suddenly zealous government. Transmitting the report of the Bureau of Corporations on the oil company to Congress, Roosevelt declared that the record showed the company had profited "enormously" from secret rail rates. Implicated also in the rebate scandal were the packing trust, the sugar trust, and the New York Central Railroad. Coincident to these public revelations was the publication of a series of popular magazine articles attacking the railroads and the recalcitrant conserva-

---

[10] Richardson, *Messages and Papers of the Presidents,* Supplement 2, pp. 1157 ff.

[11] Comments cited in the *Literary Digest,* XXXI (1905), 903, 975.

tives in the Senate who supported them. Among the authors of the articles were Henry Beech Needham, Ray Stannard Baker, and Walter Hines Page, all intimates of the President. "Much of the railroad business," Page declared in summary, "was dishonestly conducted." [12]

By the opening of Congress it appeared as if the railroads were ready to cry quits. In December the presidents of the Pennsylvania, the Reading, and the New York Central railroads announced that on January 1 no free passes would be issued to public servants, shippers, or to anyone else save their own employees. About the same time Taft reported to his brother on a confidential talk he had had with the president of the Rock Island road. This executive had admitted that the senators he had counted on for "allegiance," while still opposed to the bill, were yielding, since the President had so "roused the people that it was impossible for them to stand against the popular demand." Therefore he was in favor of a "compromise with the President." Roosevelt, Taft added, was also in favor of a compromise, provided his principles were accepted.[13]

Subsequently the railroad rate bill went sailing along in the House. The Hepburn bill was reported by a unanimous vote of the House Committee, and within a month had been passed with only seven votes cast in the negative. Its main provision, granting the Commission power to set reasonable rates on complaint of a shipper, the rates to go into effect after thirty days but subject to court review, was acceptable to the President. The bill also placed private-car lines under the Commission and empowered that body to inspect railroad books and to prescribe uniform bookkeeping methods. But the Senate, whose members were still chosen by the several state legislatures, proved far less pliable than the popularly elected House. Almost immediately a violent controversy broke out between Aldrich of Rhode Island and Dolliver of Iowa, the leader of the more progressive Republicans favorable to the bill. Seeking to embarrass the President, the Republican leader of the Senate then contrived to select Benjamin Tillman, the ranking Democrat on the committee, as the sponsor of the bill instead of Dolliver. Tillman had not been on speaking terms with the President for some months. Aldrich also won permission for any member of the

[12] Walter H. Page, "The Regulation of Railroads," *World's Work,* XI (1906), 337.
[13] *The New York Times,* December 18, 1905; Taft to Charles P. Taft, December 3, 1905, Taft MSS.

committee to offer amendments to the bill on the floor of the Senate, an almost unheard-of privilege on major legislation.

When the bill arrived on the floor it was apparent that the President had lost the support not only of the conservatives grouped around Aldrich but also of his friend Lodge and his former Attorney General Knox. In the welter of ensuing amendments it became clear that the conservatives, not daring to defeat the bill, planned to amend it into a state of innocuousness. The main legislative battle, therefore, swirled around two hotly contested points: the nature of the court review and the time at which the rates set by the Commission went into effect. The progressives in both parties supported a narrow court review of the Commission's decisions limited mainly to legal procedures and a prohibition against an injunctive suspension of the rates until the courts had established their findings. The conservatives wanted a broad court review entertaining both procedural and substantive matters, including the reasonableness of the rates and a suspension of the rates until after court action.

In the confused course of the struggle over the railroad bill tempers flared and charges of "bad faith," "traitorism," and "falsehood" were hurled. A good part of the charges resulted from the way the President worked both sides of the party street to support the bill. Roosevelt was aghast but not defeated by Aldrich's turning over the bill to Tillman and the Democrats. The Senator, the President remarked, "had lost both his head and his temper." Through an intermediary "Pitchfork" Ben Tillman was informed that he was once again *persona grata* at the White House. For weeks the President gave his support to the South Carolinian. No more dramatic shift had taken place, one newspaper commented, since Hamlet and Laertes changed rapiers. But when Roosevelt felt the Democrats could not pass the bill because of the broad review stand taken by Senator Bailey of Texas, he maneuvered his support back to Dolliver and then to the Republican Senator Long, who introduced an intended compromise amendment. By that time, however, party discipline on both sides of the chamber was so fractured and so many contending amendments were on the floor that confusion prevailed and the defeat of the bill was freely predicted. At that point Roosevelt went back to the Republican regulars and through Senator Allison asked for a compromise. Allison, after conferring with Aldrich, Knox, and Spooner, produced an amendment which won assent from all factions save radicals like Robert La Follette of Wisconsin, who had just come to the Senate, and the bitter-end conservatives like Foraker, who branded the entire bill as a "piece of populism" contrary in spirit to the Constitution and revolutionary in character. The President, who had repeatedly stated his opposition to broad review, whether of the Bailey or the Aldrich sort, now felt that the matter of review was immaterial. The courts had the review power willy-nilly, he wrote to Allison, and in the end they would determine its scope. The contest, he remarked, had finally come down to Tweedledum and Tweedledee. The important thing was the rate-making power. All else was "academic." [14]

The Hepburn Act as it finally emerged from Congress gave the Interstate Commerce Commission the power to set aside a railroad schedule on complaint of a shipper and prescribe a reasonable rate subject to court review. The review was broad in nature, empowering the courts to pass upon all details of the Commission's actions, including the question of the reasonableness of the rates. The act did, however, permit the Commission to examine railroad books and prescribe uniform bookkeeping. It placed private-car lines and terminal railroads under the supervision of the Commission and contained a commodities clause, later weakened by court interpretation, prohibiting railroads from carrying commodities not used in their own operations and made or mined by subsidiaries of the roads.

The act was a landmark in the evolution of federal control of private industry. It empowered the government to set rates and to investigate the books of interstate utilities. Between the progressive and the conservative positions it was a compromise. The more ardent radicals blamed Roosevelt for the compromise and were inclined to look upon it as a conservative bill. If the railroad senators had had their way, the courts and not the Commission would have been empowered to set rates initially. This was the intent of the original Knox amendment, as it was of that offered by Foraker; it was certainly the solution Aldrich preferred. Under the circumstances the act was a

[14] *Congressional Record*, IV, 59th Congress, 1st Session p. 3102; Foraker to Robinson Locke, June 29, 1906, Foraker MSS.; Roosevelt to W. B. Allison, April 12, 1906, and to Beveridge, June 16, 1906, Roosevelt MSS. For varying accounts of the struggle over rates, see John M. Blum, *The Republican Roosevelt* (Boston, 1954), p. 94; Henry F. Pringle, *Theodore Roosevelt, A Biography* (New York, 1931), pp. 420 ff.; Nathaniel W. Stephenson, *Nelson W. Aldrich* (New York, 1930), p. 295; and Everett Walters, *Joseph Benson Foraker, An Uncompromising Republican* (Columbus, Ohio, 1948), p. 214.

victory for the President and was recognized as such by the country at large. Even Tillman finally admitted to Beveridge that had it not been for Roosevelt's determined intervention into the legislative process, there would have been no bill. The passage of the Hepburn Act bears eloquent testimony to Roosevelt's perseverance, his marvelous political suppleness, and his willingness to settle for what was possible.[15]

The President was not yet through with the railroads. During the Hepburn battle Senator La Follette had persistently fought for the physical evaluation of the roads as the only scientific basis for rate making. The President opposed La Follette and was exceedingly uncomplimentary in his remarks to conservatives about the Wisconsin senator. A year later, however, he wrote Beveridge that "events have moved so fast in the valuation business that I think it is impossible to avoid taking conservative ground in its favor." Two months before, Roosevelt had requested the Interstate Commerce Commission to furnish him with particulars on how to obtain physical valuation, how to control the issuance of railroad securities, and how to incorporate the railroads nationally. In an Indianapolis speech on May 30, 1907, the President demanded not only physical evaluation but government control of railroad securities and federal incorporation. Roosevelt was usually willing to settle for the possible, but the horizon of the possible could always be extended with time.[16]

At the height of the Hepburn-bill struggle David Graham Phillips published his sensational article "The Treason of the Senate." Even Beveridge, who admitted that the picture of the Senate was a true one as it had existed over the past thirty years, had cautioned Phillips to modify some of his stronger statements. The article inspired the President to attack both extremes of opinion then threatening the passage of the railroad bill. At a Gridiron Club dinner and later on April 14 in a public speech Roosevelt branded the writers of such fiery articles as "muckrakers." At the same time he called for the federal control of corporation securities and the enactment of an inheritance tax. His radical remarks were largely overlooked, but his name for the writers

[15] Harrison S. Smalley, "Rate Control Under the Interstate Commerce Act," *Annals of the American Academy of Political and Social Science,* XXIX (1906), 293 ff.; Beveridge to Albert Shaw, May 20, 1906, Beveridge MSS.; Grenville M. Dodge to M. P. Dodge, Jr., April 11, 1907, Dodge MSS.

[16] Roosevelt to Beveridge, May 9, 1907, Beveridge MSS.; Roosevelt to the Interstate Commerce Commission, March 15, 1907, Roosevelt MSS.; *The New York Times,* May 31, 1907.

stuck to label forever the group exposing corruption in the popular periodicals.[17]

Although Roosevelt was often irate at the "lunatic fringe" of radical journalists and politicians, he occasionally found their efforts very useful. For years prior to 1906 a pure-food bill had been before Congress. Its patron saint, Dr. Harvey W. Wiley, the chief chemist in the Department of Agriculture, and his "poison squad" had worked incessantly for the legislation. The bill had passed the House twice in previous years, and was reintroduced again in 1905 by Senators Heyburn of Idaho and McCumber of North Dakota. Despite the support of the American Medical Association and numerous magazines, it appeared again as if it would be interned in the "graveyard of reform legislation," the Senate. Meanwhile Senator Beveridge had been attempting for a considerable time to obtain passage of a federal meat-inspection measure with an equal lack of success. Then in 1906 Upton Sinclair published *The Jungle,* a novel in form but really a tract on the incredibly filthy conditions in the Chicago packing houses. The President read the book and was as excited about its details as was the public already deeply suspicious of the "packing trust." He immediately ordered a reinvestigation of the meat packers; a previous report by the Department of Agriculture had found little wrong. Upon receiving the new study made by his labor commissioners, Charles P. Neill and J. B. Reynolds, the President fairly exploded. The report was "hideous," he wrote to the conservative chairman of the House Committee on Agriculture, James Wadsworth, and the conditions had to be "remedied at once." To move the reluctant Congress Roosevelt threatened to publish the entire "sickening report" if action were not taken. In a stinging letter to Wadsworth he said he was sorry to say that each of Wadsworth's proposed changes to the bill was "for the worse and that in the aggregate they are ruinous." At the same time he cautioned Beveridge not to insist upon his bitterly contested proposal requiring the packers to stamp the date of packing upon each piece of meat processed. So far the President had held off publication of the report, although the existence of the document was widely known and its contents speculated upon by the press. To friends of the bill urging publication of the Neil-Reynolds document, Roosevelt replied that he could not give them "any idea" of exactly when he would move. As

[17] Beveridge to Phillips, August 1, 1905, Beveridge MSS.; *The New York Times,* April 15, 1906.

Congress stalled and public clamor for action mounted to a crescendo, Roosevelt sent in the first part of the report, at the same time confidentially threatening, if action was not forthcoming, to make public the more damaging part together with a few comments of his own. At that the opposition collapsed and the pure-food bill, together with the meat-inspection provision, became a law.[18]

The administration's program scored other successes during the session. The Employers' Liability Act, applying to the District of Columbia and the common carriers, was passed, as was a statehood bill which provided for joint statehood for Arizona and New Mexico territories and for the Indian and Oklahoma territories. But since Arizona and New Mexico refused the joint arrangement, only Oklahoma profited from the legislation. Lost were most of the other social proposals the President had made for the District, including the child labor bill, which he kept supporting until the end of his term, but which he never obtained. Lost also was the Philippine tariff bill, which Roosevelt felt he had to sacrifice in order to win on the Hepburn rate measure. Still, looking at the record, the President for once thought it had been an excellent Congress. In a moment of exuberance, just before the 1906 congressional campaign, he stated he would not be afraid "to compare its record with that of any previous Congress in our history." [19]

During the congressional elections of 1906 Roosevelt felt that his efforts were directed toward defeating both political extremes and preserving the center in power. It is difficult to follow his reasoning unless one agrees that the Democrats represented both extremes and the Republicans the center. For the President showed no partiality in his support of all kinds of Republicans from the most reactionary to the moderate progressive. He had urged the re-election of Cannon in Illinois and James Watson in Indiana, he vigorously supported Hughes in New York against Hearst, and he had sent Cabinet members to both Idaho and Maine, where organized labor was trying to defeat Republican incumbents. About the only gestures he made in the direction of progressivism were in a speech at Harrisburg and his stopping of the party campaign against the Republican progressive Cummins in Iowa,

[18] Roosevelt to James M. Wadsworth, May 26, 31, and June 15, 1906, and to Beveridge, May 23, 1906, Roosevelt MSS.; Beveridge to Albert Shaw, May 26, 1906, and to J. C. Shaffer, June 18, 1906, Beveridge MSS.; *Literary Digest*, XXXII (1906), 959.

[19] Taft to Horace Taft, March 3, 1906, Taft MSS.

which was inspired, as Robert La Follette correctly reported, by Roosevelt's Secretary of the Treasury, Leslie M. Shaw, a former Iowa standpatter. At Harrisburg, after castigating both "reactionaries" and "foolish extremists," he had aroused the ire of conservatives by finding a new "inherent power" in the constitution, a power "outside of the enumerated powers" which would operate "in all cases where the object involved was beyond the power of the several states." His immediate object was to exercise "a constantly increasing supervision over and control of the great fortunes used in business" to ensure that they were used "in the interest of and not against . . . the general public." It was an inflammatory utterance, the New York *World* commented, one which outdid the radical Democrats.[20]

The President was uneasy about the election of 1906. For one thing, the Republican majority in the House had been reduced sharply. For another, organized labor seemed to be mobilizing against the party. Under its announced policy of rewarding its friends and punishing its enemies, labor had actively campaigned against a good many Republican office seekers. In a letter to one of the most regular of Republican regulars, Roosevelt cautioned him about denouncing labor as labor. The latest Congress, he felt, had not been "wise in their treatment of the labor people." It was bad business, he observed, "to solidify labor against us." [21]

Change was in the air by 1906. By that time the complex intellectual movement that had its start in the 1890's had captured a good part of the educated elite. The new economics and political science, the social gospel, pragmatism, and their tangents, had all acted as a solvent for the traditional political and ethical concepts. Four years of steady muckraking in the popular periodicals and the press, as well as odious revelations by numerous state and national investigations, were beginning to register on the popular mind. Organized labor was flexing its new-found muscles, and the Socialist party vote had been steadily climbing since the election of 1900. The local reform movements, which had started soon after the turn of the century, were now reaching up to the state level and beyond to the national government. By 1906 Wisconsin's La Follette was in the Senate, Missouri and Minnesota had

[20] La Follette to Cummins, March 19, 1906, Cummins MSS.; Roosevelt to Shaw, June 12, 1906, Roosevelt MSS.; New York *World,* October 5, 6, 1906.
[21] Roosevelt to James Watson, September 11, 1906, Roosevelt MSS.

progressive Democratic governors, and in Iowa, Albert B. Cummins was already laying plans to run against Allison in the next senatorial election. Two of the young Republican senatorial luminaries, Dolliver and Beveridge, had already crossed swords with the conservative directorate in the upper house. During the 1906 contest in Indiana, Beveridge, who had once boasted of his conservatism, openly proclaimed himself a reformer, supporting the income and inheritance taxes, a national child-labor proposal, and the institution of a direct primary system for all political offices. "You have no idea," he wrote his novelist friend, Phillips, "how profound, intense and permanent the feeling among the American people is that this great reform movement shall go on. . . ." Beveridge was not alone in his estimate of the future. In January of 1907 Sereno E. Pratt, editor of the *Wall Street Journal*, took a long look at the state of the nation. Most of what he saw he did not like. Among the special phenomena of the times Pratt reported were "the eager pursuit of sudden wealth, the shameless luxury and display, the gross and corrupting extravagance, the misuse of swollen fortunes, the indifference to law, the growth of graft, the abuses of great corporate power, the social unrest, the spread of demagogy, the advances of socialism, the appeals to bitter class hatred." Clearly, Pratt concluded, the nation was disenchanted with its present and eager to get along with the business of molding a different future.[22]

Few people were more aware of this movement of the national mind than the man in the White House. He had watched the ebb of the reform spirit under McKinley, had marked its reflux in 1902, and was conscious that it was almost at the flood by 1907. Accordingly, his tastes and ideas shifted markedly to the left. Where once he had made a distinction between the good and bad great fortunes, now he considered all great fortunes "needless and useless." By 1908 he was characterizing his chief political effort during the past six years as a fight to prevent the growth "of the least attractive and most sordid of all aristocracies," a plutocracy "which regarded power as expressed only in its basest and most brutal form, that of mere money." Ten years before he had no idea of the amount of corruption that really existed in high business and political circles. Now he knew, and knowing, he

---

[22] Beveridge to David Graham Phillips, November 13, 1906, Beveridge **MSS.**; Sereno E. Pratt, as cited by the *Literary Digest*, **XXXIV** (1907), 169.

felt as if he were living in an age like that preceding the French Revolution.[23]

As Roosevelt's attitude toward the financial rulers changed, so did his position toward their representatives in the Republican party. In his opinion, Foraker was now "a reactionary, one of the most unblushing servers and beneficiaries of corporate wealth within or without office." Prior to these days he had occasionally overlooked some of the minor peccadilloes of the powerful rulers of the Senate and their retainers. Now in 1906 he bluntly asked Senator Spooner to request his brother's resignation since he had been given many chances to reform without apparent improvement. In a burst of exasperation in 1908 he lashed out against the "ruling clique" in the Senate, the House and the National Committee, "who seemed to regard every concession to decency as merely a matter of bargain and sale." As his discomfort with the standpatters grew, he found a new appreciation for the radicals. Beveridge and Dolliver had always basked more or less in his favor. Now even Bryan, the revolutionist of 1896, was described as a "kindly, well meaning, emotional man," and whereas La Follette formerly had been "a shifty self-seeker," by 1907 Roosevelt found he liked him much better. In Roosevelt's political spectrum prior to 1907 few things were worse than a socialist. Yet a year later he wrote, "there are plenty of people who call themselves socialists, many of whose tenets are not only worthy of respect but represent real advances." Roosevelt's self-identification had changed remarkably. Once he had vociferously identified himself with the middle register of politics; by 1907 he was "trying to keep the left center together." A year later he described himself as a "radical," whose chief political task had been to lead the "ultra-conservative" party of McKinley to a position of "progressive conservatism or conservative radicalism." [24]

As Roosevelt's ideas shifted toward the left in his last two years of office, his requests for reform legislation to Congress increased. Many Presidents before him had found Congress more and more indifferent to their desires during their last months in office. Part of the reason for

[23] Roosevelt to Jacob Reis, April 18, 1906; to George O. Trevelyan, January 1, 1908; to Grafton D. Cushing, February 27, 1908; and to Lodge, September 25, 1908, Roosevelt MSS.

[24] Roosevelt to Lodge, September 27, 1906; to Spooner, August 20, 1906; to Albert Shaw, May 22, 1908; to William A. White, July 31, 1906, and January 5, 1907; to John Morley, December 1, 1908; and to Sidney Brooks, November 20, 1908, Roosevelt MSS.

the growing independence of Congress lay in the traditional diminution of power which all Presidents seem to experience. Bereft of patronage power, and no longer an important factor in future elections, their leverage with Congress diminishes rapidly as their term nears its end. Roosevelt was an especial victim of this historic erosion. His energetic use of the executive power, his impulsive personal actions, and his yearly clashes with Congress caused the movement restoring legislative independence to grow rapidly during 1907 and 1908. A small harbinger of what was to come appeared in 1906 over the President's use of "simplified spelling." The movement for phonetic spelling was quite strong even before the President took it up. On the national board of the organization were such dignified names as Nicholas Murray Butler and David Starr Jordan, the presidents of Columbia and Stanford Universities. Andrew Carnegie supported the reform, as well as Richard Watson Gilder, the respected editor of the *Century Magazine.* But a national tempest of comic proportions occurred when Roosevelt adopted the findings of the board to change the spelling of approximately three hundred words and ordered the government printer to observe the reform in all printing. Amid much editorial fun, indignant screams and portentous prophecies of disaster rent the Washington air as "night" was transformed into "nite" and "thorough" into "thoro." Heatedly Congress debated the matter, and with evident exasperation the House instructed the public printer to observe standard orthography. Admitting defeat, Roosevelt duly ordered the change, but announced that he would continue to use the new spelling in his personal correspondence. And so he did, when he remembered to use it.[25]

Much more serious both for the legal issues it involved and for the relations between the President and Congress was the Brownsville affair. On the night of August 3, 1906, a dozen or so Negro soldiers from the 25th U.S. Infantry, angered by the treatment accorded them by the citizens of Brownsville, Texas, made a shooting sortie into the town, killing one citizen. Within ten minutes they had returned to camp unobserved. But during the official investigation no one of the 160 men in the three Negro companies would inform upon his fellows. On November 5, the day before the congressional election, the President discharged "without honor" every man in the three companies, observing that if no one admitted guilt all would have to pay the

[25] Roosevelt to Charles A. Stellings, August 20, 1906, Roosevelt MSS.

penalty. This inference of guilt by association was serious, because it meant the loss of all pensions for the men, including six who had won the Medal of Honor. Since the northern Negro vote was almost solidly Republican, it had important political implications. The President's order was met with a wave of approbation from the South and with a storm of criticism from the North. Booker T. Washington wrote Taft, who was acting President while Roosevelt was in the Canal Zone, that he had never experienced a time when the Negro people were more excited. The New York Republican County Committee telegraphed a plea that the discharge of the battalion be rescinded, and protests rolled in from other northern Negro centers. Doubtful of the justice of the President's actions, Taft tried to stem the criticism by directing Roosevelt's dismissal order he held in abeyance; but on being over-ruled by the absent Roosevelt, he could do little more.[26]

Brownsville became an issue between Congress and the President when in January, 1908, Senators Tillman and Foraker introduced a resolution demanding an investigation of the affair. In the following debate most of the Republican senators joined Foraker in attacking the President, while the minority Democrats supported him. Foraker, an announced conservative candidate for the presidential nomination, was particularly bitter in his criticism of the Chief Executive. The issue between the President and the Ohio senator exploded in an open ugly quarrel at the annual Gridiron Club dinner on January 26. The scene grew tense as the President lectured the senators on their lack of respect for the office of the President. Foraker replied with a caustic and emphatic denunciation of Roosevelt, demanding that the President "have equal respect for the chosen representatives in the Senate of the Sovereign States of the Union." Roosevelt was inclined to make a "berserker speech" in reply, but finally contented himself with "a flat contradiction" and left the banquet.[27]

The miserable affair dragged on throughout the summer and fall of 1907 and into the election year of 1908. The vote on a congressional investigation diplomatically was delayed until after the presidential election. Foraker's personal prestige, together with his presidential

[26] Taft to Mrs. William Howard Taft, November 21, 1906, and to Charles P. Taft, January 1, 1907; Herbert Parsons to Taft, November 17, 1906; Washington to Taft, November 20, 1906, Taft MSS.

[27] Oscar S. Straus, "Diary" (Manuscript), January 26, 1907; Henry L. Stoddard, As I Knew Them (New York, 1927), p. 330; Roosevelt to Beveridge, January 27, 1907, Beveridge MSS.

candidacy, was all but destroyed by the revelations in the Hearst papers that he had been in the pay of the Standard Oil Company throughout his senatorial career. Irrespective of Foraker's reputation, the Brownsville episode speeded the growing estrangement between Congress and the President.[28]

Congress and the President met in head-on opposition in 1907-8 on still another issue, this time the basic one of conservation. About the turn of the century the fear that the nation was using its natural resources at too rapid a rate and that sometime in the future it would be faced with shortages became rather general, particularly in the East. The policy of setting aside nationally owned timberlands for permanent forest reserves and parks had started with Harrison and had been accelerated by Cleveland. But no comprehensive policy of conservation was adopted until the Roosevelt administration made the country acutely conscious of the problem. Credit for the rapid development was due in part to a young man, Gifford Pinchot, and in the last instance to Roosevelt, who listened to his arguments and was persuaded. A major section of Roosevelt's first message to Congress was devoted to conservation, and with his blessing the cause flourished. During the Roosevelt years the government embarked upon a major reclamation program, the Reclamation Service was established, and the forest program was consolidated under Pinchot's direction in the Department of Agriculture. Moreover, the concept of conservation was steadily widened to include not only forests but coal and mineral lands, oil reserves, and power sites. At the time Roosevelt took office some 45 million acres were included in the government reserves. Within the next seven years almost 150 million acres were added to this total. Roosevelt's conservation program was to be among his most impressive and enduring achievements.[29]

The new program was not advanced without serious opposition from the West and Congress. Only in those western urban states where the need for water was great, or in the Southwest where irrigated farming depended upon government dams and reclamation works, was there any consistent powerful support for a national conservation pro-

[28] Foraker to Judge D. Davis, May 18, 1908, and to S. F. Dwight, February 15, 1909, Foraker MSS.; Walters, *Foraker*, pp. 232 ff.

[29] Gifford Pinchot, *Breaking New Ground* (New York, 1947), pp. 190, 252, 256. See Roosevelt to James Wilson, June 7, 1907, Roosevelt MSS., for an excellent statement of the President's conservation philosophy.

gram. Elsewhere ranchers, mine operators, lumbermen, and power companies all protested against this limitation of the right to exploit the national domain. Most western fortunes had been built upon exploitation of natural resources, and the antagonism of wealthy or would-be wealthy westerners to this abrupt curtailment of opportunity was understandable. The administration incurred further opposition by its strict enforcement of existing land laws and the grazing, mining, and lumbering regulations prescribed for the new reserves. A sad farewell to the old free and easy ways with the national domain was signaled by the numerous indictments the Roosevelt administration brought against westerners on charges running from conspiracy to defraud the government to grand theft. In 1905 the indignant Senator Fulton of Oregon demanded an end to the rigorous enforcement, pointing out that through the activities of a special federal prosecutor, Francis J. Heney, a good part of the Republican party organization of the state, including his fellow senator, was in prison or under the shadow of that institution. Roosevelt replied tersely: Heney was not hurting the party but rather the senator's friends who had betrayed the party "by betraying the public service." [30]

By 1907 Senator Fulton had gathered enough support to attach a rider to a Department of Agriculture appropriation bill to the effect that no new forest reserves could be created in six western states or additions made to existing reserves without the consent of Congress. As the bill lay on the President's desk the Department of the Interior, working under forced draft by an executive order, proposed the addition to the national reserve of seventeen million acres dotted with forests, mineral deposits, and power sites. Four days before the President signed the agricultural bill, he either created or increased the size of thirty-two forest reserves. Cries of executive "impudence," "arrogance," and "dictatorship" rang through the capital, and a Public Lands Convention was called to meet in Denver to counter this assault of "government landlordism." Legally there was no recourse to the President's actions except through a formal vote of Congress, which was obviously impossible to get in face of the almost certain veto. Congressional dignity was further assaulted by the activities of Gifford Pinchot. Denied the right to withdraw power sites by any other means, the Chief Forester managed to reserve over twenty-five hundred of them from outstretched entrepreneurial hands by

[30] Roosevelt to Charles W. Fulton, May 13, 1905, Roosevelt MSS.

designating them as ranger stations. Against the expected congressional reaction to these shrewd but questionable actions the President interposed two executive vetoes.[31]

Congress, however, did not remain long without its innings. During 1908 Roosevelt created three organizations of national importance. The first of these, the National Conservation Congress, was attended by forty-four governors and some five hundred other experts and dignitaries. Acclaimed by James Hill, the Northwest railroad king, as the directors' meeting of the "great economic corporation known as the United States of America," and by the *Wall Street Journal* as "a radical new departure in government," the conference had profound results. Out of it grew a yearly meeting of the governors of the states, and within eighteen months after its adjournment some forty-one states had created conservation commissions of their own. The other two organizations met with less favorable response. They resulted in the creation of the National Country Life Commission and the Inland Waterways Commission. Although both bodies drafted impressive reports, Congress refused to support either organization. Despite, and perhaps because of, the President's pleas, the Waterways group failed to obtain the requested $20,000 to carry on its work, and the Country Life Commission, promptly dubbed "the rural uplift," was denied funds even for the publication of its report.[32]

During 1907 an adverse economic movement jarred the nation's industrial and financial institutions. The recession and the sharp New York financial panic of October and November, 1907, brought Roosevelt into further conflict with the business community and in general weakened his position with the reigning conservatives. The activities of Morgan and Company and the United States Steel Corporation in purchasing the Tennessee Coal and Iron Company during the worst days of the panic also added another controversy to the many already swirling around the President.

In January, 1907, John D. Rockefeller made a public forecast of hard times resulting from the President's attacks upon big business and finance. From that time until October the prices of stocks and other securities fell rapidly and steadily. Beginning in September, industrial production began to slump in an unseasonable trend. By October real

[31] Pinchot, *Breaking New Ground,* p. 333.
[32] Roosevelt to Cannon, May 13, 1908, Roosevelt MSS.; *Literary Digest,* XXXVII (1908), 235.

financial distress occurred throughout the country as the great New York financial institutions were unable to meet the requests for funds from interior banks. Several large industrial corporations went bankrupt, as well as many small banks in the South and West. Later in the month it became known that several leading executives of huge New York trust companies had tried and failed to corner the copper market. The resulting loss of public confidence in their institutions started runs which further strained the already tight supply of money. On October 23, the Knickerbocker Trust Company closed its doors, and in the accompanying wave of fear the withdrawal of funds from lending institutions assumed panic proportions. For a time it seemed as if the panic might not only bring down the entire New York financial structure but also have serious impact upon financial institutions the world around.[33]

As early as March, 1907, private interests were calling upon the government for help in warding off a financial panic. Through Taft, J. P. Morgan requested an interview with the President. At the meeting Morgan asked Roosevelt to meet with a group of railroad executives to reassure them that the administration would not use the recently passed rate bill against them in a vindictive fashion. After the President had considered the request and finally refused, he was asked by railroad interests to make a public statement calculated to restore confidence in the carriers and the business world in general. Again the President refused because he did not want "to seem to talk just for the effect on the stock market." Nevertheless the administration continued to keep a sharp eye on the indexes of business health, and as conditions got worse went actively to the aid of the New York financial community. In late March the Secretary of the Treasury announced that the government would not make its customary withdrawals from New York banks, and subsequently the Treasury deposited in them over $70 million of customs receipts.[34]

During the darkest days of the October panic the resources of the government were thrown even more directly into the fight for national solvency. Cortelyou, the Secretary of the Treasury, was con-

---

[33] Frederick Lewis Allen, *The Great Pierpont Morgan* (New York, 1949), pp. 186 ff.

[34] Taft to Roosevelt, March 11, 1907, Taft MSS.; Grenville Dodge to Roosevelt, March 28, 1907, Dodge MSS.; Roosevelt to Kermit Roosevelt, March 31, 1907, and to James Speyer, March 5, 1907, Roosevelt MSS.

stantly in New York during these bleak hours, where he co-operated with the group of New York bankers who, under the direction of J. P. Morgan, were switching funds from bank to bank and to the securities markets as the need to save one or another institution became critical. Among such lifesaving funds were the liquid resources of the United States government. About November 1 it became apparent that one of the more important New York brokerage houses was on the verge of bankruptcy. The firm and its associates held a good many shares of stock of the Tennessee Coal and Iron Company, some of which had been deposited with banks as collateral for loans. Had the brokerage firm closed its doors, the failure would have placed great strain on similar houses and on the New York Stock Exchange itself. But it is not so clear that the closing would critically have imperiled the banking structure. To save the firm the House of Morgan suggested that the United States Steel Corporation purchase the Tennessee Coal and Iron Company by an exchange of stock. This would lend stability to the securities firms, protect the banks holding the collateral, and enable the Steel Company, in which Morgan was deeply involved, to obtain control of the rich Tennessee coal and iron operations. There was one possible obstacle to the deal. Would the government indict the steel corporation, already a giant in its field, as a monopoly? To get the answer E. H. Gary and H. C. Frick made a hurried after-midnight journey to Washington. The next morning they met with Roosevelt and Root. Details of the conference are contained in a letter from Gary to Root written for the purpose of being placed in the government's records. According to Gary's letter the two steel executives explained that the purchase of the Tennessee firm at a price "somewhat in excess" of its real value would not materially "increase the total capacity of the steel corporation," but that the purchase "would be of great benefit to financial conditions and would probably save from failure an important business concern. . . ." The President answered, according to Gary's memory, that while he could not legally make "any binding promise or agreement," he certainly would not advise against the proposed purchase. Thereafter, Gary wrote, "The President was also kind enough to state generally his favorable opinion of our Corporation and its management as ascertained from reports from the Department of Commerce and otherwise." Root wrote back that Gary's account was accurate, but asked him to delete the President's favorable remarks as not being germane to the transaction.[35] A few days after the transaction Roosevelt had public words of praise "for those conservative and substantial business men who in this crisis have acted with such wisdom and public spirit." But even then the West held another view. "Morgan stood firm," one newspaper commented, "until every speculator had made his way to solvency." Years later, when the details of the steel corporation transaction became known, the question was raised whether the President by his actions had not materially contributed to the growth of a steel monopoly. When the Taft administration answered in the affirmative in the autumn of 1911 by initiating a suit against the corporation, the action marked a final break between Taft and his former friend Roosevelt.

During November, 1907, the government again gave substantial help in stabilizing the financial situation. By presidential authorization the Treasury issued $100 million Treasury certificates and $50 million Panama Canal bonds at low interest rates, sold them to banks on credit, and authorized the banks to issue currency with the bonds as collateral. By January the downward movement had been turned, and soon the panic, except for its political effects, was a matter of memory.

While the panic existed there was, as usual, a heated debate over its causes. To some degree the American developments, as the President pointed out, had been a part of a world movement. The inelasticity of the American currency had contributed to it, as had also overextension of credit. The loss of public faith in the nation's financial leaders, loose banking practices, especially among the New York trust companies, and the wild and harmful speculation by financiers large and small had all played their part. But to a good portion of the world of big business and finance the real reason for the debacle lay in Roosevelt's war upon business and the resulting loss of confidence. The stubborn chorus of business criticism had started back at the time of the struggle over the railroad rate and the pure-food bills. It increased in volume as the presidential utterances grew more radical in 1907, and reached a peak during the depression with the publication of James R. Day's *The Raid on Prosperity*. An unblushing reactionary, Chancellor Day of Syracuse University, accused the Roosevelt administration of destroying prosperity, of being "unconstitutional and destructive of liberty," and predicted that if the Roosevelt way were

[35] Gary to Root, November 7, 1907; Root to Gary, November 13, 1907, Root MSS.

not reversed it would end in a permanent political oligarchy controlling the government and society.[36] Many Republican leaders supported Day's general point of view. Even Root, disposed to be friendly to the President, commented the following year that there had been "much unjustifiable exaggeration in the recent talk and writing about American corporations and American business." The result had been "to destroy confidence, to discredit us abroad and to discourage enterprise." [37]

The object of this business criticism was quite unrepentant. Roosevelt was positive that much of the impetus for the depression had come from the wicked speculators. During August, 1907, he addressed himself to "certain malefactors of great wealth" who, he charged, had combined to increase the intensity of the panic "in order to discredit the policy of the government." With an upthrust arm and a baleful glance, the President shouted that there would be no letup in his campaign against "speculation, corruption and fraud," which in part had caused the panic, or in the policy of the government to control great wealth in the interests of the commonweal. Nor was there. In December Roosevelt sent his annual message to Congress. In its 35,000 words were recommendations for the adoption of an inheritance and income tax, the national incorporation and regulation of interstate business, the regulation of railroad securities, and the fixing of railroad rates based upon a scheme of physical evaluation. The President also called for the establishment of a postal savings bank, the limitation of labor injunctions, compulsory investigation of large labor disputes, and the extension of the eight-hour day and workingmen's compensation principles. Then at the end of January, 1908, as Congress seemed disinclined to consider his proposals, Roosevelt sent it the most radical message of his entire eight years of office. Included in it were all of the proposals he had recommended in December, together with a new one demanding the federal regulation of stock market gambling, which the President considered no different from gambling with cards or other mechanical devices. But the real blow to the conservatives came in Roosevelt's blasts against the federal courts and big business. The courts had just declared unconstitutional a previously passed railway

[36] For a good short analysis of the panic's causes, see Morison, *Roosevelt Letters*, V, 747 n. A summary of the anti-Roosevelt opinion is contained in *Literary Digest*, XXXV (1907), 669.

[37] Root to H. L. Higginson, November 10, 1908, Root MSS.

workingmen's compensation law. The decision had evoked bitter criticism from the left, criticism that the conservatives were seeking to silence. "No servant of the people has a right to be free from just and

To trap the mouse, don't raze the house.

honest criticism," the President declared. He also took this occasion to slap at "predatory wealth" in a way that no President had since Andrew Jackson. The panic was not caused by the administration, Roosevelt declared, but by "the speculative folly and the flagrant dishonesty of a few men of great wealth. . . ." Such men were not only responsible for a large share of the "rottenness" in business but they had also consistently fought every attempt at reform. The President then grew painfully specific, naming the executives of the Standard Oil Company and the Santa Fe Railroad as examples. "Every measure for honesty in business that has been passed during the last six years," he commented, "has been opposed by these men . . . with every resource that bitter and unscrupulous craft could suggest and the command of almost unlimited money secure." The President wrote his son that he had put into this special message his "deepest and most earnest convictions." [38]

In these two messages Roosevelt had come to the parting of the ways politically. As Professor Elting Morison rightly observes,[39] he had proposed practically every reform that was to be made during the Taft and Wilson administrations, and even a few, it might be added, that were to lie inanimate until the New Deal days. Over and beyond this Roosevelt had expressed in outline form his own political program for the next four years. Hitherto historians have assumed that Roosevelt's radical formulations of 1910 and 1912 were inspired by Herbert Croly's *Promise of American Life,* published in November, 1909, and by the sudden exigencies of his own political fortunes. A glance at his messages and speeches of 1907 and 1908 would seem to argue that Roosevelt may have had as much influence on Croly as Croly had on him. At the least this much can be said. Ideologically there was to be no great break between the Roosevelt of 1907–8 and that of the following four years. His 1907–8 observations on the need for increasing the federal regulatory powers, his indictment of the asocial nature of big business, and his criticism of the federal courts, which he expressed with far more causticity in his private letters, were to be the very essence of his radical Osawatomie speech of 1910 and his New Nationalism of 1912. Throwing past caution to the winds, Roosevelt left the center in these early years and became for a time a radical progressive. He could afford to be less cautious since he was soon to leave office and there was no need for the support of a united party in a fight for a nomination or election. A partial explanation of his courage and conviction might have been the diminishing measure of his hopes for the future. But other factors were also relevant. Roosevelt was a fighter. During the course of the previous two years he had met the constant opposition of the business community in his efforts to pass

---

[38] Roosevelt, *Works,* 7, pp. 1597 ff.; Roosevelt to Kermit Roosevelt, January 31, 1908, Roosevelt MSS.

[39] Morison, *Roosevelt Letters,* VI, 922.

reform legislation. He and his proposals had been indicted by many businessmen for causing the panic. His natural reaction was to strike back. The President also was a superb politician whose ears were sensitively attuned to swells of public sentiment. He had watched the rise of La Follette, Cummins, and all the other reformers, as well as the inexorable march of the Socialist vote and the solidifying of labor union opinion. In 1904 he had cautioned Philander C. Knox about the Republican party's going down in a wave of labor radicalism. By 1906 he was sure that the Socialist movement was more dangerous than that of the Populists had been. To a Supreme Court Justice he wrote in 1908 that if the spirit behind the decision outlawing the workingmen's compensation law was to obtain in the future, "we should not only have a revolution, but it would be absolutely necessary to have a revolution, because the condition of the worker would become intolerable." The country was moving, and Roosevelt, being a good democratic politician, was ready to move with it and guide it in the ways of moderation, expediency, and righteousness.[40]

Whatever movement was discernible in the country, businessmen were of another mind, however, about the advisability of accompanying it. In May, after the yearly meeting of the American Manufacturers Association, the organization's journal reported that the meeting had agreed that "it was better to fight than be assassinated in the interests of a coalition of politics and labor." Congress apparently felt much the same. During the 1908 session the President received bills authorizing a temporary expansion of the currency, the building of two battleships, and a workingmen's compensation measure applying only to the railroads. Roosevelt's major proposals for the relief of labor and the regulation of business were ignored.[41]

Undaunted, the President returned to the war in his December, 1908, message. It was an impolitic document and a radical one, calculated to antagonize any conservative statesman. In addition to all of his other labor proposals, he declared that the workingman should be guaranteed "a larger share of the wealth" that he produced. To the charge that he was willing to centralize power to the destruction of liberty, he replied that the chief danger to democracy lay not in the concentration of administrative power but "in having the power in-

[40] Roosevelt to William R. Day, January 11, 1908, Roosevelt MSS.
[41] *American Industries,* as quoted in the *Literary Digest,* XXXVI (1908), 181.

sufficiently concentrated so that no one can be held responsible to the people for its use." He took a final swing at the courts by designating them as "the chief lawmakers of our country" and their judges as both "competent and incompetent." The most sensational part of the message contained a rebuke to Congress itself. Seeking to restore the power of the Secret Service, which Congress had curbed in the previous session, the President declared that the congressional action could give "comfort only to criminals," and suggested that if the members of Congress were afraid of being investigated by the organization they could exempt themselves by an amendment. Angrily and by a unanimous vote the House appointed a committee to consider the remark and in the end backhandedly censured the President by refusing to accept his message of explanation. In reply Roosevelt vetoed two congressional bills, one of which he called a "fraud upon the public." In such an atmosphere the passage of any major legislation was hopeless. Recalling a friend's surmise that the last months of his administration would be a period of stagnation, Roosevelt answered that "the period of stagnation continued to rage with uninterrupted violence." And so it did almost down to the last hour of the snowy March morning when Roosevelt regretfully left the White House and became for the first time in twelve years a private citizen.[42] He was soon on his way to Africa and Europe, a trip which would keep him abroad for over a year. He looked forward to the African big game as his "last chance for something in the nature of a great adventure." At fifty he was no longer up to arduous scientific exploration; the only real worth-while struggle he looked forward to was the continuance of his fight for "political, social and industrial reform."

During the war between Congress and the White House, not all Republicans on Capitol Hill by any means were meekly following the dominant conservative leadership of the party. Against the Aldrich currency bill the votes of sixteen Midwestern Republicans were cast in the House; in the Senate, Republicans Borah of Idaho, Brown and Burkett of Nebraska, La Follette of Wisconsin, and Bourne of Oregon also voted against this party measure. Simultaneously a group of young Republicans under the leadership of Beveridge of Indiana opposed the organization's move to cut Roosevelt's request for four battleships to two. The unsuccessful efforts of Beveridge, Dolliver, and La Follette

[42] Roosevelt, *Works,* XV, 527 ff.; Roosevelt to Kermit Roosevelt, January 10, 1909, and to John St. L. Strachey, November 28, 1908, Roosevelt MSS.

to obtain consideration for Roosevelt's labor and corporation measures embittered them against the regular Senate leadership. In the House over two dozen Republicans had promised the Democratic minority that they would join in a fight against Speaker Cannon and his authoritarian rules. That fall, at the start of the presidential campaign Beveridge expressed his growing resentment against the demands of party regularity. Political life and the Republican party did not seem to be worth the effort for a man of his convictions. He was dedicated to progressive measures, but "by the ethics of party regularity" he was "compeled to go out and work for the very men who were enemies of these measures." Dolliver was already feeling some of the same strain in Iowa, and La Follette since 1900 had never felt obliged to support any regular Republican in Wisconsin.[43]

By the time Roosevelt left office a distinct cleavage had appeared in the Republican party. Roosevelt had not started the schism, and it would have developed with or without his aid. But he had abetted it, especially in his last two years. In fact, his unsatisfied legislative demands during 1907 and 1908 had provided the progressive faction with a program. Thus the inheritance Roosevelt left was a party divided between an increasingly stubborn conservative majority and a growing progressive minority whose reform claims against the party were underwritten by the most popular Republican President since Lincoln. The situation spelled trouble for Roosevelt's successor, William Howard Taft, whom the President had already designated and whom he had certified to the public as a stout defender of "my policies."

[43] Beveridge to Roosevelt, May 8, 1908, and to C. W. Miller, August 15, 1908, Beveridge MSS.; Champ Clark, *My Quarter Century of American Politics* (2 vols., New York, 1920), II, 268–270; George W. Norris in *La Follette's Magazine,* January 8, 1910.

CHAPTER 12

The Troubled Taft

THEODORE ROOSEVELT'S second term ended on March 4, 1909, but months before that date he had to decide whether he would leave the Presidency. The decision was his to make, as he well knew. From conservatives to progressives almost the whole party agreed that Roosevelt could have the nomination again for less than the asking. Even the most hopeful of the other possible candidates, William Howard Taft, observed that he had had many pledges of support provided Roosevelt declined, but that the average Republican politician regarded anyone else but the President as "a poor second choice." As late as the summer of 1907 Senator Allison of Iowa predicted that Roosevelt would be renominated again unless he "positively" refused. Few informed people in the country, whether Republicans or Democrats, seriously doubted the outcome of the election if Roosevelt decided to stand again.[1]

Of the many critical decisions Roosevelt made in his life this was among the most difficult, the one that involved the most personal agony. Few Presidents have enjoyed office as much as Roosevelt had. Temperamentally he was still a young man in 1908, energetic and ambitious, and at the top of his mental and physical powers. He was not tired, he wrote, and did not want a rest. What he wanted most was to remain master of the White House at the center of national and even world attention. "I should like to have stayed on in the Presi-

[1] Taft to Charles P. Taft, November 1, 1906, Taft MSS.; Allison to Grenville M. Dodge, July 28, 1907, Allison MSS.

dency," he observed during the campaign of 1908, "and I make no pretence that I am glad to be relieved of my official duties." [2]

But as early as 1906 Roosevelt decided that he had to give up the office he so much wanted to retain. He did more than resign; he chose his successor, and for the next two years honestly and energetically worked for his nomination and election. He acted so because he came to the conclusion that if he did not support another candidate, he himself would be renominated and elected. Why this act of resignation from a man so devoted to expediency? Because he felt obligated by his personal promise of November, 1904, because in many important things he was a man of principle, and because he was committed to democratic traditions and institutions. Roosevelt was quite aware of the power of the Presidency. He himself had measurably increased that power. "While President," he recalled, "I have *been* President, emphatically, I have used every ounce of power there was in the office. . . ." He strongly felt that the efficiency of the United States government and perhaps its very existence depended upon an exceedingly strong Executive. But Roosevelt also recognized the dangers to a democracy in granting the Executive such unqualified authority as he desired to see reside in the Presidency. His solution was to make the power terminable, to follow the two-term tradition as it had been handed down to him by his predecessors in the office. Roosevelt's act of abnegation was among his greatest contributions to his country. [3]

Convinced that he had to select his successor to stop his own nomination, Roosevelt chose William Howard Taft, his Secretary of War and his alter ego during the second term. On the ground of pure ability Roosevelt might have preferred Root. But Root's health was bad, he was too closely connected with Wall Street, and perhaps he was too conservative for the President's 1907 tastes. From the moment of Taft's choice in 1906 the whole weight of the President's office was thrown into the balance. At the start of the contest there were other candidates, among whom Foraker of Ohio and Knox of Pennsylvania carried hopes of the conservatives and Charles Evans Hughes those of more moderate views. But the weight of the federal patronage turned over to Taft, and Roosevelt's towering influence and his skillful maneuvers soon had the hopes of the remaining candidates in a permanent eclipse.

[2] Roosevelt to Arthur Hamilton Lee, December 26, 1907; to Cecil Spring-Rice, September 17, 1908, Roosevelt MSS.

[3] Roosevelt to George O. Trevelyan, June 19, 1908, Roosevelt MSS.

By the time the Republican convention met in June, 1908, the results seemed certain except for the possibility that the delegates might ignore all their promises and obligations and insist upon Roosevelt's renomination.

Mother G.O.P. "My, but it will seem quiet around the old place after Theodore is gone."

According to plan, the convention nominated Taft on the first ballot. But this was almost the only victory that the President and his nominee won. Both Roosevelt and Taft had desired either Senators Beveridge or Dolliver for the temporary chairmanship, but the conservatives insisted on one of their own for the position and won. The two also wanted a progressive for the vice-presidential nomination; but since

Dolliver and Beveridge both declined that dubious honor, the choice went again to a standpatter, James S. Sherman of New York. Both Roosevelt and Taft had "revised" and "approved" a proposed draft of the party platform, and both sent pleas to the convention for its passage as drafted. But both the controversial labor injunction and the tariff planks were substantially rewritten during the meeting by the conservative coalition headed by Senators Aldrich of Rhode Island and Crane of Massachusetts and James W. Van Cleave, president of the American Manufacturers Association. Instead of limiting the granting of injunctions, the party pledged itself to "uphold at all times the authority and the integrity of the courts. . . ." Taft had wanted a specific promise to revise the tariff downward, but the most the convention would agree to was a promise of revision without stipulating which way the revising process was to be pointed. The remainder of the platform, except for a postal-savings-bank proposal, was wholly unexceptional and extremely conservative. Although both the candidate and the incumbent expressed public satisfaction over the convention, privately neither man was too happy about the results. As for the progressive senators and representatives, they were plainly disgruntled. La Follette, whose long list of amendments to the platform had been defeated, was openly critical. Dolliver, Cummins, and Beveridge agreed with La Follette in private. "If the convention in Chicago had designedly attempted to weaken us out here," Cummins wrote, "it could not have been more effective." The consensus of the press was that the President and his friend had won the nomination and had lost everything else.[4]

Since William Randolph Hearst meanwhile had organized his own National Independence party, Bryan was left again as the unchallenged progressive leader of the Democrats. Over the protests of eastern conservatives he was nominated for the third time on a radical platform, including an anti-injunction measure, which won the unreserved support of the American Federation of Labor. The Commoner launched his usual vigorous campaign, claiming that he and not Taft was the logical heir to extend and perfect the reforms begun by Roosevelt. He spoke in favor of the federal ownership of the great interstate railroads,

[4] Taft to Wade H. Ellis, June 17, 1908, and to Charles Nagel, June 1, 1908, Taft MSS.; Roosevelt to Lodge, June 8, 1908, Roosevelt MSS.; La Follette to Dolliver, June 20, 1908, Dolliver MSS.; Dolliver to G. M. Dodge, June 24, 1908, Dodge MSS.; Cummins to Paul A. Ewart, June 27, 1908, Cummins MSS.

the dissolution of all trusts controlling 50 per cent or more of the American market, government-guaranteed bank deposits, and the gradual abandonment of the protective tariff principle so as to secure a tariff for revenue only. His consistent support of labor measures won him an official endorsement of the American Federation of Labor, which announced that it was being partisan only to labor principles and not to a political party. But long before November it was evident that Bryan was no longer exciting either the frenzied opposition or the fanatical support that he had commanded in 1896 or even in 1900. Before the election, in an unprecedented move Bryan published the amount and sources of his campaign contributions. The totals revealed that less than 350 people had given more than $100 to his campaign. So small were the Democratic funds that the party's effort was promptly called the "barefoot campaign." [5]

If the nation was less than enthusiastic about Bryan, it was certainly not pulsating with emotion for the Republican candidate. Perhaps because he had been chosen by Roosevelt, the party professionals had never been too ardent toward Taft even while supporting him. Compared with Roosevelt or even Bryan, the Republican candidate lacked personal color. Not a partisan by nature, Taft never convinced himself that the nation's decision would have real significance for the future. Both parties, he believed, were trying "to do the same thing," and the only real issue to be decided was which candidate was "the more safely to be trusted" with office. Such a spirit was not well calculated to elicit brimming enthusiasm from an electorate who had been conditioned during the Roosevelt years to expect an election to resemble something between a bull fight and a national camp meeting. The candidate did promise to work for lower tariff rates, the better control of railroads, a postal savings system, and all the Roosevelt policies in general. But his lack of fire seemed to make the once-exciting Roosevelt program about as dull as a statistical report. The campaign, one Republican paper noted, was "loaded down with calm." Roosevelt was worried about Taft's lack of appeal, about labor's mobilization against the party, about Republican finances, about Taft's campaign managers, and about the candidate's reluctance to "smash into Bryan in effective fashion." The President worked hard to pump life into the campaign. He sent off numerous suggestions to Taft, published a Taft letter without his approval, and sent out communiqués on campaign issues written

[5] *Literary Digest,* XXXVII (1908), 575.

by himself. It was a commentary on the campaign that the President's few public activities almost invariably obtained more space in the newspapers than those of the candidate's.[6]

Explaining the Republican victory of 1908, Elihu Root wrote that "it was a vote more against Bryan than for Taft." Other competent political critics felt that Roosevelt had more to do with the results than either Taft or Bryan. The truth perhaps lay somewhere in between. Although Taft's plurality was only one-half of Roosevelt's in 1904, still the new President ran well ahead of fellow Republicans in practically every state except for a few of the more progressively inclined commonwealths in the Middle West. What was especially significant in the election was the continued growth in the strength of the Democratic party and the success of the so-called progressive Republican candidates in the Midwest. The Republicans had not only lost seats in the House of Representatives but they had also lost governors in Ohio, Indiana, Minnesota, and North Dakota, all of which voted for Taft. In Wisconsin, Iowa, Nebraska, and even in Kansas self-announced progressive Republicans, who had previously defeated conservatives in the primaries, were more successful in beating their Democratic rivals. The election, *The New York Times* reported, had been punctuated with "independent voting." A closer analysis of the returns indicated that the voter in the Midwest had expressed his independence mostly from standpat Republicanism symbolized by the control of Speaker Cannon in the House and Aldrich in the Senate.[7]

William Howard Taft, the President-elect, came from an old, distinguished, and moderately wealthy Cincinnati, Ohio, family. After graduating from the Yale Law School, he entered politics in Ohio, where he was almost immediately appointed to the State Superior Court to fill an unexpired term. The following year he was elected to the position, but he never again ran for a public office, except for the Presidency. In succession he was appointed Solicitor General of the United States, a judge of the Federal Circuit Court, the president of the Philippine Commission, Governor General of the Philippines, and Secretary of War. As a judge both in Ohio and on the federal bench he won admiration from the nation's conservatives by his antilabor

[6] Taft to Charles P. Taft, July 11, 1908, to Horace Taft, August 24, 1908, Taft MSS.; Des Moines *Register and Leader,* October 4, 1908; Roosevelt to Root, September 15, 1908, to Taft, September 9 and 26, 1908, Roosevelt MSS.
[7] Root to Whitelaw Reid, November 23, 1908, Root MSS.; *The New York Times,* November 7, 1908.

decisions; as an administrator he was so successful that Roosevelt often used him as a sort of an assistant President. Taft was an overlarge man of some three hundred pounds, inclined to placidity, amiability, and the pleasures of talking, playing golf, eating, and sleeping. He was a simple man, not ambitious, with a trained mind of an unexceptional character. He was disposed to the easy, ordered life of the bench and he disliked strife.

Despite his long record of public service before the campaign, Taft was not known too well in many parts of the country. His years on the bench and in the Philippines, and his visits in Panama, Cuba, and Puerto Rico while Secretary of War had not permitted the American people too close a view of him. What the public saw personally of him during the campaign it liked. He inspired confidence by his very size. He was affable and kindly. And though most of his speeches, which he usually read, were long and dull, his infectious laugh and his genial nature helped relieve his otherwise undistinguished efforts. The nation had reason to believe that he would make an efficient Chief Executive and a progressive-minded one. He had received the President's blessing and he repeatedly remarked that the aim of his administration would be to carry out and amplify the Roosevelt policies. "I should be untrue . . . to my promises . . . if I did not make the maintenance of those reforms a most important feature of my administration," he declared solemnly at his inaugural. Roosevelt predicted that except for Washington and Lincoln he would make a record comparable to any President in history.[8]

But as honest, as public-spirited, and as experienced an administrator as Taft was, he made at best an indifferent record in the White House, and his years there were far from happy. One of the chief difficulties was that the office demanded too much time and effort for a man of Taft's personal proclivities. Compared with the Presidents that preceded and followed him Taft was lazy. He ate too much, he wanted to sleep too long, and he much preferred the quieter enjoyments of an intimate game of bridge or a legal chat with a few cronies to the exhilaration of the stump or contesting wills with Congress, or crossing intellectual rapiers with the press. Throughout his career in Washington he was always reluctant to leave a game to get back to work, he continued to eat his "normal" breakfast of beefsteak, and he never ac-

8 *The New York Times*, March 5, 1909; Roosevelt to George O. Trevelyan, June 19, 1908, Roosevelt MSS.

customed himself to the amount of wining and dining that prevented him from getting enough sleep. He made a plaintive remark to his aide that there was so much to do and so little time to do it in. The truth was that Taft was not particularly interested in many of the things he had to do. Everyone, he wrote in late December, 1908, was bored with Augusta, Georgia, where he had gone to rest, but himself. Most bored was Mrs. Taft, who thought it silly to go to a place that far from Washington where one "could not be in it or know what's doing." But that was precisely the reason why he liked it. And although the President-elect was certainly entitled to even a six weeks' rest after a campaign, the lack of an itch to know "what was doing" was portentous.[9]

Taft had never really wanted to be President, as he so often candidly stated. He was not a politician in the ordinary sense. "I don't like politics," he wrote, "I don't like the limelight." He disliked crowds; he disliked campaigning. The summer of 1908, he recalled, was "one of the most uncomfortable four months of my life." Taft was really an administrator or a jurist. He had made his reputation in these professions, not by the crowd-pleasing techniques of the professional politician. He had succeeded in politics, he wrote, because of his father's reputation, because he went to conventions and was faithful to his superiors in the party, and because, like every well-trained Ohio man, he always had his "plate the right side up when offices were falling." [10]

Taft's chief ambition was to sit on the Supreme Court. Three times Roosevelt offered him the opportunity to do so and three times he refused, the last declination coming in 1906 because Mrs. Taft was "very bitterly opposed to it." Taft was a man who was extremely loyal and easily influenced by the people he liked. His wife had had great plans for him very early in their common life. She had not wanted him to go to the Philippines; the islands were too far away from the center of power. Had he stayed in Washington, she wrote in 1905, he would have been Secretary of State instead of Root and thus would have been the President's chief adviser. Helen Herron Taft's main ambition was to

[9] Taft to Robert Taft, February 6, 1904; to Mrs. Taft, September 24, 1905; to Charles P. Taft, August 21, 1907; to Frank Hitchcock, December 22, 1908; and to David K. Watson, January 17, 1911, Taft MSS. The only really good biography of Taft is Henry F. Pringle, *The Life and Times of William Howard Taft* (2 vols., New York, 1939). Pringle disagrees with much of the following interpretation.

[10] Taft to Milton A. McRae, November 12, 1904; to Mrs. Louis W. Shaffer, July 15, 1908; to William A. White, February 26, 1908, Taft MSS.

make her husband President, and at times her eagerness caused near misunderstandings between Roosevelt and Taft. Even after the President had designated her husband as his heir, Mrs. Taft was suspicious of Roosevelt's good intentions. As late as the convention she was afraid that the President was really using her husband as a stalking-horse and would come out of the Republican meeting with the nomination. Mrs. Taft had the burning ambition that makes Presidents. She liked the limelight, the crowds, the official society, the "being in on the know." And she may have had the ability to make Taft a successful Chief Executive. Taft thought she was an excellent politician. A month after his election he wrote that if he were Chief Justice he would feel perfectly at home, but as President he was "just a bit like a fish out of water." However, the President mused, "as my wife is the politician and she will be able to meet all the issues, perhaps we can keep a stiff upper lip. . . ." It may have been one of Taft's great misfortunes that his wife could not meet many of the issues. For soon after he entered the White House, Helen Taft fell seriously ill, and for most of his term the man who did not trust his own political judgment had to look elsewhere for advice.[11]

One of Taft's lifelong troubles was that he was often persuaded to act against his own basic instincts. Taft was a conservative instinctively, emotionally, and ideologically. He revered the law, the judicial process, and the order that accompanied it. He respected the past and its institutions and disliked change, especially if that change was initiated by political pressure from below. He was not "a lover" of direct primaries, he wrote, nor of any devices that would permit the people more voice in making fundamental decisions. To him man's nearest approach to justice was the judicial process, which involved facing every question "with indifference to every consideration except to reach a right and just conclusion, and to preserve the fundamental structure of our government as our fathers gave it to us. . . ." He doubted whether human nature could be changed much, particularly by the state. Roosevelt's strong faith in state action often puzzled him. He was for promoting greater interest in the nation's children, he wrote in 1910, but he was extremely doubtful about creating a national children's bureau. He was opposed to unloading such work on the state in

11 Taft to J. D. Brannan, March 29, 1906, to Mrs. Taft, September 24, 1905, to Henry A. Merrill, December 2, 1908, Taft MSS.; Oscar S. Straus, "Diary" (manuscript), September, (?), 1908.

principle, and he questioned whether such a bureau would really be efficacious in helping children.[12]

Taft's views on the legal rights of organized labor were symptomatic of his deeply ingrained conservatism. During the panic of 1893 and the Pullman strike he had been as avid for the violent suppression of labor as Roosevelt had, hoping that the news that thirty strikers had been killed by federal troops was correct. As a member of the judiciary he had issued labor injunctions freely, earning the name of "the injunction judge." In the Roosevelt years he had changed his attitude somewhat but not profoundly. Whereas Roosevelt, certainly no enemy of capital, could argue that labor unions were a part of the evolution of modern industry and if controlled properly could be agents of social good, Taft's presuppositions were all against labor and in favor of capital. He conceded that businessmen were sometimes "arrogant" in their dealings with the unions, but he also felt that unions and their sympathizers, almost invariably "socialists," were willing "to overturn the social order." If violence broke out in any given strike, he assumed almost by faith that the unions were almost wholly responsible. In the Chicago strike of 1905, in which both sides of the struggle were probably equally guilty of resorting to violence, Taft wrote that he hoped the state troops would be used to "clean out the unions and restore order." Roosevelt was also in favor of the use of troops, but never once did he refer to "cleaning out the unions." [13]

In 1908, Taft went on record for limiting labor injunctions, but he wrote privately that he was for hedging the limitations about so "as not to do the slightest damage." It is interesting to note that Taft never energetically supported a labor injunction bill, nor was one passed during his term. At the end of the 1908 campaign, he admitted publicly that labor had the right to organize and to strike, but, he added, not the right "to injure the property or the business of their employers." Later he wrote that neither economic class ought to be favored but that each "should stand on an equality before the law." But the important point of the statement lay in the assumption that the law as then constituted afforded both sides "substantial justice." In his views on organized labor, on the increase of government services and regu-

[12] Taft to George Cromwell, August 23, 1910, to William H. Moody, October 4, 1910, to Roosevelt, July 16, 1907, and to M. P. E. Groszmann, April 12, 1910, Taft MSS.; Taft, *Popular Government* (New Haven, 1913), p. 85.

[13] Pringle, *Taft,* II, 102, 128; Taft to Elihu Root, November 10, 1906, and to Mrs. E. J. McCagg, May 12, 1905, Taft MSS.

latory powers, his antitrust attitudes, and his low-tariff preferences Taft reminds one of Grover Cleveland. Taft had been a student of William Graham Sumner of Yale. He never entirely divorced himself from his teacher's laissez-faire views.[14]

If Taft was such a philosophical conservative, how can his willingness to go along with the Roosevelt experiments and adventures be explained? Largely by his friendship for Roosevelt, his deep sense of loyalty of both a personal and party nature, and by his inclination to swim with the tide. During the Roosevelt years he was quite content to permit his superior to call the tune just as during his own Presidency he was to allow other people to make many of his decisions for him. These characteristics made him a loyal administrator but a poor President. Since Taft was neither adventurous nor creative, many of his ideas reflected those of the dominant people who immediately surrounded him. Until 1909 he had taken on much of the ideological color of the magnetic and persuasive Roosevelt. When that polar influence was removed, Taft chose advisers who more accurately reflected his own basic views. During all the years Taft was a member of the Roosevelt administration he scarcely corresponded or socially mingled with a person of the so-called progressive tendencies. Save for Roosevelt his friends were drawn from the conservative side of Congress, the bench, and official society. The habit was to continue throughout the campaign of 1908 and throughout his Presidency. Many of Roosevelt's associations, of course, had necessarily been with the same class of people. But both Roosevelt's correspondence and dinner lists had ranged practically through the spectrum of politics. Taft had few personal and political relations with reformers and progressives. The fact was that he disliked them and distrusted them even before his term began.

A portion of Taft's distaste for the left-of-center representatives in the party may have come from his realization that most of them preferred a third term for Roosevelt. In 1907 Taft was annoyed by a Roosevelt letter which indicated that Senators Bourne, La Follette, and Beveridge had been urging a third term. After his nomination he was not sure that such people would support him. They might vote for Bryan, he wrote, since many of Roosevelt's followers thought that Bryan and not he was "the legitimate successor of Roosevelt," no matter what Roosevelt himself said. On the eve of the campaign he predicted that

[14] Taft to Aaron A. Ferris, July 14, 1908, Taft MSS.; *The New York Times,* October 29, 1908; Memorandum, August 19, 1911, Taft MSS.

La Follette and Cummins would be critical of his speeches for not being radical enough. But the clearest indication of the workings of the candidate's mind came from a letter he wrote to Root urging him to busy himself with a campaign to support the selection of conservative Republican senators. Unless the Republican state legislatures selected a preponderance of conservative senators, Taft was fearful that the "Bryan wing" of the Republican party, among which he included La Follette, Cummins, Bristow, Crawford, Bourne, and Brown, would so increase its following in the coming elections that "it would not be very long until the large Republican Senatorial majority would be wiped out." Months before Taft took office he had mentally separated the progressive Republicans from the party, designating them as potential troublemakers and party deserters. Whereas Roosevelt had identified himself during the last two years of office with the "left center," Taft began by preferring the right. Since the country was obviously still moving toward the left and since Taft had promised to pursue Roosevelt's objectives, the situation in the Republican party became an interesting compound of unstable and conflicting elements.[15]

"I need a Cabinet of as many experienced lawyers as I can get . . ." Taft wrote to his newly appointed Secretary of State, Philander C. Knox, as he was trying in late December to put together his official family. He did not want "impish people" or "troublemakers," nor did he want to appoint Jews or Catholics just because of their religious qualifications. Roosevelt's function, he felt, had been to preach reform and his was to enact it. Therefore he wanted corporation lawyers who understood corporate wealth since they were the people "best fitted to do this without injury to the business interests of the country." Taft ended up with five corporation lawyers in his Cabinet, even though he was sure that he would be criticized for his selections. Together with Knox, Taft selected Franklin MacVeagh, a former anti-Bryan Democrat and a Chicago banker, as his Secretary of the Treasury; an old-time friend, railroad attorney, and another erstwhile Democrat, Jacob Dickinson, as Secretary of War; Frank H. Hitchcock, Taft's campaign manager, was made Postmaster General; George W. Wickersham, a New York corporation lawyer, Attorney General; and Charles Nagel of St. Louis, an ardent supporter in the campaign, Secretary of Commerce and Labor. James Wilson of Iowa was continued as Secretary of Agri-

[15] Roosevelt to Taft, September 3, 1907; Taft to J. D. Brannan, July 13, 1908, to Mrs. Taft, August 18, 1907, and to Root, August 15, 1908, Taft MSS.

culture and George von L. Meyer, the Postmaster General under Roosevelt, was now Secretary of the Navy. Both "Tama Jim" Wilson and Meyer were of conservative persuasion. The group, in fact, contained no reformers or progressives.

It was largely a Cabinet of Taft's own making. He had talked with Knox about his selections, with Aldrich and with Nelson Cromwell of Panama fame, but he had said very little to Roosevelt or to the other party leaders. After the elections he had told Roosevelt that he intended to keep most of his predecessor's appointments in office. At another time he had given Roosevelt to understand that he probably would retain both Garfield and Straus. But as the chips finally fell in place neither man was kept. Taft explained that he had not kept Garfield because he "knew him," and Straus, he believed, had not been a good administrator. Even Roosevelt's one direct suggestion that his personal secretary, Loeb, be appointed temporarily so as to aid him in getting a good position outside the government was turned down as smacking too much of manipulation "for personal reasons." The incoming President did offer Theodore E. Burton of Ohio a post. Burton had been one of his chief early supporters and had nominated him at the convention. But Burton was also seeking the senatorship, his chief competitor for the position being Charles Taft, the President's brother. Burton declined, as did Root and Lodge, the office of Secretary of State. Even so Taft's Cabinet was a relatively strong one, better than most Republican Cabinets of the past. If it was criticized for being overstocked with corporation lawyers, it was perhaps no more conservative than Roosevelt's first official group. Perhaps the only really strange thing about it was the way it was made. Taft had asked for precious little advice from the powerful party members and he had practically ignored the President. Roosevelt apparently had no voice in Taft's deliberations and knew nothing about the final selections until after they were made.[16]

Some years after Taft had left the Presidency he strongly criticized Roosevelt for interfering in the legislative process, where, he felt, the President had no legal powers. Strangely enough, Taft started his term in office by intervening in the affairs of the House in a far more drastic

[16] Taft to Knox, December 22, 23, 1908, and February 20, 1909, to Cromwell, December 2, 1908, to William R. Nelson, February 23, 1909, Taft MSS.; Straus "Diary," January 23, 1909; Root to Joseph A. Choate, November 21, 1908, Root MSS.; W. A. Day to P. C. Knox, December 29, 1908, Knox MSS.

and comprehensive way than Roosevelt ever had. He attempted to un-
seat Speaker Cannon, replace him with a man more congenial to his
views, and at the same time change the rules of the House, clipping the
Speaker's power. Under the existing rules the Speaker was empowered
to name all the committees of the House, including the famous Rules
Committee of which he himself was a member. His power of selection
gave him enormous influence over legislation in itself. But his power
was augmented by his position on the Rules Committee, since this body
of five members had to report a rule for each piece of legislation before
it was moved to the floor, a rule that stipulated the conditions under
which the bill would be debated. If the Speaker was sufficiently opposed to a particular bill, it had little chance of even getting a place on
the calendar, to say nothing of passage.

Taft did not start the campaigns either to dethrone the Speaker or to
change the rules of the House. He was consistent in his support of
neither, his vacillation leading to the charge that he had led his troops
to battle and then had disappeared. There is no question that he
initially gave the progressive Republicans who were opposed both to
Cannon and the rules reason for thinking that he would support them.
During the campaign of 1908 Taft complained that the greatest burden
he had to carry was Cannonism, which was synonymous with "reac-
tionaryism." He had never liked Cannon personally and thought of him
as "dirty and vulgar." And when Cannon opposed his desired planks
in the Republican platform pledging the party to tariff revision downward and a limitation of labor injunctions, Taft wrote to Roosevelt that
the Speaker would "have to go." Both Roosevelt and Root urged caution on the candidate. But in November, after Cannon had made a
high-tariff speech, Taft took the bit in his teeth. He had already formulated a plan to call an extra session of Congress to revise the tariff,
and he was delighted with the news that at least a dozen Republican
congressmen would not vote for Cannon as Speaker and that three
times that number were favorable to a revision of the dictatorial House
rules. He enthusiastically informed Roosevelt of the progress in the
movement to bring Cannon down and pledged that if by helping he
could secure the Speaker's defeat he would do so. Again Roosevelt
urged caution, doubting that Cannon could be defeated. He feared that
Taft's campaign might only result in the disaster of creating a hostile
and sullen floor leader. But the President-elect went on with his plan,
making it known rather generally in both liberal and conservative wings

of the party that he was opposed to the re-election of the Speaker. Apparently a formal statement of opposition to Cannon was prepared by Representative Burton and circulated among the party leaders. Upon receiving the statement Root was distressed. He doubted that Cannon could be beaten and warned the President-elect that he could not beat him with Burton. When Taft received similar advice from other party leaders, he gave in. By December he was admitting that Cannon probably would have to be elected. But he felt that his campaign had made the Speaker amenable both to tariff legislation and to a change in House procedures. "I am very hopeful," he told William Cromwell, "that we shall secure a change of rules so that Cannon shall not be sole tyrant in the House." [17]

Independent of Taft, but certainly heartened by his actions, a group of insurgent Republican congressmen led by George W. Norris of Nebraska, Victor Murdock of Kansas, and Augustus P. Gardner of Massachusetts had met meanwhile and determined to oppose Cannonism at the start of the next Congress. In March, 1909, thirty Republican congressmen refused to sit in the party caucus, which would have pledged them to vote for the existing rules. Since the Republican party controlled the House by a majority of only some forty votes, it appeared as if the President's desire to curb Cannon was to be fulfilled. But the tough old Speaker would not go down without a struggle. On March 9 Cannon, Senator Aldrich, and Chairman Payne of the House Ways and Means Committee called at the White House and plainly told Taft that if the Speaker was defeated on the rules, the President's plan for tariff revision at that session would be imperiled. If, on the other hand, Taft supported the party organization, the three men promised to abide by the platform and follow his "lead." Since it was a question of 30 against 180, there was little the President could do but to "deprecate" the insurrection. As much as he sympathized with the insurgent principles, he remarked, for the sake of his legislative program he had to persuade them to support the organization. After the tariff bill had been passed the issue could be fought out. Subsequently, with the President's help and with some Tammany Democratic votes purchased by the promise of tariff favors, Cannon was again selected Speaker and

[17] Taft to Roosevelt, June 15, 1908, and November 7, 1908, to William R. Nelson, August 25, 1908, to Halvor Steenerson, November 30, 1908, and to Frank L. Dingley, November 23, 1908, Taft MSS.; Roosevelt to Taft, October 9, 12, November 10, 1908, Roosevelt MSS.; Root to Taft, November 24, 1908, Root MSS.; Taft to William N. Cromwell, December 2, 1908, Taft MSS.

the rules of the House remained unchanged. Portentous of future disaster, however, thirty-one Republicans had voted with the minority on the rules, and twelve, all from the Middle West, had cast their votes against the re-election of Cannon. Taft was aware that he was "under suspicion" by the rebels, but he felt that the solution of the struggle was "extremely satisfactory" and boded well for a successful revision of the tariff.[18]

During the tariff debate, however, Taft felt that Cannon had not strictly lived up to his pledge to support the platform promise. Irritated by the Speaker, once more he let it be known that he favored a change in the House leadership. He was willing, he wrote to Root, Knox, and other party luminaries, "to have it understood that my attitude is one of hostility to Cannon and the whole crowd. . . ." But the thirty or so House insurgents were once more mystified and angered by the President's devious course. Just as Taft was again stepping up his literary campaign against Cannon, the Speaker and the official party were taking retaliatory measures against the insurgents. By the lists of the new House Committee released in December, the insurgent leaders were deprived of their most choice committee assignments. And in January, 1910, the Republican Congressional Campaign Committee announced that it would officially oppose insurgency in the coming primary elections and advocate the nomination and the election of "straight" or "loyal" Republicans. The President denied that he had approved the campaign letter. But it was only a short time afterward that a number of the insurgents reported they were no longer being blessed with presidential patronage. In a sharp interchange of letters Taft denied to George Norris that he was using the patronage to help Cannon. But he did admit that he was stopping it where it was being used "to hurt the Republican Administration and its policies." He had the most reliable information, he concluded, that his appointing power in many congressional districts was being used "to fortify the opponents of the administration and opponents of the declared policy of the Republican party." [19] What the President meant was explained more fully to an

[18] George W. Norris, *Fighting Liberal* (New York, 1945), p. 45, and "The Fight on Rules," *La Follette's Magazine*, January 8, 1910; Taft to W. A. White, March 12, 1909, to Horace Taft, March 16, 1900, and to Roosevelt, March 21, 1909, Taft MSS.

[19] Taft to Root, October 24, 1909, and to Knox, November 25, 1909, Taft MSS.; New York *Sun*, January 10, 1910; Philadelphia *North American*, January 12, 1910; Taft to Norris, January 7, 11, 1910, Taft MSS.

Indianapolis publisher. The House insurgents, along with the so-called progressives in the Senate, he wrote, had voted against the tariff; they were supporting Pinchot against Ballinger, and they were proposing crippling amendments to the administration's railroad measure then before Congress. He could only conclude that they were opposed to the administration, whereas Cannon had helped it most of the time. He did not like Cannon or his control in the House, but he would not harm those who were trying to pass his legislation or help those trying to defeat it. Thus the President again had shifted course abruptly and again had chosen to steer toward the right.[20]

Undismayed by these presidential vagaries, the insurgents, under the leadership of George Norris of Nebraska, again challenged the Speaker at the opening of the new session of Congress in March, 1910. This time they were partially successful in a dramatic session of the House which lasted through thirty-six continuous hours. A Democratic-insurgent coalition voted down a ruling from the Speaker and went on to adopt new rules for the body which enlarged the Rules Committee from five to fifteen members, made them elected by the House instead of appointed by the Speaker, and excluded the Speaker from membership. Although Cannon was not removed from his chair, the power of the Speaker over legislation was definitely limited. Even the moderate Republican papers rejoiced at the event, the New York *Tribune* remarking that the true victor in the affair was not the insurgents but the Republican party. The President, unfortunately, received no felicitations. For his share in the uprising against Cannon he received the deep mistrust of some thirty Republican members of the House, most of whom came from the Midwest, the home of the party and the section necessary to its continued dominance.[21]

Of all the campaign promises the President made, he was probably most serious about his efforts to reduce the tariff rates. Since his college days an advocate of lower rates, Taft had virtually forced the party to consider revision against the inclinations of most of its leaders. While in the Philippines he had appealed for complete free trade between the islands and the mainland. Coming home, he continued the effort and at the very start of his campaign for the Republican nomination,

[20] Taft to Lucius B. Swift, February 19, 1910, Taft MSS.
[21] New York *Tribune*, March 20, 1910. For another version of the Cannon episode, see Kenneth Hechler, *Insurgency, Personalities, and Politics of the Taft Era* (New York, 1940), pp. 27–82.

against Roosevelt's advice, he called for "a sizable reduction" in the existing Dingley rates. Taft was obviously disconcerted by the Republican Convention's reluctance to pledge the party for revision downward, and a part of his anger at Cannon was due to the Speaker's post-election remarks deprecating the possibility for a sizable reduction. In the tariff hearings following the election he felt that consumers' representatives should have a voice and cheered the remarks of Andrew Carnegie, who astounded the high protectionists by arguing that the major industries no longer needed protection since they were able to undersell the most efficient of their foreign competitors. Once elected, Taft publicly announced his intention to call a special session of Congress immediately after his inauguration for the sole purpose of considering revisions in the Dingley tariff rates.[22]

Tariff revision encountered surprisingly little difficulty in the House. The Payne bill was introduced on the floor during the third day of the session and within less than a month it had passed by a strict party vote. The House rates were not as low as the President would have liked, but he felt they represented "substantial reductions." Then on April 12, Senator Aldrich introduced a revised bill in the Senate, remarking as he did so that the Senate committee had made more reductions in the rates than had the House. The Aldrich bill contained over eight hundred amendments to the House rates, and it was soon apparent that most of the changes were in an upward direction. Upon reading the Aldrich bill, Mr. Dooley congratulated the poor senators, "steamin' away under the majestic tin dome of the capitol," trying to reduce the tariff to a weight at which it could stand on the same platform with the President without endangering his life. The Aldrich amendments, he predicted, would make living easy that year since the senator from Rhode Island had thoughtfully left curling stones, false teeth, canary-bird seed, hog bristles, and silkworm eggs on the free list. "Th' new Tariff Bill," he concluded, "put these familyar commodyties within th' reach iv all." Specifically, the rates had been boosted sharply on many products fabricated of iron and steel, on ferrous metals, textiles, and lumber. The existing rates were restored on a good many raw materials placed on the free list by the House, and a provision for an inheritance tax, also passed by the House, had been struck out. Taft

[22] Taft to Roosevelt, August 6, 1907, Taft MSS.; Andrew Carnegie, "My Experience with and Views upon the Tariff," *Century*, LXXVII (1908), 196–205.

was aghast at the "ridiculous increases," as were most of the party newspapers throughout the Midwest, a great number of which urged their senators and representatives to unite with the President to overthrow the eastern cabal headed by the Rhode Island senator.[23]

The group of Midwestern senators, who were already becoming known as progressives and who claimed they were acting in the spirit of the Roosevelt tradition, needed little urging to oppose the Aldrich rates. Forming the nucleus of this group were Robert La Follette of Wisconsin, Jonathan Dolliver and Albert Cummins of Iowa, Albert J. Beveridge of Indiana, Moses Clapp of Minnesota, and Joseph L. Bristow of Kansas. Voting with them on the tariff schedules more often than not were Norris Brown and Elmer Burkett of Nebraska, Knute Nelson of Minnesota, Coe Crawford of South Dakota, and William E. Borah of Idaho. Dolliver and Beveridge were veterans of the Senate, but the rest had come to the upper house since 1906. There was a remarkable similarity about the group. Not one had been educated in an eastern university; most had graduated from their own state institutions. All of them, except for Beveridge, were extremely parochial in their outlook. They were and remained provincial most of their lives. All of them came from states normally Republican, but primarily devoted to agriculture or to the extractive industries. A good many of them, La Follette, Cummins, Bristow, and Crawford, to name the more prominent, had won their way to the Senate over the opposition of the official party organizations in their states, an opposition aroused either because of their impetuous demands for office or because of their anti-corporation, pro-democratic programs. These newcomers had a long history of rebellion. Individualistic and uncompromising, they readily joined Dolliver and Beveridge, who had already shown signs of independence from the party directorate in the Senate. By April, 1909, La Follette, Dolliver, Cummins, Bristow, Beveridge, and Clapp had agreed to common opposition. Systematically allotting individual parts of the Aldrich bill to particular members of the group, they mastered the complexities of the intricate schedules and, beginning on May 4, took the floor of the Senate to launch perhaps the most destructive criticism of high tariffs that had been made by the elected representatives of the

[23] Taft to Horace D. Taft, June 27, 1909, Taft MSS.; *Congressional Record*, XLIV, 61st Congress, 1st Session, pt. 2, pp. 1332 ff. For more extended discussions of the tariff struggle, see George E. Mowry, *Theodore Roosevelt and the Progressive Movement* (Madison, Wis., 1946), pp. 45–65; Claude G. Bowers, *Beveridge and the Progressive Era* (Boston, 1932), p. 330.

Republican party. Most of their remarks were directed to the tariff, but in their *obiter dicta* they drew a sharp line between themselves and the regular party organization. They referred to themselves as progressives, called their opponents reactionary tools of the trusts and eastern corporations, spoke in Roosevelt's name, and called upon Taft for aid in keeping the party true to its and the President's own promises.[24]

Again Taft was in a quandary. Should he go along with the small minority of his party in the Senate who agreed with him on the particular matter under debate? Or should he support Aldrich and the organization, who reflected the views of the great majority of Republican senators? For a short time he attempted to follow the early Roosevelt pattern of working both sides of the street and crossing it when necessary. During April and May, progressive senators were invited to the White House for conferences and felt for a time that the President was with them. On occasions Taft thought about appealing to the people and occasionally talked about vetoing the bill if it was not up to his campaign promises. He might also have used patronage and he might have resorted to some of the tricks which Roosevelt had used practically to blackmail members of Congress with a threatening wave of public opinion. But Taft had neither the skill nor the inclination to play such a complex game for long. He lacked the catlike political touch of Roosevelt and he was personally disinclined to thunder publicly against the malefactors of great wealth, accusing them of thwarting the people's will. He had, moreover, constitutional scruples about interfering too much in the legislative process. "I have no disposition," he told Aldrich, "to exert any other influence than that which it is my function under the Constitution to exercise. . . ." In the end he became convinced that Aldrich, whom he had first suspected of duplicity, was sincerely trying to get as much reduction as was possible from the majority members, each committed to high tariffs for most of their local products. For the welfare of the party as well as the success of his own reform program, he concluded that it was better to remain with the party organization than to "have personal popularity." [25]

Gradually Taft's opinions changed about a number of things, about Aldrich and the controlling group in the Senate, about the progressives, and about the nature of the tariff bill itself. By the first of June he was

[24] *Congressional Record*, XLIV, 61st Congress, 1st Session, pt. 1, pp. 1450 ff.
[25] Taft to Aldrich, July 29, 1909; to John Warrington, July 26, 1909, Taft MSS.

convinced that if he could get the best features of both the House and the Senate bills, the end product would represent a substantial revision downward. Since both Cannon and Aldrich had agreed to permit him to "exert great influence" on the actions of the Conference Committee which would have to resolve the differences between the two houses, he was reasonably confident that he could secure what he desired. The President's dislike of the Speaker grew after Cannon had packed the House membership of the conference committee with high-tariff men. Cannon, he exploded, had not played fair with him. But his confidence in Aldrich increased rapidly. They became very "good friends," Taft admitted, despite their differences on individual rates. The two men found they liked each other, and soon, when he was not praising Aldrich, Taft was finding excuses for him. On the whole, he wrote his brother, Aldrich had prepared "a very scientific tariff bill." The Aldrich bill had major defects, the President admitted, but he was sure that its author had had to consent to many raises in rates, especially "to a lot of fool increases in agricultural products," to get the bill passed. He was confident that Aldrich would help him remove such errors in the Conference Committee.[26]

After a long battle, the President succeeded in getting a number of reductions in the Conference Committee. Although the final product was closer to the high Senate rates than to those of the House, it did contain, thanks largely to Taft's intervention, substantial reductions on hides, iron ore, coal, and oil, as well as on cottons, and on boots and shoes. The compromise bill also provided for the establishment of a tariff commission and a federal tax on corporations engaged in interstate business.

According to the President, the Payne-Aldrich tariff bill, as it finally emerged from the Conference Committee of the two houses, was "really a good bill" and one which he thought could be defended "as a revision substantially downward." Neither the progressive Republicans then nor scholars writing since agreed with Taft. Although there is still much debate over the precise effect of the bill, it is reasonably clear that it made little change in the over-all degree of protection afforded domestic products. It was a high-tariff measure, and if it did anything it helped eastern industry at the expense of the producers of raw ma-

[26] Taft to Mrs. Taft, June 11, July 22, 27, 1909; to Horace Taft, June 27, 1909; to J. D. Brannan, June 29, 1909; and to Charles P. Taft, July 13, August 1, 1909, Taft MSS.

terials in the West and the South. Ex-Senator Foraker, one of the most ardent high protectionists, could see nothing objectionable in the Payne-Aldrich Act. The remark of a Maine congressman that Massachusetts had never gone away from Washington "with more in her craw" was substantially correct. It was "an eastern-made bill made to protect eastern products," the regular Republican James S. Clarkson remarked, and paradoxically the President, by insisting on free raw materials, had helped along that cause. This, among other reasons, explained why seven progressive Republican senators and twenty representatives from the Middle West voted against the measure.[27]

Taft had never associated with or had much respect for the type of Middle Western Republicans known by 1909 as progressives. Before the elections of 1908 he had viewed them as possible disrupters of the party. During the tariff debate, especially after his understanding with Aldrich, his dislike of them steadily increased. Their methods, he felt, were obnoxious, particularly their "yelping and snarling" at Cannon and Aldrich, which they insisted upon "as a mark of loyalty to the Roosevelt policies." As a group they were "pretty stupid" and inclined to be "rather forward." As individuals they were worse. La Follette, he felt, was habitually given "to false and misleading statements." Dolliver and Cummins were "demagogues" and Beveridge was "self-centered, self-absorbed." After they had voted against the tariff bill, Taft was disposed to view them as enemies. They were no longer Republicans, but rather "assistant Democrats."[28]

Had the division between the Middle Western Republicans and the President been simply over a personal issue or even over the tariff schedules, the results would not have been so critical for the party. But the gulf that separated them was far more significant. During the tariff debates the progressives had steadily attacked Cannon and Aldrich as being the personal legislative representatives of big business interests which, they claimed, really dominated the party and Congress. Thus the two congressional leaders became symbols throughout the Middle West, symbols of the monopolistic railroads, of the trusts, and

[27] Taft to E. F. Baldwin, July 29, 1909, and to Mrs. Taft, July 30, 1909, Taft MSS.; Everett Walters, *Joseph Benson Foraker, An Uncompromising Republican* (Columbus, Ohio, 1948), p. 290; Clarkson to Grenville M. Dodge, September 17, 1909, Dodge MSS.; Frank W. Taussig, *The Tariff History of the United States* (New York, 1909), pp. 361–408.

[28] Taft to Horace Taft, June 27, 1909; to W. D. Foulke, July 15, 1909; and to Mrs. Taft, July 14 and 30, 1909, Taft MSS.

of high finance. To the small businessmen, the farmers, and the artisans of the midlands they came to personify the evils that had afflicted American society during the past decades, the sky-high railroad rates, the burgeoning monopolies, the rotten food sold by the Chicago packers, and the corrupt finance. These evils were all due, they believed, to "the malefactors of great wealth," as Roosevelt had trumpeted across the country, and to their legislative representatives, Aldrich and Cannon, whom Dolliver and La Follette and their friends had attacked. The proof was in Aldrich's and Cannon's betrayal of the party pledge to revise industrial protection downward. Instead, "the mother of trusts," the tariff, had been kept largely at its previous levels on manufactured goods. The major revisions downward had been on the raw products of the Middle West. This adding injury to insult was enough; the section was in revolt. With almost one accord the great newspapers of the area, the Chicago *Tribune,* the Des Moines *Register and Leader,* the Kansas City *Star,* demanded that Aldrich and his "trust serving" senators be driven out of command of the party even if that meant civil war. To underscore the point a state-wide convention of "progressive Republicans" met in Des Moines, Iowa, to hear the state's two senators and to lay plans for the overthrow of the party organization. This was the first time that the adjective "progressive" was used to qualify an official Republican gathering in the Middle West, and this in the state that Dolliver had once proudly boasted would remain loyal to the Republican party until hell went Methodist.[29]

Roosevelt had been quite aware of the rising unrest in the corn and wheat country. If the party was to have trouble, he observed before the election of 1908, it would come from the West. Peculiarly enough, the Middle Western-born Taft discounted the section's feelings. He believed that the "so-called progressives," as he designated them, had no real standing with the voters and that the newspapers, angered because they had not received free print paper in the tariff bill, were simply practicing "yellow journalism." During September and October the President gave public voice to these views. He was scheduled to make a transcontinental speaking tour, the results of which he recognized would be critical for the success of his administration. Taft hated to make speeches and disliked even more preparing for them. Their delivery frightened him. He confessed that he did not know "exactly what

[29] Mowry, *Roosevelt and the Progressive Movement,* pp. 65 ff.

to say or how to say it." During August he played golf in the mornings instead of working, and he left his summer residence in Beverly, Massachusetts, for the tour without one prepared speech and with "a barrenness of ideas," he admitted, that gave him a pallor every time he thought of the trip ahead.[30]

The President started his crucial tour by closely identifying himself with Aldrich. In Boston he described the Rhode Islander as "the real leader of the Senate," whose chief concern was the welfare of the nation and the happiness of the people at large. Next, at Winona, Minnesota, he defended James Tawney, a standpatter and a high-tariff member of the House. At Winona he also addressed himself directly to the Payne-Aldrich Act. In a speech he had prepared the day before on the train, he defended the supporters of the bill, attacked its critics, and ended by describing the measure as "the best tariff act" that had ever been passed. During the rest of his autumn trip the President had lavish praise for many regular Republicans, including such conservatives as Senators Smoot of Utah and Carter of Montana. Although his itinerary took him through Wisconsin, Minnesota, Iowa, and Kansas, he failed to utter one public word about any Republican who had voted against the Payne-Aldrich Act. La Follette, Clapp, Dolliver, Cummins, and Bristow, the press noted, were not even invited to take the customary ride on the presidential train.[31]

Until the address at Winona very little public criticism had been leveled against Taft. The progressives had confined their bitter remarks to private occasions and the Middle Western Republican press had remained silent. After Winona, however, a sharp change occurred. The President, the Des Moines *Register and Leader* stated, had chosen his side. Apparently, he was for Aldrich and Cannon for the East and for the monopolistic corporations, and against the land of his birth, the Middle West. Roosevelt, the newspaper observed, could have the 1912 nomination for the asking.[32]

---

[30] Taft to W. H. Miller, July 13, 1909; to W. D. Foulke, July 15, 1909; to Nancy Roelker, September 11, 1909; and to F. H. Gillett, September 13, 1909, Taft MSS.

[31] Taft to Mrs. Taft, September 17, 1909, Taft MSS.

[32] Des Moines *Register and Leader,* September 23, 24, 1909.

CHAPTER 13

The Progressive Rebellion

HAD the Ballinger-Pinchot conservation controversy of 1909–10 simply involved Taft's Secretary of the Interior and Roosevelt's personal friend at the head of the Forestry Bureau in the Department of Agriculture, the squabble, like so many such in politics, might soon have been forgotten. But the argument between the two men quickly developed into a clash that made national headlines for months, a clash between progressives and conservatives, between the anti-Roosevelt people and the ex-President's friends, between conservationists and anticonservationists. In the first instance much of this was due to Gifford Pinchot.

By law the Interior Department was responsible for the administration of all public lands; of effecting transfers from the public domain to private ownership; of reserving, under congressional authority, national forests and parks; and of prescribing rules and regulations for the preservation and exploitation of the national reserves. Its relations with the Bureau of Forestry, located in the Agriculture Department and charged with the preservation and administration of the national forests, have thus been traditionally intimate and often vexatious. Under Roosevelt, relations between the two agencies were superb largely because both Pinchot and Secretary of the Interior James R. Garfield were friends as well as intimates of the President, with whom they played tennis almost weekly.

Admittedly Gifford Pinchot was something of a zealot, a "Sir Galahad of the woodlands," as Harold Ickes referred to him years afterward. Admittedly also he was predisposed to dislike Richard Achilles

Ballinger, who as Taft's appointee had taken the place of his friend, Garfield, as Secretary of Interior. Garfield had wanted to stay on in Taft's Cabinet and Pinchot, who had ambitions of his own to become Secretary of Agriculture, had very much wanted him to stay. Both Garfield and Pinchot were intensely disappointed when Ballinger was selected. And the closing of the White House doors after March 4, 1909, after he had been so welcome there before, must have offended Pinchot's sensitive and ambitious nature, and inclined him to see threats against the Roosevelt-Garfield-Pinchot conservation policies out of all real proportions. Pinchot was, no doubt, an intensely prejudiced man. But not all the threats against his sacred forests were products of his imagination. A good many, perhaps most, wealthy Westerners had been fervently opposed to Roosevelt's conservation policies. A number of western senators and their powerful constituents were still smarting from Roosevelt's withdrawal of millions of acres of potentially rich mining, lumber, and grazing lands before he had to capitulate to the legislative mandate barring the creation of all future reservations without the express consent of Congress. Many of them were still indignant over the method by which Pinchot and Garfield had withdrawn hundreds of water-power sites by designating them as needed ranger stations. Roosevelt's great popularity and party loyalty had silenced a direct attack upon him. But Pinchot, a wealthy, educated Easterner, was an ideal substitute, and "Pinchotism" became an emotional epithet in the West even while Roosevelt was President. Now that he had gone and a western man was Secretary of the Interior, the time had come to overthrow the "accursed Pinchotism" and "throw open the public domain," thereby ensuring the survival of traditional western individualism against the threat of eastern socialism. The summer of 1909 saw the birth of two organizations, the National Domain League in Colorado and the Western Conservation League in Spokane, Washington. The stated purpose of the Colorado organization was to restore the rights of farmers, stockmen, and miners in the national domain, which the League claimed had been usurped by the Forest Service. The Spokane organization was opposed to "bureaucracy, government ownership and centralization." It proposed to destroy "Federal tenantry" by supporting a state conservation movement which would "free" the natural resources from the clutches of the eastern Socialists. Among its chief supporters were Washington's governor, Marion E. Hay; the state's two senators, Samuel H. Piles and Wesley L. Jones; and Erastus Brainerd, editor of the Seattle *Post-Intelligencer*. All of these men were conservative Republicans, all were more or less opposed to the federal conservation policy, and all were political friends of Ballinger. Brainerd, the most vocal of the anticonservationists, had in fact been Ballinger's most consistent supporter since he had entered politics. As long as Ballinger was Secretary of the Interior, one of Brainerd's employee's held a position in the Interior Department and reported back the news to his boss in Seattle. Ballinger had been a most successful mayor of Seattle before coming to the nation's capital in 1907 as Commissioner of the Land Office. He resigned that office in 1908 after serving well and had gone back to practicing law in Seattle, from where he was recalled as Secretary of the Interior by Taft.[1]

Ballinger had not been long in his new office until he called to the President's attention Garfield's and Pinchot's wholesale withdrawal of water-power sites as ranger stations, arguing that their actions were illegal and that the land should be returned to the public domain. At about the same time Ballinger also charged that the Bureau of Reclamation under Roosevelt had grossly exceeded its legal authority by committing itself to plans for current and future works, the costs of which far exceeded existing funds. In both instances, Taft agreed with the conclusions of his Secretary, ordering him to return the water-power sites to the public domain until each site could be specifically investigated by geologists, and to "put the breaks down" on the Reclamation Service until Congress met. Taft observed that Garfield had "gone far beyond legal limitations" and Pinchot and his fellow "transcendentalists" in the Reclamation Service had permitted their enthusiasm to lead them into lawlessness. At the President's direction, Ballinger returned more than a million acres of land to the public domain and ordered a stop to further expenditures by the Reclamation Service.[2]

Gifford Pinchot was not slow in criticizing Ballinger's activities, and

[1] Elmo Richardson, "Early Conservation Policy in the Western States," unpublished doctor's thesis, University of California, Los Angeles. The preceding paragraphs are based upon this illuminating thesis.

[2] Taft to William Kent, June 29, 1909; to Ballinger, August 10, 1909; and to T. E. Burton, June 9, 1910, Taft MSS. For more extended accounts of the affair, see Henry F. Pringle, *The Life and Times of William Howard Taft* (2 vols., New York, 1939), II, 470 ff., which is sympathetic to Taft and Ballinger; George E. Mowry, *Theodore Roosevelt and the Progressive Movement* (Madison, Wis., 1946), pp. 73 ff.; and Alpheus T. Mason, *Bureaucracy Convicts Itself* (Princeton, 1941), which lean in the other direction.

in early August, at a Spokane Conservation League meeting, he virtually charged the Secretary of the Interior with being an enemy of Roosevelt's conservation policies. As a result of a conference Pinchot had with an investigator of the General Land Office, Louis Russell Glavis, the complicated issue of the Cunningham claims became an important part of the developing controversy. The Cunningham claims, held by a group of Seattle men, some of whom were Ballinger's friends, were on the national domain and comprised about 15 per cent of the Bering River coal fields in Alaska. Back in 1907 Ballinger, as Commissioner of the General Land Office, had ordered them validated. But an investigation by federal agents, among whom was Glavis, charged that the claimants had broken the law by collusive actions and intended further violations by proposing to sell a part of the coal lands, once they were clear-listed to a Morgan-Guggenheim Syndicate organized the year before. Nevertheless Ballinger clear-listed the claims, only to reverse his actions on direction of Secretary of Interior Garfield, who order a further investigation. In August of 1909 Garfield wrote the President that he was just as satisfied now, as he was in 1907, that the claims were illegal.[3]

In 1908 Ballinger left office and Glavis was put in full charge of the Cunningham investigation. During the next twelve months Glavis obtained further evidence that collusion did exist, a fact later substantiated by the printing of a contract between the Cunningham group and the Morgan-Guggenheim Syndicate, dated July 20, 1907, by which David Guggenheim agreed to purchase a half-interest in the coal claims. Meanwhile Ballinger accepted a fee to represent the Cunningham group before his old office in Washington. A short time after Ballinger became Secretary of the Interior, Glavis was removed from his investigations on the grounds that he was working too slowly. Although Glavis' successor also claimed that more time was needed to conclude the investigation, the Interior Department ordered an immediate hearing on the case. It was then that Glavis appealed to Pinchot. Already predisposed against Ballinger, the Forester accepted Glavis' story, sent it to Taft, and obtained an interview for the investigator with the President.[4]

[3] Garfield to Taft, August 28, 1909, Taft MSS.
[4] Investigation of the Department of the Interior and of the Bureau of Forestry, Senate Document 719, 61st Congress, 1st Session, Vol. 2, pp. 60–63; Vol. 5, pp. 2132–2133.

As Taft looked into the charges he grew increasingly "indignant" at Glavis and Pinchot. On September 13, just before he left on his western speaking tour, he prepared a thirteen-page letter ruling with Ballinger on every charge made, calling him a friend of conservation, and stating that he was "in full sympathy with the attitude of this administration." Glavis was to be discharged, but Taft had not included a discussion of Pinchot's part, so that the Forester would not have to enter the controversy unless he chose to do so. Along with his decision Taft sent a long, gracious letter to Pinchot asking him not to make Glavis' cause his. If Pinchot were to leave, the President stated, it would be "one of the greatest losses" his administration would sustain.[5]

Taft had never really liked Pinchot. Before the Ballinger trouble he had thought of him as "a radical and a crank." The best that could be said for him was that he might act "as a kind of conscience in certain directions to be followed when possible." After the Ballinger row Taft's suspicions of Pinchot increased, and finally in September, 1909, he came to the conclusion that the Forester was "heading a conspiracy among the muckrakers" to impeach Ballinger's "honesty and purity of motive." When Pinchot kept up his assault both publicly and privately, the President became convinced that he was planning some kind of a coup, forcing Taft to dismiss him and making him a martyr.[6]

Taft's suspicions were quite correct. In November two articles attacking Ballinger and the administration appeared in *Collier's Weekly*. Much of the material for the articles came from Pinchot's office. The Forester also kept bombarding all of his progressive friends with anti-Ballinger material. He now stated unequivocally that Ballinger was "the most effective opponent the conservation policies have yet had." But in spite of everything he could do, Pinchot feared that unless Congress took action the whole controversy would "pass quietly away. . . ." To ensure that it did not, Pinchot wrote a letter which Dolliver read on the floor of the Senate. The letter admitted that the Forest Service had been supplying confidential anti-Ballinger information to the press. It praised Glavis and indicted the Secretary of the Interior as a foe of conservation. The letter, of course, ensured Pinchot's dismissal. It was meant to. It also focused public attention on the congressional investi-

<hr>

[5] Taft to Horace Taft, September 11, 1909; to Ballinger, September 13, 1909; and to Pinchot, August 22, September 23, 1909, Taft MSS.

[6] Taft to Roosevelt, December 24, 1908; to Horace Taft, June 6, 1909; and to Mrs. Taft, October 3, 1909, Taft MSS.

·gation of the Interior Department. What might have been a routine
activity now became the subject of heated discussion all over the nation.[7]

Taft had not wanted to dismiss Pinchot. He fully realized the implications of the action. In the eye of the public Pinchot was the personal
symbol of Roosevelt's conservation policy. He was also one of Roosevelt's closest political friends and thus intimately associated with the
progressive Republicans in the Senate and the insurgents in the House
who were already showing a distressing sense of independence from
party regularity. The President recognized that by a process of simple
transference the public would interpret his defense of Ballinger before
the Joint Congressional Committee as evidence of his opposition to
conservation and the Roosevelt policies. This was precisely what happened.

In the long deliberations of 1910 Ballinger was exonerated from all
charges of fraud and corruption. The majority of the Joint Committee,
carefully selected to reflect the administration's viewpoint, also found
him an efficient Secretary of the Interior and a promoter of sound conservation policies. Unfortunately for Taft, the majority of the country
and certainly most of the progressive Republicans decided the other
way. Part of the reason for this negative decision lay in the rather inept
way with which the administration had presented its case. Louis D.
Brandeis, the attorney for the opposition, was, on the other hand,
adroit. Brandeis proved that the Lawlor Memorandum on which the
President had presumably based his decision favorable to Ballinger—a
document presented as evidence to support the President's action—was
really prepared after the decision had been made. The predating of reports is not too unusual in government, but the public chose to interpret the predating of the Lawlor Memorandum as evidence of
administrative chicanery. Years after the hearing, Brandeis felt that the
misdating of the document was the factor that won for the opposition
in the court of public opinion.[8]

There were other factors. The connection between the Morgan-Guggenheim Syndicate and the Cunningham claimants was indisputably
proved, although there was no evidence that Ballinger knew of the

[7] Pinchot to Charles R. Crane, November 29, 1909; to James R. Garfield,
December 5, 1900; to Roosevelt, December 31, 1909; to Dolliver, January 5,
1910, Pinchot MSS.

[8] Minutes of conversation between Brandeis and Pinchot, December 30, 1939,
Pinchot MSS.

concert. Ballinger's acceptance of a fee to represent the Cunningham group before the governmental office he had just left hurt the administration's case, which was largely based upon the claim that it was just as zealous for conservation as were Garfield and Pinchot, but that it insisted its action be based upon legal authority, authority which the Roosevelt lieutenants had repeatedly flouted. There happened to be an administrative rule in the Department of the Interior forbidding former employees to represent claimants before the department. But perhaps the public judgment came mostly from its great confidence in Roosevelt and his young reformers and its suspicion of anyone or any cause connected with great corporate enterprises or with such names as Morgan and Guggenheim. As Henry Stimson wrote, there were a great many honest friends of Taft who had complete confidence in Garfield and Pinchot but who "were in doubt as to Ballinger." [9]

Was the administration really a foe or a friend of conservation? Of Taft there can be no doubt. After Ballinger resigned he replaced him with Walter Fisher, a friend of Pinchot, whose conservation views were beyond suspicion. The President also won back from Congress the power that had been taken away from Roosevelt to remove public-domain lands from entry by a simple executive declaration. His energetic use of the power eventually resulted in the removal of more lands from entry than Roosevelt had removed in a comparable period of time. The judgment on Ballinger is more difficult. Senator Francis J. Newlands, a Nevada Democrat and an ardent conservationist, consistently held that Ballinger was a conservation advocate and that he had been unjustly maligned. On the other hand, in 1908 Ballinger argued with the Republican platform committee for the reaffirmation "of the Republican policy for the free distribution of the available areas of the public domain to the landless settlers." And after he had resigned as Secretary of the Interior, he proposed repeatedly that all federal-held lands exclusive of the national parks be turned over to the states. Twice Taft had to ask him not to associate himself with the known foes of the federal conservation policy.[10] Before his appointment, Taft had written that Ballinger was acceptable "to the people" in the West, and a man whose views were "reasonable" about government rights there. But what was reasonable to the "people" in the West was often down-

[9] Stimson to Root, November, (?), 1909, Root MSS.

[10] Arthur H. Darling (ed.), *The Public Papers of Francis J. Newlands* (2 vols., Boston, 1932), I, 112; Ballinger to Wade Ellis, June 11, 1908, Taft to Ballinger, July 31, 1911, Taft MSS.

right heresy to eastern conservationists. Ballinger came from a group of men who traditionally had viewed the public lands as a source of private income. In exploiting public wealth for private gain such "people" in the West had been rather free and easy with their interpretation of government restrictions. Ballinger's casual concern with the legal compliance by the Cunningham group, compared to his strict demand for legality in the Garfield power-site transfers, illustrated his bent of mind. Elihu Root, a lawyer of some ability without a reputation for crusading, was a member of the congressional committee. He voted for the majority report, but he had serious private reservations about some of its conclusions. Specifically, he did not agree with Ballinger and Taft that the withdrawal of water-power sites by Garfield was either illegal or unjustified by the public interest. "It would have been better," he wrote to the committee chairman, "for Mr. Ballinger to have left the old withdrawals standing. . . ."[11]

In the end the Ballinger-Pinchot affair had more impact upon politics than it did on conservation. At its opening, Root realized that the controversy was bound to place the more zealous supporters of Roosevelt in a grim conflict with the administration. It was pregnant, he predicted, "with immense evil for the Administration and the Republican Party." So it was. With the introduction of the Morgan and Guggenheim names into the piece, the muckrake periodical press took off in full cry after "the despoilers of the national heritage." *Colliers' Weekly* in particular featured the developing affair with articles and editorials all heavily weighted against Ballinger and the administration. The Middle Western progressive Republicans rallied around Pinchot. So did many of the Forester's personal friends in the East and the Far West. James R. Garfield, Henry Stimson, Albert Shaw, editor of the *World's Work*, the Abbott brothers of *The Outlook*, and William Kent and Chester Rowell from California all were militantly opposed to Ballinger. The group had something else in common beyond their support of Pinchot. They were all ardent Roosevelt men. They would have been less than human had they not contrasted the existing administration most unfavorably with the preceding one. More significantly, some of them began to talk about the possibility of substituting Roosevelt for Taft in 1912.[12]

[11] Taft to Knox, December 22, 1908, Taft MSS.; Root to Knute Nelson, August 27, 1910, Root MSS.
[12] Root to Henry Stimson, November 18, 1909, Root MSS.; Garfield to Pinchot, December 5, 1909, Pinchot MSS.; Stimson to Root, February 20, 1910,

The President himself, as much as he was to try to avoid it, was unable to escape the driving wedge of events that was slowly but surely opening a chasm between himself and Roosevelt. When the Ballinger-Pinchot affair started, he felt it was no more serious than a quarrel between governmental departments. But in three weeks' time he concluded that a "conspiracy" existed, a conspiracy among the zealous Roosevelt people to bring about "an open rupture" between himself and his former chief. He was determined to avoid that. Apparently he never considered that in criticizing the illegality of Garfield's and Pinchot's setting aside water-power sites, he was at the same time criticizing Roosevelt, their chief. But as the quarrel went on and Roosevelt's name was frequently used as a sort of a talisman by Pinchot's supporters, Taft's attitudes toward Roosevelt shifted perceptibly. The shift was probably unconscious, but it was also understandable. Before the fall of 1909, in all of Taft's correspondence there is probably not one sharp word about Theodore Roosevelt. But after the Ballinger-Pinchot controversy the President began to see certain flaws in his predecessor. His "whole administration" had been "demoralized by his dealing directly with subordinates." Both he and Pinchot had a "socialistic tendency." And although Taft never once believed that Roosevelt was directly connected with his troubles, he did conclude that indirectly Roosevelt had contributed to them. Some of the people attacking him were those who had been "carried off their feet by Roosevelt's sermons and preachments. . . ." They were essentially lawless and emotional, he observed, having very little respect "for making progress through statutes and by lawful steps." With those remarks the first crack in a seemingly enduring friendship had appeared, an almost inevitable result when Taft's conservative and legalistic attitudes came in conflict with Roosevelt's adventurous and political spirit.[13]

During the Ballinger-Pinchot controversy, the national magazines which had contributed so much to the progressive movement were almost a unit against the administration. In part their position is explained by their devotion to the cause of conservation, in part to their intense opposition to the President's attempt to raise second-class post-

---

Root MSS.; Albert Shaw to Beveridge, November 13, 1909, Beveridge MSS.; Dolliver to Beveridge, September 14, 1909, Dolliver MSS.

[13] Taft to Nicholas Longworth, August 30, 1909; to Mrs. Taft, October 3, 15, 1909, Taft MSS.

age rates. During these years, as usual, the Post Office Department was incurring its annual deficit. And, as usual, a part of the loss was explained by the low second-class rates afforded to newspapers and magazines. After Roosevelt's muckrake speech in 1906, the Senate appointed a committee to investigate the subject of second-class rates. The Penrose report issuing from the investigation concluded that the government was really subsidizing magazines and newspapers by the low postage rate and proposed a revision whereby magazines but not newspapers would be made to pay more. During the Roosevelt years the matter was pushed neither by the President nor by the members of his Cabinet. Soothing their unnecessary fears, Secretary of the Treasury Cortelyou assured a publishers' committee that no postal rate changes were contemplated.[14]

With an almost unerring penchant for creating powerful enemies, Taft in his first annual message to Congress alluded to the "enormous subsidy" given to newspapers and periodicals and indicated that he favored a sharp raise in rates. The measure proposed by his Postmaster General, Hitchcock, and introduced into Congress would have effectively raised the old magazine rate in existence since 1889 from one to four cents a pound, while leaving the newspaper charge substantially alone. The periodical publishers angrily charged that the administration desired "not revenue but revenge," revenge for their opposition to the Payne-Aldrich Tariff and to Ballinger. The newspapers, not affected by the measure, joined the chorus of opposition, and by means of a Democratic-Progressive-Republican coalition the postal bill was defeated. Showing a characteristic vein of stubbornness, the President declared that he would continue to recommend the rate increase until he was removed from office. He did and eventually won. His losses were much more significant. He had incurred the hostility of most of the popular periodical press. At the beginning of the 1912 campaign the two chief speakers invited to address the periodical publishers' dinner at Philadelphia were Robert La Follette and Woodrow Wilson.[15]

Until well into 1910 Taft's record appeared to be almost wholly characterized by one serious political contretemps after another. During the following three years, however, it was punctuated by a series

---

[14] Albert Shaw to Beveridge, January 26, February 6, 9, 1907, Shaw MSS.
[15] Taft to Boies Penrose, February 15, 1911, Taft MSS.; *The Outlook*, XCIII (1909), 8946; *Literary Digest*, "Doubling the Postal Tax on Print," XLIV (1912), 7; *The New York Times*, March 2, 1911.

260 THE ERA OF THEODORE ROOSEVELT

of solid reform achievements, which in their sum went far toward fulfilling Taft's promises during the campaign of 1908. Taft had never had much sympathy with the railroads. They were run, he wrote before coming to office, in a highly monopolistic fashion by a group of eight or nine men who were "exceedingly lawless in spirit." As a candidate Taft supported all of Roosevelt's proposed amendments to the Hepburn Act save for the physical evaluation scheme, and added a few new features of his own. The President was particularly insistent that a special Commerce Court be created whose main function would be to hear appeals from the rate decisions of the Interstate Commerce Commission. He also desired that the power to supervise and regulate the issuance of railroad securities be lodged with the Commission. The bill, which was to become the Mann-Elkins Act of 1910, met immediate objections from the progressives when it was introduced into the House in January, 1910. Prepared under the direction of Attorney General Wickersham, the bill endowed the Interstate Commerce Commission with real additional powers of setting rates on its own initiative and of supervising the issuance of securities. But the progressives objected to the very broad powers of review given to the new Commerce Court; to the setting aside of the Sherman Law, permitting certain types of railroad mergers; and to the lack of a provision for physical evaluation. In the House they amended the bill substantially, striking out the merger provision and adding amendments providing for physical evaluation and defining telephone and telegraph companies as common carriers. The President's favored Commerce Court was barely saved by a tie vote. In the Senate the bill received rougher handling; over two hundred progressive-sponsored amendments were offered. So entangled did the bill become in the three-way battle between the regular and the progressive Republicans and the minority Democrats that it finally had to be withdrawn and entirely rewritten. During the interval Senator Aldrich, who was in charge of the bill, made a bargain with the Democratic minority. In return for regular Republican support of a statehood bill adding the presumed Democratic states of Arizona and New Mexico to the Union, enough Democrats promised their votes to pass the measure against progressive opposition. The Commerce Court was retained and physical evaluation was defeated along with Taft's proposal to regulate securities. But the bill was a real advance in railroad regulation. Under its provisions the Commission was given the power to initiate rate changes and to regulate railroad and telegraph companies. Furthermore, the burden of proof to show that a specific rate was inequitable was now placed upon the defending carrier. The measure improved the Hepburn Act to such a degree that the progressive Republicans voted for it to a man.[16]

The President deserved some of the credit for the receiving of the more effective railroad regulation, but not all. The progressives had defeated a good many retrograde features of the original Mann-Elkins bill. They had also contributed to the bill's more positive virtues, as in the case of the addition of telephone and telegraph companies to the Interstate Commerce Commission's purview. They had fought valiantly for the President's proposed regulation of securities, only to be defeated by Aldrich's bargain with the Democrats. The peculiar part of the affair was Taft's conclusion that the opposition of the progressives to the original Mann-Elkins bill was proof enough that they were thoroughly antiadministration and wanted to see it defeated. Upon the basis of that judgment the President sought to read them out of the party by defeating them in the primaries of 1910.

On railroad legislation the President and the progressive Republicans had started largely with the same preconceptions but had ended seriously quarreling with one another. They were to repeat the queer performance over the issue of a postal-savings-bank system. Roosevelt had recommended the establishment of such a system in 1907 and again in 1908. Both Taft and the progressive Republicans were heartily for the reform measure, whereas more conservative Republicans were against it. But pressure by Taft and Roosevelt, plus the need to meet the Democratic proposal for government-guaranteed bank accounts, had persuaded the Republican platform makers to include postal savings in the party's list of promises. Even so, Aldrich was so opposed to the bill that it was bottled up in the Senate Finance Committee under his chairmanship for over six months. But in January, 1910, Aldrich changed his mind about the measure. The reason for his shift lay in the fact that in 1910 the national banks held over $730 million worth of 2 per cent government bonds upon which they had issued national bank notes, the issue constituting a major part of the circulating paper me-

[16] Taft to Horace Taft, October 27, 1905; to Robert La Follette, July 19, 1908; to Wharton Baker, June 11, 1910; and to Nicholas Longworth, July 15, 1910, Taft MSS. For more extended discussions, see Mowry, *Roosevelt and the Progressive Movement,* pp. 93 ff.; Pringle, *Taft,* I, 523 ff.; and especially James R. Mann, "Personal Legislative History of the Interstate Commerce Act," an unpublished volume in the Library of Congress which includes original letters.

dium. By 1910 the Aldrich Monetary Commission had determined to recommend a central unitary bank to issue a new currency. But before the private banks could be induced to support the new plan, some way had to be devised for the banks to unload their relatively low-interest-bearing government bonds, then selling at a discount. When the postal-savings bill was reported in the Senate, it called for a payment of 2 per cent interest on deposits as compared to the 3 to 5 per cent rates offered by banks and new government issues. The progressives immediately attached two amendments to the bill, the first calling for a minimum interest rate of $2\frac{1}{4}$ per cent, the second stipulating that the funds collected in any district should be deposited in the local banks of that district. Highly irritated by the maneuvers, the President charged Senator Cummins, who had presented the amendments, with "loading down the bill with impossible conditions" almost as "socialistic" as the Democratic scheme for guaranteeing bank deposits. After an acrimonious exchange between Taft and the progressives the bill was passed with the 2 per cent rate and without the geographical limitation on the reinvestment of funds. The progressives voted against the act, and once again the President and the radicals found themselves in antipodal final positions after having started from approximately the same reform assumptions.[17]

The years from 1910 to 1913 produced a surprising number of minor social reforms for which Taft, as his biographer states, has never been given proper credit. Measures regulating safety in mines and on railroads, the abolition of phosphorus matches, an act creating a Children's Bureau in the federal government, an Employers' Liability Act covering all work done on government contracts, and one limiting government labor to eight hours were inscribed in the federal statutes. Most of these acts were supported by the President, and yet most of them were passed by a Democratic-controlled House and a Democratic-progressive Republican coalition in the Senate, both ends of which were, to understate it, at extreme odds with Taft. Meanwhile, the President's supporters, the regular Republicans, were usually found opposed to the majority of these reforms. The eight-hour bill offered an interesting example of this involved misalliance. Two similar measures

[17] *Circular of the National City Bank,* July, 1910; Taft to Knute Nelson, January 1, 1910, to Horace Taft, March 5, 1910, and to Nicholas Longworth, July 15, 1910, Taft MSS.; Cummins to James D. Land, March 9, 1910, Cummins MSS.

had been approved by Congress in 1868 and 1892. But in each instance the acts had been so weakened by court interpretation that they needed repassing. Between 1896 and 1908 four limitation-of-hours bills were passed by the House but defeated by the regular Republican organization in the Senate. It was not until the Democrats controlled the House and the regular domination of the Senate was ended that the measure was finally passed and signed by the President.[18]

As the President often failed to reap where he had sown, he occasionally was given debits he did not fully deserve. Although he was a conservative, Taft was partially responsible for the passage of perhaps the most profound reform passed in the course of recent American history, the income tax. It is almost impossible to see how most of the social legislation passed since 1912 could have been financed without the income tax. Lack of the tax must also have meant the almost complete frustration of any government seeking to redistribute income in an orderly fashion. The modern democratic social service state, in fact, probably rests more upon the income tax than upon any other single legislative act. This graduated tax was started on its way to enactment during the Taft administration with a partial presidential blessing. As a part of the Payne-Aldrich bill a graduated inheritance tax, which the President had asked for in his inaugural address, had been passed in the House. When it was defeated in the Senate, Senators William E. Borah of Idaho and Joseph W. Bailey of Texas offered a graduated income tax starting with incomes over $5,000. Most conservatives, of course, viewed the income and the inheritance taxes as the last steps before socialism. But in face of a Democratic-progressive coalition they could not find the votes to defeat the measure outright. Back in 1895 the Supreme Court had held an existing income tax unconstitutional. Opposed to the use of a graduated tax except in times of war and unwilling to embarrass the Court, Taft proposed a compromise entailing a corporation tax and the initiating of a constitutional amendment legalizing the income tax. Because he was instrumental in stopping the vote on the income tax, and because he refused to support the inheritance tax, Taft was accused of being against both and thus in favor of the accumulation of major large fortunes. This was partially true. But it was also true that later, when three-fourths of the states

[18] Taft to Borah, March 4, 1910, Taft MSS.; Pringle, *Taft*, II, 621; Selig Perlman, *The History of Trade Unionism in the United States* (New York, 1922), p. 199.

were needed to ratify the amendment, the President wrote earnest letters to his friends in the Ohio legislature asking them to support the income tax resolution so that a federal bill could be passed in the future in case it were needed. The controversy illustrates again Taft's inability to ride with the buoyant reform tide. Under pressure the President would move, but not too far, and certainly not far enough to escape censure from the rising left.[19]

The President had very little to do with, and took no public position on, the passage of another basic reform, the direct election of United States senators. Since the turn of the century the reputation of the upper house had steadily decreased in stature. The body had consistently opposed most progressive reforms. What advances had been made were largely wrung out of the Senate by presidential or public pressure. At one time in the decade three senators were under indictment of the federal courts for accepting bribes, and a dozen or so more were smeared with charges of corruption. The process of selection by the state legislatures was notoriously a matter of purchase. In 1907 Simon Guggenheim candidly revealed how he had been elected in Colorado: he had contributed so much to the campaign fund of the Republican members of the legislatures that none of them was out of pocket for his expenses. By 1911, twenty-nine states had moved to select their senators by popular vote. Even so, the reform press stated, the body was still an "obstructive, spoils-seeking, courtesy-bound, corporation-fed" group. The time had come either to abolish or reform it. After a long legislative struggle lasting over two years, a progressive-Democratic coalition passed the enabling resolution for the necessary constitutional amendment.[20]

By permission of the Enabling Act of 1910 the territories of Arizona and New Mexico had framed constitutions and presented them for congressional approval in 1911. The basic law of New Mexico was unexceptional, but the Arizona document included provisions for the initiative, the referendum, and the recall, including the recall of judges. Popular opposition to the courts was steadily rising in the nation for many of the same reasons that led to criticism of the Senate. As in the

[19] Taft to F. J. Newlands, May 14, 1909, to J. D. Brannan, June 25, 1909, and to Arthur I. Vorys, June 3, 1910, Taft MSS.; Lodge to Roosevelt, July 31, 1909, Roosevelt MSS.; Robert M. La Follette, *Autobiography* (Madison, Wis., 1911), p. 440.

[20] *Literary Digest*, XXXIV (1907), 121; Kansas City *Star*, January 21, 1911.

case of most fast-running reform movements in American history, the state and federal courts had interposed so many legal objections to the new legislative formulations that the judiciary as a whole had grown extremely unpopular. The use of the injunction and contempt procedures had won it the hostility of organized labor. Reformers were antagonized at the courts' repeated frustration of their efforts through the power of judicial review. The judiciary, Roscoe Pound wrote, "do nothing and obstruct everything." William Allen White observed that the institution was "one of the most ruthless checks on democracy permitted by any civilized people." At Osawatomie, Roosevelt himself had implied that the courts were the chief existing obstruction to the development of social justice. It was time, William Kent argued, "to dispense with the fallacy that by the accident of appointment or election to office they [judges] became an order of superior beings, infallible and answerable to nobody." When such respected people spoke the public responded. A spate of measures to reform the judiciary was advanced, among them the recall of judges.[21] Led by Lodge and Root, the Senate conservatives bitterly denounced this proposal to make judges more responsive to the popular will, only to be beaten once again by progressive-Democratic votes. It was then that Taft interposed his veto. He had never been a friend of direct government, he said, and he was particularly hostile to any move that might curtail the independence of the judiciary. A popular government, his veto message read, was not a government of, by, and for a majority of the people but a "government of the whole people, by a majority of the whole people, under such rules and checks as will secure a wise, just and beneficent government for all the people." The veto had little effect, for Arizona accepted the amendment temporarily and then, after having become a state, readopted the recall. But Taft's action earned him the reputation for being a foe of popular government at a time when the word democracy had the power to inspire almost religious veneration. By 1914, twelve states had adopted some of the principles of direct democracy; of these six had incorporated in their constitutions the device for the recall of judges.[22]

[21] Pound, cited in Walter Lippmann, *Drift and Mastery* (New York, 1914), p. 157; William Allen White, *The Old Order Changeth* (New York, 1910), p. 57; William Kent to Rudolph Leonart, August 17, 1911, Kent MSS.

[22] Taft to Chandler Harper, January 23, 1908, Taft MSS.; *The New York Times,* August 15, 1911; John A. Garraty, *Henry Cabot Lodge* (New York,

Among the dominant characteristics of the ordinary legal mind is the impulse to operate from relatively fixed principles, the desire to be consistent with the precepts of the past, and perhaps the disposition to see men and issues in the polar aspects of wrong or right. All of these qualities lead to a rather strong inflexibility which is admirable at times but which scarcely aids a politician in days of rapidly running reform. Taft had a sound but fairly ordinary legal mind. His disposition was to adopt a hard-and-fast position. Unlike Roosevelt, he had little of that facility for running with the reform hares and hunting with the conservative hounds. Once Taft had adopted a position, moreover, the opposition appeared to be in the situation of the defeated before the bar of justice. If the litigants were sensible men they should accept their defeat and change their ways without further protest. Given the President's mentality and that of the progressive Republicans, a clash and even a permanent schism were all but inevitable.

The President's low opinion of progressives at the end of the Payne-Aldrich Tariff fight was intensified during the rest of the year and the beginning of 1910. By the end of the discussion over railroad regulation, Taft had come to the fixed conclusion that the progressives were out to ruin the party and him. Day by day he found them personally more obnoxious. La Follette was a fanatic, Dolliver and Cummins blatant demagogues, Clapp an unstable lightweight, and Beveridge an egotist and a liar whose name might more appropriately be spelled "Beverage." The President pointedly refused to meet the progressives socially, and remarked that for "perfectly unscrupulous Jesuitical methods" there was nothing to touch the man who was given to uplifting by muckraking and denunciation. He would play golf with either a Republican or a Democrat, but he drew the line at professional demagogues.[23]

The conservatives, of course, were gleeful at the President's new attitude. For some time they had been waiting for an opportunity to rid the party of the progressive "evil." As far back as 1909, before the successful insurgent assault on Cannon, the Speaker told the press that plans were under way to defeat the progressives in the 1910 primaries

---

1953), pp. 287 ff.; Philip C. Jessup, *Elihu Root* (2 vols., New York, 1938), II, 243.

[23] Taft to Lucius B. Swift, February 12, 1910; to Lafayette Young, February 28, 1910; to Frank H. Shaffer, March 26, 1910; to C. P. Taft, April 19, 1910; and to Horace Taft, February 1 and March 26, 1910, Taft MSS.

and that the administration would support the regulars in "their snake hunt." Taft himself wrote injudicious letters promising that once he got his legislative program through he "would separate the sheep from the goats" in his dispensation of patronage. Just before the fight with the Speaker, patronage was denied to the progressives and the insurgents, the President explaining that he was preserving the *status quo* to impress the mavericks "with their obligations." And then, at the height of the debate over the Mann-Elkins bill, the Attorney General plainly stated in a Chicago speech that if the progressives did not support the President and the Republican organization they would "read themselves out of the party." Even before Wickersham's speech Taft had agreed with a proposal by Aldrich that a regular party fund be raised to help "orthodox Republicans" and to defeat progressives in the primaries. Taft himself called together a meeting of the Iowa regulars to map out such a campaign. He took much the same action in Kansas and Nebraska. In Washington, where the insurgent member of the House, Miles Poindexter, was running for the Senate, the President used his personal influence to persuade all but one of a group of regulars to retire from the race so that conservative strength could be "consolidated" against Poindexter. The pattern was repeated in California. There the progressive movement was finally challenging the Southern Pacific Railroad machine for the control of the state. Without definite proof the President assumed that the reformers, headed by Hiram Johnson, would be against him. He asked Murray Crane to see that effective speakers were sent to help out Governor Gillett, the machine candidate. But the most obvious presidential intervention was in Wisconsin. Hoping to control the state convention, the regular Republicans organized a "true Republican meeting." The meeting was addressed by Vice-President Sherman, who had not wanted to go and had refused twice, but changed his mind because of Taft's "repeated urgent request." Sherman bore greeting from the President to the regularly constituted Republican party of Wisconsin. In Wisconsin, as in Iowa, Kansas, Nebraska, and Washington, statewide networks of Taft Republican Clubs were formed to support the regulars attempting to overthrow the incumbent La Follette progressives. A vote for the progressives or insurgents, the party faithful were instructed by the regular Republican newspapers during the campaign, was a vote for Bryan and "democratic radicalism." [24]

[24] J. C. Burrows to James S. Sherman, September 17, 1910, Sherman MSS.;

The progressive Republicans were, of course, quite aware of what Taft and his conservative friends were doing. They struck back by organizing "Progressive Republican" clubs in answer to the Taft clubs. In Congress they were much more daring in their criticism of both the President and the regular leaders. Dolliver, who had already described Taft as a large, ineffectual person completely surrounded by men who knew exactly what they wanted, challenged the Chief Executive to "push" the progressives from the party. Their only crime, Dolliver said in his last speech to the Senate, had consisted "of taking the President's campaign speeches seriously" and of considering the Republican platform "as a binding moral obligation." In the summer's primaries throughout the Middle West, it was obvious that the Republican party was confronted with a full-size rebellion against the President and the regular organization. The stakes concerned both office and principle. La Follette, Beveridge, Dolliver, and Cummins were already on record as being opposed to Taft's renomination in 1912.[25]

In the uncertain balance between the forces contending for the future control of the Republican party, there was still one great uncommitted factor—Roosevelt. He had been away for over a year, but was due to return in June, 1910. Although he had written Lodge two years before that when he stopped being President he would "stop completely," the carrying out of that resolve was fraught with almost insuperable difficulties. Months prior to his landing and before he had made one statement, his name was already a political counter of no small weight. In February, 1910, the Chicago *Tribune* announced that the great majority of Middle Western newspaper editors preferred Roosevelt to Taft for 1912. This announcement was followed by appeals by Miles Poindexter, William Allen White, and Henry Allen for his nomination. By June "Roosevelt Republican" clubs had appeared in progressive dominated states, and the "back from Elba" cry became a chorus.[26]

Taft to Otto C. Bannard, December 20, 1909, to Elbert F. Baldwin, January 14, 1910, to Lafayette Young, February 17, 1910, to Murray Crane, July 14, 1910, to John L. Wilson, August 27, 1910, and to Frank H. Hitchcock, April 6, 1910, Taft MSS.; James S. Sherman to William L. Ward, June 2, 1910, Sherman MSS. See also Mowry, *Roosevelt and the Progressive Movement,* pp. 98 ff.

[25] *Congressional Record,* XLV, 61st Congress, 2nd Session, pt. 8, p. 7908; Beveridge to Pinchot, March 23, 1910, Beveridge MSS.

[26] Roosevelt to Lodge, July 19, 1908, Roosevelt MSS.

From the day that Roosevelt emerged from the jungle he was besieged by appeals from the champions of both sides of the Republican argument. Pinchot met him at Porto Maurizio with a sheaf of bitter letters from progressive senators and other anti-Taft people. Lodge wrote that the only two ways he could save the party from disaster were either to support Taft or to run for the Presidency himself. Root met him in London to advise that he remain silent until after he had thoroughly studied the situation at firsthand. Finally, just before he sailed for America, he received a long handwritten letter of greeting from the President. It was a warm letter but also a deeply pessimistic one full of troubles, both personal and political. He had conscientiously been trying to implement Roosevelt's policies, the President wrote, but he had had "a hard time." He did not presume to influence Roosevelt's judgment on the Pinchot matter, but he did accuse the progressive senators, including Borah, with systematically attempting to defeat the party, a policy that would probably result in a Democratic victory in the fall elections. On top of it all, Mrs. Taft, the President wrote, had had a complete "nervous collapse" soon after she entered the White House, which at first had brought on a partial "paralysis" and later an "almost complete aphasia." The harassed Taft did not ask for Roosevelt's support, but he obviously expected it.[27]

It is a very difficult matter for even complacent men willingly to transfer the pomp and power of the Presidency to another; the process must have been twice as difficult for Roosevelt. He was not too happy with Taft when he sailed for Africa. Taft had ignored all of his few suggestions about the Cabinet. But until Roosevelt met Pinchot in Europe there is no evidence in his letters that he had taken a position against his former friend. Thereafter things were greatly different. Taft, he wrote after the Pinchot conference, had not only "twisted around" his policies, but had so aligned himself with the reactionaries that he had alienated Roosevelt's friends as well as a great majority of the voters. The Pinchot conference ended a friendship. From that day on Roosevelt's cordial personal feelings for Taft rapidly disappeared. Returning home, he refused Taft's hearty invitation to be a guest at the White House in a formal note coldly ending "most sincerely yours." [28] Once in the United States, Roosevelt announced that he would make

[27] Taft to Roosevelt, May 26, 1910, Roosevelt MSS.
[28] Roosevelt to Lodge, April 11, 1910, and to Taft, June 8, 1910, Roosevelt MSS.

no political comments for at least two months. But then within a week
his home at Oyster Bay became a mecca for politicians, particularly
those, as Taft noted, of the progressive variety. At the end of a month,
he definitely re-entered politics by taking a leading part in the New
York State Convention and by scheduling a speaking tour through the
West. That decision was Roosevelt's crossing of the Rubicon. For although he undoubtedly believed that his purpose was to bring the warring factions of the Republican party together again—a move that would
aid the administration—the decision inevitably meant conflict with
Taft and with the reigning conservatives in the party. True, he avoided
all but one intraparty fight in the primaries, and in the following general election he spoke for both the progressive Beveridge in Indiana
and the conservative Lodge in Massachusetts. But the aim of his mission as well as his personal attitudes kept him from praising the administration and constrained him, at least in theoretical terms, to
endorse progressivism. Since Taft was President and head of the party
and was determined to remain so, friction was unavoidable. Roosevelt's
one direct intervention in the intraparty fight was in New York, where
he felt he could co-operate with the President in defeating the New
York party bosses, who were intent upon stopping the introduction of
a direct primary system and upon nominating a reactionary candidate
for governor. He and Taft were successful in New York, but only at
the cost of increasing the mutual suspicion with which they now
viewed each other.[29]

In the subtle and complex relationship between Roosevelt and Taft,
the personal factor obviously lay close to the heart of their growing
difficulties. Roosevelt, perhaps, could not have thoroughly approved
of the leadership of any successor, much less that of a personal friend.
Taft naturally expected at the least a public endorsement from Roosevelt, the absence of which he interpreted as something akin to a betrayal of a long partnership. But there were other reasons for their
growing misunderstanding. The two men in 1910 had different attitudes toward what constituted desirable party and governmental policy.
Taft came to office pledged to achieve the Roosevelt policies as enunciated in 1906 and 1907. He had conscientiously worked to obtain
them, and by 1910 had been successful to a surprising degree. But the

[29] For a detailed account of Roosevelt's involved maneuvering during the
summer of 1910, see Mowry, *Theodore Roosevelt and the Progressive Movement*, pp. 120 ff.

reform movement had not stood still. As it made increasingly more radical demands, Taft began to react and draw limits beyond which he would not go. With Roosevelt's impelling personal influence removed, he had drifted steadily toward the right. First his friends and then more slowly his policies were taken from that sector. Faced with the rapidly widening differences in the party that had started under Roosevelt, he had neither the inclination nor the skill to play the middle against the ends. In the late summer of 1910 he made his choice. He was a conservative, Taft admitted, and had been when Roosevelt was President. He was opposed to insurgency which demanded "that everybody should have the same amount of wealth and comfort and education, leading to discontent with everything." Roosevelt and the insurgents whom he headed were assaulting the Supreme Court and challenging the basic law of the land with their "wild ideas." The time had come to "stand by the Constitution" and Taft meant to do just that. As President, he wrote his brother, he could do one thing that neither the insurgents nor "the active statesman at Oyster Bay" could prevent. By the end of the term he would have the opportunity to appoint a majority of the Supreme Court. In view of the agitation to change the Constitution, he felt that his selections would be of the utmost importance.[30]

Taft's reference to the assaults on the Constitution were generally applicable to the progressive program of direct government and further regulation of business. More specifically, they were pointed to Roosevelt's call for a New Nationalism at Osawatomie, Kansas. Just as Taft had drifted right since 1908, Roosevelt, who then had thought of himself as the leader of the left center, had moved in an opposite direction. His last message to Congress had been radical enough even in 1908 to call forth protests from Taft. But in his 1910 speeches at Denver and at Osawatomie he went much further in his attacks on the courts, in his demands for the augmentation of federal power, and in his defense of human rights as against property rights. Before the Colorado state legislature he described the federal courts as one of the fundamental barriers to the securing of social justice. Not only had the courts traditionally overprotected property rights, he declared in Kansas, but they had also created "the neutral area" where neither the power of

[30] Taft to C. P. Taft, September 10, 1910; to Edward Colston, September 8, 1910; to Horace Taft, September 18, 1910; and to H. A. Lawrence, October 11, 1910, Taft MSS.

the state nor the nation could act upon lawless corporations and lawless wealth. The answer to the problem was sensibly to increase the power of the federal government and to make the courts subsidiary to Congress and to the Chief Executive, who would then become the "steward of the public welfare." Since the nation faced a new relationship between property and human rights, the old rules of the game had to be changed so as to produce "a more substantial equality of opportunity, and of reward for equally good service." In sum, Roosevelt asserted, the community should have the power to regulate property "to whatever degree the public welfare may require. . . ." [31]

Roosevelt tempered his New Nationalism by more moderate speeches in the East designed to attract the moderate conservatives. But his effort to bring the clashing factions of the party together on "a sound progressive" program, which would also win public support, failed. His more conservative efforts in the East got a cold reception among the western progressives, and his New Nationalism won for him the almost hysterical criticism of the right. The whole affair emphasized the almost hopeless split in the party, and in view of the "irresponsible folly" of both the "ultra-insurgents" and the "Bourbon-Reactionaries," Roosevelt concluded that any further effort of his to unite the two factions was "pointless." [32]

If Roosevelt had a bad summer in 1910, Taft had a far worse one. In the battle of the primaries between progressive and standpat Republicans, the administration had suffered an almost unbroken string of reverses. Forty incumbent regular Republican congressmen had been defeated, most of them by announced progressives. Moreover, all of the progressive Republican senators were victorious, and in California, North Dakota, and Washington three more progressive names were placed on the final ballot by Republican voters. The effort by Taft and his regular following to purge the party lists of the troublesome rebels had failed. In the wake of these disheartening returns came the great disaster of the November general elections.

The congressional election of 1910 was one of those significant divides in American history which signalize a reversal in political trends before a complete transfer of power occurs. For the first time in sixteen years the Democratic party controlled the House of Representatives, and

---

[31] *The New York Times,* August 30, September 1, 1910.
[32] Roosevelt to Lodge, September 20, 1910, Roosevelt MSS.

although the Republicans kept their majority in the Senate it was purely a nominal one, since the group of eight or nine progressive senators held the balance of power between the almost evenly divided regular Republican and Democratic forces. The election also went far to rehabilitate the Democratic party because it furnished it with a group of new reform-minded leaders, most of whom, coming from the East, were unattached to Bryan and his unrivaled record of consecutive defeats. Among them was the erstwhile president of Princeton University and the new governor of New Jersey, Woodrow Wilson. The results of the 1910 canvass also radically changed the balance of power between the contesting groups within the Republican party. Paralleling the series of regular defeats in the East was the string of progressive victories of the West. Maine, Massachusetts, Connecticut, New York, New Jersey, Ohio, and Indiana had all been lost, but the progressive-held states in the West remained in Republican hands. Both of Roosevelt's favored candidates, moreover, Henry L. Stimson in New York and Beveridge in Indiana, had been defeated. Seemingly the voters had repudiated both Taft's conservative principles and Roosevelt's attempt to reconsolidate the party somewhere left of center, but had given the new Republicanism of La Follette and Cummins a rousing vote of confidence. The election left Roosevelt deeply disappointed and decidedly irritated with Taft. It was even more of a blow to the President. For he now faced the last two years of his term with a hostile majority in the House of Representatives and with the more victorious elements of his own party ready to repudiate him.[33]

---

[33] *The New York Times,* November 10, 1910.

CHAPTER 14

Republican Decline

JUST before Roosevelt left office he gave Philander C. Knox, Taft's incoming Secretary of State, a long summary statement of America's relations with the rest of the world. Except with Japan, Roosevelt wrote, American foreign relations were good and peaceful. Friction with Germany had abated, he could not imagine trouble with England, and only minor irritations existed in the Caribbean. With Japan the case was far different. Japan was a formidable military power, "humiliated and sensitive," and the anti-Japanese feeling on the West Coast might provoke trouble at almost any time. Roosevelt cautioned Knox to treat Japan with "extreme consideration," keep the navy powerful, and be prepared for a war.[1]

Roosevelt's predictions met the usual mixed fate of such guesses. Except for customary minor troubles the next four years produced no crisis with Europe largely because Taft and Knox avoided intervention in the rapidly mounting intra-European tensions. The continuing Jewish pogroms in Russia did bring demands from American Jewry for the denunciation of the 1832 commercial treaty with Russia and the breaking off of diplomatic relations. Taft proposed, however, to substitute "steady diplomatic pressure" for the more drastic action of severing relations and annulling a treaty under which $60 million of American trade was carried on yearly. "Why cut the limb on which we sit?" he queried. Contrary to Roosevelt's predictions, American relations with

[1] Roosevelt to Knox, February 8, 1909, Knox MSS.

274

Japan remained peaceful, while those with the Caribbean area were exceedingly troublesome.[2]

Writing in 1930, Elihu Root believed that Taft and Knox had reversed his Latin-American policy, thereby causing much later trouble. Root implied, and his biographer states, that whereas Root's efforts had been toward conciliating the Latin Americans by less intervention, Taft and Knox had embarked upon an entirely new aggressive policy of "dollar diplomacy" in the Caribbean, which was fundamentally inspired by the profits it would bring for American investors. Root cited the treaties Knox negotiated with Honduras and Nicaragua as cases in point. The treaties, which were not ratified by the Senate, provided for the appointment of an American director of finance and the transference of European-held debt to United States banks. The treaty with Nicaragua also contained a new "Platt Amendment." In each case the negotiations were accelerated by the threat of force, and by March 4, 1913, American marines had landed not only in Nicaragua but in Santo Domingo as well.[3]

Root was perhaps right in his criticism of the Taft Caribbean policy as long as he compared it to his own and not to Roosevelt's. But Taft and Knox had invented nothing basically new in Nicaragua and Honduras. The precedent for their actions had been set in Santo Domingo years before under Roosevelt. If there was a difference it was in the emphasis that the new administration placed upon the commercial advantages which would accrue to Americans by the new arrangements and upon the de-emphasis of strategic aims as reasons for their creation. It is interesting to note that whereas Taft boasted in his 1912 message to Congress about the new business which State Department aides had helped to obtain in the Latin-American region, he was not inclined to accept the further extrapolation of the Roosevelt Corollary to the Monroe Doctrine involved in the Magdalena Bay affair.[4]

When Taft learned about the intention of a Japanese syndicate to purchase a large amount of land around Magdalena Bay in Baja California, he was not worried by the strategic implications of the transaction; but in the Senate Lodge offered a resolution to stop the sale on the grounds that the syndicate might be acting for the Japanese gov-

[2] Taft to Jacob H. Schiff, February 23, 1911, and to Hart Lyman, April, (?), 1911, Taft MSS.
[3] Philip C. Jessup, *Elihu Root* (2 vols., New York, 1938), I, 563; II, 250.
[4] Taft, *Addresses*, Vol. 18, p. 240.

ernment, proposing an addition to the Monroe Doctrine that would virtually require the consent of the United States to the transfer of any significant parcels of land around strategic sites in the Western Hemisphere to non-Americans. Although the Senate passed the resolution incorporating the so-called Lodge Corollary, the President declared that since the Senate was without power to make foreign policy, he would not feel "any obligation" to follow the meaning of the resolution in the future.[5]

Taft was equally cautious in his relations with the much more significant Mexican Revolution, which imperiled not only a strategic stake in the region but billions of dollars of American capital. For years prior to 1911 Mexico had been ruled by a tough and very efficient dictator-president, Porfirio Díaz. Sympathetic with the army, the nobility, the established church, and the upper economic registers of society, Díaz had encouraged foreign investment, and by 1910 American money constituted almost half of the more than $4 billion in foreign capital invested there. At the same time almost seventy thousand American citizens were Mexican residents. Under the Díaz regime almost everyone was happy except the great bulk of the native population. In the midst of the land's rich resources they had remained illiterate, diseased, impoverished. Díaz had met the many prior revolutionary challenges to his regime with stern repression; but by 1909, 90 per cent of the Mexican people, according to the American ambassador, were supporting a revolt, and soon the Mexican Revolution had started in earnest. Although the rebels' long-time aspirations were often confused, their immediate aims were clear: to dispossess both the foreign and domestic exploiters. Since the United States was geographically near and American capital was so dominant in the country, anti-Americanism was rampant.[6]

The immediate sympathies of the United States government were with Díaz. Taft had little regard for the Americans who complained about the actions of foreign capitalists in Mexico. They were "uplifters, without any sense" and among the "most annoying" of people. Díaz, he felt, had done more for the people of Mexico than had been accomplished in any other Latin-American country. His methods might be a

---

[5] Taft to Knox, August 5, 1911, and to David Starr Jordan, August 5, 1911, Taft MSS.

[6] Henry L. Wilson to Taft, quoted in Taft to Henry Taft, July 26, 1911; Taft to General Leonard Wood, March 12, 1911, Taft MSS.

bit rough, but then the Mexican people needed "a firm hand." The President tried to help the tottering Díaz in 1909 by meeting him in a public ceremony on the Texas border, and during the following confused months the American government officially gave the regime every possible support through normal diplomatic channels. But in May, 1911, under the leadership of Francisco Madero, the revolutionary forces overthrew Díaz, and the United States was confronted with a government in Mexico City antipathetic to all foreigners and foreign capital, but not strong enough to preserve order in the shattered country. Consequently, attacks upon Americans and American property were frequent.[7]

When it became apparent that the old Díaz regime could no longer keep order in Mexico, Taft was sorry. He had hoped that the dictator would make some compromises to quiet the turmoil. But then and afterward he refused to use more than diplomatic pressure to protect American interests. He ordered the mobilization of twenty thousand men north of the border, but he consistently discounted the possibility of intervention. Moreover, he ordered American forces to avoid any provocative acts that might elicit retaliation. When the American navy persisted in sending small ships of war into Mexican waters, he ordered his Secretary of the Navy to keep the "small fry" out of Mexican waters and to conduct all maneuvers north of the border line. The navy was "anxious for a contest," he felt, and had to be restrained. Even when shots were fired across the southern border and demands for retaliation mounted in the Southwest, the President refused to be diverted from his peaceful course. He could not order intervention, he wrote the governor of Arizona, or even authorize a return of fire across the border, because that would only produce greater bloodshed in the end. Instead of retaliation he asked the local authorities of the threatened towns to direct the people to place themselves where the Mexican bullets could not reach them. This "temporary inconvenience," he thought, was a small price to pay for the sake of safety and peace.[8]

It is one of history's ironies that, just at the time when world friction was mounting to climax shortly before the First World War, the international peace movement was energetic and confident of ultimate suc-

[7] Taft to Henry W. Taft, July 26, 1911, and to Horace Taft, January 19, 1911, Taft MSS.

[8] Taft to James Creelman, March 21, 1911; to George Von L. Meyer, March 14, 1911; to Roosevelt, March 22, 1911; and to M. S. Sloan, April 18, 1911, Taft MSS.

cess. By 1910 the European movement to establish an association of nations for the enforcement of peace had chapters in almost every civilized country. Roosevelt gave the movement his qualified endorsement in a speech at Christiana, Norway. The American Society for the Judicial Settlement of International Disputes was organized, and Congress passed a resolution authorizing the President to establish a peace commission to inquire into the possibility of the limitation of international armaments and the establishment of an international naval force for the maintenance of world peace. Late in the year Andrew Carnegie, supremely confident in the power of money to order human affairs, established his Peace Fund with an initial gift of $10 million.

President Taft was profoundly dedicated to world peace. While Carnegie placed his confidence in money, Taft was certain that courts and the judicial procedure, even though unsustained by anything more than public opinion, could accomplish this dream of centuries. When international arbitration became accepted, he believed, then the world could count on the disappearance of war. Taft proposed to do more than his share during his term to make such arbitration procedures a reality. In a series of speeches in late 1910 and early 1911, he elaborated on the idea. He had already directed his Secretary of State to negotiate arbitration treaties "broader in their terms than any . . . heretofore ratified, and broader than any that now exist between nations." In August, 1911, the President submitted to the Senate treaties with Great Britain and France calling for the contracting nations to arbitrate all differences between them that were "justiciable in their nature by reason of being susceptible of decision by the application of the principles of law or equity." All such difficulties, which included even matters of "national honor" and "territory," the President explained, were to be settled in the future at The Hague or a similar court of arbitration.

Signing the arbitration treaties and submitting them to the Senate was probably the most popular act of the administration in its four years. *The New York Times* called the treaties "the crowning achievement of Mr. Taft's Administration," [9] and if one can believe the press, an overwhelming majority of all sections of the nation and political faiths was exuberantly commendatory. But the Senate held another

[9] Taft to Dr. L. S. Rowe, December 15, 1911, Taft MSS.; *The New York Times,* January 22, 1911.

opinion. So did Theodore Roosevelt. Blithely overlooking his stout de-fense of arbitration a few years back, he exerted himself in opposition as he had in few other instances after leaving office. Roosevelt com-posed numerous antitreaty articles for *The Outlook;* repeatedly wrote long letters to Lodge and Root, both on the Senate Foreign Relations Committee, urging them to denounce the Taft proposals; and spoke to public gatherings, often using words "really offensive" to Taft. Long afterward Roosevelt recalled that of all the errors of the Taft ad-ministration no misconduct was greater than that relating to foreign affairs. The President also bestirred himself by making a cross-country tour in behalf of his treaties. But though he won the plaudits of the crowds, in the end the Senate triumphed, as it had over Cleveland, McKinley, and Roosevelt on similar treaties. As that body amended his proposals out of all recognition, the President sadly gave up the effort.[10]

Although compared to Roosevelt's foreign policy Taft's seemed to be the essence of consistency, it was not entirely innocent of paradoxes. Contrasted to Taft's vigorous stand for international arbitration, his position on the Panama tolls question is difficult to explain. The tolls question arose over what rates were to be charged ships using the nearly completed Panama Canal. In the Hay-Pauncefote Treaty with Eng-land the United States had agreed to permit passage on equal terms to the ships of all nations in both peace and war. Defending the seizure of the Canal Zone, both Roosevelt and Hay had appealed to the world right of passage across the Isthmus obstructed by Colombia. The United States, they declared, had acted on that right as mandatary of civilization for the equal benefit of all mankind. But now that the Canal had been built and paid for, Taft took the position that the nation might legally discriminate in favor of its own shippers by allow-ing them free passage; the equal-terms clause he interpreted as meaning equality for all other nations save the United States. Upon strenuous British objections the President denied that the quarrel was rightfully a matter for arbitration under the arbitral agreements signed by Elihu

[10] For representative press opinion on the treaties, see *The New York Times,* August 4, 1911; the Philadelphia *Record,* August 9, 1911; the Washington *Herald,* August 6, 1911. Roosevelt to Henry White, October 5, 1911, Roosevelt MSS. The manuscripts of Taft, Knox, Roosevelt, and Root are particularly voluminous on the arbitration treaties. Perhaps no other particular legislative issue in the Taft administration occasioned so much letter writing from so many important people.

Root. With the President's encouragement Congress approved of the discrimination. The nation changed its stand and finally lived up to its clearly stated international obligation in 1913. Taft, however, never admitted that he was wrong. As late as 1914 he explained Root's and Lodge's votes to reverse his stand by their "snobbish" London society viewpoint.[11]

In contrast to Taft's cautious, patient, peaceful policy with Mexico, his actions in China also present something of a paradox. Taft had more firsthand knowledge of the Orient than any other ranking American statesman. He had lived in the Philippines for years and had traveled extensively in East Asia. It is strange, therefore, that he so severely misjudged the Oriental political situation when he came to power in 1909. Possibly the administration's Oriental policy was more Knox's than it was Taft's, as both Taft and Root's biographers suggest. Much of the President's trouble came from his disinclination to overrule a member of his Cabinet. Or perhaps Taft felt the urge to differ from Roosevelt in a field where he was not pledged to follow his predecessor's program. Whatever the reason, the Taft-Knox Oriental policy departed from Roosevelt's opportunistic one and as a consequence encountered serious difficulties.

Although an expansionist, Roosevelt had given up the thought of acquiring territory in China because he realized that the American people would not support it with the requisite force needed to equal that of the powers already established there, particularly that of Russia and Japan. As a substitute he relied upon the Open Door, which, if it could be held open, would permit commercial expansion. But Roosevelt also realized the close identity between military and commercial power in the Far East and recognized that an aggressive commercial policy without a corresponding political equivalent was doomed to failure. Denied military support by public sentiment, he sought a substitute in attempting to balance Russian and Japanese power, even giving up the Open Door principle in Korea to gain his countervailing forces in the Portsmouth Treaty. Meanwhile he had dabbled in what was to become known as "dollar diplomacy" by promising the Morgan railroad syndicate State Department support. But by 1910 the Oriental pattern of power had been changed drastically. Japan had grown

---

[11] Root to Henry F. Stimson, February 27, 1913, to Elbert F. Baldwin, June 8, 1914, Root MSS.; Taft to Elbert F. Baldwin, June 26, 1911, to Knox, April 30, 1914, Taft MSS.

immensely in national strength. And the anti-German European Alliance partners, headed by Britain and France, had encouraged their Far Eastern partners, Russia and Japan, to come to an understanding that had divided up Manchuria, had destroyed Roosevelt's Portsmouth counterpoise, and had isolated both Germany and the United States in East Asia. Roosevelt seemed to sense the importance of the need for a changed American policy. In a 1910 interchange with Knox and Taft he proposed that the United States virtually give up its commercial ambitions in Manchuria and China in return for an understanding with Japan over the West Coast immigration problem. In particular, he cautioned against supporting a "weak and unreliable" China against Japanese ambitions in Manchuria, which he felt could not be obstructed with anything less than force.[12]

The President and his relatively uninformed Secretary of State, however, had previously agreed upon an aggressive commercial policy, which Taft more than hinted at in May, 1910. In a public speech the President declared that there was nothing inconsistent in pursuing a foreign policy which would still be determined by principles of national interest and abstract justice but which would also be made to "include active intervention to secure for our merchandise and our capitalists opportunity for profitable investment. . . ." Such a policy was pursued in Latin America and elsewhere, but nowhere was it given more emphasis than in that curious repository of America's nebulous and unsatisfied commercial dreams, China. At the insistence of the State Department American bankers agreed to participate in at least three Chinese projects, two of them for the construction of railroads and the third a scheme for the support of Chinese national currency. To obtain the right of participation, the American government put pressure on the Chinese government as well as the governments of foreign powers whose nationals were already operating in the area. With China Taft took the almost unprecedented step of writing directly to the Prince Regent to ask for equal opportunity for American capital. In one of his most expansive moments Secretary Knox proposed a plan to all nations holding railroad concessions that a vast international consortium be formed to loan China enough money with which to purchase all the foreign-held railroads. This particular scheme was received with meager enthusiasm in the various European capitals, but the United

[12] Roosevelt to Taft, December 8 and 22, 1910, Roosevelt MSS.; Knox to Taft, December 19, 1910. Taft MSS.

States did obtain entry for its bankers in two more modest financial enterprises. But in 1913, when the Wilson administration announced that the American bankers would not be supported by the State Department, the American financiers hastily withdrew from the projects, leaving the rewards and perils of Chinese investments to others.[13]

In his 1912 annual message to Congress, Taft described his investment policy as one of "substituting dollars for bullets." No doubt the President was sincere in his hope that he could advance American business and investment interests, save China, and thereby allay international tensions. It should be noted that right at the start of his administration the State Department issued a memorandum stating: "The nations that finance the great Chinese railroads and other enterprises will be foremost in the affairs of China and the participation of American capital . . . will give the voice of the United States more authority in that country, which will go far toward the preservation of the administrative entity of China." This easy combination of profits and virtue was a noble dream but utterly futile. It gathered the fruit before the planting of the tree. The legally minded Taft and Knox apparently never did understand the extent to which Chinese investments flowed from political power and not the reverse. Nor did they appear to realize that such power had to be established on a firmer base than note writing. With Roosevelt's balance of power in the Orient gone, the only available substitute was force or the threat of it, and this neither Taft nor the American people were prepared to use.[14]

Taft's dollars-for-bullets utterances won for his foreign policy the name of "dollar diplomacy," which was described in some quarters as the placing of the power of the government at the disposal of foreign investors, with the implication that the President was ready to risk war for the benefit of a few. Nothing could be further from the truth, as Taft's Mexican policy clearly indicates. The President was profoundly a man of peace. What was wrong with the Taft-Knox version of dollar diplomacy was not that it worked evil but rather that, except in a few small Latin-American countries, it could and did not work at all.

In 1910 the Taft administration was confronted with another foreign question intimately tied with domestic politics. Even before the pas-

[13] Taft, *Addresses,* Vol. 18, p. 240; Taft to Knox, September 1, 1910, and to Prince Chun, July 15, 1909, Taft MSS.
[14] Alfred W. Griswold, *The Far Eastern Policy of the United States* (New York, 1938), pp. 87–132.

sage of the Payne-Aldrich Tariff, the threat of a Canadian-American trade war had been mounting yearly. Roosevelt had toyed with the idea of negotiating lower rates by means of a reciprocity treaty, but had given up his efforts because of opposition both in the United States and in Canada. On the surface the economies of the two countries seemed to be complementary. Canada was overwhelmingly an exporter of agricultural goods and raw products and an importer of manufactured wares. Yearly the exportable surplus of American manufactures grew, as did the need for cheap raw products. The only insect in the reciprocity ointment seemed to be the yearly American agricultural surplus. But then, it was argued by some theorists, the prices of such goods, since they were in oversupply, were set by the international markets. A mutual lowering of the tariffs, this thesis continued, would thus aid American manufacturers at little or no cost to American agriculture. Taft said his attention was first drawn to the subject by the remark of Senator Aldrich that Canadian reciprocity could be had with no cost to the protective principle and with great benefits to both nations. The continued demand of the West for tariff reductions and the increasing clamor in the East about the rising cost of living might also be satisfied, the President felt, by a Canadian treaty. Consequently in January, 1911, a treaty negotiated by Knox was presented to Congress which placed on the free lists of both nations most agricultural goods, some minerals, iron, and steel plate, and paper pulp. Sizable reductions were to be made also in prepared meats, canned vegetables, flour, and a long list of other manufactured products not originating on the farm.[15]

The tariff treaty immediately won the acclaim of most eastern manufacturers and merchants, but it encountered bitter opposition from both eastern and western farmers. Root, who kept a statistical record of his correspondence on reciprocity, reported that whereas 548 of a total of 551 New York merchants and manufacturers favored the treaty, 435 New York granges plus 10 other farm organizations had written denouncing it. His agricultural constituents almost to a man thought of the treaty as a "sacrifice of their interests." And as they had "furnished the backbone of the Republican vote," Root reflected, the passing of the reciprocity treaty would be a serious thing for the party and the

[15] Roosevelt to C. W. Fairbanks, November 12, 1904, Roosevelt MSS.; Taft to Aldrich, January 29, 1911, and to Knox, January 14, 1911, Taft MSS. See Lewis E. Ellis, *Reciprocity, 1911* (New York, 1939).

administration. Further opposition came from the Republican West. Except for Beveridge every progressive Republican senator was against the measure. Pointing out that most of the United States reductions were on farm goods and raw materials, whereas manufactured products were to benefit by the freer market in Canada, they argued that this was just one more indication of the President's willingness to sacrifice the western farmer for the benefit of the eastern manufacturer. And then, curiously enough, a good many Republicans from industrial states began to change their original good opinion of the treaty. Fearing that this was just a first step in a Taft-sponsored crusade against the protective principle, they joined the American Protective Tariff League and the Iron and Steel Association in opposing it. In the Senate, regular Senators Bradley, Gallinger, Frye, Hale, and Smoot joined in an opposition powerful enough to prevent the treaty from coming to a vote.[16]

At times Taft could be a very stubborn man. He was delighted with the opposition of the progressive Republicans to reciprocity. It proved to him the hypocrisy in the past demands of these "defenders of God's patient poor" for tariff reductions. He was not even bothered by the grave reservations of the majority of his party. "The whole Republican party," he wrote, would "have to go for it if they propose to save their bacon." He had already warned his Republican colleagues that he would call a special session of the new Congress if the treaty was not passed. Ignoring Root's advice to let reciprocity drop, he made a deal with the Democratic majority in the incoming House. The following special session, which lasted all through the hot Washington summer, presented a strange spectacle. Aligned against the Republican President were most of the congressional Republican leaders plus the progressives. But in the end, by co-operating with southern Democrats whose cotton, tobacco, and corn were not threatened by Canadian competition, the President won a temporary victory. Together with the Democrats he won over enough regular Republican votes to pass the treaty.[17]

In January, 1911, Taft confessed that he believed in the reciprocity

[16] Root to Robert Bacon, June 7, 1911, Root MSS.; *La Follette's Weekly,* August 5, 1911; James M. Swank to Foraker, March 29 and June 10, 1911, Foraker MSS.; *Congressional Record,* XLVII, 62nd Congress, 1st Session, pt. 1, p. 395.

[17] Taft to Aldrich, January 29, 1911; to E. J. Hill, March 22, 1911; and to Robert Taft, August 22, 1911. Oscar Underwood, *The Drifting Sands of American Party Politics* (New York, 1928), p. 166.

principle so much that he was not troubled by his guess that his support of the treaty would eliminate him in 1912 from "the consideration of practical politicians." The President had very logical reasons for the guess. By 1911 the progressives were implacably opposed to his re-nomination. Now with the reciprocity measure he had angered the farmers and had alienated a good share of the party regulars devoted to the protective principle. The conservative fears of a coming attack on high protection were realized. Immediately after the passage of the reciprocity treaty, a Democratic-progressive Republican coalition suc-ceeded in passing a number of "popgun" tariff bills which would have substantially lowered the existing rates on farm machinery, iron and steel goods, woolens, and shoes had not the President interposed a veto. Thus Taft opened himself to the charge that he favored lowering the tariff for the benefit of the manufacturers but not for the farmers or consumers. Conservative Republicans were also able to mutter with satisfaction that this was what came from the President's dealings with the Democrats. The major blow against Taft, however, was not struck in Washington but in Ottawa. Had reciprocity simply been an economic issue for Canadians, the prairie provinces would probably have tri-umphed over the manufacturers of Ontario and Quebec to approve the treaty. But politics were injected into the debate, empire politics, and the question of Canadian independence. Fears were voiced in both Canada and Britain that the treaty would lead to Canada's dependence upon the United States and that thus she eventually would lose her self-identity and her membership in the British Empire. There were good grounds for such fears, both historic and current. The desires of the "War Hawks" of 1812 and of Polk, Seward, and Blaine had not been forgotten north of the border. And there was no doubt that the idea of "Continental Union," as Henry Stimson called it, lurked in many a mind in the United States. The current of business set up by the treaty, Taft wrote privately, would eventually "make Canada only an adjunct of the United States." Unfortunately, such sentiments were not confined to private correspondence. In defending the treaty the Presi-dent ineptly referred to Canada as being "at the parting of the way." Many other speeches and articles were far less discreet. In the end a combination of Canadian nationalism, empire sentiment, and manu-facturing interests defeated the treaty. At the cost of alienating the American farmer, irritating the friends of high protection, and the further fragmentation of his party, Taft had achieved nothing save an additional loss of prestige and public confidence.[18]

Had Taft been a good politician, he would have done everything possible after 1910 to placate the conservative element in his party, which usually reflected rather faithfully the attitudes of business. Instead, simultaneously with his support of Canadian reciprocity, he and his Attorney General, Wickersham, were pushing possibly the most active antimonopoly campaign that the nation has ever witnessed. Taft had always been more of an ardent supporter of competitive capitalism than Theodore Roosevelt, and was more sanguine about the possibility of its restoration through the zealous use of the Sherman Anti-Trust Law against evolving monopolies. Roosevelt had used the Sherman Law, had in fact restored its vitality, but from the first moments of his administration he had lacked confidence in it. He soon concluded that it was a retrograde and not a progressive instrument. The consolidation movement in both business and labor Roosevelt believed to be a normal and inevitable evolutionary growth, the stoppage of which would do great harm to the country. He had used the Sherman Law then only as an indirect weapon to get what he really wanted, federal control, and also possibly because of the political value of its use. In his first message to Congress he asked for federal incorporation of interstate businesses. From there as the years progressed he successively asked for more stringent federal regulation. By 1910 he was proposing the creation of a body for the regulation of business not unlike the Interstate Commerce Commission, and in 1911 the federal control of prices of trust-made goods.

Taft, on the other hand, was dedicated to the virtues of the competitive system and felt that there was no way station between true competition and socialism. "We must get back to competition," he argued at Pocatello in October, 1911. "If it is impossible, then let us go to socialism, for there is no way between." But the President believed that socialism was not necessary since the effective use of the Sherman Law would in fact restore effective competition. The Sherman Law, he wrote in 1911, "is a good law that ought to be enforced, and I propose to enforce it." True enough, in the 1908 campaign, when he was still

[18] Stimson to Root, February, (?), 1911, Root MSS.; Taft to Roosevelt, January 10, 1911, and to Knox, June 2, 1911, Taft MSS.; W. S. Fielding to Knox, September 29, 1911, Knox MSS. For a good survey of the American desire for a union with Canada, see "Making Canada an Adjunct," *Literary Digest*, XLIV (1912), pp. 1029–1030.

under the ideological shadow of Roosevelt, he had argued for national incorporation of large businesses. When he eventually presented his measure to Congress, however, it was a voluntary and not a compulsory measure. Taft made it clear that he wanted the law as a "supplement" to and not in place of the Sherman Act.[19]

Taft never got his incorporation statute, in part because he did not really push the measure and in part because western Republicans, notwithstanding the President's assurances, feared that the bill might weaken the Sherman Act. Grounds for such fears certainly existed. As the antimonopoly movement grew, a good many large industrialists looked with more favor at regulatory schemes. For years in and out of Congress there had been talk that the Sherman Law was too rigid in its inclusive application to all restraint of interstate commerce whether the intent was toward monopoly or not, and whether the restraint was reasonable or not. Perhaps Roosevelt's distinction between "good and bad" trusts had stimulated the movement toward a more flexible interpretation of the law. At any rate, in 1911 the Supreme Court in the Standard Oil and the American Tobacco cases enunciated its famous "rule of reason." The Court found both the oil and the tobacco companies to be monopolies guilty of violating the antitrust act and ordered their dissolution. But in its argument the Court fundamentally changed the nature of the Sherman Act. Within the bounds of "reasonable contention" the Court found the intent of both companies had been to effect a monopoly and that their actions had placed an "undue restraint" on the free flow of interstate and foreign commerce. By its use of the words "reasonable" and "undue" the Court, in effect, had amended the original law, and had arrogated unto itself the power to decide whether a business restraining interstate commerce was guilty of violating the Sherman Act.[20]

Before the Standard Oil decision the President had opposed the suggestion that the Court be allowed to exercise the power to decide what was or what was not reasonable restraint. Afterward, however, he reversed his position and reconciled himself to the decision, finally claiming that the Court had really strengthened the law rather than weakened it. This strange but characteristic reversal of the President

[19] *The New York Times,* October 7, 1911; Taft to A. R. Kimball, November 21, 1911, Taft MSS.
[20] Des Moines *Register and Leader,* January 19, 1910; Taft to J. C. Hemphill, November 16, 1911, Taft MSS.

had no effect, however, on the temper of his own antitrust activities. To objections that his and Wickersham's overzealous use of the Sherman Act were bringing on an industrial panic, he grimly replied, "We are going to enforce that law or die in the attempt." And although Taft's antitrust campaign was never as comprehensive as he believed it to be, by the end of his four years his administration had obtained far more indictments against business concerns than were secured in the Roosevelt span of seven. So vigorous indeed was the campaign that within a short time big business began to wonder whether Roosevelt, after all, was not preferable to Taft. The administration, the New York *Sun* lamented, was doing more to injure established institutions than even the Socialists and the anarchists.[21]

Among the many antitrust suits initiated by the Taft administration, by far the most important was that against the United States Steel Corporation. It had little effect on the pattern of American industry, for after dragging on for years the suit was finally decided against the government. But politically its results were almost catastrophic, both for Taft personally and for the Republican party. During the campaign of 1908 Taft had been asked by one of the contributors to the party whether the government had any plans for taking action against the steel corporation. The trust was not then under investigation by the government, Taft replied, and he did not know of any reason for investigation or prosecution. "Indeed," the candidate added, "Secretary Garfield tells me there is not." But in June, 1910, the President changed his mind. Upon the passage of a congressional resolution asking for an investigation, Taft ordered one. And then sometime in 1911, exactly when is not clear, Taft, after several interviews with Solicitor General Frederick W. Lehmann, decided that a suit was in order. The Secretary of War, Jacob M. Dickinson, was appointed as a special counsel to prepare the government's case, announced on October 26, 1911. In the government's attempt to prove monopoly one of its main points of evidence was the steel corporation's acquisition of the Tennessee Coal and Iron Company in 1907, of which Theodore Roosevelt had tacitly, if not actually, approved. The only conclusions that could be drawn from the charge were painfully obvious. Either the administration felt

[21] Taft to R. D. Silliman, December 31, 1909, to Horace Taft, November 5, 1911, and to H. L. Higginson, July 28, 1911, Taft MSS.; Worthington C. Ford (ed.), *The Letters of Henry Adams, 1892–1918* (Boston, 1932), p. 534; New York *Sun*, October 28, 29, 31, 1911.

that Roosevelt had been duped in 1907 or that he was guilty of collusion in the formation of a monster monopoly.[22]

Taft apparently knew nothing about the inclusion of Roosevelt and the Tennessee Coal and Iron Company in the government charges. Attorney General Wickersham had read the relevant documents, but not the President. He also apparently remained curiously blind to the implications of Roosevelt's inclusion in the case. Ten days after the steel suit was announced, he wrote a long letter to his brother in which he discussed the action at length without once mentioning the ex-President. A month later he confessed that introducing Roosevelt's name into the suit had not helped it. But, he protested, he was not consulted at the time and he could not do anything about it at that late date.[23] Taft was a man of monumental honesty, but the whole story of the preparation of the steel suit is extremely curious. Until the drawing up of the government's formal case, the President took an active interest in it. On March 6, for example, he had written the Solicitor General that he wanted to go over the steel investigation thoroughly with him. Moreover, the President was aware, or should have been, of the dynamite hidden in Roosevelt's connection with the steel company. Just a little over two months before the steel suit was announced, a committee of the House of Representatives also investigating the steel trust had requested that Roosevelt appear before it and testify as to his part in the acquisition of the Tennessee Coal and Iron Company. Taft and Roosevelt had even talked over the matter previous to the committee's request and the President had advised Roosevelt not to testify. Although the Colonel felt the request was a sheer piece of effrontery by a group of "dishonest jacks," he insisted on appearing. Before the Stanley Committee, Roosevelt admitted that the steel corporation might have had more than benevolent motives in the purchase of the Tennessee corporation. But he insisted with all the fire and emphasis which he could summon up, a not altogether negligible quantity, that he as President had acted in the best interests of the nation and had been entirely consistent with both the spirit and the letter of the law. Had he read the newspapers, Taft could not have avoided being aware of Roosevelt's indignation. Yet a month later,

[22] Taft to George R. Sheldon, September 19, 1908, and to Lehmann, January 22, 1911, March 6, 1911, Taft MSS.

[23] Taft to Horace Taft, November 5, 1911, and to George B. Edwards, December 3, 1911, Taft MSS.

when he was informed the steel suit was to be filed within the next six weeks, the President did not ask to see the bill of particulars. One is forced to conclude that Taft was either an incredibly dull student of human reactions or that he intentionally avoided looking at the steel suit documents.[24]

Roosevelt's reaction to the steel suit was as predictable as the relations of the celestial spheres. Before, he had been irritated by the President, but only with the modulated ire that comes with a difference over issues. Now he was thoroughly enraged. He strenuously disagreed with the administration's arguments in the suit. But what angered him most was the President's lack of any sense of obligation to his own word in the past. He had talked over the steel matter with Taft in 1907 two or three times, he recalled. Since Taft had been "enthusiastic in praise of what was done," then it ill became him now to disagree. He should have objected immediately, Roosevelt wrote with certain venom, "or else from every consideration of honorable obligation never under any circumstances afterwards." He was forced to conclude that Taft and Wickersham were "playing small, mean and foolish politics. . . ."[25]

All such remarks Roosevelt made in letters conspicuously marked private and confidential. His public rejoinder appeared in *The Outlook* in mid-November. He opened with some sharp retorts to the government's claims in the steel suit. But most of the article was devoted to a blistering attack upon Taft's "archaic" attempt to restore the competitive system, an attempt no more logical than a return "to the flintlocks of Washington's Continentals." The only way to cure the industrial problem without doing irretrievable harm to the country, Roosevelt argued, was to accept the combination movement as inevitable and indeed necessary to modern life. To protect the consumer and the laboring man in this new concentrated society, a vast augmentation of federal regulatory power was needed. With such regulation, Roosevelt admitted, he was ready to go as far as the setting of industrial prices.[26]

[24] Taft to Lehmann, March 6, 1911, Taft MSS.; Roosevelt to Nicholas Longworth, June 19, 1911, and to James Garfield, August 9, 1911, Roosevelt MSS. The Roosevelt testimony before the committee is given in *The Outlook,* XCVIII (1911), 866.

[25] Roosevelt to Everett P. Wheeler, October 27, 1911, and to James Garfield, October 30, 1911, Roosevelt MSS.

[26] Roosevelt, "The Trusts, the People and the Square Deal," *The Outlook,* XCIX (1911), 649.

The steel suit and the personal involvement of Roosevelt provoked a multilevel crisis in the Republican party and in the progressive movement. Immediately after the congressional elections of 1910 the so-called progressive Republicans had met in the home of Senator La Follette to draw up a declaration of principles and a call for a national meeting. At the meeting on January 21, 1911, the National Progressive Republican League was organized. Included in its membership were eight Republican senators, six state governors, numerous congressmen, and many non-officeholders. Its purpose was to defeat William Howard Taft for the Republican nomination in 1912 by supporting the candidacy of Robert La Follette. The League tried desperately to obtain the public support of Roosevelt; many of its members, in fact, would have been overjoyed to forget La Follette immediately and support Roosevelt for the nomination had he been willing. But the Colonel not only refused to permit his name to be used; he also declined to align himself with the League. Roosevelt was sure that the progressives and La Follette would not be able to defeat Taft for the Republican nomination. He was also equally certain that Taft would be defeated in the election. The split in the Republican party was so great, he concluded, that 1912 would inevitably be a Democratic year. Between the warring factions he felt that the views of the conservatives on the balance "offered a little more promise for good. . . ." Nevertheless, as far as he personally was concerned, he was determined in the summer of 1911 to remove himself from all intraparty hostilities. He would not, he declared in a public statement in late June, be a candidate himself, nor would he support any other man for the nomination.[27]

Roosevelt retained his midsummer position unwaveringly until the day of the steel suit; thereafter he changed it rapidly. On the day the suit was announced he intimated to the governor of California that he might be persuaded to run for the nomination were he convinced that the masses of the people liked and trusted him. Within a little more than a month, by not saying either yes or no to a proposal by his former Secretary of the Interior, James R. Garfield, he left the way open for his friends to work for his candidacy. From that moment, given Roosevelt's great popularity and his competitive spirit, the rest was inevitable. By February, 1912, he declared that his hat was in the

[27] George E. Mowry, *Theodore Roosevelt and the Progressive Movement* (Madison, Wis., 1946), pp. 172–182.

ring, and he had become a zealous competitor for the Republican nomination along with Taft and La Follette.

So much of the story was personal. Other matters of ideology existed, however, that cut far deeper into Republican unity than the conflicting personalities and ambitions of Roosevelt, Taft, and La Follette. For by 1911–12 the Republican party had come to a crisis over the basic question of the future of the United States. What were the tomorrows to be like? Was big business to be allowed to go on developing unhindered by either the government or the labor movement until the whole nation was dominated by industrialists? Were their values of a highly differentiated and plutocratic society, roughly equating social power and worth with wealth, to become the values of the nation? Or was the burgeoning labor movement to produce the rulers of the future? The labor movement had as its theoretical end an equality of economic rewards, but had shown neither much of a disposition to democratic principles within its own ranks nor a concern for social or cultural affairs outside the small realm of the shop. By 1910 Americans had lived with big capital for a generation. The Socialist party was making phenomenal gains, and its vote was to be well over a million in the next election. Organized labor at the same date counted over two million members. Big capital and growing labor were in critical conflict in 1911–12, both demanding that the government act in ways that would permit their own steady development at the expense of the other. In the midst of the 1912 presidential campaign, the president of one of the major railroads proposed that the courts grant a "perpetual injunction force at all times" against labor interference with the operation of the transportation industry. A short while before, Samuel Gompers, president of the American Federation of Labor, had demanded that the courts be stripped of all powers to grant labor injunctions. "The courts," Gompers wrote, "are on the point of finding out that final decisions of justice must come not from one class in a republic, but from all of its people." [28]

There were other groups that held different views about the future. The farmer, the small businessman, the professional, and the self-employed had little sense of allegiance to either corporate business or corporate labor. These middle registers, from which most of the progressives came, wanted neither big-business nor big-labor domination.

[28] S. M. Felton to Root, July 9, 1912, Root MSS.; *American Federationist,* XVIII (1911), 999.

A portion of this group, devoted to a small America in which power was fragmented and unorganized, looked back longingly toward the past and wanted to recreate it. Emotionally they were disposed toward the country and the town as against the city, toward the workshop as against the factory, toward the individual as against the regimented mass, toward a small Jeffersonian government as against a leviathan state, and toward an isolated nation as against a mobilized state exerting its power in the far corners of the world. Coming mostly from the Midwest and beyond, these agrarian reformers wanted to crush the power of big business without creating an equivalent focus of centralized power elsewhere. Because no force adequate to the task existed outside that of government, they were forced to rely upon an increasingly potent state. But the ultimate goal was in the past. Their yardstick was not what could be, but what had been. To such a degree they reluctantly walked backward into the future.

An equally important progressive faction had caught a vision from the new organization of capital and labor, from the new science, religion, and technology. Urban-minded and collectivists, although not Socialists, these progressives were critical of the "chaotic individualism" of the past. They decried the "mutilation" of productive capacity, which they saw as a direct result of the attempt to restore competition. The new collective industrial system of corporations and labor unions, they argued, was capable of enormous social good, provided it was properly organized for a higher social good. What was wanted was not destruction but reconstruction through the introduction of public management. They envisioned a productive machine that would remain capitalistic in function but almost socialistic in purpose and result. The major aim, Herbert Croly suggested, was to secure the maximum production from a private system with the most widespread diffusion of benefits possible.[29] As these progressives thought in terms of concentrated power internally, so they also thought in the realm of foreign affairs. Isolation, with its invidious distinction between Americanism and Europeanism, contributed nothing to society except to flatter the American vanity. If the nation was to live up to its democratic promise, then it must of necessity use its power abroad for the construction of an international "system of public laws." The securing of such a system in the Western Hemisphere would be relatively easy, Croly thought. Elsewhere, because powerful nations existed which

[29] Herbert Croly, *The Promise of American Life* (New York, 1909), p. 367.

would benefit by strife, the task would be more difficult. But the United States could, by "an alliance with the pacific European powers," namely, Great Britain and France, first project the system across the North Atlantic and then work for "its establishment throughout the world." [30]

Successful democratic politicians rarely ever can afford to take their doctrines from one ideological font. But in a very rough and imprecise way Taft, La Follette, and Roosevelt reflected the triangular ideological struggle for supremacy within the Republican party. By 1912, Taft, a self-announced conservative, was leaning for support upon the still dominant, pro-big-business element among the party's officeholders and its suppliers of funds. The President was not the automatic voice of big business. By principle he was devoted in some ways to a shadowy laissez-faire state that had disappeared many years before. But his dislike of a powerful government, his fear of direct democracy, his reverence for the courts, and his mental confusion, as attested by his foreign policy, made it practically impossible for him successfully to challenge the enormous strength of the new industry. He had neither the will to return to the past nor the inclination to disturb the present.

La Follette also only roughly reflected the more microcosmic attitudes of the farmers and the small merchants in the Midwestern states where his candidacy was strongest. He was a university-trained man, influenced by the new social science and religion. Under his leadership Wisconsin had gone further than any other state along the path toward a social democracy. But although he used the new techniques of control, his goals were mainly those of the past, those of the people among whom he had grown up in the smaller village of Primrose, Wisconsin. Like the Gracchi of Rome, he was ready to use new political power to return the state to its ancient rural, democratic, freeholding ways. In 1912 Robert La Follette desired a small America both internally and externally. So he remained for the rest of his life. Later, in the debates of the League of Nations, he expressed both his fears and his faith: "I do not covet for this country a position in the world which history has shown would make us the object of endless jealousies and hatred. . . ." [31]

For Roosevelt the facts speak more clearly. A twentieth-century

[30] *Ibid.*, p. 314.

[31] Belle Case La Follette and Fola La Follette, *Robert M. La Follette* (2 vols., New York, 1953), II, 981.

urban man, Roosevelt was extremely sensitive and responsive to the new doctrines abroad in the United States and the world. He recognized the reactionary impulse of much of Midwest progressivism. It was really "a kind of rural toryism," he remarked. Being a good politician, he compromised with the agrarians, but his heart and head were elsewhere. An admirer of organization, a seeker of power, and a glorifier of strength, Roosevelt was really devoted to the New Nationalism. In the interstices of that bundle of doctrines first expounded at Osawatomie and later in the campaign of 1912 lay the seeds of much of the promise and most of the peril of the next fifty years.[32]

Ideology, of course, is only one of many elements that decide national political contests. Personality, organization, money, myth, and chance are all weighty counters in the final result. But the conflicting ideas within the Republican party were significant factors in its temporary disintegration. In the three-cornered fight for the Republican nomination Roosevelt defeated La Follette, only to be defeated in turn by Taft at the national nominating convention. In an angry burst of ambition and conviction, Roosevelt founded his Progressive party in an attempt to rally all progressive sentiment to his support. Neither La Follette nor enough of the country responded. Roosevelt ran well ahead of Taft but considerably behind Woodrow Wilson and the Democrats. And with Wilson's election the Republican phase of the progressive movement had come to an end.[33]

[32] Roosevelt to A. W. Cooley, August 29, 1911, Roosevelt MSS.

[33] For a detailed account of the 1912 primary and general election contest, see the following volume of this series, Arthur S. Link, *Woodrow Wilson and the Progressive Era, 1910–1917* (New York, 1954).

Bibliography

Manuscripts

Among the most important sources for tracing the rise and fall of the progressive mind as contrasted to progressive politics are the Papers of Oswald Garrison Villard, Houghton Library, Harvard University; the Papers of William Allen White, Library of Congress; the Albert Shaw Manuscripts, New York Public Library; the Papers of Louis D. Brandeis, Law School Library, University of Louisville; and the Papers of Ray Stannard Baker, Charles Edward Russell, and Louis F. Post, all in the Library of Congress. Shaw was the editor of *World's Work,* Baker and Russell were muckraking periodical writers, and Post was for four years the editor of *The Public,* the Midwestern reform magazine dedicated to the fortunes of the Democratic party. Of lesser importance on the same subject are the Papers of Amos Pinchot, the Papers of Finley Peter Dunne, and the small group of letters of Clarence Darrow, all in the Library of Congress. The Papers of Samuel Gompers, American Federation of Labor Archives, Washington; the Papers of Frank Parsons, Yale University; and the unfortunately small Lincoln Steffens Collection, Bancroft Library, University of California, Berkeley, should also be consulted. For special phases of the rise of the reform spirit, see the large Benjamin B. Lindsey Collection, the Papers of Jane Addams, and the Papers of Susan B. Anthony in the Library of Congress.

For the growth of eastern progressivism in the cities and the states, see the Papers of William E. Chandler, New Hampshire Historical Society, Concord; the Seth Low Collection, Columbia University; and the Papers of John Purroy Mitchell and the Jacob A. Riis Manuscripts in the Library of Congress. The Papers of Bainbridge Colby, Library of Congress, were mostly written after 1912; those of Charles Evans Hughes, Library of Congress, are disappointingly thin; and the Woodrow Wilson Manuscripts, Library of Congress, contain very few letters to and from progressives until after 1910.

The evolution of progressivism in the Midwest can be traced in the Papers of Hazen Pingree, Detroit Public Library, and the Chase S. Osborne Papers,

University of Michigan. The Albert J. Beveridge Papers, Library of Congress, form a huge and valuable collection. The Papers of Herbert S. Hadley, University of Missouri; the John A. Johnson Papers, Minnesota Historical Society; and the Coe I. Crawford, S. X. Way, and Peter Norbeck Collections, University of South Dakota, are valuable for their particular states. Some of the Papers of Robert M. La Follette on his state career are open in the State Historical Society of Wisconsin. For Wisconsin also see the Papers of Francis E. McGovern, James O. Davidson, and Charles R. McCarthy in the State Historical Society. In Iowa, the Papers of Albert B. Cummins, Historical Memorial and Art Department of Iowa, Des Moines, and the Papers of Jonathan P. Dolliver, Iowa State Historical Society, Iowa City, are best. The Walter R. Stubbs and Joseph H. Bristow Collections, Kansas State Historical Society, are slight but informative.

On the mountain region the Papers of Edward P. Costigan, University of Colorado, Boulder; the John A. Shafroth Papers, Colorado State Archives, Denver; and the George Curry Papers, Historical Society of New Mexico, Santa Fe, are useful. In the Northwest the Papers of Miles Poindexter, University of Washington, Seattle (on microfilm), and the Jonathan Bourne, Jr., Papers, University of Oregon, Eugene, supply evidence of the mounting protest against the old politics especially after 1910.

For California developments, see especially the Papers of Hiram Johnson, and the Chester Rowell Manuscripts, Bancroft Library, University of California, Berkeley; the Papers of Meyer Lissner, Stanford University; and the William Kent Collection, Yale University. The Papers of George C. Pardee and John D. Works, Bancroft Library, University of California, Berkeley; the John D. Works Collection, Stanford University; and the Papers of John Randolph Haynes, and the Edward A. Dickson Collection, Haynes Foundation, University of California, Los Angeles, are also useful.

The South has not been as fortunate in the collection of manuscripts in the recent period as have other sections. For various southern aspects of the revolt against the old politics, see the Thomas E. Watson Papers, University of North Carolina; the Papers of Benjamin R. Tillman, University of South Carolina; the disappointing William Jennings Bryan Papers, Library of Congress and the National Archives; and the very large collection of Josephus Daniels Papers, Library of Congress. For other manuscript material on the rise of local movements across the nation, see the entries under the Roosevelt and Taft administrations.

THE ROOSEVELT ADMINISTRATIONS

On Theodore Roosevelt's administrations three large collections are of prime importance. The Papers of Theodore Roosevelt, Library of Congress, and subsidiary collections in the New York Historical Society and the Harvard College Library, are invaluable. Roosevelt was a prodigious letter writer, and his correspondence touched upon most of the cultural and political questions of the day. The William Howard Taft Papers, Library of Congress, are also of great significance for the Roosevelt years, as well as the Papers of Elihu Root, Library of Congress. The papers of most of the other members of Roosevelt's Cabinets are available. The Papers of John Hay, the Philander C. Knox Collection, the Papers of James R. Garfield, and the Papers of Charles J. Bonaparte, all in the Library of Congress, are essential. Either because of their meager quantity or quality, the Papers of Oscar S. Straus, which include a manuscript diary, the Papers of William Henry Moody, and the Lyman J. Gage Collection, in the Library of Congress, are of lesser importance. Of particular value for the conservation movement are the voluminous manuscripts of Gifford Pinchot, Library of Congress. Of the lesser important figures in the Roosevelt administration the following collections are useful: the Harvey W. Wiley Papers, the Papers of Frederick H. Newell, the Journals of W. Cameron Forbes, the Henry White Papers, the Papers of Whitelaw Reid, the Chandler P. Anderson Papers, the Philippe Bunau-Varilla Papers, the Cecil Spring-Rice Correspondence with Theodore Roosevelt, the Leonard Wood Papers, the George Goethals Papers, and those of James H. Wilson and General Robert Lee Bullard, all in the Library of Congress. The papers of William W. Rockhill, Harvard College Library, are useful for Chinese affairs.

THE TAFT ADMINISTRATION

Of primary importance is the huge Collection of William Howard Taft, Library of Congress, numbering over a thousand portfolios. The President's manuscripts are of particular importance because very few collections of his Cabinet members are available. Among these are the Knox papers already mentioned; the Papers of Franklin Mac Veagh, Library of Congress; and the Henry L. Stimson Papers, Yale Library. The manuscripts of James W. Wickersham are in possession of the family in New York City and are not open to students. The above may be supplemented by the James S. Sherman Papers, New York Public Library, a large collection but of minor value, by the papers of many of the less significant figures of the Roosevelt administration, and by the papers of congressmen and senators listed below.

CONGRESS

The nature and philosophy of the conservative leadership of the Senate are well documented in the Nelson W. Aldrich Papers, Library of Congress, which will be opened in the immediate future to scholars; the large collection of William B. Allison Papers, Historical, Memorial and Art Department of Iowa, Des Moines; the rather unsatisfactory Papers of John C. Spooner, Library of Congress; and the small collection of political letters to and from Orville H. Platt, State Library, Hartford, Connecticut. The important papers of Henry Cabot Lodge, Massachusetts Historical Society, are temporarily closed. But the Papers of Joseph Benson Foraker, Library of Congress and the Historical and Philosophical Society of Ohio, Cincinnati, although showing signs of family editing, are extremely interesting. The above may be supplemented by the Papers of Thomas H. Carter, Library of Congress; the Papers of Jacob H. Gallinger, New Hampshire Historical Society; the Francis E. Warren Papers, University of Wyoming, Laramie; and the already noted collections of Philander C. Knox and James S. Sherman. For the House of Representatives the best equivalent collections are the Papers of James A. Tawney, Minnesota Historical Society, St. Paul; the James R. Mann Collection, Library of Congress; and the Papers of John C. Lacey and James T. Hull, both in the Historical, Memorial and Art Department of Iowa, Des Moines.

For the progressive Republicans the most useful are the large collection of Albert J. Beveridge Papers, Library of Congress; the similar extensive but incomplete Papers of Albert B. Cummins, Historical, Memorial and Art Department of Iowa; the small but valuable Jonathan P. Dolliver Papers, Iowa State Historical Society, Iowa City; the massive Papers of Miles Poindexter, University of Virginia, which are also on microfilm at the University of Washington, Seattle; and the Papers of Knute Nelson, Minnesota Historical Society, St. Paul; and of Joseph L. Bristow, Kansas Historical Society, Topeka. Two important collections are not yet open: the major part of the Robert M. La Follette Papers in possession of Fola La Follette, and the William Borah Collection, Library of Congress. Of lesser significance but still important are the Papers of Moses Clapp, Minnesota Historical Society; the Jonathan Bourne Collection, Oregon Historical Society; the Elmer J. Burkett Manuscripts, in possession of the family, Lincoln, Nebraska; and the Coe I. Crawford Papers, University of South Dakota. For the Republican progressives in the House the most useful are the Papers of George W. Norris and Augustus P. Gardner, Library of Congress; the Papers of Nils P. Haugen and John Jacob Esch, State Historical Society of Wisconsin; the Charles A. Lindbergh Collection, Minnesota Historical Society, St. Paul; and the Charles D. Willard Collection, Huntington Library, San Marino, California.

Democratic strategy and policies in the Senate are well revealed in the Lee S. Overman Papers, University of North Carolina; the Francis J. Newlands Collection, Yale University; the Benjamin R. Tillman Papers, University of South Carolina; the Furnifold M. Simmons Manuscripts, Duke University Library; and the Papers of Gilbert M. Hitchcock, Library of Congress. Hitchcock was a member of the House until 1911 and thereafter in the Senate. For the House of Representatives, Democratic policy can best be seen in the John Sharp William Papers, Library of Congress; the Papers of Henry T. Rainey, Library of Congress; and the important Carter Glass Collection, Alderman Library, University of Virginia. Of particular value for the period after 1910 are the Claude Kitchen Papers, University of North Carolina. Of less use for the Roosevelt and Taft periods are the Henry D. Flood Papers, Library of Congress; the John H. Bankhead Manuscripts and the Oscar W. Underwood Papers, Alabama Department of Archives, Montgomery; the Francis B. Harrison papers and the Papers of Richard P. Hobson, both in the Library of Congress; and the Bourke W. Cochran Collection, New York Public Library.

MISCELLANEOUS

Among the papers of newspaper editors and writers not already mentioned, the most important are the Henry Watterson Collection, Library of Congress; the Papers of Lucius B. Swift, Indiana Historical Society, Bloomington; the William D. Foulke Collections, Library of Congress and the Indiana Historical Society; and the Papers of Owen Wister, Library of Congress.

Among the great manuscript collections of the United States few are more important for their total history than that of the Adams Family Papers, Massachusetts Historical Society. This recently opened collection contains the manuscripts of Brooks and Henry Adams, both close friends of Roosevelt, who influenced the President on several important matters of policy. The Nicholas Murray Butler Papers, Columbia University Library, contain the thought of this important low-tariff conservative Republican. The Richard Olney Papers, Library of Congress, reflect both the thought and the influence of this influential conservative Democrat. The large Booker T. Washington Collection, Library of Congress, is invaluable for Negro opinion and contains information about Roosevelt's southern racial policy. For business opinion, see the Henry Lee Higginson Papers, Houghton Library, Harvard University; the George Foster Peabody Collection, Library of Congress; and the Papers of General Grenville M. Dodge, Historical, Memorial and Art Department of Iowa, Des Moines. The Dodge Letters are particularly useful for railroad matters and for Midwestern conservative business attitudes. After Andrew Carnegie sold his steel mills he turned to world peace and business reform. The Carnegie Papers, Library of Congress, are valuable as the record of a social Darwinist who became a progressive.

The very few items in the Alfred Mahan Papers, Library of Congress, are important for naval and world policy. The Papers of Lafayette Young, Historical, Memorial and Art Department of Iowa, reflect the conservatism of a Midwest publisher and politician, as do the Papers of George Perkins in the same institution. Moreton Frewen was a British subject who carried on a large transatlantic correspondence on United States affairs. His Papers, Library of Congress, are significant for their relatively detached view of men and issues.

Published Letters and Writings

Elting E. Morison and John M. Blum (eds.), *The Letters of Theodore Roosevelt* (8 vols., Cambridge, 1951–54), is superbly edited. These volumes contain about one-fifth of Roosevelt's letters, extremely well selected and annotated. They also include a number of brilliant essays on the President and his policy. They should be supplemented by *The Works of Theodore Roosevelt* (20 vols., National Edition, New York, 1926), which contain most of Roosevelt's important public speeches. Henry Cabot Lodge (ed.), *Selections from the Correspondence of Theodore Roosevelt and Henry Cabot Lodge, 1884–1918* (2 vols., New York, 1925), has strange omissions and should be checked with Roosevelt's own manuscripts. Will Irwin (ed.), *Letters to Kermit from Theodore Roosevelt, 1902–1908* (New York, 1946), gives an intimate view of Roosevelt.

Unfortunately neither the letters nor speeches of William Howard Taft have been published. But a number of volumes exist which contain the correspondence of lesser figures. Among the more important of these are Arthur H. Darling (ed.), *The Public Papers of Francis G. Newlands* (2 vols., Boston, 1932); Colin B. Goodykoontz (ed.), *The Papers of Edward P. Costigan Relating to the Progressive Movement in Colorado, 1902–17* (Boulder, 1941); Anne W. Lane and Louis H. Wall (eds.), *The Letters of Franklin K. Lane, Personal and Political* (Boston, 1922); Constance Gardner (ed.), *Some Letters of Augustus Peabody Gardner* (Boston, 1920); Stephen Gwynn (ed.), *The Letters and Friendships of Sir Cecil Spring-Rice* (2 vols., Boston, 1929); and T. B. Moore, *The Collected Papers of John Bassett Moore* (7 vols., New Haven, 1945). Moore was America's leading scholar on international law, a frequent adviser to the State Department.

Among the printed collections for the nonpolitical figures, Ella Winter and Granville Hicks (eds.), *The Letters of Lincoln Steffens* (2 vols., New York, 1938), are perhaps of most consequence to the student of progressivism. The volumes supplement the few letters of Steffens which are available in manuscript collections. Also of importance is Walter Johnson (ed.), *Selected Letters of William Allen White, 1899–1943* (New York, 1947). These letters, selected to depict White rather than his views, are nevertheless extremely informative. Allen Nevins (ed.), *The Letters and Journal of Brand Whitlock* (2 vols., New York, 1936), gives a good insight into the mentality of one of the early municipal reformers. Burton J. Hendrick, *The Life and Letters of Walter Hines Page* (3 vols., Garden City, N.Y., 1924–26), should be used with caution.

Among the more strictly literary figures, Mildred Howells (ed.), *Life in Letters of William Dean Howells* (2 vols., New York, 1928), is of great value in assaying middle-class thought of the period. Worthington C. Ford (ed.), *The Letters of Henry Adams, 1892–1918* (Boston, 1932), throws light upon an important and original mind. Newton Arvin (ed.), *The Selected Letters of Henry Adams* (New York, 1951), is of less use. Donald Hazen (ed.), *The Letters of William Roscoe Thayer* (New York, 1926), prints the correspondence of a friend and a biographer of Theodore Roosevelt.

Newspapers

The New York Times during the period was by far the most comprehensive newspaper in its coverage and one of the most objective. Unfortunately its published index was not started until 1912 and that of the New York *Tribune* stopped in the early years of the decade. Of all the pro-administration papers between 1901–12, the New York *Tribune* was probably the best, although it was inclined to be more favorable to Taft than to Roosevelt. Among the more consistent Roosevelt papers were the Kansas City *Star,* the Chicago *Tribune,* and the Des Moines *Register.* The New York *Sun* was the voice of extreme conservatism on the East coast, the Los Angeles *Times* on the West. Two independent papers worthy of note are the Springfield *Republican* and the New York *Post.*

Of the Democratic papers, the New York *World* was probably the best, especially after 1904, when Frank Cobb joined its editorial staff. Other representative Democratic papers included the Baltimore *Sun,* the Louisville *Courier Journal,* the St. Louis *Post Dispatch,* and the Raleigh *News and Observer.*

Most ardent and consistent in their progressive policy were the Philadelphia *North American,* the Kansas City *Star,* the Des Moines *Register,* the San Francisco *Bulletin,* and the Los Angeles *Express.* The Hearst chain was both extremely radical and nationalistic in the early years of the decade, but its social policy became less vigorous as the years progressed. The most important Hearst papers were the original paper of the chain, the San Francisco *Examiner,* and the New York *American* and the Chicago *American.*

The left-wing position was well reflected by the New York *Call.* Of vast importance in reflecting the conservative-radical, anarchistic-socialistic, agrarian opinion was the Girard (Kansas) *Appeal to Reason.*

Periodicals

The first decade of the twentieth century was the golden day of the magazine with a political message, the most outstanding development in such publishing being the rise of the so-called muckrake journals, magazines cheap in price but devoted to a clinical and critical study of phases of life and politics. The sober and serious *Arena,* with a small circulation, was the first in the field, and is important because of its New England religious flavor. Others with far more circulation, color, and influence were *McClure's, Pearson's, Everybody's, American,* and *Cosmopolitan.* Because it took the lead in the Ballinger-Pinchot controversy, *Collier's* is especially important for the Taft period.

Two middle-of-the-road progressive journals inclined to support the Roosevelt policies were *The Outlook* and *World's Work*. Edited by the Abbott brothers, *The Outlook* was the popular voice of the evangelical Protestant reform. Roosevelt wrote regularly for the magazine after 1910. Dr. Albert Shaw, editor of *World's Work,* was particularly interested in civic reform and civic planning. Two ardent regional progressive periodicals were the Midwestern *Public* and the *California Weekly and Pacific Outlook. The Nation* continued its traditional classical liberal attitudes. *La Follette's Magazine* was the personal voice of the Wisconsin senator after 1909, and *The Commoner,* Lincoln, Nebraska, retailed the views of William Jennings Bryan.

The conservative approach can be seen in George Harvey's *North American Review* and in the *San Francisco Argonaut.* The *Literary Digest* and the old *Current Opinion* are useful for their excellent summary of press opinion from around the world. More specialized in their interests are the *American Federationist,* the voice of the trade unions; *Capper's Weekly,* a leading farm journal; and the *Commercial and Financial Chronicle,* the *Wall Street Journal,* and the *New York Journal of Commerce. The Scientific American* is especially valuable for its excellent articles on technical and scientific developments.

Memoirs

The period is rich in personal memories of the leading figures of the age. Among the most important of such volumes are Theodore Roosevelt, *An Autobiography* (New York, 1921), which should be used with considerable caution; Archie Butt, *Taft and Roosevelt; The Intimate Letters of Archie Butt* (New York, 1930), informative but also at times misleading; Owen Wister, *Roosevelt: The Story of a Friendship* (New York, 1930); and John S. Leary, Jr., *Talks with T.R.* (New York, 1920). Robert M. La Follette, *Autobiography* (Madison, Wis., 1911), was written in part as a campaign document. George W. Norris, *Fighting Liberal: The Autobiography of George W. Norris* (New York, 1945), only hints at the real stature of the man. Gifford Pinchot, *Breaking New Ground* (New York, 1947), is a partisan but essential source for the history of conservation. Much useful material can be obtained from Nicholas Murray Butler, *Across the Busy Years* (2 vols., New York, 1939–40); Henry L. Stimson, *On Active Service in Peace and War* (New York, 1948), gives some information on New York politics and on the Taft administration.

Mary B. Bryan (ed.), *The Memoirs of William Jennings Bryan* (Philadelphia, 1925), is useful for a study of Bryan's motivation and purposes. Champ Clark, *My Quarter Century of American Politics* (2 vols., New York, 1920), is extremely disappointing. Other minor books by major political figures include Joseph B. Foraker, *Notes of a Busy Life* (Cincinnati, 1911); Shelby M. Cullom, *Fifty Years of Public Service* (Chicago, 1911); Oscar S. Straus, *Under Four Administrations; From Cleveland to Taft* (New York, 1922); and Mrs. William H. Taft, *Recollections of Full Years* (New York, 1914).

The personal accounts of less important political participants are also plentiful. Among the more essential are Tom L. Johnson, *My Story* (New York, 1911); James E. Watson, *As I Knew Them* (Indianapolis, 1936); Isaac Stephenson, *Recollections of a Long Life* (Chicago, 1915); Philippe Bunau-Varilla, *Panama, the Creation, Destruction and Resurrection* (London, 1913), and *From Panama to Verdun; My Fight for France* (Philadelphia, 1940); William S. Vare, *My Forty Years in Politics* (Philadelphia, 1933); Oscar W. Underwood, *Drifting Sand of Party Politics* (New York, 1928); Cyrenus Cole, *I Remember, I Remember* (Iowa City, 1936); James M. Cox, *Journey Through My Years* (New York, 1946); Harold L. Ickes, *Autobiography of a Curmudgeon* (New York, 1943); Carter Henry Harrison, *Stormy Years* (New York, 1935); and Dr. Harvey Wiley, *An Autobiography* (Indianapolis, 1930).

Four most essential books for sampling the spirit, if not the facts, of the period are Lincoln Steffens, *The Autobiography of Lincoln Steffens* (2 vols., New York, 1931), one of the great autobiographical efforts of recent history; William Allen White, *The Autobiography of William Allen White* (New York, 1946); Henry Adams, *The Education of Henry Adams* (New York, 1918); and Oswald Garrison Villard, *Memoirs of a Liberal Editor* (New York, 1939). Other important works by journalists or publishers are Brand Whitlock, *Forty Years of It* (New York, 1914); Charles E. Russell, *Bare Hands and Stone Walls: Some Recollections of a Sideline Reformer* (New York, 1933); S. S. McClure, *My Autobiography* (New York, 1914); Frederic C. Howe, *The Confessions of a Reformer* (New York, 1925); Fremont Older, *My Own Story* (New York, 1926); Ida Tarbell, *All in the Day's Work* (New York, 1939); and Ray Stannard Baker, *American Chronicle* (New York, 1945). The last is not as complete on the progressive period as the student might wish.

Largely because of their relations with major political figures, the following are useful: Henry L. Stoddard, *As I Knew Them* (New York, 1927); H. H. Kohlsaat, *From McKinley to Harding* (New York, 1923); Arthur W. Dunn, *From Harrison to Harding* (2 vols., New York, 1922); Oscar King Davis, *Released for Publication* (New York, 1945); and Josephus Daniels, *Editor in Politics* (Chapel Hill, 1941).

Samuel Gompers, *Seventy Years of Life and Labor: An Autobiography* (2 vols., New York, 1925), is the revealing work of the dean of American labor. Equally important is the remembrance of Morris Hillquit, *Loose Leaves from a Busy Life* (New York, 1934), giving the point of view of a Socialist labor leader. Thomas J. Coolidge, *The Autobiography of T. Jefferson Coolidge,* gives a good portrait of the mind of a conservative Republican man of affairs. A conservative Democratic business viewpoint can be found in Perry Belmont, *An American Democrat, The Recollections of Perry Belmont* (New York, 1940). Richard T. Ely, *Ground Under Our Feet; An Autobiography* (New York, 1938); John R. Commons, *Myself* (New York, 1934); and Edward A. Ross, *Seventy Years of It* (New York, 1937), bear the testimony of scholar-reformers.

Other personal records include Lyman Abbott, *Reminiscences* (New York, 1915); William D. Foulke, *A Hoosier Autobiography* (New York, 1922); Henry Watterson, *"Marse Henry"* (2 vols., New York, 1919); Alice Longworth Roosevelt, *Crowded Hours* (New York, 1933); Victor Rosewater, *Backstage in 1912* (Philadelphia, 1932); Julia Foraker, *I Would Live It Again* (New York, 1932); and Charles R. Flint, *Memoirs of a Busy Life* (New York, 1933).

General Works

No attempt will be made to list all the books dealing with each particular subject. To do so would require far more pages than are available. Therefore only books that the author used which are either not mentioned in the footnotes or which have a much wider importance than particular citation indicates will appear in the following sections. Among the few general works covering the entire period in detail, by far the best are two by Harold U. Faulkner, *The Decline of Laissez-Faire, 1897–1917* (New York, 1951), and *The Quest for Social Justice, 1898–1914* (New York, 1931). As the titles indicate, the first deals mainly with economic and social phenomena and the second with the more general aspects of the progressive movement. Mark Sullivan, *Our Times, The United States 1900–1925* (6 vols., New York, 1926–35), is the work of an intelligent journalist, valuable among other reasons for its observations on popular culture. Two most necessary biographies are by Henry F. Pringle, *Theodore Roosevelt, A Biography* (New York, 1931), and *The Life and Times of William Howard Taft* (2 vols., New York, 1939). One of the most readable books of its kind, the Roosevelt volume is slight and perhaps underestimates the importance of its subject. Although much more detailed and scholarly, the Taft volume also needs corrections here and there. A sectional study, Russel B. Nye, *Midwestern Progressive Politics* (East Lansing, 1951), is excellent within its limits.

Henry S. Commager, *The American Mind, An Interpretation of American Thought and Character Since the 1880's* (New Haven, 1952), is invaluable for its field, as is Morton G. White, *Social Thought in America, the Revolt Against Formalism* (New York, 1949). By far the finest single interpretation of twentieth-century American literature is Alfred Kazin, *On Native Grounds* (New York, 1942), but the student should also consult Oscar Cargill, *Intellectual America* (New York, 1941), and John Chamberlain, *Farewell to Reform* (New York, 1932).

Not confined to the progressive period but containing extremely valuable and brilliant insights into the progressive mind are Richard Hofstadter, *The Age of Reform, From Bryan to F.D.R.* (New York, 1955), and Eric F. Goldman, *Rendezvous With Destiny* (New York, 1952). Three other fine works which contribute in the same manner are Daniel Aaron, *Men of Good Hope* (New York, 1951); Louis Hartz, *The Liberal Tradition in America* (New York, 1954); and Arthur Ekirch, Jr., *The Decline of American Liberalism* (New York, 1956).

Material America

The only good detailed survey of the farmer and his problems in this period is Theodore Saloutos and John D. Hicks, *Agricultural Discontent in the Middle West, 1900–1939* (Madison, Wis., 1951). But see also Fred A. Shannon, "The Status of the Midwestern Farmer in 1900," *Mississippi Valley Historical Review*, XXXVII (1950), 491. For the status of labor, see John R. Commons and associates, *History of Labor in the United States* (New York, 1918), V, and Foster R. Dulles, *Labor in America: A History* (New York, 1949). On the business mind, the rise of monopoly, and finance capitalism, see Edward C. Kirkland, *Dream and Thought in the Business Community, 1860–1900* (Madison, Wis., 1956), and T. C. Cochran and William Miller, *The Age of Enterprise* (New York, 1942). More technical are Eliot Jones, *The Trust Problem in the United States* (New York, 1924), and Arthur R. Burns, *The Decline of Competition* (New York, 1936). On the new immigration, John Higham, *Strangers in the Land* (New Brunswick, N.J., 1955), and Oscar Handlin, *The Uprooted* (Boston, 1951), are excellent.

Intellectual Tides

The appropriate chapters in Richard Hofstadter, *Social Darwinism in American Thought, 1860–1905* (Philadelphia, 1944); Sidney Fine, *Laissez Faire and the General Welfare State* (Ann Arbor, 1956); and Joseph Dorfman, *The Economic Mind in American Civilization* (New York, 1949), III, offer an excellent start for an examination of the American political mind in the twentieth century. See also Merle Curti, *The Growth of American Thought* (New York, 1943), and Ralph H. Gabriel, *The Course of American Democratic Thought* (New York, 1940). For the academician's contributions to the rational discussion, see Merle Curti, *The Social Ideals of American Educators* (New York, 1935). Joseph Dorfman, *Thorstein Veblen and His*

America (New York, 1934); James R. Everett, *Religion in Economics: A Study of John Bates Clark, Richard T. Ely and Simon Patten* (New York, 1946); and Sidney Fine, "Richard T. Ely, Forerunner of Progressivism," *Mississippi Valley Historical Review*, XXXVII (1951), 599, are also worth while. Among other important biographies that contribute to the subject are Charles A. Barker, *Henry George* (New York, 1955); Arthur F. Beringause, *Brooks Adams* (New York, 1955); William H. Jordy, *Henry Adams: Scientific Historian* (New Haven, 1952); Catherine D. Bowen, *Yankee from Olympus: Justice Holmes and His Family* (Boston, 1944); and Felix Frankfurter, *Mr. Justice Holmes and the Supreme Court* (Cambridge, 1938). Of seminal importance for this chapter is Ralph B. Perry, *The Thought and Character of William James* (2 vols., Boston, 1935). Mark A. DeWolfe Howe, *The Correspondence of Mr. Justice Holmes and Sir Frederick Pollock* (Cambridge, 1941), is rewarding, as is M. H. Fisch, "Justice Holmes, the Prediction Theory of Law and Pragmatism," *Journal of Philosophy*, XXXIX (1942), 312.

Among a number of very good studies of the change in religion are Charles H. Hopkins, *The Rise of the Social Gospel in American Protestantism, 1860–1915* (New Haven, 1940); Henry F. May, *Protestant Churches and Industrial America* (New York, 1949); Stow Persons, *Free Religion: An American Faith* (New Haven, 1947); and Edward A. White, *Science and Religion in American Thought: The Impact of Naturalism* (Stanford, Calif., 1952). More specific studies include V. P. Bodein, *The Social Gospel of Walter Rauschenbusch and Its Relation to Religious Education* (New Haven, 1944); Ira V. Brown, *Lyman Abbott, Christian Evolutionist* (Cambridge, 1953); and Sidney Warren, *American Free Thought, 1860–1914* (New York, 1943), the study of free-thought press and literature.

There is no good study of the American woman as a social and intellectual group in existence. One has to depend therefore mostly on biographies. Among the best of these are Mary Earhart, *Frances Willard* (Chicago, 1944); Jane Addams, *My Friend Julia Lathrop* (New York, 1935); Josephine Goldmark, *Impatient Crusader; Florence Kelley's Life Story* (Urbana, 1953); Mary G. Pick, *Carrie Chapman Catt: A Biography* (New York, 1944); and R. L. Duffus, *Lillian Wald, Neighbor and Crusader* (New York, 1938). Jane Addams, *Twenty Years at Hull House* (Chicago, 1910), and Lillian D. Wald, *The House on Henry Street* (New York, 1915), are relevant memoirs.

Conservative, Radical, and Progressive

Until very recently scholars have paid little attention to conservatism. Since no good study of recent conservatism exists, the student is forced to go to the scattered writings and utterances of the period's major figures. Among the biographies particularly helpful are Philip C. Jessup, *Elihu Root* (2 vols.,

New York, 1938); Richard W. Leopold, *Elihu Root and the Conservative Tradition* (Boston, 1954); John A. Garraty, *Henry Cabot Lodge* (New York, 1953); Nathaniel W. Stephenson, *Nelson W. Aldrich* (New York, 1930); and Hermann Hagedorn, *Leonard Wood* (2 vols., New York, 1931). Of special interest are Bernard E. Brown, *American Conservatives: The Political Thought of Francis Lieber and John W. Burgess* (New York, 1951), and H. E. Barnes, "William Graham Sumner," *Sociological Review,* XIV (1922), 209. For judicial conservatism, see Louis B. Boudin, *Government by Judiciary* (2 vols., New York, 1932); Max Lerner, *The Mind and Faith of Justice Holmes* (New York, 1943); and Willard L. King, *Melville Weston Fuller* (New York, 1950).

Compared to the literature on conservatism, that on radicalism is rich. Among the good general works are the comprehensive Donald D. Egbert and Stow Persons (eds.), *Socialism and American Life* (2 vols., Princeton, 1952); David A. Shannon, *The Socialist Party of America* (New York, 1955); Howard H. Quint, *The Forging of American Socialism* (Columbia, S.C., 1953), which covers only the earliest period; Ira Kipnis, *The American Socialist Movement, 1897–1912* (New York, 1952); and Paul F. Brissenden, *The I.W.W.* (New York, 1919). Students should also see *The Writings and Speeches of Eugene V. Debs* (New York, 1948), and Marvin Wachman, *History of the Social Democratic Party of Milwaukee, 1897–1910* (Urbana, 1945). Among the better biographies are Ray Ginger, *The Bending Cross: A Biography of Eugene V. Debs* (New Brunswick, N.J., 1944), and Matthew Josephson, *Sidney Hillman* (New York, 1952). Chester M. Destler, *American Radicalism, 1865–1901* (New London, Conn., 1946), just approaches the period, but contains a number of interesting observations on the early Socialist developments.

For an analysis of progressive political thought, see Hofstadter, *The Age of Reform,* and Goldman, *Rendezvous with Destiny,* already cited. But the student should not overlook Thomas H. Greer, *American Social Reform Movements: Their Pattern Since 1865* (New York, 1949), and Chapter 4 of George E. Mowry, *The California Progressives* (Berkeley and Los Angeles, 1952). Arthur M. Schlesinger, *The American as a Reformer* (Cambridge, 1950), and *Paths to the Present* (New York, 1949), are both useful. C. Vann Woodward, *Origins of the New South* (Baton Rouge, La., 1951), contains some exceptionally pertinent material on southern developments.

The Struggle for the Cities and the States

Some excellent works deal with the older and more corrupt municipal politics. Among the best of them are Walton E. Bean, *Boss Reuf's San Francisco: The Story of the Union Labor Party, Big Business and Graft Prosecution* (Berkeley and Los Angeles, 1952); G. M. Reynolds, *Machine Politics in*

New Orleans 1897–1926 (New York, 1936); Howard Zink, *City Bosses in the United States* (Durham, N.C., 1930); and L. Wendt and H. Kogen, *Lords of the Levee: The Story of Bath House John and Hinky Dink* (Indianapolis, 1943). James T. Salter, *The American Politician* (Chapel Hill, 1938), also contains pertinent material.

For the period before 1900, Clifford W. Patton, *The Battle for Municipal Reform: Mobilization and Attack, 1875–1900* (Washington, 1940), is adequate. But for the twentieth century no really good study of the municipal reform crusade exists. Nye, *Midwestern Progressive Politics,* already mentioned, contains some excellent material on the Middle Western reform mayors. L. Ware, *Jacob Riis, Police Reporter, Reformer, Useful Citizen* (New York, 1938), covers one phase of the New York City movement. Arthur Mann, *Yankee Reformers in the Urban Age* (Cambridge, 1954), is much wider in scope. For a comprehensive view, consult the autobiographies of the city reformers, municipal histories, and contemporary magazine articles.

The reform movement in the states is more adequately covered. Ransome E. Noble, *New Jersey Progressivism Before Wilson* (Princeton, 1946); George E. Mowry, *The California Progressives,* already mentioned; and Winston A. Flint, *The Progressive Movement in Vermont* (Washington, 1941), are satisfactory. Less so are Elizabeth Ring, *The Progressive Movement of 1912 and the Third Party Movement of 1924 in Maine* (Orono, Me., 1933); E. N. Doan, *The La Follettes and the Wisconsin Idea* (New York, 1947); and Robert S. Maxwell, *La Follette and the Rise of the Progressives in Wisconsin* (Madison, Wis., 1956). A. D. Kirwan, *The Revolt of the Rednecks; Mississippi Politics, 1876–1925* (Lexington, Ky., 1951), is of special value for its study of poor-white sentiment. Much other material will be found in state histories and biographies too numerous to mention here individually.

C. C. Regier, *The Era of the Muckrakers* (Chapel Hill, 1932), and Louis Filler, *Crusaders for American Liberalism* (Yellow Springs, Ohio, 1950), do justice to the muckrakers as a group. Special mention should also be made of Elmer Ellis, *Mr. Dooley's America; A Life of Finley Peter Dunne* (New York, 1941).

Among the better biographies of state reformers are Arthur S. Link, *Wilson: The Road to the White House* (Princeton, 1947); Merlo J. Pusey, *Charles Evans Hughes* (2 vols., New York, 1951); Dexter Perkins, *Charles Evans Hughes and American Democratic Statesmanship* (Boston, 1956); C. Vann Woodward, *Tom Watson, Agrarian Rebel* (New York, 1938); Francis B. Simkins, *Pitchfork Ben Tillman, South Carolinian* (Baton Rouge, La., 1944); Winifred G. Helmes, *John A. Johnson* (Minneapolis, 1949); and E. A. Fitzpatrick, *McCarthy of Wisconsin* (New York, 1944). For the reform movement in the South, Dewey W. Grantham, Jr., "Hoke Smith; Progressive

Governor of Georgia," *Journal of Southern History*, XV (1949), 423, should also be consulted.

The Progressive Mind

Three very important works on progressive theory of this period should not be overlooked: W. Herbert Croly, *The Promise of American Life* (New York, 1909); Walter Lippmann, *Drift and Mastery* (New York, 1914); and Walter Weyl, *The New Democracy* (New York, 1912). Two other books of major importance to the subject are Simon Patten, *The New Basis of Civilization* (New York, 1907), and William G. Brown, *The New Politics and Other Papers* (Boston, 1914). In addition to the titles cited under sections entitled General Works and Conservative, Radical, and Progressive, see the definitive John D. Hicks, *The Populist Revolt* (Minneapolis, 1931), and Walter Johnson, *William Allen White's America* (New York, 1947).

Roosevelt, The First Years

For varying interpretations of the character of Roosevelt in addition to the one by Pringle, see the brilliant John M. Blum, *The Republican Roosevelt* (Boston, 1954), and, by the same author, "Theodore Roosevelt: The Years of Decision" in Morison and Blum, *Roosevelt Letters*, II, 1484. Richard Hofstadter, *The American Political Tradition and the Men Who Made It* (New York, 1948), contains an able chapter on Roosevelt. Matthew Josephson, *The President Makers* (New York, 1940), should also be consulted as well as the older works: J. B. Bishop, *Theodore Roosevelt and His Times Shown in His Own Letters* (New York, 1920); William R. Thayer, *Theodore Roosevelt* (Boston, 1919); and Lawrence F. Abbott, *Impressions of Theodore Roosevelt* (New York, 1920).

On the Northern Securities Case, Balthasar Meyer, *A History of the Northern Securities Case* (University of Wisconsin Bulletin, No. 142, Madison, 1906), is an almost contemporary account. Other useful material is found in the court record, *Northern Securities Co. et al. v. United States*, 193 U.S. 360, 1904; Henry Clews, *Fifty Years on Wall Street* (New York, 1915); James G. Pyle, *The Life of James J. Hill* (New York, 1917); and Frederick L. Allen, *The Great Pierpont Morgan* (New York, 1949). For Roosevelt's trust policy, see Hans B. Thorelli, *Federal Antitrust Policy: Organization of an American Tradition* (Baltimore, 1955); the already-mentioned Moody, *The Truth About the Trusts;* James D. Clark, *The Federal Trust Policy* (Baltimore, 1931); and, for the nineteenth-century background, Sidney Fine, *Laissez Faire and the General Welfare State* (Ann Arbor, 1956).

Much useful information on the anthracite coal industry is found in the *Report* of the Anthracite Coal Commission, U.S. Department of Labor Bulletin No. 46 (Washington, 1903). Eliot Jones, *The Anthracite Coal Combi-*

nation in the United States (Cambridge, 1914), and Arthur E. Suffern, *Conciliation and Arbitration in the Coal Industry of America* (Boston, 1915), are helpful. Useful works for Roosevelt's labor policy as a whole are H. L. Hurwitz, *Theodore Roosevelt and Labor in New York State* (New York, 1943); Edward Berman, *Labor Disputes and the President of the United States* (New York, 1924); L. L. Lorwin, *The American Federation of Labor, History, Policies, and Prospects* (Washington, 1933); and Marguerite Green, *The National Civic Federation and the American Labor Movement, 1900–1925* (Washington, 1956).

Hemisphere Diplomacy

For highly suggestive discussions of the attitudes of Roosevelt and the progressives toward foreign politics, see Chapter 1 of Howard Beale, *Theodore Roosevelt and the Rise of America to World Power* (Baltimore, 1956), and William E. Leuchtenburg, "Progressivism and Imperialism: The Progressive Movement and American Foreign Policy, 1898–1916," *Mississippi Valley Historical Review,* XXXIX (1952), 483. Roosevelt's naval policy can be found in G. C. O'Hara, *Theodore Roosevelt and the Rise of the Modern Navy* (Princeton, 1943). But see also W. E. Livezey, *Mahan on Sea Power,* (Norman, Okla., 1947), and D. W. Mitchell, *History of the Modern American Navy* (New York, 1946).

Few subjects have been covered so well as recent Caribbean policy. Among the large number of good general works on the subject, perhaps the best are Dexter Perkins, *The United States and the Caribbean* (Cambridge, 1947), and *The Monroe Doctrine, 1867–1907* (Baltimore, 1937); Samuel F. Bemis, *The Latin American Policy of the United States* (New York, 1943); H. C. Hill, *Roosevelt and the Caribbean* (Chicago, 1927); Dana G. Monroe, *The United States and the Caribbean* (Boston, 1934); and W. H. Callcot, *The Caribbean Policy of the United States, 1890–1920* (Baltimore, 1942). For Santo Domingo, see M. M. Knight, *The Americans in Santo Domingo* (New York, 1928). On the Venezuelan incident, S. W. Livermore, "Theodore Roosevelt, The American Navy and the Venezuelan Crisis," *American Historical Review,* LI (1946), 452, and J. F. Rippy, "The Antecedents of the Roosevelt Corollary of the Monroe Doctrine," *Pacific Historical Review,* IX (1940), 267, are of special interest. D. C. Miner, *The Fight for the Panama Route; The Story of the Spooner Act and the Hay-Herran Treaty* (New York, 1940), is excellent. M. P. Du Val, *And the Mountains Will Move* (Stanford, 1947), is adequate for the subsequent history of the Canal. Other useful works on the subject are J. F. Rippy, *The Capitalists and Colombia* (New York, 1931), and Arthur P. Wittaker, *The United States and South America: The Northern Republics* (Cambridge, 1948). Thomas A. Bailey, "Theodore Roosevelt and the Alaskan Boundary Settlement," *Canadian*

Historical Review, XVIII (1937), 123, should be compared with Beale, *Theodore Roosevelt and the Rise of America to World Power.* For Cuban relations, see especially Russell H. Fitzgibbon, *Cuba and the United States, 1900–1935* (Menasha, Wis., 1935).

Among the biographies of special value for this subject not already mentioned are Tyler Dennett, *John Hay, From Poetry to Politics* (New York, 1933); William R. Thayer, *The Life and Letters of John Hay* (2 vols., Boston, 1915); Karl Schriftgeisser, *The Gentleman from Massachusetts: Henry Cabot Lodge* (Boston, 1954); and William D. Puleston, *The Life and Work of Alfred Thayer Mahan* (New Haven, 1943).

The Drive for Election

Roosevelt's intricate political moves in 1903 and 1904 can best be studied in the already-mentioned biographies by Pringle and Blum. But A. Bower Sageser, *The First Two Decades of the Pendleton Act* (Lincoln, Neb., 1935), contains some material on patronage. Garel A. Grunder and William E. Livezey, *The Philippines and the United States* (Norman, Okla., 1951), traces the evolution of American policy. Three studies by Philippine officials should also be noted: C. C. Worcester, *The Philippines Past and Present* (New York, 1914); W. C. Forbes, *The Philippine Islands* (Boston, 1928); and C. B. Elliot, *The Philippines to the End of the Commission Government* (New York, 1917).

Among the biographies dealing with this subject are Thomas Beer, *Hanna* (New York, 1929); E. J. Scott and L. B. Stone, *Booker T. Washington, Builder of a Civilization* (New York, 1917); G. C. Osborn, *John Sharp Williams; Planter Statesman of the Deep South* (Baton Rouge, La., 1943); James McGurrin, *Bourke Cockran* (New York, 1948); and S. H. Acheson, *Joe Bailey: The Last Democrat* (New York, 1932).

The Orient and the World

In addition to many of the volumes listed under the section Hemisphere Diplomacy, the following general works should be consulted: Alfred W. Griswold, *The Far Eastern Policy of the United States* (New York, 1938), and Tyler Dennett, *Americans in Eastern Asia* (New York, 1941). Tyler Dennett, *Roosevelt and the Russo-Japanese War* (New York, 1925), should be compared with Beale, *Theodore Roosevelt and the Rise of America to World Power.* M. J. Bau, *The Open Door Doctrine in Relation to China* (New York, 1923), and E. C. Sandmeyer, *The Anti-Chinese Movement in California* (Urbana, 1939), cover Chinese relations, while Thomas A. Bailey, *America Faces Russia* (New York, 1950), does the same for that country. Thomas A. Bailey, *Theodore Roosevelt and the Japanese American Crisis* (Stanford, Calif., 1934), is particularly valuable, as is also O. J. Clinard,

Japan's Influence on American Naval Power (Berkeley and Los Angeles, 1947), and Yamato Ichihashi, *Japanese in the United States* (Stanford, Calif., 1932). Thomas A. Bailey, "The World Crisis of the American Battleship Fleet, 1907–1909," *Pacific Historical Review*, I (1932), 389, and "The Root-Takahira Agreement of 1908," *Pacific Historical Review*, IX (1940), 19, are of interest on their special subjects.

David A. Lockmiller, *Magoon in Cuba: A History of the Second Intervention, 1906–1909* (Chapel Hill, 1938), is an admirable study. J. B. Scott, *The Hague Peace Conference of 1899 and 1902* (2 vols., New York, 1909), was written without the aid of any of the pertinent manuscripts. Eugene N. Anderson, *The First Moroccan Crisis, 1904–1906* (Chicago, 1930), is a fine study written from European sources. For the developing Anglo-American understanding, see Lionel M. Gelber, *The Rise of Anglo-American Friendship* (New York, 1938).

Roosevelt, the Final Years

I. L. Sharfman, *The Interstate Commerce Commission: A Study in Administrative Law and Procedure* (New York, 1931), is still the authoritative work on this important railroad regulatory agency. In addition, for the Hepburn Act see William Z. Ripley, *Railroads: Rates and Regulation* (New York, 1912). A number of biographies are also important for the politics of the act. Among them are George Keenan, *E. H. Harriman* (2 vols., Boston, 1922); Claude G. Bowers, *Beveridge and the Progressive Era* (Boston, 1932); Eric F. Goldman, *Charles J. Bonaparte; Patrician Reformer, His Early Career* (Baltimore, 1943); L. B. Richardson, *William B. Chandler, Republican* (New York, 1940); and Everett Walters, *Joseph Benson Foraker: An Uncompromising Republican* (Columbus, Ohio, 1948).

On Roosevelt's conservation policies the already-cited Pinchot, *Breaking New Ground,* is indispensable. But see also the scholarly Louise E. Peffer, *The Closing of the Public Domain: Disposal and Reservation Policies, 1900–50* (Stanford, Calif., 1951), and two articles, W. R. Cross, "Ideas in Politics: The Conservation Policies of the Two Roosevelts," *Journal of the History of Ideas,* XIV (1953), 421, and J. A. O'Callaghan, "Senator Mitchell and the Oregon Land Frauds, 1905," *Pacific Historical Review,* XXI (1952), 255.

For the Panic of 1907, William C. Schluter, *The Pre-War Business Cycle, 1907–1914* (Columbia University Studies in History, Economics and Public Law, New York, 1923), is technical; Alfred D. Noyes, *Forty Years of American Finance, 1865–1907* (New York, 1909), is less so.

The Troubled Taft

Pringle, *Taft,* already cited, and George E. Mowry, *Theodore Roosevelt and the Progressive Movement* (Madison, Wis., 1946), give good if somewhat different estimates of Taft. Kenneth W. Hechler, *Insurgency: Personalities and Politics of the Taft Era* (New York, 1940), is a good political study of the first two years of the Taft administration. For Taft's own view of the Presidency, see his *The Presidency* (New York, 1916). F. W. Taussig, *The Tariff History of the United States* (New York, 1914), and *Free Trade, the Tariff and Reciprocity* (New York, 1920), contain material on the Payne-Aldrich Tariff. C. Chiu, *The Speaker of the House of Representatives Since 1898* (New York, 1928), is a study of the Speakers as well as their office. Two germane biographies are Blair Bolles, *Tyrant From Illinois: Uncle Joe Cannon's Experiment with Personal Power* (New York, 1951), and Claudius O. Johnson, *Borah of Idaho* (New York, 1936).

The Progressive Rebellion

The Ballinger-Pinchot affair is still a controversial subject among historians. For one interpretation, see Pringle, *Taft;* for others, see Alpheus T. Mason, *Bureaucracy Convicts Itself: The Ballinger-Pinchot Controversy of 1910* (New York, 1941), and Mowry, *Theodore Roosevelt and the Progressive Movement.* Rose M. Stahl, *The Ballinger-Pinchot Controversy* (Northampton, Mass., 1926), is an older and less critical work. Of interest also are Pinchot, *Breaking New Ground,* mentioned before; J. T. Ganoe, "Some Constitutional and Political Aspects of the Ballinger-Pinchot Controversy," *Pacific Historical Review,* III (1934), 323; Thomas Dreier, *Heroes of Insurgency* (New York, 1910); and Alpheus T. Mason, *Brandeis: A Free Man's Life* (New York, 1946). C. A. M. Ewing, *Congressional Elections, 1896–1944: The Sectional Basis of Political Democracy in the House of Representatives* (Norman, Okla., 1947), contains some interesting observations relevant to the election of 1910.

Republican Decline

Howard F. Cline, *The United States and Mexico* (Cambridge, 1953); R. D. Gregg, *The Influence of Border Troubles on Relations Between the United States and Mexico* (Baltimore, 1937); and J. M. Callahan, *American Foreign Policy in Mexican Relations* (New York, 1932), are of value for a study of Taft's Mexican policy. For Taft's Oriental policy, see the works listed under the previous section, The Orient and the World. Edward Berman, *Labor and the Sherman Act* (New York, 1930), and Felix Frankfurter and N. Green, *The Labor Injunction* (New York, 1930), give useful background material for relations between Taft and organized labor. W. L. King, *Melville Weston Fuller* (New York, 1950), says more about the Chief Justice than it does about the decisions made during the first two Taft years.

L. E. Ellis, *Reciprocity, 1911* (New Haven, 1939), gives the full story of the reciprocity struggle. Richard E. Leopold, "The Mississippi Valley and American Foreign Policy, 1890–1941: An Assessment and an Appeal," *Mississippi Valley Historical Review,* XXVII (1951), 625, indicates the devotion of the prewar Middle West to a small and isolated America. Two other useful works are J. G. Reid, *The Manchu Abdication and the Powers, 1908–1912* (Berkeley, Calif., 1935), and Herbert Croly, *Willard Straight* (New York, 1924).

Index